Rick Steves'

AMSTERDAM, BRUGES & BRUSSELS

2003

KEY

- Pedestrian Street / Square
- Famous for Shopping
- Jordaan Walk
- Landmark; Point of Interest
- *i* Tourist Information

0 — 250 meters
0 — 250 yards

JORDAAN

Lindengracht
Lindenstraat
Boomstraat
Westerstraat
Anjeliersstraat
Tuinstraat

Egelantiersstraat
Egelantiersgracht
Egelantiersgracht

Nieuwe Lelliestraat
Bloemstraat
Bloemgracht
Bloemgracht
Bloemstraat

ROZENGRACHT
Rozenstraat

Laurierstraat
Lauriergracht
Lauriergracht
Lauriergracht

Elandsstraat
Elandsgracht
Elandsgracht
Elandsgracht

Looiersgracht
Looiersgracht

MARNIXSTRAAT

WESTERMARKT

RAADHUISSTRAAT

POST

HARTENSTRAAT

NIEUWE WESTERDOKSTRAAT
HAARLEMMERSTRAAT
Brouwersgracht

Prinsengracht
Herenstraat
Singel

Spuistraat
NIEUWEZIJDS VOORBURGWAL

16

26
PALEISSTRAAT

Dam Square

DAMRAK
Beurs

Damstraat

Oudezijds Voorburgwal
Oudezijds Achterburgwal

2
4

SPUI

Nieuwe Zijds Voorburgwal
Singel

6
Oude Turfmarkt

Mint Tower

AMSTEL

Flower Market
Reguliersdwarsstraat

10 **31**

Leidsegracht
Leidsegracht

Korte
Lange LEIDSESTRAAT

Leidseplein
15 *i*

MARNIXSTRAAT

OVERTOOM

STADHOUDERSKADE

VONDEL PARK Zandpad
Vossiusstraat
Schapenburgerpad
Pieter Cornelisz Hooftstraat
Jan Luijken-Straat

CONSTANTIJN HUYGENSTRAAT

PAULUS POTTERSTRAAT
32 **Van Gogh Museum**
Stedelijk Museum **28** **MUSEUM PLEIN**
18

KERKSTRAAT
Keizersgracht
Prinsengracht
Leidsegracht
Leidsedwarsstraat
Nieuwe Spiegelstraat

WETERINGSCHANS

POST

VIIZELSTRAAT

25 **Rijksmuseum**
HOBBEMAKADE
HOBBEMASTRAAT
STADHOUDERSKADE
Honthorststraat

WETERINGSCHANS
Tweede Weteringdwarsstraat
Lijnbaansgracht
Noorderstraat
Nieuw Looiersstraat
F Simonszstraat

Den Texstraat
Nicolaas Witsenkade
Singelgracht

12

to U.S. Consulate & Concertgebouw

3
34

13

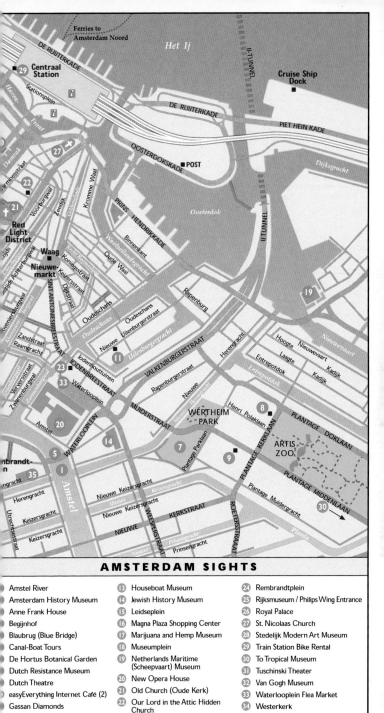

Ferries to Amsterdam Noord

DE RUIJTERKADE

Het Ij

I-TUNNEL

Cruise Ship Dock

29 **Centraal Station**

Stationsplein

DE RUIJTERKADE

PIET HEIN KADE

OOSTERDOKSKADE ■ POST

Dijksgracht

27

PRINS HENDRIKKADE

Oosterdok

I-TUNNEL

22

21

Red Light District

Binnenkant

Oude Waal

Rapenburg

19

Waag

Nieuwe-markt

SINT ANTONIESBREESTRAAT

Oudeschans

Oudeschans

Nieuwe Uilenburgerstraat

Hoogte Nieuwevaart

Laagte

Entrepotdok

Kadijk

Kadijk

JODENBREESTRAAT

Nieuwe Uilenburgergracht

11

VALKENBURGERSTRAAT

Herengracht

23

33

Waterlooplein

Rapenburgerstraat

Nieuwe

Henri Polaklaan

8

MUIDERSTRAAT

WERTHEIM PARK

PLANTAGE DOKLAAN

20

WATERLOOPLEIN

14

7

Plantage Parklaan

PLANTAGE KERKLAAN

ARTIS ZOO

5

9

Rembrandt-n

Amstel

35

I

Herengracht

PLANTAGE MIDDENLAAN

Nieuwe Keizersgracht

Nieuwe Keizersgracht

Plantage Muidergracht

30

Keizersgracht

Nieuwe Keizersgracht

KERKSTRAAT

ROETERSSTRAAT

Keizersgracht

NIEUWE

WIJDE

Prinsengracht

AMSTERDAM SIGHTS

Amstel River

Amsterdam History Museum

Anne Frank House

Begijnhof

Blaubrug (Blue Bridge)

Canal-Boat Tours

De Hortus Botanical Garden

Dutch Resistance Museum

Dutch Theatre

easyEverything Internet Café (2)

Gassan Diamonds

Heineken Brewery

13 Houseboat Museum

14 Jewish History Museum

15 Leidseplein

16 Magna Plaza Shopping Center

17 Marijuana and Hemp Museum

18 Museumplein

19 Netherlands Maritime (Scheepvaart) Museum

20 New Opera House

21 Old Church (Oude Kerk)

22 Our Lord in the Attic Hidden Church

23 Rembrandt's House

24 Rembrandtplein

25 Rijksmuseum / Philips Wing Entrance

26 Royal Palace

27 St. Nicolaas Church

28 Stedelijk Modern Art Museum

29 Train Station Bike Rental

30 To Tropical Museum

31 Tuschinski Theater

32 Van Gogh Museum

33 Waterlooplein Flea Market

34 Westerkerk

35 Herengracht Canal Mansion

LEGEND

═══ A7 ═══	Freeway/Motorway
────────	Major Rail Line
············	Ferry Lines
✈	Airport
Haarlem	Recommended location*
Nijmegen	Just passing through**
■	Ruin, Museum, other Point of Interest

* Black locations are places of interest to tourists, sized by importance. Many are covered in this guidebook.

** Gray locations are places of little or no interest to tourists and are sized by population.

0 km	50 km	100 km

0 mi	50 mi

North Sea

Wadden Islands

Waddenzee

Emd

Groningen

Leeuwarden

Den Helder • *Afsluitdijk* • **Hindeloopen**

NETHERLANDS

Alkmaar • ■ *Open-Air Museum* **Enkhuizen** **Hoorn**

Zaanse Schans ■ **Edam** Lelystad *Flevoland*

Haarlem

Keukenhof ☆ **Amsterdam**

Aalsmeer ✈ *Schiphol*

Scheveningen Leiden

The Hague • **Utrecht** *Kröller-Müller Museum*

• **Delft** Open-Air ■ *Museum*

Hoek van Holland **Arnhem** ■

Rotterdam *Waal* Nijmegen Emmerich

Maas

Eindhoven

Venlo Duisburg Esse

Düsseldorf

GERMANY

to Dover, Zeebrugge England

Ostende • **Bruges** • **Antwerp**

Flanders Fields Museum **Ghent**

Brussels Hasselt Maastricht **Köln**

Waterloo ☆ • **Aachen**

BELGIUM Liège Remagen

Lille Namur

Arras Cambrai Aulnoye *WALLONIE* Cochem

ARDENNES

FRANCE **LUXEMBOURG**

St. Quentin • Trier

Charleville-Mézières

Laon Longwy ☆ **Luxembourg City**

Soissons Thionville Saarbrücke

• **Senlis** *Verdun Battlefield*

✈ *Charles de Gaulle* **Reims**

to Harwich, England

FLANDERS

Bad Benthei

Hengelo

Lelystad

Mons

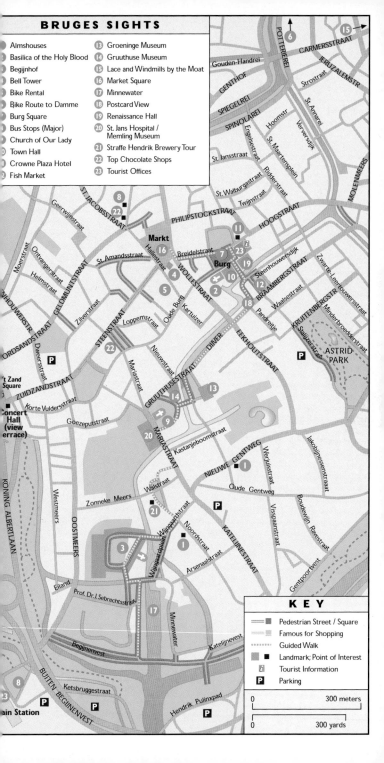

BRUGES SIGHTS

- Almshouses
- Basilica of the Holy Blood
- Begijnhof
- Bell Tower
- Bike Rental
- Bike Route to Damme
- Burg Square
- Bus Stops (Major)
- Church of Our Lady
- Town Hall
- Crowne Plaza Hotel
- Fish Market

13 Groeninge Museum
14 Gruuthuse Museum
15 Lace and Windmills by the Moat
16 Market Square
17 Minnewater
18 Postcard View
19 Renaissance Hall
20 St. Jans Hospital /
   Memling Museum
21 Straffe Hendrik Brewery Tour
22 Top Chocolate Shops
23 Tourist Offices

KEY

- Pedestrian Street / Square
- Famous for Shopping
- Guided Walk
- Landmark; Point of Interest
- *i* Tourist Information
- P Parking

0   300 meters

0   300 yards

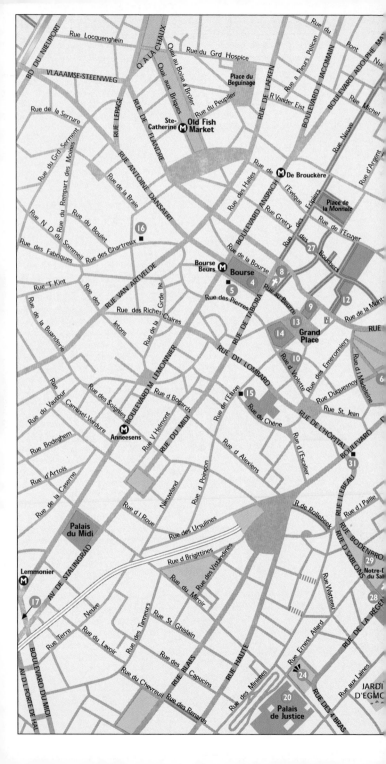

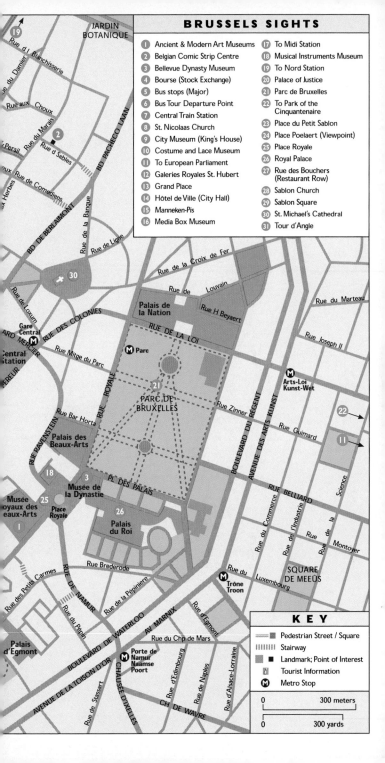

BRUSSELS SIGHTS

1. Ancient & Modern Art Museums
2. Belgian Comic Strip Centre
3. Bellevue Dynasty Museum
4. Bourse (Stock Exchange)
5. Bus stops (Major)
6. Bus Tour Departure Point
7. Central Train Station
8. St. Nicolaas Church
9. City Museum (King's House)
10. Costume and Lace Museum
11. To European Parliament
12. Galeries Royales St. Hubert
13. Grand Place
14. Hôtel de Ville (City Hall)
15. Manneken-Pis
16. Media Box Museum
17. To Midi Station
18. Musical Instruments Museum
19. To Nord Station
20. Palace of Justice
21. Parc de Bruxelles
22. To Park of the Cinquantenaire
23. Place du Petit Sablon
24. Place Poelaert (Viewpoint)
25. Place Royale
26. Royal Palace
27. Rue des Bouchers (Restaurant Row)
28. Sablon Church
29. Sablon Square
30. St. Michael's Cathedral
31. Tour d'Angle

KEY

- ▬■ Pedestrian Street / Square
- ‖‖‖ Stairway
- ■ Landmark; Point of Interest
- 𝘪 Tourist Information
- Ⓜ Metro Stop

| 0 | 300 meters |
| 0 | 300 yards |

Rick Steves'
AMSTERDAM, BRUGES & BRUSSELS 2003

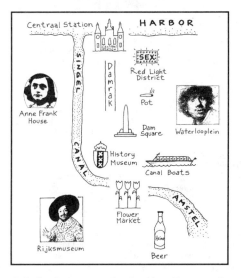

Centraal Station — HARBOR

SINGEL

Damrak

SEX
Red Light District

Pot

Dam Square

Anne Frank House

History Museum

Canal Boats

CANAL

Waterlooplein

AMSTEL

Flower Market

Rijksmuseum

Beer

by Rick Steves & Gene Openshaw

AVALON
TRAVEL

Other ATP travel guidebooks by Rick Steves
Rick Steves' Best of Europe
Rick Steves' Europe 101: History and Art for the Traveler (with Gene Openshaw)
Rick Steves' Europe Through the Back Door
Rick Steves' Mona Winks: Self-Guided Tours of Europe's Top Museums
   (with Gene Openshaw)
Rick Steves' Postcards from Europe
Rick Steves' France (with Steve Smith)
Rick Steves' Germany, Austria & Switzerland
Rick Steves' Great Britain
Rick Steves' Ireland (with Pat O'Connor)
Rick Steves' Italy
Rick Steves' Scandinavia
Rick Steves' Spain & Portugal
Rick Steves' Florence (with Gene Openshaw)
Rick Steves' London (with Gene Openshaw)
Rick Steves' Paris (with Steve Smith and Gene Openshaw)
Rick Steves' Rome (with Gene Openshaw)
Rick Steves' Venice (with Gene Openshaw)
Rick Steves' Phrase Books: French, German, Italian, Portuguese, Spanish, and
   French/Italian/German

Avalon Travel Publishing, 1400 65th Street, Suite 250, Emeryville, CA 94608

Text © 2003 by Rick Steves
Maps © 2003 by Europe Through the Back Door

Printed in the United States of America by R.R. Donnelley
First printing January 2003

Portions of this book were originally published in *Rick Steves' Mona Winks* © 2001,
1998, 1996, 1993, 1988 by Rick Steves and Gene Openshaw; and in *Rick Steves'
France* © 2003, 2002, 2001, 2000, 1999 by Rick Steves and Steve Smith.

ISBN 1-56691-453-1 • ISSN 1543-012X

For the latest on Rick's lectures, books, tours, and television series, contact Europe
Through the Back Door, Box 2009, Edmonds, WA 98020, tel. 425/771-8303,
fax 425/771-0833, www.ricksteves.com, e-mail: rick@ricksteves.com.

Europe Through the Back Door Managing Editor: Risa Laib
Europe Through the Back Door Editor: Jill Hodges, Cameron Hewitt
Avalon Travel Publishing Editor and Series Manager: Laura Mazer
Copy Editor: Kate McKinley
Research Assistance: Amy McKenna (Netherlands Day Trips)
Production & Typesetting: Kathleen Sparkes, White Hart Design
Cover and Interior Design: Janine Lehmann
Maps and Graphics: David C. Hoerlein, Rhonda Pelikan, Zoey Platt
Photography: Rick Steves, Dominic Bonuccelli, Gene Openshaw
Front matter color photos: p. i, Amsterdam, © Rick Steves;
   p. viii, Grand Place, Brussels, Belgium © Lee Foster

Distributed to the book trade by Publishers Group West, Berkeley, California

CONTENTS

The Netherlands and Belgium

INTRODUCTION

Congratulations! You've made a very good choice. Amsterdam, Bruges, and Brussels—the three greatest cities of the Low Countries—are a delight to experience. Rattling on your bike over the cobbles, savoring fresh pralines, lingering in flower-carpeted squares, you'll find a slow-down-and-smell-the-tulips world that enchants. Any time of year, the well-organized traveler can enjoy the intimate charms of these cities.

Amsterdam—that retired sea captain of a city—is called "the Venice of the North," both for its canals and for its past position as an economic powerhouse. Bruges—once mighty, now mighty cute—comes with fancy beers in fancy glasses, lilting carillons, and lacy Gothic souvenirs of a long-gone greatness. Brussels—the capital of Europe, with a low-rise Paris ambience—exudes fine living, from its famous cuisine to its love of comics and chocolate.

Belgium and the Netherlands are called the Low Countries because nearly half their land is below sea level. Surrounded by mega-Europe, it's a region that's easy to overlook. But travel here is a snap, the area is steeped in history, and all the charming icons of the region—whirring windmills, Dutch Masters, dike hikes, one-speed bikes, and ladies tossing bobbins to make fine lace—line up for you to enjoy. If ever an area were a travel cliché come true, it's the Low Countries.

This book covers the predictable biggies in and around Amsterdam, Bruges, and Brussels—and mixes in a healthy dose of Back Door intimacy. Along with taking in Rembrandt's *Night Watch*, you'll climb through Captain Vincent's tiny houseboat museum. And after touring Brussels' European Parliament glass skyscraper, you'll rummage through a rough-and-tumble flea market. And you'll meet intriguing people: In one morning, Joos will show you how to swallow that pickled herring, Majel will paddle you in a canoe through the *polderland* to her stuck-in-the-mud (and stuck-in-the-past) village, and Frans will pop a taste of his latest chocolate into your mouth.

This book is a tour guide in your pocket—laying out just the best of these three great cities in hopes that you'll enjoy the trip of a lifetime. The best is, of course, only our opinion. But after more than 25 busy years of travel writing, lecturing, and guiding, we've developed a sixth sense for what tickles the traveler's fancy.

This Information Is Accurate and Up-to-Date

This book is completely up-to-date for 2003. And, like all our city and country guidebooks, it will be updated every year. Most publishers of guidebooks that cover a region from top to bottom can afford an update only every two or three years (and even then, the research is rarely done in person). Since this book is selective, covering only the places we think make the best month of sightseeing, we can update it each summer. Of course, even with an annual update, things change. But if you're traveling with this book in 2003, we guarantee you're using the most up-to-date information available in print (for the latest, see www.ricksteves.com/update).

Our guidebooks are designed to help you have an inexpensive, hassle-free trip. Your trip costs at least $10 per waking hour. Your time is valuable. This guidebook saves lots of time.

Welcome to Our Guide

The information on each city—Amsterdam, Bruges, and Brussels—is organized in the following way:

Each **Orientation** chapter has all the details on tourist information offices (TIs) and city transportation, plus an easy-to-read map designed to make the text clear and your arrival smooth.

Planning Your Time, a suggested schedule with thoughts on how to best use your limited time in each place.

Sights provides a succinct overview of the city's most important sights, with ratings: ▲▲▲—Don't miss; ▲▲—Try hard to see; ▲—Worthwhile if you can make it; No rating—Worth knowing about.

The **Self-Guided Tours** are easy-to-follow walks or tours through the big must-see attractions. This book covers the major sights in Amsterdam (Rijksmuseum, Van Gogh Museum, Anne Frank House, a city walk, Jordaan neighborhood, Red Light District, and more), Haarlem (the Grote Kerk and the Frans Hals Museum), Bruges (a city walk, Groeninge Museum, and Memling Museum), and Brussels (a city walk, Upper Town walk, and Ancient and Modern Art Museums). Throughout this book, when you see a ✪ in a listing, it means that the sight is covered in much more depth in a self-guided walk or one of our museum tours—a page number will tell you where to look to find more information.

The **Sleeping** and **Eating** chapters cover our favorite hotels and restaurants—from budget bargains to worthwhile splurges—and provide an introduction to the region's cuisine. With these, you'll know just where to eat and sleep well in each city.

Transportation Connections covers train and bus connections among these cities and to nearby destinations, as well as information on getting to and from the airport.

The **appendix** includes telephone tips and a climate chart.

With this book you'll become your own guide, traveling like a temporary local and getting the absolute most out of every mile, minute, and dollar. You won't waste time on mediocre sights because, unlike other guidebooks, we cover only the best. When you get to a key sight, you'll have exactly the information you need to properly understand it. Since your major financial pitfall is lousy, expensive hotels, we've worked hard to assemble the best accommodation values for each stop.

Trip Costs

Five components make up your total trip cost: airfare, surface transportation, room and board, sightseeing/entertainment, and shopping/miscellany.

Airfare: Don't try to sort through the mess. Find and use a good travel agent. A basic round-trip United States–Amsterdam flight costs $700–1,100 (even cheaper in winter), depending on where you fly from and when. While we generally consider saving time and money in Europe by flying "open jaw" (into one city and out of another), if you're sticking to the Low Countries, you're never more than about three hours from Amsterdam's airport.

Surface Transportation: If you plan to venture beyond the cities covered in this book, you may want a rental car (driving in the Low Countries is a breeze), but if you're just touring Amsterdam, Bruges, and Brussels, you're best off enjoying the region's excellent train system. Trains leave at least hourly between each of the cities. It costs about $35 for a ticket from Amsterdam to Brussels or Bruges.

Room and Board: You can thrive in the Low Countries on $80 a day per person for room and board. That allows $10 for lunch, $20 for dinner, and $50 for lodging (based on 2 people splitting the cost of a $100 double room that includes breakfast). To live and sleep more elegantly, we'd propose a budget of $120 per day per person ($10 for lunch, $40 for dinner, and $70 each for a $140 hotel double with breakfast). Students and tightwads do it on $45 a day ($25 per bed, $20 for meals and snacks). Budget sleeping and eating requires the skills and information covered later in this chapter (and in much greater depth in *Rick Steves' Europe Through the Back Door*).

Sightseeing and Entertainment: In big cities, figure $8 per major museum (Van Gogh Museum, Memling Museum); $3 for minor ones (climbing church towers or windmills); $10 for guided walks, boat tours, and bike rentals; and $30 for bus tours and splurge experiences such as concerts. An overall average of $15 a day works for most. Don't skimp here. After all, this category directly powers most of the experiences all the other expenses are designed to make possible.

Shopping and Miscellany: Figure $2 per ice-cream cone, coffee, or soft drink. Shopping can vary in cost from nearly nothing to a small fortune. Good budget travelers find that this category has little to do with assembling a trip full of lifelong and wonderful memories.

Exchange Rates
We've priced things throughout this book in the local currency: the euro.

> 1 euro (€) = about $1.

One euro is broken down into 100 cents. You'll find coins ranging from 1 cent to 2 euros, and bills from 5 euros to 500 euros.

Prices, Times, and Discounts
The prices in this book, as well as the hours and telephone numbers, are accurate as of October 2002. Europe is always changing, and we know you'll understand that this, like any other guidebook, starts to yellow even before it's printed.

In Europe you'll be using the 24-hour clock. After 12:00 noon, keep going—13:00, 14:00, and so on. For anything over 12, subtract 12 and add p.m. (for example, 14:00 is 2 p.m.).

While discounts for sights and transportation generally are not listed in this book, seniors (60 and over) and students (with International Student Identification Cards) may get discounts—but only by asking. Those under 18 nearly always receive generous discounts. Teachers with an International Teacher ID Card are also given discounts or free admission to many sights. To get a Teacher or Student ID Card, contact STA Travel (U.S. tel. 800/777-0112, www.statravel.com or www.isic.org).

When to Go
Though Bruges and Amsterdam can be plagued by crowds, the

long days, lively festivals, and sunny weather make summer a great time to visit. It's rarely too hot for comfort. Brussels' fancy business-class hotels are deeply discounted in the summer.

Late spring and fall are also good times to visit, with generally mild weather and lighter crowds (except during holiday weekends— for details, see "Red Tape and Holidays," below). If you're counting on seeing the tulip fields in their full glory, go in the spring.

Winter travel is cold and wet in this region. It's fine for big cities, but smaller towns and countryside sights feel dreary and lifeless. Some sights close for lunch, tourist information offices keep shorter hours, and some tourist activities (like English-language windmill tours) vanish altogether.

Sightseeing Priorities— The Netherlands and Belgium

With cheap flights from the United States, minimal culture shock, almost no language barrier, and a well-organized tourist trade, the Low Countries are a good place to start a European trip. Depending on the length of your trip, here are our recommended priorities.

2 days:	Amsterdam, Haarlem
3–4 days, add:	Bruges
5–6 days, add:	Brussels and another day in Amsterdam
7 days, add:	Side-trips from Amsterdam (e.g., Enkhuisen, The Hague)

Red Tape and Holidays

You need a passport but no visa or shots to travel in the Netherlands and Belgium.

In 2003, these dates can be busy anywhere in Europe: Easter weekend through Monday (April 19–26), Labor Day weekend (May 1–4), VE Day (May 8), Ascension weekend (May 29–31), Pentecost weekend (June 7–9), Assumption (Aug 15), All Saints' Day weekend (Oct 30–Nov 1, holiday on Nov 1), Armistice Day (Nov 11), and the winter holidays (late Dec–early Jan). Many sights close on the actual holiday (check with the local TI). In the Netherlands, remember these dates: Queen's Day (April 30), Remembrance Day (May 4), and Liberation Day (May 5). Belgium's Independence Day is July 21.

VAT Refunds for Shoppers

Wrapped into the purchase price of your souvenirs is a Value Added Tax (called VAT in English, BTW in Dutch) of around 15 percent in the Netherlands and 17 percent in Belgium. If you make a single purchase of more than €125 in Belgium or €135 in the Netherlands at a store that participates in the VAT refund scheme, you're entitled to get most of that tax back. Personally, we've never felt that VAT refunds are worth the hassle, but if you do, here's the scoop.

If you're lucky, the merchant will subtract the tax when you make your purchase (this is more likely to occur if the store ships the goods to your home). Otherwise, this is what you'll need to:

1) **Get the paperwork.** Have the merchant completely fill out the necessary refund document, called a "cheque." You'll have to present your passport at the store.

2) **Have your cheque(s) stamped at the border** as you leave your last stop in the European Union by the customs agent who deals with VAT refunds. It's best to keep your purchases in your carry-on for viewing, but if they're too large or dangerous (such as knives) to carry on, then track down the proper customs agent to inspect them before you check your bag. You're not supposed to use your purchased goods before you leave. If you show up at customs wearing your new clogs, officials might look the other way—or deny you a refund.

3) **To collect your refund,** you'll need to return your stamped documents to the retailer or its representative. Many merchants work with a service, such as Easy Tax-Free (www.easytaxfree.com), which has offices at major airports, ports, and border crossings. These services, which extract a 4 percent fee, usually can refund your money immediately in your currency of choice or credit your card (within two billing cycles). If you have to deal directly with the retailer, mail the store your stamped documents and then wait. It could take months.

Banking

Smart travelers plan on spending euros while in Europe. Get euros at the best rates at a cash machine. Bring your ATM, credit, or debit card, along with a couple hundred dollars in cash as a backup. Traveler's checks are a waste of your time and money.

Bank machines are everywhere now (always open, lower fees, quick processing; you'll need a PIN code—numbers only, no letters—with your Visa or MasterCard). Before you go, verify with your bank that your card will work. Bring two cards in case one gets damaged.

Just like at home, credit (or debit) cards work easily at hotels, restaurants, and shops, but small businesses (B&Bs) accept payment only in the local currency. Visa and MasterCard are far more widely accepted than Diners or American Express. Travelers with euros have the easiest time and can sometimes get discounted prices for their accommodations by paying in cash rather than using a credit card.

The Language Barrier

People speak Dutch in Amsterdam, Flemish in Bruges, and
French in Brussels. But you'll find almost no language barrier
anywhere, as all well-educated folks, nearly all young people,
and nearly everyone in the tourist trade speak English. Still,
take a few minutes to learn some polite Dutch pleasantries.

English	*Dutch*	*Pronunciation*
Hello.	**Hallo.**	hol-LOH
Good day.	**Dag.**	tock
Please?	**Alstublieft?**	AHL-stoo-bleeft
You're welcome.	**Alstublieft.**	AHL-stoo-bleeft
Thank you.	**Dank u wel.**	dahnk yoo vehl
Excuse me?	**Pardon?**	par-DOHN
Do you speak English?	**Sprekt u Engels?**	spraykt yu ENG-gels
Yes. / No.	**Ja. / Nee.**	yah / nay
Okay.	**Oké.**	okay
Cheers!	**Proost!**	prohst
Goodbye.	**Tot ziens.**	toht zeens
one / two / three	**een / twee / drie**	ayn / t'vay / dree

Travel Smart

Your trip is like a complex play—easier to follow and really
appreciate on a second viewing. While no one does the same
trip twice to gain that advantage, reading this book in its entirety
before your trip accomplishes much the same thing.

Reread this book as you travel. Visit local tourist information
offices. Upon arrival in a new town, lay the groundwork for a smooth
departure. Slow down and ask questions. Most locals are eager to
tell you about their town's history and point you in their idea of
the right direction. Buy a phone card, and use it for reservations
and confirmations. Those who expect to travel smart, do.

While museums are open daily in Amsterdam, they close
on Monday in Bruges, Brussels, and Haarlem. Note that on any
day, major sights stop admitting people 30–60 minutes before
they close. Many smaller sights close for lunch off-season.

As you peruse this book, note special days (holidays, festivals, market days, and days when sights are closed). Plan ahead
for laundry, post office chores, picnics, and Sundays (particularly
if traveling by train). Sundays have pros and cons for travelers,
as they do in the United States (special events and weekly markets, limited hours, shops and banks closed, limited public transportation, no rush hours). Saturdays are like weekdays.

Tourist Information

The tourist information office is your best first stop in any new city. In this book, we refer to them as TIs. Throughout the Low Countries, you'll find TIs are usually well organized and have English-speaking staffers.

Tourist Offices, U.S. Addresses

National tourist offices in the United States are a wealth of information. Before your trip, request any specific information you may want (such as city maps and schedules of upcoming festivals).

Netherlands Board of Tourism: 355 Lexington Avenue, 19th floor, New York, NY 10017, tel. 888-GO-HOLLAND, fax 212/370-9507, www.goholland.com, e-mail: info@goholland.com. They have a great country map, events calendar, and seasonal brochures—they request a $5 donation for mailing (pay on receipt).

Belgian National Tourist Office: 780 3rd Avenue, Suite #1501, New York, NY 10017, tel. 212/758-8130, fax 212/355-7675, www.visitbelgium.com, e-mail: info@visitbelgium.com. They have hotel and city guides, a list of Jewish sites, and brochures for ABC—antiques, beer, and chocolate—lovers. Ask for a Brussels map.

Recommended Guidebooks

For most travelers, this book is all you need. But consider some supplemental travel information, especially if you're traveling beyond our recommended destinations. Considering the improvements they'll make in your $3,000 vacation, $25 or $35 for extra maps and books is money well spent. One simple budget tip can easily save the price of an extra guidebook.

Historians like the green Michelin guides and the Cadogan series; both have individual books on all three cities—Amsterdam, Bruges, and Brussels. Art lovers go for the *Eyewitness Travel Guide to Amsterdam* and the *Eyewitness Travel Guide to Brussels, Bruges, Ghent & Antwerp*. The Lonely Planet series (which has a book on Amsterdam, and another on Brussels, Bruges & Antwerp) is well-researched and geared for a mature audience but is not updated annually. Vagabonds enjoy *Let's Go Amsterdam* (updated annually) for its coverage of hosteling, nightlife, and the student scene.

Rick Steves' Books and Videos

Rick Steves' Europe Through the Back Door 2003 gives you budget travel tips on minimizing jet lag, packing light, planning your itinerary, traveling by car or train, finding budget beds without reservations, changing money, avoiding rip-offs, outsmarting thieves, using cell phones, hurdling the language barrier, staying healthy, taking great photographs, what to do in your bidet, and lots more. The book also includes chapters on 35 of Rick's favorite Back Doors.

Rick Steves' Country Guides are a series of eight guidebooks covering the Best of Europe, France, Great Britain, Ireland, Germany/Austria/Switzerland, Italy, Spain/Portugal, and Scandinavia. All are updated annually; most are available in bookstores in December, the rest in January.

Rick's **City Guides,** which include this book, cover London, Paris, Venice, Florence, and Rome. These practical guides offer in-depth coverage of the sights, hotels, restaurants, and nightlife in these grand cities along with illustrated tours of their great museums. They're updated annually and come out in December and January.

Rick Steves' Europe 101: History and Art for the Traveler (with Gene Openshaw) gives you the story of Europe's people, history, and art. Written for smart people who were sleeping in their history and art classes before they knew they were going to Europe, *101* really helps Europe's sights come alive.

Rick's new public TV series, *Rick Steves' Europe,* keeps churning out shows. Of 82 episodes (the new series plus *Travels in Europe with Rick Steves*), three feature Amsterdam, Bruges, and Brussels. These air nationally on public television. They're also available in information-packed home videos and seven- or eight-episode DVDs (order online at www.ricksteves.com or call us at 425/771-8303 for our free newsletter/catalog).

Rick Steves' Postcards from Europe, Rick's autobiographical book, packs 25 years of travel anecdotes and insights into the ultimate 2,000-mile European adventure. Through his guidebooks, Rick shares his favorite European discoveries with you. *Postcards* (set partly in the Netherlands) introduces you to his favorite European friends.

All of Rick's books are published by Avalon Travel Publishing (www.travelmatters.com).

Maps

The complete color maps at the front of this book will guide you to any sight or city. The black-and-white maps in this book, drawn by Dave Hoerlein, are concise and simple. Dave is well traveled in the Low Countries and has designed the maps to help you locate recommended places and get to the TIs, where you'll find more in-depth maps (often free) of the cities or regions. Maps of all the cities are readily available (generally for free or cheap) upon arrival.

Transportation

Because of the short distances and excellent public transportation systems in the Low Countries, and the fact that this book covers three big cities, connect Amsterdam, Bruges, and Brussels by train, not by car. You absolutely do not want or need a car in any of these cities.

Hourly trains connect each of these towns faster and easier than you could by driving. Just buy tickets as you go. You don't need advance reservations to ride a train between these cities unless you take the (avoidable) Amsterdam–Brussels–Thalys train. For more extensive travels beyond the Low Countries, you may want to study your railpass options (see www.ricksteves.com).

Telephones, Mail, and E-mail

You cannot travel smartly without using the telephone—to reserve and confirm hotel rooms, make restaurant reservations, check sightseeing plans, and call home. Phone cards have replaced coin-operated phones in most of Europe. Each country has its own phone cards, and you buy them there. There are two basic types: one that you insert into pay phones, and one with a scratch-off PIN code that you can use from any phone. Either card can be purchased at post offices, newsstands, and some tobacco shops. These cards only work in the country where they're purchased, so don't try to use a Dutch card to make calls in Belgium.

When you use an insertable phone card, simply take the phone off the hook, insert the prepaid card, wait for a dial tone, and dial away. The price of the call (local or international) is automatically deducted while you talk. They are sold in several denominations starting at about €5. Calling the United States with one of these phone cards is reasonable (about 3 minutes per euro).

International calling cards (PIN cards) give you the cheapest calls possible to the United States. There are a variety of prepaid PIN cards that work like PIN cards sold in the United States, allowing you to dial from the comfort of your hotel (or anywhere else). These cards all work the same way and are simple to use, once you carefully read the rules. Dial the toll-free access number listed on the card, then follow the prompts, dialing your scratch-to-reveal personal identification number (PIN), and finally the number you want to call.

U.S. Calling Card Services: Since direct-dialing rates have dropped, calling cards (offered by AT&T, MCI, and Sprint) are no longer a good value. In fact, they are a rip-off. You'll likely pay $3 for the first minute with a $4 connection fee; if you get an answering machine, it'll cost you $7 to say "Sorry I missed you." Simply dialing direct (even from your hotel room) is generally a much better deal.

Dialing Direct: The **Netherlands**' phone system uses area codes. To make a call within a city, you dial the local number without the area code. To make a long distance call within the country, include the area code. To make an international call to the Netherlands, dial the international access code (011 if you're calling from the United States or Canada, 00 if you're calling from Europe), then the Netherlands' country code (31), the area code without its initial 0, and the local number. Example: The number of a recommended hotel in Haarlem is 023/532-4530. To call it within Haarlem, dial 532-4530. To call it from Amsterdam, dial 023/532-4530. To call it from the United States, dial 011 (U.S. international access code), 31 (Netherlands country code), 23 (Haarlem's area code without the initial 0), and 532-4530.

Belgium uses a direct-dial system (no area codes). To call anywhere within Belgium, you dial the same nine-digit number. To make an international call to Belgium, dial the international access code (011 if you're calling from the United States or Canada, 00 if calling from Europe), then Belgium's country code (32), then the local number without its initial 0.

To make an international call from the Netherlands or Belgium, start your call with Europe's international access code (00), then dial the country code of the country you're calling. To call our office in the United States, dial 00 (Europe's international access code), 1 (U.S. country code), then 425/771-8303 (our area code plus local number).

For a list of **international access codes and country codes,** see the appendix. European time is six/nine hours ahead of the East/West Coast of the United States.

Cell Phones: Many travelers buy cheapie cell phones—about $70 on up—to make local and international calls. The cheapest phones work only in the country where they're sold; the pricier phones work throughout Europe (but it'll cost you about $40 per country for the necessary chip to operate in that country and for prepaid phone time). Because of their expense, cell phones are most economical for travelers staying in one country for two weeks or more.

If you're interested, stop by one of the ubiquitous phone shops or at a cell-phone counter in a department store. Confirm with the clerk whether the phone works only in Belgium or the Netherlands or throughout Europe. To understand all the extras, get a brand that has instructions in English. Make sure the clerk shows you how to use the phone—practice making a call to the store or, for fun, to the clerk's personal cell phone. You'll need to pick out a policy; different policies offer, say, better rates for making calls at night or for calling cell phones rather than fixed phones. We get the basic fixed rate: a straight 30 cents per minute to the United States and 15 cents per minute to any fixed or cell phone in the home country at any hour. Receiving calls is generally free. When you run out of calling time, buy more time at a newsstand. Upon arrival in a different country, purchase a new chip (which comes with a new phone number). Remember, if you're on a tight budget, skip cell phones and buy PIN phone cards instead.

Mail: While you can arrange for mail delivery to your hotel (allow 10 days for a letter to arrive), phoning and e-mailing are so easy that we've dispensed with mail stops altogether.

E-mail: Almost all hotels recommended in this book are enthusiastic about e-mail. Internet service providers (ISPs) can change with alarming frequency, so if your e-mail message to a hotel bounces back, search for the hotel's name in a search engine such as Google (www.google.com) to see if it has a new Web site. If that doesn't work, call or fax the hotel.

Cybercafés and little hole-in-the-wall Internet access shops (offering a few computers, no food, and cheap prices) are popular in most cities. Many hotels offer Internet access to their guests for a reasonable price. The dominant cybercafé chain in Brussels and Amsterdam is easyEverything (open 24/7 with the best rates and fastest connections in town). If the extension .com doesn't work at the end of a URL, try .nl for the Netherlands and .be for Belgium.

If you're planning to log on from your laptop in your hotel room, you'll need an Internet service provider that has local phone numbers for each country you'll visit. While an American modem cable plugs into European phone jacks, you may have to tweak your settings to make your computer recognize a pulse instead of the U.S. dial tone. Bring a phone jack tester that reverses line polarity as needed.

Sleeping

Hotels

We like places that are clean, small, central, traditional, inexpensive, friendly, and not listed in other guidebooks. Most places we list have at least five of these seven virtues. In this book, the price for a double room will range from $50 (very simple, toilet and shower down the hall) to $180 (maximum plumbing and more), with most clustering around $100.

Most hotels have lots of doubles and a few singles, triples, and quads. While groups sleep cheap, traveling alone can be expensive. Singles (except for the rare closet-type rooms that fit only a twin bed) are simply doubles used by one person—so they often cost nearly the same as a double.

Rooms are safe. Still, keep cameras and money out of sight. Towels aren't routinely replaced every day; drip-dry and conserve.

Sleep Code

To give maximum information in a minimum of space, we use these codes to describe accommodations listed in this book. Prices listed are per room, not per person.

S = Single room (or price for one person in a double).

D = Double or Twin.

T = Triple (generally a double bed with a single).

Q = Quad (usually two double beds).

b = Private bathroom with toilet and shower or tub.

s = Private shower or tub only (the toilet is down the hall).

CC = Accepts credit cards (Visa and MasterCard, rarely American Express or Diners).

no CC = Does not accept credit cards; pay in local cash.

According to this code, a couple staying at a "Db-€80, CC" hotel would pay a total of 80 euros (about $80) for a double room with a private bathroom. The hotel accepts credit cards or cash in payment.

A hearty breakfast with cereal, meats and local cheeses, fresh bread, yogurt, juice, and coffee or tea is standard in hotels.

Bed-and-Breakfasts

B&Bs offer double the cultural intimacy and often nicer rooms for a good deal less than most hotel rooms. Hosts usually speak English and are interesting conversationalists.

In the Low Countries, B&Bs are common in well-touristed areas outside of the big cities. While they are rare in Amsterdam and Brussels, you'll find B&Bs in Bruges and Haarlem.

Local TIs have lists of B&Bs and can book a room for you, but you'll save money by booking direct with the B&Bs listed in this book.

Making Reservations

It's possible to travel at any time of year without reservations, but given the high stakes, erratic accommodations values, and the quality of the gems we've found for this book, we'd highly recommend calling ahead for rooms several days in advance.

If you know exactly which dates you need and really want to stay in a particular place, reserve before you leave home. If you prefer to book rooms as you go, make a habit of calling between 10:00 and 12:00 on the day you plan to arrive, when the hotelier knows who'll be checking out and just which rooms will be available.

Don't be afraid to call. We've taken great pains to list telephone numbers with long-distance instructions (see "Telephones, Mail, and E-mail," above, and the appendix). Most hotels listed are accustomed to English-only speakers. A hotel receptionist will trust you and hold a room until 16:00 without a deposit, though some will ask for a credit-card number. Hotels are likely to charge the first night of your stay to your credit card as a deposit.

When reserving from home, phone and fax costs are reasonable, e-mail is a steal, and simple English works. To fax, use the form in the appendix (online at www.ricksteves.com/reservation). A two-night stay in August would be "2 nights, 16/8/03 to 18/8/03." Europeans write the date as day/month/year, and European hotel jargon uses your day of departure.

If you receive a response from the hotel stating their rates and room availability, it's not a confirmation. You must confirm that you indeed want a room at the given rate. One night's deposit is generally required. A credit card is often accepted as a deposit (though you may need to send a signed traveler's check or, rarely, a bank draft in the local currency). To make things easier on yourself and the hotel, be sure you really intend to stay at the hotel on the dates you requested.

If you must cancel, tell the hotelier as soon as possible. These family-run businesses lose money if they turn away customers while holding a room for someone who doesn't show up. Understandably, some hotels bill no-shows for one night (and if you cancel without giving enough advance notice, you may not receive your entire deposit back). Long distance is cheap and easy from public phone booths. Don't let these people down—I promised you'd call and cancel if for some reason you won't show up.

Reconfirm your reservations a few days in advance for safety. Don't needlessly confirm rooms through the tourist office; they'll take a commission.

Hostels

There are excellent hostels in all three cities covered in this book. Hostels charge about $15 per bed. Get a hostel card before you go (contact Hostelling International, tel. 202/783-6161, www.hiayh.org). Travelers of any age are welcome if they don't mind dorm-style accommodations or meeting other

Tips on Tipping

Tipping in Europe isn't as automatic and generous as it is in the United States, but for special service, tips are appreciated, if not expected. As in the United States, the proper amount depends on your resources, tipping philosophy, and the circumstance, but some general guidelines apply.

Restaurants: Almost all restaurants include tax and a 15 percent service charge in their prices, but it's polite to round up for a drink or meal well served. This bonus tip is usually about 5 percent of the bill (e.g., if your bill is €19, leave €20). For exceptional service, tip up to 10 percent. Even if you pay with your credit card, it's best to tip in cash to make sure the tip reaches your server. If you order your food at a counter, don't tip.

Taxis: To tip the cabbie, round up. For a typical ride, round up to the next euro on the fare (to pay a €13 fare, give €14); for a long ride, to the nearest 5 (for a €52 fare, give €55). If the cabbie hauls your bags and zips you to the airport to help you catch your flight, you might want to toss in a little more—but not more than €5. If you feel like you're being driven in circles or otherwise ripped off, skip the tip.

Special services: Tour guides at public sites sometimes hold out their hands for tips after they give their spiel; if we've already paid for the tour, we don't tip extra, though some tourists do give a euro or two, particularly for a job well done. We don't tip at hotels, but if you do, give the porter a euro for carrying bags and leave a couple of euros in your room at the end of your stay for the maid if the room was kept clean. In general, if someone in the service industry does a super job for you, a tip of a couple of euros is appropriate... but not required.

When in doubt, ask. If you're not sure whether (or how much) to tip for a service, ask your hotelier or the TI; they'll fill you in on how it's done on their turf.

travelers. Travelers without a hostel card can generally spend the night for a small, extra "one-night membership" fee. Cheap meals are sometimes available, and kitchen facilities are usually provided. Expect youth groups in spring, crowds in the summer, and snoring. In official IYHF-member hostels, family rooms are sometimes available on request, but it's basically boys' dorms and girls' dorms. You usually can't check in before 17:00 and must be out by 10:00. There's often a 23:00 curfew. Official hostels are marked with a triangular sign that shows a house and a tree.

The Low Countries have plenty of private hostels where you'll find no mid-day lockout, no curfew, co-ed dorms, simple double rooms, and a more easygoing and rowdy atmosphere.

Stranger in a Strange Land

We travel all the way to Europe to enjoy differences—to become temporary locals. Still, you'll experience frustrations. Certain truths that we find God-given or self-evident, such as French fries with ketchup, ice in drinks, bottomless cups of coffee, hot showers, and the bigger the better, are not so true. Suddenly, you're in a land where decent people see the neighborhood prostitute as just one of many hardworking service providers, and mothers stop by the coffee-shop for a baggie of marijuana after picking up the kids at piano lessons. One of the benefits of travel is the eye-opening realization that there are logical, civil, and even better alternatives. The fact that Americans treat time as a commodity can lead to frustrations when dealing with other cultures. For instance, while an American "spends," "wastes," or "kills" time, a Belgian merely "passes" it. You will find no cup holders in Belgian cars—drinks are to be enjoyed slowly, with friends. A willingness to go local (and at a local tempo) ensures that you'll enjoy a full dose of European hospitality.

If there is a negative aspect to the European image of Americans, it's that we can appear big, loud, aggressive, impolite, rich, and a bit naive. While Europeans look bemusedly at some of our Yankee excesses—and worriedly at others—they nearly always afford us individual travelers all the warmth we deserve.

Back Door Manners

While updating this book, we heard over and over again that our readers are considerate and fun to have as guests. Thank you for traveling as temporary locals who are sensitive to the culture. It's fun to follow you in our travels.

Send Us a Postcard, Drop Us a Line

If you enjoy a successful trip with the help of this book and would like to share your discoveries, please fill out the survey at the end of this book and send it to us at Europe Through the Back Door, Box 2009, Edmonds, WA 98020. We personally read and value all feedback. Thanks in advance—it helps a lot.

For our latest travel information, tap into our Web site: www.ricksteves.com. For any updates to this book, check www.ricksteves.com/update. Rick's e-mail address is rick @ricksteves.com. Anyone is welcome to request a free issue of our *Back Door* quarterly newsletter.

Judging from all the positive feedback and happy postcards we receive from travelers who have used our books, it's safe to assume you'll enjoy a great, affordable vacation—with the finesse of an independent, experienced traveler.

From this point, "we" (your co-authors) will shed our respective egos and become "I."

Thanks, and happy travels!

BACK DOOR TRAVEL PHILOSOPHY
From *Rick Steves' Europe Through the Back Door*

Travel is intensified living—maximum thrills per minute and one of the last great sources of legal adventure. Travel is freedom. It's recess, and we need it.

Experiencing the real Europe requires catching it by surprise, going casual ... "Through the Back Door."

Affording travel is a matter of priorities. (Make do with the old car.) You can travel—simply, safely, and comfortably—anywhere in Europe for $80 a day plus transportation costs. In many ways, spending more money only builds a thicker wall between you and what you came to see. Europe is a cultural carnival, and time after time, you'll find that its best acts are free and the best seats are the cheap ones.

A tight budget forces you to travel close to the ground, meeting and communicating with the people, not relying on service with a purchased smile. Never sacrifice sleep, nutrition, safety, or cleanliness in the name of budget. Simply enjoy the local-style alternatives to expensive hotels and restaurants.

Extroverts have more fun. If your trip is low on magic moments, kick yourself and make things happen. If you don't enjoy a place, maybe you don't know enough about it. Seek the truth. Recognize tourist traps. Give a culture the benefit of your open mind. See things as different but not better or worse. Any culture has much to share.

Of course, travel, like the world, is a series of hills and valleys. Be fanatically positive and militantly optimistic. If something's not to your liking, change your liking. Travel is addictive. It can make you a happier American, as well as a citizen of the world. Our Earth is home to six billion equally important people. It's humbling to travel and find that people don't envy Americans. They like us, but, with all due respect, they wouldn't trade passports.

Globetrotting destroys ethnocentricity. It helps you understand and appreciate different cultures. Travel changes people. It broadens perspectives and teaches new ways to measure quality of life. Many travelers toss aside their hometown blinders. Their prized souvenirs are the strands of different cultures they decide to knit into their own character. The world is a cultural yarn shop. And Back Door travelers are weaving the ultimate tapestry. Come on, join in!

THE NETHERLANDS

- 36,000 square kilometers (14,000 square miles), a little larger than Maryland
- 15 million people (1,100 people per square mile; 15 times the population density of the United States)
- €1 = about $1

Holland: Windmills, wooden shoes, tulips, cheese, and great artists. In its 17th-century glory days, tiny Holland was a world power—politically, economically, and culturally—with more great artists per kilometer than any other country.

Today, the Netherlands is Europe's most densely populated country and also one of its wealthiest and best organized. A generation ago, Belgium, the Netherlands, and Luxembourg formed the nucleus of a united Europe when they joined economically to form Benelux.

Efficiency is a Dutch custom. The average income is higher than in the United States. Though only 8 percent of the labor force is made up of farmers, 70 percent of the land is cultivated, and you'll travel through vast fields of barley, wheat, sugar beets, potatoes, and flowers.

"Holland" is just a nickname for the Netherlands. North Holland and South Holland are the largest of the 12 states that make up the Netherlands. The word Netherlands means "lowlands," and the country is so named because half of it is below sea level, reclaimed from the sea (or rivers). That's why the locals say, "God made the Earth, but the Dutch made Holland." Modern technology and plenty of Dutch elbow grease have turned much

The Netherlands

of the sea into fertile farmland. Though a new, 12th state—Flevoland, near Amsterdam—has been drained, dried, and populated in the last 100 years, Dutch reclamation projects are essentially finished.

The Dutch can generally speak English, they pride themselves on their frankness, and they like to split the bill. Traditionally, Dutch cities have been open-minded, loose, and liberal (to attract sailors in the days of Henry Hudson). And today, Amsterdam is a capital of alternative lifestyles—a city where nothing's illegal as long as nobody gets hurt. While freewheeling Amsterdam does have a quiet side, travelers who prefer more sedate Dutch evenings sleep in a small town nearby (see Haarlem chapter) and side-trip into the big city.

The country is so small, level, and well-covered by trains and buses that transportation is a snap. Major cities are connected by speedy trains that come and go every 10 or 15 minutes. Connections are excellent, and you'll rarely wait more than a few minutes. Round-trip tickets are discounted. Buses take you where trains don't, and bicycles take you where buses don't. Bus stations and bike-rental shops cluster around train stations. The national bus system, both within and between cities, runs on a uniform system of magnetic-strip cards that act as debit cards, deducting the fare of a ride each time you board (though single-ride tickets are also available). You can buy strip cards on the bus or more cheaply at train stations, post offices, and some tobacco shops. If you're caught riding without a card, you have to take off your clothes.

Holland is a biker's dream. The Dutch, who average four bikes per family, have put small bike roads (with their own traffic lights) beside nearly every big auto route. You can rent bikes at most train stations and drop them off at most others. And you can take bikes on trains, outside of rush hour, for €6 per day.

AMSTERDAM

ORIENTATION

Amsterdam is a progressive way of life housed in Europe's most 17th-century city. Physically, it's built upon millions of pilings. But more than that, it's built on good living, cozy cafés, great art, street-corner jazz, stately history, and a spirit of live-and-let-live. It has more than 700,000 people and about as many bikes. It also has more canals than Venice and about as many tourists.

During its Golden Age in the 1600s, Amsterdam was the world's richest city, an international sea-trading port, and the cradle of capitalism. Wealthy, democratic burghers built a planned city of canals lined with trees and townhouses topped with fancy gables. Immigrants, Jews, outcasts, and political rebels were drawn here by its tolerant atmosphere, while painters like young Rembrandt captured that atmosphere on canvas. But all this history is only the beginning.

Approach the city not as a historian but as an ethnologist observing a strange culture. Stroll through any neighborhood, and see things that are commonplace here but rarely found elsewhere. Carillons chime quaintly in neighborhoods selling sex, as young professionals smoke pot with impunity next to old ladies in bonnets selling flowers. Observe the neighborhood's "social control," where a man feels safe in his home knowing he's being watched by the hookers next door.

The Dutch people are unique. They may be the world's most handsome people—tall, healthy, and with good posture—and the most open, honest, and refreshingly blunt. As connoisseurs of world culture, they appreciate Rembrandt paintings, Indonesian food, and the latest French film—but with an unsnooty, blue-jeans attitude.

Be warned: Amsterdam, a bold experiment in freedom, may box your Puritan ears. Take it all in, then pause to watch the sunset— at 10:00 p.m.—and see the Golden Age reflected in a quiet canal.

Orientation
(area code: 020)

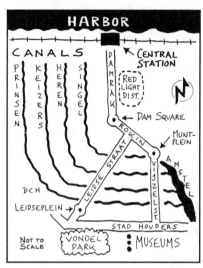

Amsterdam Overview

Amsterdam's central train station, on the north edge of the city, is your starting point (TI, bike rental, and trams fanning out to all points). Damrak is the main street axis, connecting the station with Dam Square (people-watching and hangout center) and its Royal Palace. From this spine, the city spreads out like a fan, with 90 islands, hundreds of bridges, and a series of concentric canals (named "Prince's," "Gentleman's," and "King's") that were laid out in the 17th century, Holland's Golden Age. Amsterdam's major sights are within walking distance of Dam Square.

To the east of Damrak is the old part of the city (today's Red Light District), and to the west is the new part, where you'll find the Anne Frank House and the Jordaan neighborhood. Museums and Leidseplein nightlife cluster at the southern edge of the city center.

Planning Your Time

Amsterdam is worth a full day of sightseeing on even the busiest itinerary. While the city has a couple of must-see museums, its best attraction is its own breezy ambience. The city's a joy on foot—and it's a breezier and faster joy by bike.

Amsterdam in a Day

9:00 Follow our self-guided Amsterdam Walk, which takes you from the train station to the Rijksmuseum, with stops at the peaceful Begijnhof, Amsterdam Historical Museum, and flower market. Break the walk in the middle with a relaxing hour-long canal cruise (departs from Spui dock).

14:00 Visit Amsterdam's two great art museums, side by side: the Van Gogh and the Rijksmuseum.

18:00 Tour the Anne Frank House (visiting at 18:00 or later saves an hour in line in summer).

19:00   Wander the Jordaan, finding dinner in this idyllic side of town.

21:00   Stroll the Red Light District for some of Europe's most fascinating window shopping.

Amsterdam in Two or More Days

Day 1

9:00   Follow our self-guided Amsterdam Walk, which takes you from the train station to the Rijksmuseum, via the quiet Begijnhof, Amsterdam Historical Museum (make time to tour this), and flower market.

12:00   Stop for lunch in the Spui neighborhood before completing the walk.

14:00   Visit Amsterdam's two outstanding art museums, side by side: the Van Gogh and the Rijksmuseum.

18:00   Dinner.

21:00   Stroll the Red Light District for some memorable window-shopping.

Day 2

9:00   Start your day with a one-hour canal-boat tour.

10:00   Tour the sights that interest you around Rembrandtplein (Rembrandt's house, Waterlooplein flea market, Gassan Diamond polishing demo, Dutch Resistance Museum).

13:00   Lunch and afternoon free to shop and explore.

17:00   Tour the Anne Frank House.

18:30   Take self-guided Jordaan Walk.

20:00   Dinner in Jordaan.

Day 3

Visit Haarlem.

Day 4

Side-trip by train to an open-air folk museum (either Zaanse Schans or Enkhuizen's Zuiderzee), and visit Edam.

Arrival in Amsterdam

By Train: Amsterdam swings, and the hinge that connects it to the world is its perfectly central Centraal Station. Walk out the door, and you're in the heart of the city. You'll nearly trip over trams ready to take you anywhere your feet won't. Straight ahead is Damrak street, leading to Dam Square. With your back to the entrance of the station, the TI and GVB public-transit offices are just ahead and to your left. And on your right is a vast, multistoried bike garage.

By Plane: From Schiphol Airport, take the direct train to Amsterdam (6/hr, 20 min, €3). A taxi from Schiphol to Amsterdam's Centraal Station costs €35. The KLM Hotel Bus departs from lane A7 in front of the airport (2 routes—ask the attendant which is best for you, 3/hr, 20 min, €10). The bus stops in front of the Westerkerk near the Anne Frank House and many recommended hotels.

If you're staying in Haarlem, take a direct express bus to Haarlem (4/hr, 40 min, €3.50, #300 from lane B2 in front of the airport).

Tourist Information

There are four VVV offices ("VVV" is Dutch for TI—tourist information office): inside the train station (Mon–Sat 8:00–20:00, Sun 9:00–17:00), in front of the train station (daily 9:00–17:00), on Leidsestraat (less crowded, daily 9:00–19:00), and at the airport (daily 7:00–22:00).

Avoid the crowded, inefficient offices if you can. For €0.60 a minute, you can save yourself a trip by calling the TI toll line at 0900/400-4040 (Mon–Fri 9:00–17:00). If you're staying in nearby Haarlem, use the helpful, friendly, and rarely crowded Haarlem TI (see Haarlem chapter) to answer most of your Amsterdam questions and provide you with the brochures. Consider buying a city map (€2), *Day by Day* entertainment calendar (€1.50), and any of the €1 walking-tour brochures ("Discovery Tour through the Center," "The Former Jewish Quarter," "Walks through Jordaan").

At Amsterdam's Centraal Station, GWK Change has hotel reservation windows whose clerks sell phone cards (local and international) and cheaper city maps (€1.60) and can answer basic tourist questions with shorter lines (one office is at track 4/5, the other is in west tunnel at the right end of station as you leave platform, tel. 020/627-2731).

Don't use the TI (or GWK) to book a room; you'll pay €5 per person and your host loses 13 percent—meaning you'll likely pay a higher rate. The phone system is easy, everyone speaks English, and the listings in this book are a better value than the potluck booking you'd get from the TI.

Helpful Hints

Theft Alert: Tourists are considered green and rich, and the city has more than its share of hungry thieves—especially on trams and at the many hostels. Wear your money belt.

Street Smarts: Most canals are lined by streets with the same name. When walking around town, beware silent transportation—trams and bicycles. (Don't walk on tram tracks or pink bicycle paths.)

Shop Hours: Many shops close all day Sunday and Monday morning.

Pronunciation of Place Names

Dam (pron. dahm) Amsterdam's main square

Damrak (DAHM-rock) main street between train station and Dam Square

Spui (shpow, rhymes with cow) both a street and square

Rokin (roh-KEEN) street connecting Dam Square and Spui

Kalverstraat (KAL-ver-strot) pedestrian street

Leidseplein (LIDE-zuh-pline) lively square

Jordaan (zhor-DAHN) neighborhood in southwest Amsterdam

Museumplein (myoo-ZAY-um-pline) square with Rijks and Van Gogh museums

gracht (hhkkrockt, guttural) canal

straat (strot) street

plein (pline) public square

huis (house) house

kerk (kerk) church

Maps: The free and cheap tourist maps can be confusing. Consider paying a bit more (€2) for a top-notch map. I like the Carto Studio Centrumkaart Amsterdam or, better yet, the "Amsterdam: Go where the locals go" map by Amsterdam Anything.

Telephones: Calling the United States from a phone booth is now very cheap—you'll get about five minutes for a euro. Handy telephone cards (€5 or €10) are sold at TIs, the GVB public-transit office (in front of train station), tobacco shops, post offices, and train stations.

Happy Birthday: On the Queen's Birthday, April 30, Amsterdam turns into a gigantic garage sale/street market.

Internet Access: It's easy at cafés all over town. Two huge easyEverything Internet cafés offer hundreds of terminals with fast and cheap access all day, every day (€1/40 min, Damrak 33, a block in front of train station, and at Reguliersbreestraat 22, between Mint Tower and Rembrandtplein). "Coffeeshops," which sell marijuana, also offer Internet access, letting you surf the Net with a special bravado.

Useful Phone Numbers and Web Sites

Amsterdam's Emergency Telephone Number: 112

Schiphol Airport: toll tel. 0900/7244-7465

Taxi: 020/677-7777

Entertainment (AUB Ticket Office): toll tel. 0900/0191

Tourist Information: toll tel. 0900/400-4040
Tourist Information Online: www.amsterdam.nl (City of
    Amsterdam), www.holland.com (Netherlands Board
    of Tourism).

Getting around Amsterdam

The helpful GVB transit-information office is in front of the train
station and next to the TI. Its free multilingual *Public Transport
Amsterdam Tourist Guide* includes a transit map and explains ticket
options and tram connections to all the sights.

By Bus, Tram, and Métro: Trams #2 and #5 travel the
north-south axis from Centraal Station to Dam Square to Leidseplein to Museumplein. Tram #14
goes east–west (Westerkerk–
Dam Square–Muntplein–
Waterlooplein–Plantage). If
you get lost in Amsterdam, 10
of the city's 17 trams take you
back to the central train station.

The Métro (underground
train) is used mostly for commuting to the suburbs, but it does co
nect Centraal Station with some
sights east of Damrak (Nieuwemarkt–Waterlooplein–Weesplein).
Individual **tickets** cost €1.50 and give you an hour on the buses,
trams, and Métro system (pay as you board on trams and buses;
for the Métro, buy tickets from machines).

Strip cards are cheaper than individual tickets. Any downtown bus or tram ride costs two strips (good for 1 hour of transfers). A card with 15 strips costs €6 and can be purchased at the
GVB public-transit office, machines at the train station, post
offices, airport, or tobacco shops throughout the country. Shorter
strip tickets (2, 3, and 8 strips) are also sold on some buses and
trams. Strip cards are good on buses all over the Netherlands (the
further you go, the more strips you'll use, such as 6 strips for
Haarlem to the airport), and you can share them with your partner.

A €5.50 **Day Card** gives you unlimited transportation on the
buses and Métro for a day in Amsterdam; you'll almost break even
if you take three trips (valid until 6:00 the following morning; buy
as you board or at the GVB public-transit office, which also sells a
better-value 2-day version for €8.50; sometimes costs €0.50 more
if you buy it on board).

The **Amsterdam Pass** offers unlimited use of the tram, bus,
and Métro as well as free or discounted admissions to many city
sights and boat rides (€26/1 day, €36/2 days, €46/3 days, sold at

Amsterdam

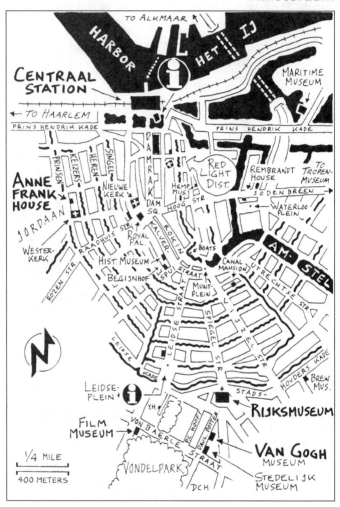

GVB public-transit office and TIs). If you'll be using the tram a lot and visiting lots of museums, this pass can save you about a third on your transportation and sightseeing. (It doesn't include the Anne Frank House).

By Foot: The longest walk a tourist would take is 45 minutes from the station to the Rijksmuseum. Watch out for silent but potentially painful bikes, trams, and crotch-high curb posts.

By Bike: Everyone—bank managers, students, pizza delivery boys, and police—uses this mode of transport. It's *the* smart way to travel, where 40 percent of all traffic rolls on two wheels. You'll get around town by bike faster than you can by taxi. On my last visit,

I rented a bike for five days, parked it outside my hotel, enjoyed wonderful mobility, and felt pretty smart. I highly encourage this for anyone who wants to get maximum fun per hour in Amsterdam. One-speed bikes, with "brrringing" bells and two locks (use them both; bike thieves are bold and brazen here), rent for about €8 per day (cheaper for longer periods) at any number of places. Hotels can send you to the nearest spot.

MacBike is the bike-rental powerhouse, with a huge and efficient outlet at Centraal Station (daily 9:00–17:45, €4/2 hrs, €7/day, €9/24 hrs, €11.50/2 days, more for 3 gears, at west end of station just before Ibis Hotel, tel. 020/625-3845, can reserve online, www.macbike.nl). MacBike gives out a free basic "Great Waterland Bicycle Tour" brochure (3 hr, 20 km) and sells several booklets outlining bike tours in and around Amsterdam for €1. For those staying near the Anne Frank House, Frederic Rent a Bike is also good (€10/24 hours, cheaper longer, daily 9:00–17:30, Brouwersgracht 78, tel. 020/624-5509).

No one wears helmets. For safety: Use arm signals, stay in the obvious and omnipresent bike lanes, yield to traffic on the right, and fear tram tracks. Cross tram tracks at a perpendicular angle to avoid catching your tire in the rut. You must walk your bike through pedestrian zones. Lock your bike to something immovable—or lose it. Warning: Police are ticketing bikers as drivers. Obey traffic signals.

By Boat: While the city is great on foot or bike, another option is the Museum Boat, which shuttles tourists from sight to sight on an all-day ticket. Tickets cost €13.50 (with sight discounts worth about €2.25). The sales booths in front of the Centraal Station (and the boats) offer handy free brochures with museum times and admission prices. The narrated ride takes 90 minutes if you don't get off (every 30 min in summer, every 45 min off-season, 7 stops, live quadrilingual guide, departures 9:30–17:00, discounted after 13:00 to €11.50, tel. 020/530-1090). A similar Canal Bus is nearby. If you're looking for a floating nonstop tour, the regular canal tour boats (without the stops) give more information, cover more ground, and cost less (see "Tours of Amsterdam," below).

By Taxi: Amsterdam's taxis are expensive (€2.50 drop and €1.50 for each kilometer). You can wave them down, find a rare taxi stand, or call one (tel. 020/677-7777) for a pick-up. Given the fine tram system, taxis are rarely a good value.

By Car: Forget it—frustrating one-ways, terrible parking, and meter maids with a passion for booting cars wrongly parked.

Tours of Amsterdam

▲▲Canal Boat Tours— These long, low, tourist-laden boats leave continually from several docks around the town for a relaxing, if uninspiring, one-hour quadrilingual introduction to the city (€6.50, 2/hr, more frequent in summer). One very central company is at the corner of Spui and Rokin streets, about  five minutes from Dam Square (daily 10:00–22:00, tel. 020/623-3810). No fishing allowed—but bring your camera. Some prefer to cruise at night, when the bridges are illuminated.

Bike Tours—The Yellow Bike Tour company offers a three-hour-long city tour (€17, at 9:30 and 13:00) and a six-hour tour of the countryside (€23, April–Nov daily at 11:00, 35 km; Nieuwezijds Kolk 29, 3 blocks from Centraal Station, tel. 020/620-6940).

Wetlands Safari, Nature Canoe Tours near Amsterdam— If you'd like to get some exercise and a dose of the *polder* country and village life, consider this tour. Majel Tromp, a young villager who speaks great English, takes groups limited to 15 people. The program: Meet at the VVV tourist office outside Centraal Station at 9:30, catch a bus, stop for coffee, take a canoe trip with several stops, tour a village by canoe, munch a rural canal-side picnic lunch (included), then canoe and bus back into the big city by 14:30 (€30, 10 percent off with this book, May–mid-Sept Mon–Fri, reservations required, tel. 020/686-3445 or cellular 06/5355-2669, www.wetlandssafari.nl).

Adam's Apple Tours—This walking tour offers a 90-minute English-only look at the historic roots of Amsterdam. You'll have a small group and a caring guide starting at Centraal Station, ending at the Dam Square (€12, 10:00, 13:00, and 15:00 most days May–Sept, call 020/616-7867 to check times and book, www.adamsapple.nl).

Private Guide—Ab Walet is a likeable, hard-working, and know-ledgeable local guide who enjoys personalizing tours for Americans interested in knowing his city better. He specializes in history and architecture and exudes a passion for Amsterdam (€70/half-day, €120/day, tel. 020/671-2588, cellular 06/2069-7882, e-mail: abwalet@yahoo.com).

Do-It-Yourself Bike Tour of Amsterdam—A day enjoying the bridges, bike lanes, and sleepy off-the-beaten-path canals on your own one-speed is an essential Amsterdam experience. The real joys of Europe's best-preserved 17th-century city are the count-less intimate glimpses it offers: the laid-back locals sunning on their porches under elegant gables, rusted bikes that look as if they've been lashed to the same lamppost since the 1960s, wasted hedonists planted on canal-side benches, and happy sailors perma-nently moored but still manning the deck.

For a good day, rent a bike at Centraal Station (see "By Bike" on page 31). Head west down Haarlem-merstraat, working your wide-eyed way down the Prinsengracht (drop into Café 't Papeneiland at Prinsengracht 2) and detouring through the gentrified small streets of the Jordaan neighborhood before popping out at Westerkerk under the tallest spire in the city.

Pedal out to the lush and peaceful Vondelpark, and then cut back through the center of town (Leidseplein to the Mint Tower, down Rokin street to the Dam Square). From there, cruise the Red Light District, following Oudezijds Voorburgwal past the Oude Kerk (Old Church) to Zeedijk street and return to the train station.

From Centraal Station, you can escape into the countryside by hopping on the free ferry behind the station. In five minutes, Amsterdam will be gone, and you'll be rolling through your very own Dutch painting (get free "Great Waterland Bicycle Tour" brochure from MacBike rental shop, on west side of train station).

SIGHTS

These sights are arranged by neighborhood for handy sight-seeing. When you see a ⭐ in a listing, it means the sight is covered in much more depth in my self-guided walks or one of the museum tours.

Sights—Southwest Amsterdam

▲▲▲**Rijksmuseum**—Built to house the nation's greatest art, the Rijksmuseum packs several thousand paintings into 200 rooms. To survive, focus on the Dutch masters: Rembrandt, Hals, Vermeer, and Steen.

Follow the museum's chronological layout to see painting evolve from narrative religious art, to religious art, to the Golden Age, when secular art dominated. With no local church or royalty to commission big canvases in the post-1648 Protestant Dutch republic, artists had to find their own patrons. They specialized in portraits of the wealthy city class (Hals), pretty still-lifes (Claesz), and nonpreachy slice-of-life art (Steen). The museum has four quietly wonderful Vermeers. And, of course, there's a thoughtful brown soup of Rembrandt, including *Night Watch*. Works by Rembrandt show his excellence as a portraitist for hire *(De Staalmeesters)* and offer some powerful psychological studies, such as *The Denial of St. Peter*—with a betrayed Jesus in the murky background (€8, free if under 18, helpful audioguide-€3.50, daily 10:00–17:00, great bookshop, decent cafeteria, tram #2 or #5 from train station, Stadhouderskade 42, tel. 020/674-7000, www.rijksmuseum.nl). ⭐ See Rijksmuseum Tour, page 91.

Note: When the main part of the Rijksmuseum closes for renovation in the fall of 2003, its masterpieces will be on display in the Phillips Wing (south wing—the part of the huge building nearest the Van Gogh museum).

Amsterdam Sights

▲▲▲**Van Gogh Museum**—Near the Rijksmuseum, this remarkable museum showcases 200 paintings by the troubled artist whose art seemed to mirror his life. The new exhibition hall (usually included with admission) features temporary exhibits of 1840–1920 art (€7.25, €2 if under 18, daily 10:00–18:00, good audioguide-€3, Paulus Potterstraat 7, tel. 020/570-5200, www.vangoghmuseum.nl).
⭐ See Van Gogh Museum Tour, page 112.

Museumplein Neighborhood

Stedelijk Modern Art Museum—Next to the Van Gogh Museum, this place is fun, far-out, and refreshing. It has mostly post-1945 art but also a sometimes-outstanding collection of Monet, van Gogh, Cézanne, Picasso, and Chagall, and a lot of special exhibitions. Unfortunately, it's closed until 2005.

▲**Museumplein**—Bordered by the Rijks, Van Gogh, and Stedelijk museums and the Concertgebouw (classical music hall), this square is interesting even to art haters. Amsterdam's best acoustics are

found underneath the Rijksmuseum, where street musicians perform everything from chamber music to Mongolian throat singing. Mimes, human statues, and crafts booths dot the square. Coster Diamonds offers tours showing stone cutting and polishing. Skateboarders careen across a concrete tube, while locals enjoy a park bench or a coffee at the Cobra café.

▲**Heineken Brewery**—The leading Dutch beer is no longer brewed here, but this old brewery now welcomes visitors to a slick and entertaining beer-appreciation experience. It's really the most enjoyable beer tour I've encountered in Europe. You'll learn as much as you want, marvel at the huge vats and towering ceilings, see videos, and go on rides. "What's it like to be a Heineken bottle and be filled with one of the best beers in the world? Try it for yourself." An important section recognizes a budding problem of our age—vital to people as well as beer—this planet's scarcity of clean water. With globalization, corporations are well on the way to owning the world's water supplies (€7.50 for self-guided hour-long tour and 3 beers or soft drinks, must be over age 18, Tue–Sun 10:00–18:00, last entry 17:00, closed Mon, tram #16, #24, or #25 to Stadhouderskade 78, an easy walk from the Rijksmuseum, tel. 020/523-9666).

▲**Leidseplein**—Brimming with cafés, this people-watching mecca is an impromptu stage for street artists, accordionists, jugglers, and unicyclists. Sunny afternoons are liveliest. The Boom Chicago theater fronts this square. Stroll nearby Lange Leidse-dwarsstraat (1 block north) for a taste-bud tour of ethnic eateries from Greek to Indonesian.

▲▲**Vondelpark**—This huge and lively city park is popular with the Dutch—families with little kids, romantic couples, strolling seniors, and hippies sharing blankets and beers. It's a popular venue for free summer concerts. On a sunny afternoon, it's a hedonistic scene that seems to say "parents…relax."

Amsterdam Film Museum—It's actually not a museum but a movie theater. In its three 80-seat theaters, it shows several films a day, from small foreign productions to 70 mm classics drawn from its massive archives (€6.25, always in the original language, often English subtitles, Vondelstraat 69, tel. 020/589-1400, www.filmmuseum.nl).

Houseboat Museum Amsterdam—Small sail-powered cargo ships became uneconomical with the advent of modern cargo boats in the 1930s. Almost worthless, they found a new use—as houseboats lining the canals of Amsterdam. Today 2,500 such boats—their cargo holds turned into elegantly cozy living rooms—are called home by locals. For a peek into this *gezellig* (cozy) world, visit this tiny museum. Captain Vincent enjoys showing visitors around the museum, which feels lived in because until 1997 it was (€2.50, March–Oct Wed–Sun 11:00–17:00, closed Mon–Tue, Nov–Feb Fri–Sun 11:00–17:00, closed Mon–Thu, Prinsengracht opposite #296 facing Elandsgracht, tel. 020/427-0750).

Sights—Central Amsterdam, near Dam Square

▲▲▲**Anne Frank House**—A pilgrimage for many, this house offers a fascinating look at the hideaway of young Anne during the Nazi occupation of the Netherlands. Pick up the English pamphlet at the door. Recently expanded, the exhibit now offers more thorough coverage of the Frank family, the diary, the stories of others who hid, and the Holocaust. In summer, skip the hour-long daytime lines by arriving after 18:00 (last entry is 20:30) and visit after dinner (€6.50, April–Aug daily 9:00–21:00, Sept–March daily 9:00–19:00, Prinsengracht 263, near Westerkerk, tel. 020/556-7100, www .annefrank.nl). ✪ See Anne Frank House Tour, page 125.

For an interesting glimpse of Holland under the Nazis, rent the powerful movie *Soldier of Orange* before you leave home.
Westerkerk—Near the Anne Frank House, this landmark church (generally open April–Sept 11:00–15:00) has a barren interior, Rembrandt's body buried somewhere under the pews, and Amsterdam's tallest steeple. The tower is open by tour only. The mandatory €3 guided tour (in English and Dutch) tells of the church and its carillon and takes you up to see the view (45 min, departures on the hour, April–Sept Mon–Sat 10:00–17:00, last trip at 17:00, closed Sun and in winter, tel. 020/689-2565).
Royal Palace (Koninklijk Paleis)—The palace, right on Dam Square, was built as a lavish city hall for Amsterdam, when the country was a proud new republic and Amsterdam was awash in profit from trade. When constructed (around 1660), this building was one of Europe's finest. Today it's the official (but not actual) residence of the queen and has a sumptuous interior (while it pretends that it's open to the public, this is rare—and for the near future it's closed because of an asbestos problem, tel. 020/624-8698). For more information, see page 54 of the Amsterdam City Walk chapter.
▲**Begijnhof**—Stepping into this tiny, idyllic courtyard in the city center, you escape into the charm of old Amsterdam. Notice house #34, a 500-year-old wooden structure (rare since repeated fires taught city fathers a trick called brick). Peek into the hidden Catholic church, dating from the time when post-Reformation Dutch Catholics couldn't worship in public. It's opposite the English Reformed church, where the Pilgrims worshiped while

Central Amsterdam

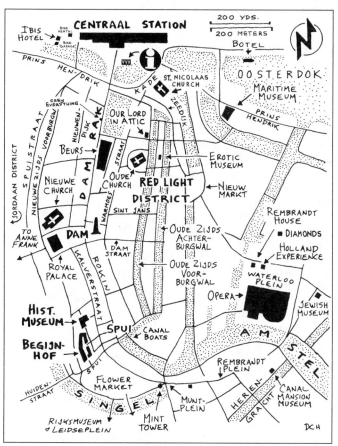

waiting for their voyage to the New World (marked by a plaque near the door). Be considerate of the people who live around the courtyard (free, daily 10:00–17:00, on Begijnensteeg lane, just off Kalverstraat between #130 and #132, pick up flier at office near entrance, open weekdays 10:00–16:00). For more information, see page 61 of the Amsterdam City Walk chapter.

▲**Amsterdam History Museum**—Follow the city's growth from fishing village to world trader to hippie haven. This creative and hardworking museum features Rembrandt's paintings, fine English descriptions, and a carillon loft. The loft comes with push-button recordings of the town bell tower's greatest hits and a self-serve carillon "keyboard" that lets you ring a few bells yourself (€6.50, Mon–Fri 10:00–17:00, Sat–Sun 11:00–17:00, good-value restaurant, next to Begijnhof, Kalverstraat 92, tel. 020/523-1822). The museum's free pedestrian corridor—lined with old-time group portraits—is a powerful teaser. ⚫ See Amsterdam History Museum Tour, page 140.

Sights—Southeast Amsterdam

To reach these sights from the train station, take tram #9 or #14. All of these sights except the last two (Tropenmuseum and Maritime Museum) are close to each other and could easily be connected into an interesting walk.

▲**Rembrandt's House**—Tour the place this way: See the 10-minute introductory video (Dutch and English showings alternate); tour Rembrandt's reconstructed house (filled with exactly what his bankruptcy inventory of 1656 said he owned); imagine him at work in his reconstructed studio; ask the printer to explain the etching process; then, for the finale, enjoy several rooms of original Rembrandt etchings. You'll find no paintings, but the etchings are marvelous and well described (€7, Mon–Sat 10:00–17:00, Sun 13:00–17:00, Jodenbreestraat 4, tel. 020/520-0400).

Holland Experience—Bragging "Experience Holland in 30 minutes," this show takes you traveling with three clowns through an idealized montage of Dutch clichés. There are no words but lots of images and special effects as you rock with the boat and get spritzed with perfume while viewing the tulips (€8, 2 enter for price of 1 with this book, or show this book and get €1.25 off the €11.50 combo-ticket with Rembrandt's House, daily 10:00–18:00 on the hour, adjacent to Rembrandt's house at Jodenbreestraat 8, tel. 020/422-2233). The men's urinal is a trip to the beach. Plan for it.

▲**Diamonds**—Many shops in the "city of diamonds" offer tours. These tours come with two parts: a chance to see experts behind magnifying glasses polishing the facets of precious diamonds, fol-

lowed by a visit to an intimate sales room to see (and perhaps buy) a tiny shiny souvenir. The handy and professional Gassan Diamonds facility fills a huge warehouse a block from Rembrandt's House. You'll get a security sticker and join a tour to see a polisher at work and hear a general explanation of the process (free, 15 min). Then you'll have an opportunity to sit

Waterlooplein Neighborhood

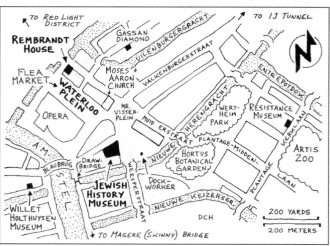

down and have color and clarity described and illustrated with diamonds ranging in value from $100 to $30,000. Afterwards you can bring your free cup of coffee from the café to the Delftware painting exhibit across the parking lot (daily 9:00–17:00, Nieuwe Uilenburgerstraat 173, tel. 020/622-5333, www.gassandiamonds.com).
Waterlooplein—Several of the sights in southeast Amsterdam cluster near this large square, dominated by the modern opera house.

Survey the neighborhood from the lamp-lined **Blaubrug** ("Blue Bridge")—a modest, modern version of Paris' Pont Alexandre III. The bridge crosses the **Amstel River.** From this point, the river is channeled to form the city's canals.

Pan clockwise. The big, curved modern facade belongs to the new opera house (commonly called the "Stopera," after a public outcry wanting to stop its construction). Behind the Stopera is the daily Waterlooplein flea market (not visible from here; listed below). One block beyond that (not visible from here) are Rembrandt's House, the Holland Experience, and Gassan Diamonds (all mentioned above). To the right of the Stopera are the twin gray steeples of the Moses and Aaron church, which sits roughly in the center of the former Jewish Quarter.

Several **Jewish sights** cluster to the right of the Moses and Aaron church: the Jewish History Museum, Portuguese Synagogue, and dockworker memorial. Just east of those is the De Hortus Botanical Garden.

The modern drawbridge in the foreground, though not

famous, is photogenic. Crossing the Amstel upstream is one of the city's romantic spots—the Magere Brug ("Skinny Bridge"). And a block away is the city's best look at a Golden Age mansion, the Herengracht Canal Mansion (a.k.a. Willet Holthuysen Museum; listed under "Sights—Rembrandtplein," below).

Waterlooplein Flea Market—
For more than a hundred years, the Jewish Quarter flea market has raged daily except Sunday behind the Rembrandt House. The long narrow park is filled with stalls selling cheap clothes, hippie stuff, old records, tourist knick-knacks, and garage-sale junk.

Jewish History Museum—Four historic synagogues have been joined by steel and glass to make one modern complex telling the story of the Jews in Amsterdam through the centuries (€5, daily 11:00–17:00, good kosher café, Jonas Daniel Meijerplein 2, tel. 020/626-9945).

De Hortus Botanical Garden—This is a unique oasis of tranquility within the city (no cell phones allowed because "our collection of plants is a precious community, treat it with respect"). One of the oldest botanical gardens in the world, it dates from 1638, when medicinal herbs were grown here. Today, among its 6,000 different kinds of plants—most of which were collected by the Dutch East India Company in the 17th and 18th centuries—you'll find medicinal herbs, cacti, several greenhouses (one with a fluttery butterfly house—a hit with kids), and a tropical palm house. Much of it is thoughtfully described in English: "A Dutch merchant snuck a coffee plant out of Ethiopia, which ended up in this garden in 1706. This first coffee plant in Europe was the literal granddaddy of the coffee cultures of Brazil—long the world's biggest coffee producer." (€5, Mon–Fri 9:00–17:00, Sat–Sun 11:00–17:00, Plantage Middenlaan 2A, tel. 020/625-8411.)

▲Dutch Theater (Hollandsche Schouwburg)—This is a moving memorial. Once a lively theater in the Jewish neighborhood, this was used as an assembly hall for local Jews destined for Nazi concentration camps. On the wall, 6,700 family names pay tribute to the 104,000 Jews deported and killed by the Nazis. Upstairs is a small history exhibit on local Jews during World War II. The ruined theater actually offers little to see but plenty to think about—notice the hopeful messages that visiting school groups attach to the wooden tulips (free, daily 11:00–16:00, Plantage Middenlaan 24, tel. 020/626-9945).

▲▲Dutch Resistance Museum (Verzetsmuseum)—This is

Jews in Amsterdam

In 1940, one in ten Amsterdamers was Jewish, and most lived in the neighborhood behind Waterlooplein. Jewish traders had long been welcome in a city that cared more about business than religion. In the late 1500s, many Sephardic Jews from Spain and Portugal immigrated, fleeing persecution. (The philosopher Baruch Spinoza's ancestors were among them.) In the 1630s, Yiddish-speaking Eastern European Jews (Ashkenazi) poured in. By 1700, the Jewish Quarter was a bustling, exotic, multicultural world, with more people speaking Portuguese, German, and Yiddish than Dutch.

Jews were not first-class citizens. They needed the city's permission to settle there, and they couldn't hold public office (but then neither could Catholics under Calvinist rule). Still, the Jewish Quarter was not a ghetto (enforced segregation), there were no special taxes, and cosmopolitan Amsterdam was well acquainted with all types of beliefs and customs.

In 1796, Jews were given full citizenship. In exchange, they were required to learn the Dutch language and submit to the city's legal system...and the Jewish culture began assimilating into the Dutch.

In 1940, Nazi Germany occupied the Netherlands. On February 22, 1941, the Nazis began rounding up Jews—herding hundreds of them to Jonas Daniel Meyerplein to be shipped to extermination camps in Eastern Europe. The citizens responded with a general strike that shut down the entire city, a heroic gesture honored today with a statue of a striking dockworker on Jonas Daniel Meyerplein. Despite the strike, the roundups continued. By war's end, more than 100,000 of the city's 130,000 Jews had died.

Today, about 25,000 Jews live in Amsterdam, and the Jewish Quarter has blended in with the modern city.

an impressive look at how the Dutch resisted their Nazi occupiers from 1940 to 1945. You'll see propaganda movie clips, study forged ID cards under a magnifying glass, and read of ingenious, clever, and courageous efforts to hide local Jews from the Germans. And at the end of the war, Nazi helmets were turned into bedpans (€4.50, Tue–Fri 10:00–17:00, Sat–Mon 12:00–17:00, closed April 30, well described in English, recommended café adjacent, tram #9 from station, Plantage Kerklaan 61, tel. 020/620-2535). Amsterdam's famous zoo is just across the street.

Amsterdam's Story

Visualize the physical layout of this manmade city, built on trees, protected by dikes, and laced with canals in the marshy delta at the mouth of the Amstel River. Location, location, location. Boats could arrive here from Germany by riverboat down the Rhine, from England across the Channel and down the IJ River, and from Denmark entering the Zuiderzee inlet of the North Sea. St. Nicholas, protector of water travelers, was the city's patron.

As early as 1300, Amsterdam was already an international trade center of German beer, locally caught herring, cloth, bacon, salt, and wine. Having dammed and canalized the Amstel, and diked out the sea tides, they drained land, sunk pilings, and built a city from scratch. When the region's leading bishop granted the town a charter (1300), Amsterdamers could then set up their own law courts, judge their own matters, and be essentially autonomous. The town thrived.

By 1500, Amsterdam was a walled city of 12,000, with the Singelgracht serving as the moat. Mid-century, the city got a growth spurt when its trading rival Antwerp fell to Spanish troops and a flood of fellow Flemish headed north fleeing the chaos and religious persecution.

In 1602, hardy Dutch sailors (and the Englishman Henry Hudson) tried their hand at trade with the Far East. When they returned, they brought with them valuable spices, jewels, luxury goods...and the Golden Age.

The Dutch East India Company (abbreviated V.O.C. in Dutch), a state-subsidized import/export business, combined nautical skills with capitalist investing. With 500 or so 150-foot ships cruising in and out of Amsterdam's harbor, it was the first great multinational corporation. Amsterdam's Golden Age (c. 1600–1650) rode the wave of hard work and good fortune. Over the next two centuries, the V.O.C. would send a half-million Dutch people on business trips to Asia, broadening their horizons.

The city of the Golden Age was perhaps the wealthiest on earth, thriving as the "warehouse of the world." Goods came from

▲**Tropical Museum (Tropenmuseum)**—As close to the Third World as you'll get without lots of vaccinations, this imaginative museum offers wonderful re-creations of tropical-life scenes and explanations of Third World problems. Ride the elevator to the top floor, and circle your way down through this immense collection opened in 1926 to give the Dutch a peek at their vast colonial hold-

everywhere. The V.O.C.'s specialties were spices (pepper and cinnamon), coffee and tea, Chinese porcelain (Delftware's Eastern inspiration), and silk. Meanwhile, the Dutch West India Company concentrated on the New World, trading African slaves for South American sugar. With its wealth, Amsterdam built in grand style, erecting the gabled townhouses we see today. The city expanded west and south, adding new neighborhoods.

But by 1650, Amsterdam's overseas trade was being eclipsed by new superpowers England and France. Inconclusive wars with Louis XIV and England drained the economy, destroyed the trading fleet, and demoralized the people. Throughout the 1700s, Amsterdam was a city of backwater bankers rather than international traders, although it remained the cultural center of Holland.

In 1795, the city was beached at low tide. Napoleon's French troops occupied the country and the economy was dismal.

A revival in the 1800s was spurred by technological achievements. The Dutch built a canal reconnecting Amsterdam directly with the North Sea (1824–1876), railroads laced the small country, and the city expanded southward by draining new land. The Rijksmuseum, Centraal Station, and Magna Plaza were built as proud monuments to the economic upswing.

The 1930s Depression hit hard, followed by four years of occupation under the Nazis, aided by pro-Nazi Dutch. Its large Jewish population was decimated by Nazi deportations and extermination (falling from 130,000 Jews in 1940 to 30,000 in 1945).

With post-war prosperity, in the 1960s Amsterdam became a world cultural capital again as the center for Europe's hippies, who came here to smoke marijuana. Grassroots campaigns by young, artistic, politically active people promoted free sex and free bikes.

Today, Amsterdam is a city of 727,000 people jammed into small apartments (often with the same floor plan as their neighbors'). Since the 1970s, many locals are immigrants. One in 10 Amsterdamers is Surinamese, and one in 10 bows toward Mecca.

ings. Don't miss the display case allowing you to see and hear the world's most exotic musical instruments. The Ekeko cafeteria serves tropical food (€7, daily 10:00–17:00, tram #9 to Linnaeusstraat 2, tel. 020/568-8215).

Netherlands Maritime (Scheepvaart) Museum—This huge collection of model ships, maps, and sea-battle paintings fills the 300-year-old Dutch Navy Arsenal. Given the Dutch seafaring heritage, I expected a more interesting museum. Sailors may disagree, but—even with its recreation of an 18th-century Dutch East India Company ship manned by characters in old costumes—I found the place pretty lifeless (€6.75, daily 10:00–17:00, closed Mon off-season, English explanations, don't waste your time with 30-min movie, bus #22 or #32 to Kattenburgerplein 1, tel. 020/523-2222).

Sights—Rembrandtplein and Neighborhood

One of the city's premier nightlife spots is the leafy Rembrandtplein (his modest statue stands here) and the adjoining Thorbeckeplein. Several late-night dance clubs (such as IT, a half-block east down Amstelstraat) keep the area lively into the wee hours. Utrechtsestraat is lined with upscale shops and restaurants.

▲**Herengracht Canal Mansion (Willet Holthuysen Museum)**— This 1687 patrician house offers a fine look at old Amsterdam's wealthy, with a good 15-minute English introductory film and a 17th-century garden in back (€4.50, Mon–Fri 10:00–17:00, Sat–Sun 11:00–17:00, tram #4 or #9 to Herengracht 605, 1 block southeast of Rembrandtplein, tel. 020/523-1870).

Tuschinski Theater—This movie palace from the 1920s glitters inside and out. Still a working theater, it's a delightful old place to see first-run movies (a half-block from Rembrandtplein down Reguliersbreestraat). The exterior is an interesting hybrid of styles, forcing the round peg of Art Nouveau into the square hole of Art Deco. The stone-and-tile facade features stripped-down, functional Art Deco squares and rectangles but is ornamented  with Art Nouveau elements—Tiffany-style windows, garlands, curvy iron lamps, Egyptian pharaohs, and exotic gold lettering over the door. Inside, the sumptuous decor features red carpets, nymphs on the walls, and semi-abstract designs. Grab a seat in the lobby and watch the ceiling morph (Reguliersbreestraat 26–28).

Sights—Red Light District

▲▲**Amstelkring Museum (Our Lord in the Attic)**—Near the train station in the Red Light District, you'll find a fascinating hidden Catholic church filling the attic of 17th-century merchants' houses (€4.50, Mon–Sat 10:00–17:00, Sun 13:00–17:00, Oudezijds

Voorburgwal 40, tel. 020/624-6604). ✪ See Amstelkring Museum Tour, page 132.

▲▲**Red Light District**—Europe's most touristed ladies of the night shiver and shimmy, as they have since 1700, in 450 display-case windows around Oudezijds Achterburgwal and Oudezijds Voorburgwal, surrounding the Oude Kerk (Old Church). Drunks and druggies make the streets uncomfortable late at night, but it's a fascinating walk between noon and nighttime.

The neighborhood, one of Amsterdam's oldest, has had prosti-tutes since 1200. Prostitution is entirely legal here, and the prostitutes are generally entrepreneurs, renting space and running their own businesses. Popular prostitutes net around €300 a day (S&F, €25–50) and fill out tax returns. ✪ See Red Light District Walk, page 68.

The **Prostitution Information Center,** open to the public, offers a small booklet that answers most of the questions tourists have about the Red Light District (free, Tue, Wed, Fri, and Sat 11:30–19:30, facing Oude Kerk at Enge Kerksteeg 3).

Sex Museums—Amsterdam has two sex museums: one in the Red Light District and one a block in front of the train station on Damrak. While visiting one can be called sightseeing, visiting both is hard to explain. Here's a comparison:

The Erotic Museum in the Red Light District is less offen-sive; its five floors rely heavily on badly dressed dummies of prostitutes in various acts. It also has a lot of uninspired paintings, videos, phone sex, old photos, and sculpture (€5, daily 11:00–24:00, along the canal at Oudezijds Achterburgwal 54, tel. 020/624-7303; also see Red Light District Walk, page 68).

The Damrak sex museum goes farther, telling the story of pornography from Roman times through 1960. Every sexual devia-tion is revealed in various displays, and the nude and pornographic art is a cut above that of the other sex museum. Also interesting are the early French pornographic photos and memorabilia from Europe, India, and Asia. You'll find a Marilyn Monroe tribute and some S&M displays, too (€5, daily 10:00–23:30, Damrak 18, a block in front of station).

▲**Marijuana and Hemp Museum**—This is a collection of dope facts, history, science, and memorabilia (€6, daily 11:00–22:00, Oudezijds Achterburgwal 148, tel. 020/623-5961). While small, it has a shocking finale: the high-tech grow room in which dozens of varieties of marijuana are cultivated in optimal hydroponic (among other) environments. Some plants stand five feet tall and shine under the intense grow lamps. The view is actually through glass walls into the neighboring Sensi Seed Bank Grow Shop, which sells carefully cultivated seeds and all the gear needed to grow them. It's an interesting neighborhood.

The **Cannabis College Foundation,** "dedicated to ending the global war against the cannabis plant through public education," is a half a block away at #124 (free, daily 11:00–19:00, tel. 020/423-4420, www.cannabiscollege.com). For more, see the Red Light District Walk, page 68, and Smoking, page 161.

AMSTERDAM
CITY WALK

From the Train Station to the Rijksmuseum

Amsterdam today looks much as it did in its Golden Age, the 1600s. It's a retired sea captain of a city, still in love with life, with a broad outlook and a salty story to tell.

Take a Dutch-sampler walk from one end of the old center to the other, tasting all that Amsterdam has to offer along the way. It's your best single stroll through Dutch clichés, democratic squares, businesses, afternoon happy-hour hangouts, and, yes, Amsterdam's 800-year history.

Orientation

Route Overview: The walk starts at the central-as-can-be train station. You'll walk about five kilometers (3 miles), heading down Damrak to Dam Square, continuing south down Kalverstraat to the Mint Tower, then wafting through the Bloemenmarkt (flower market), before continuing south to Leidseplein and jogging left to the Rijksmuseum. To return to Centraal Station, catch tram #2 or #5 from the southwest corner of the Rijksmuseum.

Tips: Find public toilets at fast-food places (€0.25) and near the entrance to the Amsterdam History Museum. Beware of silent transport—trams and bikes. Stay off the tram tracks and bike paths, and yield to bell-ringing bikers.

Length of Our Tour: Allow three hours for this walk.

Nieuwe Kerk: Fee if exhibition scheduled, daily 10:00–18:00, Dam Square, tel. 020/638-6909, www.nieuwekerk.nl.

Amsterdam Diamond Center: Free, daily 9:30–18:00, shorter hours off-season, Rokin 1, tel. 020/624-5787.

De Papegaai Catholic Church: Free, daily 10:00–17:00, on Kalverstraat.

Amsterdam History Museum: €6.50, Mon–Fri 10:00–17:00, Sat–Sun 11:00–17:00, Kalverstraat 92, tel. 020/523-1822.

City Walk Overview

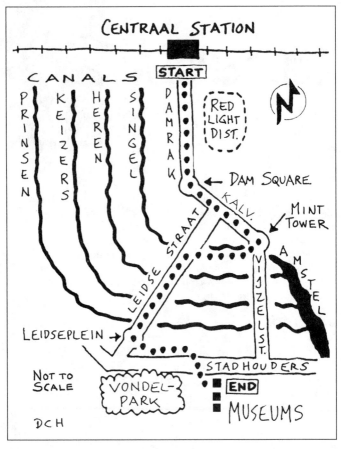

CENTRAAL STATION

START

CANALS

PRINSEN

KEIZERS

HEREN

SINGEL

DAMRAK

RED LIGHT DIST.

DAM SQUARE ←

KALV.

MINT TOWER

LEIDSE STRAAT

VIJZELST.

AMSTEL

LEIDSEPLEIN →

STADHOUDERS

NOT TO SCALE

VONDEL-PARK

END

MUSEUMS

DCH

Begijnhof: Free, daily 10:00–17:00, on Begijnensteeg lane, just off Kalverstraat between #130 and #132.

House of Hajenius: Free, Rokin 92, tel. 020/623-7494, www.hajenius.com.

When Nature Calls: Free, daily 10:00–22:00, Keizersgracht 508, www.whennaturecalls.nl.

Delft Shop: Free, Prinsengracht 440, tel. 020/627-8299.

Rijksmuseum: €8, free if under 18, daily 10:00–17:00, tel. 020/674-7000, www.rijksmuseum.nl.

Van Gogh Museum: €7.25, €2 if under 18, daily 10:00–18:00, Paulus Potterstraat 7, tel. 020/570-5200, www.vangoghmuseum.nl.

Centraal Station

Here where today's train travelers enter the city, sailors of yore disembarked from seagoing ships to be met by street musicians, pickpockets, hotel-runners, and ladies carrying red lanterns. When the station was built at the former harbor mouth, Amsterdam lost some of its harbor feel, but it's still a bustling port of entry.

Centraal Station, with warm red brick and prickly spires, is the first of several neo-Gothic buildings we'll see from the late

1800s, built during Amsterdam's economic revival. One of the towers has a clock dial; the other tower's dial is a weathervane. Watch the hand twitch as the wind gusts.

As you emerge from the train station, the city spreads out before you in a series of concentric canals. Ahead of you stretches the street called Damrak, leading south to Dam Square, a kilometer away. To the left of Damrak is the city's old *(oude)* side, to the right is the new *(nieuwe)*.

The big church towering above the old side (at about 10 o'clock) is the St. Nicholas church, built in the 1880s when Catholics—after two centuries of oppression—were finally free to worship in public. The church marks the beginning of the Red Light District. The city's biggest bike garage, a multi-storied wonder, is on your right (in front of the Ibis Hotel). If you'd like to make this "walk" a much faster "roll," there's a handy bike-rental place in the station (Mac-Bike, daily 9:00–17:45, across from bike garage, Stationsplein 33, online reservations possible, tel. 020/625-3845, www.macbike.nl).

• *We'll basically walk south from here to the Rijksmuseum. The art museum and the station—designed by the same architect—stand like bookends holding the old town together. Follow the crowds south on Damrak, walking along the right side of the street.*

Damrak

Stroll past every Dutch cliché at the tourist shops: wooden shoes, plastic tulips, Heineken fridge magnets, and windmill saltshakers. Listen to a hand-cranked barrel organ. Order French fries (called *Vlaamse frites*, or Flemish fries, since they were invented in the Low Countries) and dip them in mayonnaise, not ketchup. Eating international cuisine (Indonesian *rijsttafel*, Argentine steaks, Middle-Eastern *shoarma*, pron. SHWAHR-mah) is like going local in cosmopolitan Amsterdam. And you'll find the city's most notorious commodity displayed disease-free at the Amsterdam sex museum.

Amsterdam City Walk, First Half

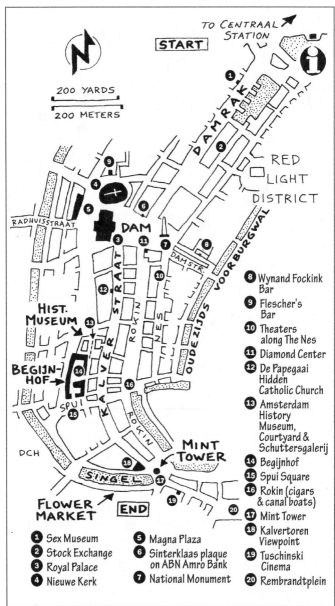

TO CENTRAAL STATION

START

RED LIGHT DISTRICT

DAMRAK

200 YARDS
200 METERS

RADHUISSTRAAT

DAM

HIST. MUSEUM

BEGIJN-HOF

SPUI

DCH

KALVER STRAAT

ROKIN

NES

OUDEZIJDS

VOORBURGWAL

DAM STR.

MINT TOWER

SINGEL

FLOWER MARKET

END

8 Wynand Fockink Bar

9 Flescher's Bar

10 Theaters along The Nes

11 Diamond Center

12 De Papegaai Hidden Catholic Church

13 Amsterdam History Museum, Courtyard & Schuttersgalerij

14 Begijnhof

15 Spui Square

16 Rokin (cigars & canal boats)

17 Mint Tower

18 Kalvertoren Viewpoint

19 Tuschinski Cinema

20 Rembrandtplein

1 Sex Museum

2 Stock Exchange

3 Royal Palace

4 Nieuwe Kerk

5 Magna Plaza

6 Sinterklaas plaque on ABN Amro Bank

7 National Monument

The street was once a riverbed, where the Amstel River flowed north into the IJ river (pron. eye) behind today's train station. Both rivers then emptied into a vast inlet of the North Sea (the Zuiderzee), making Amsterdam a major seaport. Today, the Amstel is channeled into canals, its former mouth has been covered by Centraal Station, the North Sea inlet has been diked off to make an inland lake, and 100,000 ships a year reach the open waters by sailing west through the North Sea Canal.

• *The long brick building with the square clock tower, along the left side of Damrak, is the...*

Stock Exchange (Beurs)

Built of nine million bricks on 4,880 tree trunks hammered into the marshy soil, the Beurs van Berlage (named for an early 20th-century Amsterdam architect with vision) stands as a symbol of the city's long tradition as a trading town.

Back when "stock" meant whatever could be loaded and unloaded onto a boat, Amsterdamers gathered to trade. Soon, rather than trading goats, chickens, and kegs of beer, they were exchanging slips of paper and "futures" at one of the world's first stock exchanges. Traders needed money-changers, who needed bankers, who made money by lending money...and Amsterdam of the 1600s became one of the world's first great capitalist cities, loaning money to free-spending kings, dukes, and bishops.

This impressive building, built in 1903 in a geometric, minimal, no frills style, is one of the world's first modern buildings, emphasizing function over looks. In 1984, the stock exchange moved next door (see the stock-exchange read-out) to the Euronext complex—a joint attempt by France, Belgium, and the Netherlands to compete with the power of Britain's stock exchange. The old Beurs building now hosts concerts and a museum for temporary exhibits.

Amsterdam still thrives as the center of Dutch businesses such as Heineken, Shell Oil, Philips Electronics, KLM Airlines, and Unilever. Amsterdamers have always had a reputation of putting business above ideological differences, staying neutral while trading with both sides.

• *Damrak opens into...*

Dam Square

The city got its start right here, around 1250, when fishermen in this marshy delta settled along the built-up banks of the Amstel River. They blocked the river with a *damme*, and created a small village called "Amstel-damme." Soon the fishermen were trading with German riverboats traveling downstream and with seafaring boats from Stockholm, Hamburg, and London. Dam Square was the center of it all.

The dam on the Amstel divided the *damrak* (meaning "outer harbor"—for sea traffic) from the *rokin* ("inner harbor"—for river traffic). Land trade routes converged here as well, and a customs house stood here. Today the Damrak and Rokin (pron. roh-KEEN) are major roads and the city's palace and major department stores face the square, where mimes, jugglers, and human statues mingle with locals and tourists. This is the historic heart of the city. As

the symbolic center of the Netherlands, it's where political demonstrations begin and end.

Pan the square clockwise to see the following: the Royal Palace (the large domed building on the west side), the Nieuwe Kerk (New Church), an ABN Amro bank, Damrak, the proud old De Bijenkorf ("The Beehive") department store, the Krasnapolsky Hotel, the white phallic obelisk of the National Monument, the Rokin, touristy Madame Tussaud's, and the entrance to pedestrian-only Kalverstraat.

Royal Palace

The name is misleading, since Amsterdam is one of the cradles of modern democracy. For centuries, this was the Town Hall of a self-governing community that prided itself on its independence and thumbed its nose at royalty. The current building, built in 1652, is appropriately classical (like the democratic Greeks), with a triangular pediment featuring—fittingly for Amsterdam—denizens of the sea cavorting with Neptune (with his green copper trident.)

After the city was conquered by the French, Napoleon imposed a monarchy on Holland, making his brother Louis the king of the Netherlands (1808). Louis used the city hall as his "royal palace," giving it the current name. When Napoleon was defeated, the victorious powers dictated that the Netherlands remain a monarchy, under a noble Dutch family called the House of Orange.

City on a Sandbar

Amsterdam is built upon millions of wooden pilings. The city was founded on unstable mud, which sits on stable sand. In the Middle Ages, buildings were made of wood, which rests lightly and easily on mud. But devastating fires repeatedly wiped out entire neighborhoods, so stone became the building material of choice. Stone is fire-resistant but was too heavy for a mud foundation. For more support, pilings were driven 9 meters (30 feet) through the mud and into the sand. The Royal Palace sits upon 13,000 such pilings—still solid after 300 years. (The wood survives fine if kept wet and out of the air.) Since World War II, concrete rather than wood has been used for the pilings, with foundations driven 18 meters (60 feet) deep through the first layer of sand, through more mud, and into a second layer of sand. And today's biggest buildings have foundations sinking as much as 36 meters (120 feet) deep.

If the current Queen Beatrix is in town, this is, technically, her residence (her permanent home is in the Royal Palace at The Hague). Amsterdam is the nominal capital of the Netherlands, but all governing activity is at The Hague (a city 50 km southwest). Today, because of an asbestos problem, Amsterdam's Royal Palace is closed to the public.

Nieuwe Kerk

In 1980, Queen Beatrix said "I do" in the Nieuwe Kerk, where the Netherlands' monarchs are crowned, wed, and buried. The "new" church is 600 years old (newer than the 700-year-old "old" church in the Red Light District). The sundial above the entrance once served as the city's official timepiece.

The church's bare, spacious, well-lit interior (often occupied by temporary art exhibits) looks quite different from the Baroque-encrusted churches found in the rest of Europe. In 1566, clear-eyed Protestant extremists throughout Holland marched into Catholic churches (like this once was), lopped off the heads of holy statues, stripped gold-leaf angels from the walls, urinated on Virgin Marys, and shattered stained glass windows in a wave of anti-Catholic vandalism.

This Iconoclasm (icon-breaking) of 1566 started an 80-year war against Spain and the Hapsburgs, leading finally to Dutch independence in 1648. Catholic churches like this one were converted to the new dominant religion, Calvinist Protestantism (today's Dutch Reformed Church). From then on, Dutch churches downplayed the "graven images" and "idols" of ornate religious art.

The Nieuwe Kerk is now the symbolic religious center of the Netherlands. When Beatrix dies or retires, her son, Crown Prince Willem Alexander, will parade to the center of the church, sit in front of the golden choir screen, and—with TV lights glaring and flashbulbs popping—be crowned the next sovereign.

• *Looking between the Royal Palace and the Nieuwe Kerk, you'll see the fanciful brick facade of the Magna Plaza shopping center, the start of the walk to the Anne Frank House and the Jordaan neighborhood (see Jordaan Walk, page 81). Back in Dam Square, on the wall of the ABN Amro bank, find the colorful little stone plaque of...*

Sinterklaas—St. Nicholas

Jolly old St. Nicholas (Nicolaas in Dutch) is the patron saint of sea-farers (see the three men in a tub) and of Amsterdam, and is also the model for Sinterklaas—the guy we call Santa Claus. Every year in late November, Holland's Santa Claus arrives by boat near Centraal Station (from his legendary home in Spain), rides a white horse up Damrak with his black servant, Peter, and arrives triumphant in this square while thousands of kids cheer.

December 5, the feast day of St. Nicholas, is when the Dutch exchange presents and Sinterklaas leaves goodies in good kids' wooden shoes. (Smart kids maximize capacity by putting out big boots.) Many Dutch celebrate Christmas on December 25, as well.

Around the corner in Damrak, the bank has an ATM and a chip-loader (*Oplaadpunt*). The ATM is familiar, but what's that small keypad next to it? It's for loading up the Dutch cash card—an attempt to eliminate the need for small change. With the keypad, the Dutch transfer money from their accounts onto a card with a computer chip. Then they can make purchases at stores by insert-ing the card into a pay-point, the way Americans buy gas from the pump.

National Monument

The obelisk, which depicts a crucified Christ, men in chains, and howling dogs, was built in 1956 as a WWII memorial. Now it's considered a monument for peace.

The Nazis occupied Holland from 1940 to 1945. They

deported 100,000 Amsterdam Jews, driving many—including young Anne Frank and her family—into hiding. Near the end of the war, the "Hunger Winter" of 1944–1945 killed thousands and forced many to survive on tulip bulbs. Today, Dutch people in their 70s—whose growth-spurt years coincided with the Hunger Winter— are easy to identify because they are uniformly short.

Circling the Square

You're at the center of Amsterdam. To the east a few blocks is the top of the Red Light District (see Red Light District Walk, page 68). Amsterdam is the world capital of experimental theater, and several edgy theaters line the street called the Nes (stretching south from Hotel Krasnapolsky).

Office workers do afternoon happy-hours at crowded bars that stock *jenevers* and liqueurs in wooden kegs. De Drie Fleschjes, a particularly casual pub, is tucked right behind the Nieuwe Kerk. The more upscale Wynand Fockink (100 meters down the alley along the right side of Hotel Krasnapolsky) serves fruit brandies produced in its adjoining distillery (which you can visit). Though the brew is bottled and distributed all over Holland, what you get here in the home-office bar is some of the best Fockink liqueur in the world.

At the Amsterdam Diamond Center (where Rokin street meets Dam Square), see cutters and jewelry-setters handling diamonds, plus some small educational displays and fake versions of big, famous stones. Since the 1500s, the city has been one of the world's diamond capitals. Eighty percent of industrial diamonds (for making drills and such) pass through here, as do many cut and polished jewels, like the Koh-i-Nohr diamond.

• *From Dam Square, head south on . . .*

Kalverstraat

This pedestrian-only street is lined with many familiar franchise stores and record shops. (If you're on a bike, you must dismount and walk it.) This has been a shopping street for centuries and today is notorious among locals as the place for cheesy, crass materialism. For

Amsterdam City Walk, Second Half

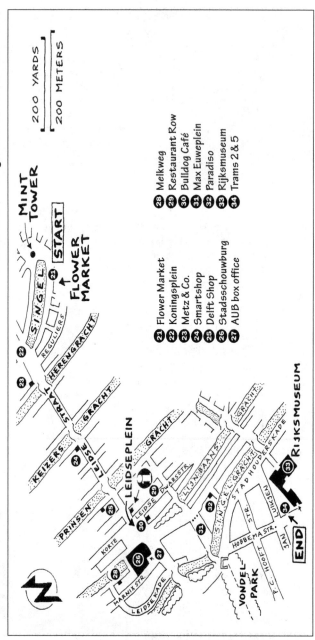

200 YARDS
200 METERS

MINT TOWER

START

FLOWER MARKET

S·I·N·G·E·L

REGULIERS

KEIZERSGRACHT

HERENGRACHT

LEIDSESTRAAT

PRINSENGRACHT

LEIDSEGRACHT

LEIDSEPLEIN

KORTE

MARNIX STR.

LEIDSEKADE

LEIDSE DWARSSTR.

LIJNBAANSGRACHT

SINGELGRACHT

STADHOUDERSKADE

HOBBEMASTR.

P.C. HOOFTSTR.

JAN LUIJKEN STR.

VONDEL PARK

RIJKSMUSEUM

END

21 Flower Market
22 Koningsplein
23 Metz & Co.
24 Smartshop
25 Delft Shop
26 Stadsschouwburg
27 AUB box office

28 Melkweg
29 Restaurant Row
30 Bulldog Café
31 Max Euweplein
32 Paradiso
33 Rijksmuseum
34 Trams 2 & 5

smaller and more elegant stores, try the adjacent district called De Negen Straatjes ("The Nine Little Streets"), where 190 shops mingle by the canals (about 4 blocks west of Kalverstraat).

• *About 120 meters along (across from the McDonald's), pop into . . .*

De Papegaai Hidden Catholic Church (Petrus en Paulus Kerk)

This Catholic church (daily 10:00–17:00), while not exactly hidden (you found it), keeps a low profile even now that Catholicism has been legalized in Amsterdam. In the late 1500s, with Protestants fighting Catholics and the Dutch fighting Spanish invaders, Amsterdam tried to stay neutral, doing business with all parties. Finally in 1578, Protestant extremists (following the teachings of Reformer John Calvin) took political control of the city. They expelled Catholic leaders and bishops, outlawed the religion, and allied Amsterdam with anti-Spanish forces in an action known to historians as The Alteration.

For the next two centuries, Amsterdam's Catholics were driven underground. Catholicism was illegal but tolerated, as long as it was not done in public, but in humble, unadvertised places like this, and for personal use only.

Today the church, which asks for a mere "15 minutes for God" (*een kwartier voor God*), stands as a metaphor for how marginal religion has always been in highly commercial and secular Amsterdam. (For more on hidden churches, see Amstelkring Museum Tour, page 132.)

• *Seventy meters farther along, at #92, where Kalverstraat crosses Wijde Kapel Steeg, look to the right at an archway leading to the . . .*

Courtyard of the Amsterdam History Museum

On the arch is Amsterdam's coat of arms—a red shield with three Xs and a crown. Not a reference to the city's sex trade, the X-shaped crosses (which appear everywhere in the city) represent the crucifixion of St. Andrew, the patron saint of fishermen, and symbolize heroism, determination, and mercy. The crown dates to 1489, when Maximilian I (the Low Countries' first Hapsburg ruler and later Holy Roman Emperor) paid off a big loan from city bankers and, as thanks for the cash, gave the city permission to use his prestigious trademark, the Hapsburg crown, atop its shield.

In the middle of the alleyway stands an alms box with a sealed-over coin slot (see photo previous page). The relief above the door (dated 1581) shows boys around a dove, reminding all who pass that this was an orphanage and asking for charity. Go inside.

The pleasant David and Goliath café (with a shady courtyard) is watched over by a giant statue of Goliath and a knee-high David (from 1650). In the courtyard are the lockers for the orphan's uniforms and a pay toilet.

• *The courtyard leads to another courtyard with the best city history museum in town, the Amsterdam History Museum (see tour on page 140). In between the two courtyards (on the left) is a glassed-in passageway (daily 10:00–17:00) lined with paintings, called the...*

Schuttersgalerij (Civic Guard Gallery)

In these group portraits from Amsterdam's Golden Age (early 1600s), look into the eyes of the frank, dignified men (and occasionally women) with ruffs and lace collars who made Amsterdam the most prosperous city in Europe, sending trading ships to distant colonies and pocketing interest from loans. The weapons they carry are mostly symbolic, since these "Civic Guards" who once protected the town had become more like fraternal organizations of business bigwigs.

Civic Guard of Captain Arent ten Grootenhuys from 1608 (the fourth painting on the left wall, bottom level) is typical of this highly stylized genre. The company sits in two rows. In the center is the young flag-bearer (with rolled-up flag). Just to the left is Captain G., recognizable because he holds the traditional captain's pike (a long axe-like weapon topped with a spearhead-shaped tip). This "captain" was really a successful businessman, one of the founders of the Dutch East India Company. His lieutenant (right of center, with elaborate armor) cocks a partisan (pike with a sword-like tip). Others wield hatchet-headed halberds.

Everyone looks straight out, and every face is lit perfectly. Each paid for his own portrait and wanted it right. It took masters like Rembrandt and Frans Hals to take the starch out of the collars and compose more natural scenes.

• *The gallery offers a shortcut to the Begijnhof, 70 meters farther south. But if the gallery is closed, backtrack to Kalverstraat, continue south, then turn right on Begijnensteeg. This leads to the entrance of the walled courtyard (daily 10:00–17:00) called the...*

Begijnhof

This quiet courtyard (pron. gutturally: buh-HHHINE-hof) lined with houses around a church, has sheltered women since 1346. In early times, rich women gave up their wealth to live in Christian poverty here as part of the lay order called Beguines. Poor women and widows lived here as well, spinning wool and making lace to earn their keep.

In 1578, when Catholicism was outlawed, the Dutch Reformed Church (and the city) took over many Catholic charities—such as this place. Many Dutch women, widowed by the hazards of overseas trade, found a retirement home here. The last Beguine died in 1971, but the Begijnhof still provides subsidized housing to single women in need (mostly Catholic seniors and students). The Begijnhof is just one of about 75 *hofjes* (housing projects surrounding courtyards) that dot Amsterdam.

Begin the Beguine visit at the statue of one of these charitable sisters. She faces the wooden house *(houten huys)* at #34. The city's oldest, it dates from 1477. Originally the whole city was built of wood. To the left of the house is a display of carved gable stones that once adorned house fronts and served as street numbers (and still do at #19 and #26, the former Mother Superior's house).

The brick-faced **English Church** (Engelse Kerk, from 1420) was the Beguine church until 1607, when it became Anglican. The Pilgrims (strict Protestants), fleeing persecution in England, stopped here in tolerant Amsterdam and prayed in this church before the *Mayflower* carried them to religious freedom at Plymouth Rock in America. (It remains a welcoming place, with English services on Sundays at 10:30.)

The "hidden" **Catholic Church** faces the English Church (enter through a low-profile doorway). Amsterdam's oppressed 17th-century Catholics, who refused to worship as Protestants, must have eagerly awaited the day when, in the 19th century, they were legally allowed to say Mass. Step inside.

Today, Holland is still divided religiously, but without the bitterness. Roughly a third are Catholic, a third Protestant... and a third list themselves as "unchurched."

• *From the Begijnhof, backtrack to busy Kalverstraat, then turn right, continuing south. Pause at the busy intersection with Spui Straat and get oriented.*

Spui and the Rokin

To the right down Spui Straat is the square called **Spui** (rhymes with "cow"). Lined with cafés and bars, it's one of the city's more popular spots for nightlife and sunny afternoon people-watching.

A half-block to the left is the busy street called **Rokin** (pron. ro-KEEN). A statue of Queen Wilhelmina (1860–1962) on the Rokin shows her riding daintily sidesaddle. In real life, she was the iron-willed inspiration for Dutch Resistance against the Nazis. The present Queen Beatrix is Wilhelmina's granddaughter.

Canal cruises depart from the Rondvaart Kooij dock.

The **House of Hajenius,** at Rokin 92, is a temple of cigars, a "paradise for the connoisseur" showing "175 years of tradition and good taste." To enter this sumptuous Art Deco building with its painted leather ceilings is to step back into 1910. The brown-capped canisters are for smelling fine pipe tobacco. Take a whiff. The personal humidifiers (read the explanation) allow locals to call in an order and have their cigars waiting for them in just the right humidity. Upstairs in back is a small, free museum (Rokin 92, www.hajenius.com).

• *Continue up Kalverstraat toward the...*

Mint Tower (Munttoren)

The tower, which marks the limit of the medieval walled city, served as one of the original gates (the steeple was added later, in 1620). The city walls were girdled by a moat—the Singelgracht. Until about 1500, the area beyond here was nothing but marshy fields and a few farms on reclaimed land.

On the way to the Mint Tower, you'll pass department stores with cafeterias. At the end of Kalverstraat, the Vroom & Dreesman

department store is one of Holland's oldest chains. The Kalvertoren shopping complex offers a top-floor viewpoint and café (venture into the glass atrium and slide up in the wild elevator). Across the street, inside La Marché department store, La Place is a sprawling self-service cafeteria—handy for a quick and healthy lunch.

From the busy intersection at Muntplein, look left (at about 10 o'clock) down Reguliersbreestraat. A long block east of here (where you see trees) is Rembrandtplein, another major center for nightlife. Halfway down the block (past the massive easyEverything Internet Café—open all day, every day, €1/40 min, Reguliers Breestraat 33), the twin green domes mark the exotic Tuschinski Theater, where you can see modern movies in a sumptuous Art Deco setting. Sit inside and stare at the ever-changing ceiling, imagining this place during the Roaring '20s.

• *Just past the Mint Tower, turn right and walk west along the south bank of the Singelgracht, which is lined with the greenhouse shops of the ...*

Flower Market (Bloemenmarkt)

Cut flowers, plants, bulbs, seeds, and garden supplies attest to Holland's reputation for growing flowers. Tulips, imported from Turkey in the 1600s, grew well in the sandy soil of the dunes and reclaimed land. By the 1630s, the country was in the grip of a full-blown tulip mania, when a single bulb sold for as much as a house, and fortunes were won and lost. Finally, in 1637, the market plummeted, and the tulip became just one of many beauties in the country's flower arsenal. Today Holland is a major exporter of flowers. Certain seeds are certified and OK to bring back into the United States (merchants have the details).

• *The long Flower Market ends at the next bridge, where you'll see a square named ...*

Koningsplein

Choke down a raw herring—the commodity that first put Amsterdam on the trading map—with locals who flock to this popular outdoor herring stand. (*Hollandse nieuwe* means the herring are in season.)

• *From Koningsplein, we'll turn left, heading straight to Leidseplein. At first the street southward is just labeled Koningsplein (Scheltema, Amsterdam's leading bookstore, is at Koningsplein 20), but it soon becomes . . .*

Leidsestraat

Between here and Leidseplein you'll cross several grand canals, following a street lined with fashion and tourist shops, and crowded with shoppers, tourists, bicycles, and trams. Trams must wait their turn to share a single track as the street narrows.

The once-grand, now-frumpy Metz & Co. department store (where Leidsestraat crosses Herengracht) offers a rare above-the-rooftops panorama of the city from its sixth-floor café.

Looking left down Herengracht, you'll see the "Golden Curve" of the canal, lined with grand, classical-style gables.

• *Past the posh stores of Laura Ashley, DKNY, and Lush, find a humble establishment where Leidsestraat crosses the Keizersgracht.*

When Nature Calls Smartshop

"Smartshops" like this one are clean, well-lighted, fully professional retail outlets that sell powerful drugs, many of which are illegal in America. Their "natural" drugs include harmless nutrition boosters

(royal jelly), harmful but familiar tobacco, herbal versions of popular dance-club drugs (herbal Ecstasy), powerful psychoactive plants (psilocybin mushrooms), and joints that are an unpredictable mix of marijuana and other substances, sold under exotic names like "Herbal Love." The big item: marijuana seeds.

Prices are clearly marked, with brief descriptions of the drugs, their ingredients, and effects. The knowledgeable salespeople can give more information on their "100 percent natural products that play with the human senses."

Still, my fellow Americans, *caveat emptor!* We've grown used to thinking, "If it's legal, it must be safe. (If it's not, I'll sue.)"

While perfectly legal and aboveboard, some of these

Canals

Amsterdam's canals tamed the flow of the Amstel River, creating pockets of dry land to build on. The city's 100 canals are about three meters (10 feet) deep, crossed by some 1,200 bridges, fringed with 100,000 Dutch elm and lime trees, and bedecked with 2,000 houseboats. A system of locks (back near Centraal Station) controls the flow outward to (eventually) the North Sea and the flow inward of the incoming tide. The locks

are opened periodically to flush out the system.

It is amazing how quiet and peaceful this big city of more than 700,000 can be. Some of the boats in the canals look pretty funky by day, but Amsterdam is an unpretentious, anti-status city. When the sun goes down and the lights come on, people cruise the sparkling canals with an on-board hibachi and a bottle of wine, and even scows can become chick magnets.

substances can cause powerful, often unpleasant reactions. Even if you've smoked marijuana (itself a potent mind-alterant), use caution with less familiar drugs. (Keizersgracht 508, daily 10:00–22:00, www.whennaturecalls.nl).

• *Where Leidsestraat crosses the Prinsengracht, just over the bridge on the right, you'll find...*

The Delft Shop (Prinsengracht 440)

The distinctive blue-and-white design characterizes glazed ceramics made in Delft (50 km southwest of here). Dutch traders learned the technique from the Chinese of the Ming dynasty, and many pieces have an oriental look. The doodads with arms branching off a trunk are popular "flower pagodas," vases for displaying tulips.

• *Leidsestraat empties into the square called...*

Leidseplein

Filled with outdoor tables under trees, ringed with cafés, theaters, and nightclubs, bustling with tourists, diners, trams, mimes, and fire-eaters, and lit by sun- or lantern-light, Leidseplein is the city's liveliest square.

Do a 360-degree spin: Leidseplein's south side is bordered by the city's main serious theater, the **Stadsschouwburg,** which dates back to the 17th-century Golden Age (present building from 1890). To the right, down a lane behind the big

theater, stands the **Melkweg** (Milky Way), the once-revolutionary, now-institutional entertainment complex housing all things youth-oriented under one roof (Lijnbaansgracht 234a); step into the lobby or check out posters plastered on walls to find out who's playing tonight. On Leidseplein's west side is the Boom Chicago nightclub theater (at #12), presenting English-language spoofs of politics, Amsterdam, and tourists. The neighborhood beyond Haagen Dazs and Burger King is the **Restaurant Row,** featuring countless Thai,

Brazilian, Indian, Italian, Indonesian, and even a few Dutch eateries. Next, on the east end of Leidseplein, is the **Bulldog Café and Coffeeshop,** the flagship of several café/bar/coffeeshops in town. (Notice the sign above the door: It once housed the police bureau). A small green-and-white decal in the window indicates that it's a city-licensed "coffeeshop," where marijuana is sold and smoked legally (for more information, see Smoking, page 161).

• *From Leidseplein, turn left and head along the taxi rank down the broad, busy, tram-filled boulevard called Kleine-Gartman Plantsoen, which becomes Weteringschans. At the triangular garden filled with iguanas, cross the street and pass under a row of tall, gray, Greek-style columns, entering . . .*

Max Euweplein

The Latin inscription above the colonnade—*Homo Sapiens non urinat in ventum*—means "Don't pee into the wind." Pass between the columns and through a passageway to reach a pleasant interior courtyard of cafés and a large chessboard with knee-high kings. (Max Euwe was a Dutch world chess champion.) The square gives you access to the Casino, and just over the small bridge is the entrance to **Vondelpark.**

• *Return to Weteringschans street. Continue 75 meters east to a squat red-brick building called . . .*

Paradiso

Back when rock-and-roll was a religion, this former church staged intimate concerts by big-name acts such as the Rolling Stones. In the late 1960s, when city fathers were trying hard to tolerate hordes of young pot-smokers, this building was redecorated with psychedelic colors and opened up as the first place where marijuana could be smoked—not legally yet, but it was tolerated. Today the club hosts live bands and DJs and sells marijuana legally (for current shows, see www.paradiso.nl).

• *Continue down Weteringschans to the first bridge, where you'll see the Rijksmuseum across the canal.*

The Rijksmuseum and Beyond

The best visual chronicle of the Golden Age is found in the Rijksmuseum's portraits and slice-of-life scenes. For a tour of the Rembrandts, Vermeers, and others, see the Rijksmuseum Tour, page 91.

On this walk, we've seen landmarks built during the city's late-19th-century revival: Centraal Station, the Stadsschouwburg, and now the Rijksmuseum. They're all similar, with red brick and Gothic-style motifs (clock towers, steeples, prickly spires, and stained glass). Petrus Cuypers (1827–1921), who designed the train station and the Rijksmuseum, was extremely influential. Mainly a builder of Catholic churches, he made the Rijksmuseum, with its stained glass windows, a temple to art.

The Rijksmuseum has been much celebrated for its open and airy design, but its once-spacious courtyards have been consumed by the vast museum's ever-growing need for more gallery space. In the fall of 2003, the Rijksmuseum will be closed for several years while the gangly add-ons are removed and the building returns to its original elegant simplicity.

Behind the Rijksmuseum is the always entertaining Museumplein and the Van Gogh Museum (see tour on page 112). The Heineken Brewery museum is a kilometer east of the Rijks on Stadhouderskade (see page 37).

To return to Centraal Station (or to nearly anyplace along this walk), catch tram #2 or #5 from the southwest corner of the Rijks. Trams #6, #7, and #10 (catch them on Weteringschans) can take you farther south, east, or west. Or walk north on Nieuwe Spiegel Straat, which leads (with a little detour) back to the Mint Tower.

RED LIGHT DISTRICT WALK

Amsterdam's oldest neighborhood has hosted the world's oldest profession since 1200. The district lies between Damrak and Nieuwemarkt. Amsterdamers call it De Wallen, or "The Walls," from the old city walls that once stood here. On our walk, we'll see history, sleaze, and cheese—chickens in Chinatown windows, drunks in doorways, cruising packs of foreign twenty-somethings, cannabis in windows, and sex for sale.

The sex trade runs the gamut, from sex shops selling porn and accessories to blue video arcades, from glitzy nightclub sex shows featuring strippers and sex acts to the real deal—prostitutes in bras, thongs, and high heels, standing in window displays, offering their bodies. Amsterdam keeps several thousand prostitutes employed—and it's all legal.

Not for everyone: The Red Light District has something offensive for everyone. Whether it's in-your-face images of graphic sex, exploited immigrant women, whips-and-chains, passed-out drug addicts, wafting pot smoke and urine smells, or just the shameless commercialism of it all, it's not everyone's cup of tea. While I encourage people to expand their horizons—that's a great thing about travel—it's perfectly OK to say "No, thank you."

Orientation

Route Overview: The walk starts at the centrally located Dam Square. Two parallel streets with similar names—Oudezijds Voorburgwal and Oudezijds Achterburgwal—run north–south through the heart of De Wallen. We'll walk a big long loop: north on Voorburgwal ("Voor") street past the Old Church, hook around on Zeedijk street, and return on Achterburgwal ("Achter"), ending two blocks from Dam Square.

Length of Our Tour: Allow two hours for this walk.

Photography: Consider leaving your camera in your bag. Absolutely avoid taking photos of ladies in windows, or you may have your film forcibly ripped from the camera and shredded by a snarling bouncer. Taking even seemingly harmless of ordinary people is frowned upon by privacy-loving locals. Photos of landmarks like the Oude Kerk church and wide shots of distant red lights from the bridges are certainly OK, but remember that cameras are a prime target in this high-theft area.

When to Go: Mornings are quiet, but that's also when you see more passed-out-drunk-in-a-doorway scenes. Afternoons bring out more prostitutes, and evenings are actually quite festive, with many tourists and out-of-towners.

Safety: Coming here is asking for trouble, but if you're on the ball and smart, it's perfectly safe. While there are plenty of police on horseback keeping things orderly, there are also plenty of rowdy drunks, drug-pushing low-lifes, con-artists, and pickpockets (not to mention extremely persuasive girls in windows). Assume any fight or commotion in the streets is a ploy to distract innocent victims who are about to lose their wallets. As always, wear your money belt and keep a low profile.

Old Church (Oude Kerk): €5, Mon–Sat 11:00–17:00, Sun 13:00–17:00.

Prostitution Information Center: Free, open Tue, Wed, Fri, and Sat 11:30–19:30, www.pic-amsterdam.com.

Lotus Flower Buddhist Temple: Free, daily 12:00–17:00, Zeedijk street.

Banana Bar (Bananenbar): Nightly, Ouedezijds Achterburgwal 37, tel. 020/622-7640.

Erotic Museum: €5, daily 11:00–24:00, O.Z. Achterburgwal 54, tel. 020/624-7303.

Casa Rosso: Nightly until 2:00, Achterburgwal 106-108, tel. 020/627-8954.

Cannabis College: Daily 11:00–19:00, O.Z. Achterburgwal 124, tel. 020/423-4420, www.cannabiscollege.com.

The Hash, Marijuana, and Hemp Museum: €6, daily 11:00–22:00, O.Z. Achterburgwal 130.

Sensi Seed Bank Store: Free, daily 11:00–18:00, O.Z. Achterburgwal 150.

The Tour Begins

From Dam Square, go east one block on Damstraat, past shops selling little wooden shoes and little wooden hash pipes. At the first bridge, turn left on Oudezijds Voorburgwal.

Red Light District

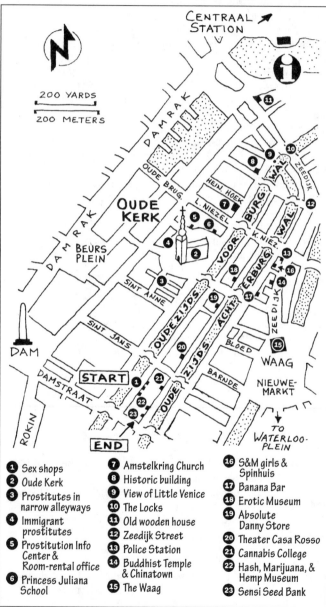

1. Sex shops
2. Oude Kerk
3. Prostitutes in narrow alleyways
4. Immigrant prostitutes
5. Prostitution Info Center & Room-rental office
6. Princess Juliana School
7. Amstelkring Church
8. Historic building
9. View of Little Venice
10. The Locks
11. Old wooden house
12. Zeedijk Street
13. Police Station
14. Buddhist Temple & Chinatown
15. The Waag
16. S&M girls & Spinhuis
17. Banana Bar
18. Erotic Museum
19. Absolute Danny Store
20. Theater Casa Rosso
21. Cannabis College
22. Hash, Marijuana, & Hemp Museum
23. Sensi Seed Bank

Oudezijds Voorburgwal

Amsterdam's oldest canal was once lined with its richest houses and nicknamed "The Velvet Canal" for the fancy clothes of its wealthy inhabitants. The first city wall ran along the right-hand side, and this canal was before *(voor)* the city wall *(burgwal)*, while the next canal over was after *(achter)*.

• *Along the right-hand side of Voor street, you'll find . . .*

Sex Shops and Video Arcades

Dildos, dirty playing cards, penis-headed lipstick, S&M starter kits, kinky magazines, and blue videos—welcome to De Wallen. While the Red Light District is notorious throughout the Netherlands, even small rural towns often have a sex shop like this to satisfy their citizens' needs. Browsers are welcome inside the sex shops.

Video arcades—giving access to dozens of porn films—charge by the minute.

• *A block farther north is the impressive . . .*

Oude Kerk

Returning from a long sea voyage, sailors of yore would spy the steeple of the Old Church on the horizon, and know they were home. They thanked St. Nicholas—the patron of this church, seafarers, and Amsterdam—for their safe return.

Begun around 1300 (some of the tower is original) and dedicated to St. Nicholas, the gangly church was built in fits and starts over the next 300 years. Even when the rival Nieuwe Kerk (New Church) was built on Dam Square, Amsterdam's oldest church still had the tallest spire, biggest organ, and most side-altars, and remained the neighborhood's center of activity, bustling inside and out with merchants and street markets.

The tower (70 meters high, or 290 feet), with an octagonal steeple atop a bell tower, is an 18th-century update of the original 1300 tower, which was the model for many other Dutch churches. The carillon's 47 bells chime mechanically or can be played by one of Amsterdam's three official carillonneurs.

Inside, the church is spacious and stripped-down, thanks to iconoclastic vandals. In the 16th century, rioting anti-Spanish Protestants gutted the church, smashed windows, and removed politically incorrect "graven images" (religious statues). One renowned girl threw her shoe at the Virgin statue. (Strict Calvinists at one point even removed the organ as a senseless luxury, until they found they couldn't stay on key singing hymns without it.) The church, permanently stripped of "popish" decoration, was transformed from Catholic to Dutch Reformed, the name St. Nicholas' Church was dropped, and it became known by the nickname everyone called it anyway—the Oude Kerk (Old Church). Today, there's not much to see inside (€5, Mon–Sat 11:00–17:00, Sun 13:00–17:00).

Around the Oude Kerk

The church is surrounded by prostitution, yes, but there are other things, as well—namely, everyday life. Attached to the Oude Kerk like barnacles are small buildings, originally homes for priests, church offices, or rental units. The house to the right of the entrance (#25), inhabited by an elderly woman, is very tiny—10 by 2.5 meters (32 x 8 feet). Remember, someone lives here—be discreet.

Though the Red Light District is considered prime real estate, the ugly, 1970s-style apartments (near the church tower) offer a few lucky residents cheap subsidized housing. Along the canal is a green, metal urinal that gets a lot of use. And, a few steps to the left of the Oude Kerk's entrance, look down to find boobs in the pavement.

• *From the Oude Kerk, backtrack a half-block south on Voor street to the Bulldog Café and turn right at a narrow alleyway. Take a deep breath and squeeze into this tight opening.*

Prostitutes in Narrow Alleyways

You're right in the thick of high-density sleaze. Several narrow streets are lined with panty-and-bra-clad girls in the windows winking at horny men, rapping on the window to attract attention, or looking disdainfully at sightseers. The area sure looks rough, but, aside from tricky pickpockets, these streets are actually very safe, overseen by surveillance cameras.

The entire Red Light District is dotted with teeny-tiny video surveillance cameras, located above doorways and in tiny alleys. If prostitutes have or notice any trouble, they press a buzzer that swiftly unleashes a burly, angry bouncer or the police.

There are other pockets of prostitution around, but this is one of the most concentrated. Explore.

• *Now circle the church clockwise. Around the back you'll see older, plumper (cheaper) prostitutes.*

Prostitution

Prostitution has been legal here since the 1980s. The women are often entrepreneurs, renting space and running their own businesses. Women usually rent their space for eight-hour shifts. A good spot costs €75 for a day shift and €150 for an evening. The rooms look tiny from the street ("Do they have

to do it standing up?"), but most are just display windows, opening onto a room behind or upstairs with a bed, a sink, and little else.

Prostitutes are licensed. To get a license, you have to have no criminal record, keep your premises hygienic, use condoms, and avoid minors. Most prostitutes opposed legalization, not wanting taxes and bureaucratic regulations.

Popular prostitutes charge €50 for a 20-minute visit and make around €300 a day. They fill out tax returns, and many belong to a loose union called the Red Thread. The law, not pimps, protects prostitutes.

While many women choose prostitution as a lucrative career, many others are forced into it by circumstance—poverty, drug addiction, abusive men, and immigration scams. Since the fall of the Iron Curtain, many East Europeans have flocked here for the high wages. The line between victim and entrepreneur grows finer and less clear.

• *On Enge Kerk Steeg, around the back of the Oude Kerk, is the . . .*

Prostitution Information Center (#3)

Doling out information, condoms, and souvenir T-shirts, the P.I.C. welcomes visitors (open Tue, Wed, Fri, and Sat 11:30–19:30). They have a map showing exactly where prostitution is legal and offer a small and frank booklet answering the most common questions tourists have about Amsterdam's Red Light District.

• *Next door is a . . .*

Room-Rental Office *(Kamerverhuurbedrijf)*

Women come here to rent window-space and bedrooms to use for prostitution. Several of the available rooms are just next door. In return for their 8-, 12-, or 24-hour rental, they get security—

the man at the desk keeps an eye on them via video surveillance. (See the monitors inside, and the small cameras and orange alarm lights above the doors.) The office also sells supplies (condoms by the case, lubricants, Coca-Cola).

This man does not arrange sex. The women who rent space from this business are self-employed. Customers negotiate directly with a woman at her door.

How does it work? A customer browses around. A prostitute catches his eye. If the prostitute is interested in his business (they are selective for their own safety), she winks him over. They talk at the door as she explains her price. Many are very aggressive at getting the man inside, where the temptation game revs up. A price is agreed and paid in advance.

Are there male prostitutes? Certainly anything you might want is available somewhere in the Red Light District, but an experiment in the 1990s to put male prostitutes in windows didn't stand up. There are, however, "reconstructed women"—gorgeous transvestites who may (or may not) warn customers, to ward off any rude surprises.

• *Continue circling the church. At the back side of the church, amid prostitutes in windows, you'll pass the ...*

Princess Juliana School

Life goes on, and locals need some place to send their kids. This was built in the 1970s when the idea was to mix all dimensions of society together, absorbing the seedy into the decent. The location of this preschool (for kids from newborn to 4 years old) would be a tough sell where I come from.

• *Turn left and continue north on Voor street to the end of the canal.*

Pill Bridge and Little Venice

The first bridge you pass is nicknamed "Pill Bridge" for the retail items sold by the seedy guys who hang out here. Beyond that is the fascinating Amstelkring Museum—Our Lord in the Attic Church (at #40, one of the city's most visit-worthy museums—see Amstelkring Museum Tour, page 132).

Where Voor street intersects Oudezijds Armsteeg street (at #14) is a historic building from 1580 (two years after the Alteration, and two decades before the Dutch East India Company formed, but built during a time of

increasing overseas trade). Notice the small gap between this building and the neighboring building—these tiny alleys were for water
drainage during rainstorms.

On the right, a view of Little Venice shows houses rising
directly from the water (no quays or streets). Like Venice, the city
was built in a marshy delta area, on millions of pilings. And like
Venice, it grew rich on sea trade.

• *From here, Voor street climbs slightly uphill (passing a collection of
fine gable stones embedded in the wall on the right) to Zeedijk street.
Twenty meters to the right (east) on Zeedijk street are the locks.*

The Zeedijk and the Locks

The street called Zeedijk runs
along the top of the "sea dike"
that historically protected sea-
level Amsterdam from North
Sea tides. The locks here (and
elsewhere along the water's edge)
are opened once a day with the
tides to flush out the city's canals.
If the gate is open, you may see
water flowing in or out.

• *At the west end of the block, Zeedijk street opens to a view of Damrak,
the marina, and Centraal Station. On the corner, you'll find an . . .*

Old Wooden House (Zeedijk #1)

Picture the scene in the 1600s, when this café was a tavern, sitting
right at what was then the water's edge. (Centraal Station sits on
reclaimed land.) Sailors tied up in today's marina, arriving from,
say, a two-year voyage to Bali, bringing home fabulous wealth.
They spilled into Zeedijk street, were greeted by swinging ladies
swinging red lanterns, stopped by St. Olaf's chapel to say a prayer
of thanks, then anchored in this tavern for a good Dutch beer.

• *Head east along Zeedijk street, which soon curves to the south.*

Zeedijk Street

In the 1970s and 1980s, this street was unbelievably sleazy (I live
to tell)—a no man's land of junkies fighting amongst themselves.
Today, it's increasingly trendy and upscale, fast becoming a
Sesame Street neighborhood of urban diversity. In fact, the entire
Red Light District is becoming a popular place for young urban
professionals to call home.

The street is a mix of ethnic restaurants (Thai and Portuguese) and bars, like the gay-oriented Queen's Head (#20).
The new building at #30, built in "MIIM" (1998), offers

Social Control

The buzzword in Holland is "social control" *(soziaal kontrool)*, meaning that neighborhood security comes not from iron shutters, heavily armed cops, and gated communities but from neighbors looking out for each other. Everyone knows everyone in this tight-knit neighborhood. If Magrit doesn't buy bread for two days, the baker asks around. Unlike in many big cities, there's no chance that anyone here could lie dead in his house unnoticed for weeks. Video surveillance cameras watch prostitutes, while prostitutes survey the streets, buzzing for help if they spot trouble. Watch the men who watch the women who watch out for their neighbors across the street who watch the flower shop on the corner—"social control."

apartments for rent and sale to the neighborhood's new, upscale inhabitants. The Barbizon Palace Hotel was part of a coordinated effort by business and city to bring legitimate commerce into this once dangerous and dreary area.

The former Café t' Mandje (#63) was perhaps Europe's first gay bar (opened in 1927 and closed in 1985). It stands as a memorial to owner Bet van Beeren (1907–1967), "Queen of the Zeedijk." The original Zee-dyke, Bet cruised the street in leather on her motorcycle.

Amsterdam's Chinatown is just around the corner, featuring chickens in windows, some of the city's best Chinese restaurants, and Oriental gift shops.

It's easy to miss the police station (#80), which is deliberately low-profile. In addition to patrolmen on foot, the neighborhood is peppered with plainclothes cops.

• *From the police station, this walk turns right, back to the canalside red lights. But first, you may wish to venture a block or two farther south, where you'll find a temple and a prison...*

The Lotus Flower Buddhist Temple

Enter this colorful, red-and-yellow, open-air temple by climbing the stairs, passing through one of the three entry arches representing the Buddhist Threefold Path (clean living, meditation, and wisdom). Under the roof, on lotus flowers, sits a statue of Guan Yin, whose thousand hands are always busy helping Buddha.

Monks and nuns (who live in the monastery to the right and convent to the left) and Chinatown's faithful kneel before the goddess, burn incense, and offer her fruit and flowers. The walls hold terracotta panels bearing the names of donors to this new addition to the neighborhood (free, daily 12:00–17:00).

The Waag and Nieuwemarkt

In 1488, this tower was the main gate of the city's eastern wall, later it became a weighing house *(Waag)*, then a prison. In the 1600s, the octagonal tower was an operating theater for med students, where Rembrandt sat, sketchpad in hand, to see a criminal's body dissected. The painting that resulted *(The Anatomy Lesson of Dr. Deijman)* now hangs in the Historisch Museum (see Amsterdam History Museum Tour, page 140).

Today, the Waag is a café, sitting in the middle of Nieuwemarkt Square (which sports a modern public urinal), a scene that is somewhat seedy, but hip, bar-filled, and very local.

• *From Zeedijk street (at the police station), head west on Korte Stormsteeg, then left on Oudezijds Achterburgwal street.*

Oudezijds Achterburgwal

This beautiful, tree-lined canal is the heart of Red Light District nightlife, holding the main nightclubs. Most of the sights we'll see are along the right-hand side of the street.

• *But first, on the left-hand side, find . . .*

"S. M." Sign (#11)

The yellow sign over the girls in the windows advertises prostitutes specializing in sadomasochistic sex. Formerly, the international code for rough sex was "Russian Massage." ("French" meant oral, "Greek" meant anal, and "British," I believe, meant sharing tea.)

Banana Bar (Bananenbar, at #37)

The facade of this nightclub is decorated with Art Nouveau eroticism classier than what's offered inside. For €40, you get admission for an hour, with drinks included. Undressed ladies serve the drinks, perched atop the bar. Touching is not allowed, but you can order a banana, and the lady will serve it to you any way you like.... For a full description, step into the lobby (open nightly, tel. 020/622-7640).

• *And on the right side of the street is the ...*

Erotic Museum (#54)

"Wot a rip-off!" said a drunk British lout to his mates as he emerged from the Erotic Museum. If it's graphic sex you seek, this is not the place (perhaps try the Damrak sex museum, see page 47).

What you will see, besides the self-pleasuring bicycle girl in the lobby, is mannequins acting out the Banana Bar specialty (on the ground floor); some mildly risqué John Lennon sketches of him and Yoko Ono, a collage from Madonna's book *Sex*, and erotic statuettes from Asian cultures (on the first floor); a collection of racy comic books, photos, and old French literature (on the second floor); reconstructions of what you see in today's Red Light District, including a prostitute's chambers, sex-shop window displays, and videos of nightclub sex shows (on the third floor); and finally, the S&M room, where you're greeted by a mannequin urinating on you (on the top floor). S-mannequins torment M-mannequins for their mutual pleasure, and there are photos of America's raunchy 1950s pinup girl, Betty Page, in black hair, stockings, garters, and high heels (€5, daily 11:00–24:00, O.Z. Achterburgwal 54, tel. 020/624-7303).

Absolute Danny (#76)

This shop "for all your sensual clothing" sells leather and rubber outfits with dog collars suggesting bondage scenarios, in a full array of colors from red to black to ... well, that's about it.

• *If you missed the Waag café, look east across the Achter canal and down Bloedstraat (lined with prostitutes) for a view. Continuing south on Achter street you'll find ...*

Theater Casa Rosso

The area's best-known nightclub for live sex shows is fronted by a continuously ejaculating penis fountain with rotating testicles. Unlike some sex shows that draw you in to rip you off with hidden charges, the Casa Rosso is a legitimate operation. Fixed-price tickets offer evening performances featuring strippers and live sex acts, some simulated, some real (nightly until 2:00, Achterburgwal 106–108, tel. 020/627-8954).

• *Along the right side of the next block, you'll find three cannabis sights, starting with the...*

Cannabis College

This free public study center explains the positive industrial, medicinal, and recreational uses of cannabis. Books and newspaper clippings tell about practical hemp products, the medical uses of marijuana, and police prosecution/persecution of cannabis users. The pride and joy of the college is downstairs— the organic flowering cannabis garden "where you can admire the plant in all her beauty." The garden—access by donation— happens to fit the Dutch legal limit of three plants per person or five per household (daily 11:00–19:00, O.Z. Achterburgwal 124, tel. 020/423-4420).

The Hash, Marijuana, and Hemp Museum (#130)

Though informative, this earnest museum is small and overpriced (€6, daily 11:00–22:00), with much to teach but little to entertain. But if you patiently read the displays, you'll learn plenty about cannabis and its various uses through history.

The leafy, green cannabis plant was grown by (among others)

Golden Age Dutch merchants on large plantations. They turned the fibrous stalks (hemp) into rope and canvas for ships, and used it to make clothing and lace.

Some cannabis plants— particularly mature females of the *sativa* and *indica* species— contain the psychoactive alkaloid tetrahydrocannabinol (THC) that makes you high. The buds, flowers, and leaves of the plant (marijuana) and the brown sap/ resin/pitch that oozes out of the leaves (hashish, or hash) can be dried and smoked to produce effects ranging from euphoria to paranoia to the munchies.

Some cultures, from ancient Scythians and Hindus to modern Nepal and Afghanistan, have used cannabis as a sacred, ritual drug. Modern Rastafarians, following a Bible-based religion centered in Jamaica, smoke cannabis, bob to reggae music, and praise God for creating "every herb" and calling them all "good" (Gen. 1:11–12).

The museum's highlight is the grow room, where you look through windows at real live cannabis plants in various stages of growth, some as tall as my mom. Grown hydroponically (in water, no soil) under grow lights, at a certain stage they're "sexed" to weed out the boring males and "selected' to produce the most powerful strains.

Sensi Seed Bank Store

Also known as the Cannabis Connoisseurs Club, this is a shop geared toward cannabis growers, selling seeds, grow lights, climate-control devices, bug sprays, how-to books, and CDs of music to grow dope by (free, daily 11:00–18:00, O.Z. Achterburgwal 150).
• *Where Achter street intersects Oude Doelen street, look to the right to see the Royal Palace on Dam Square, two blocks away.*

Tour Over

We've peeked at locals—from prostitutes to drug pushers to Buddhists to politically active heads with green thumbs—and survived. Congratulations. Now, go to your hotel and take a shower.

JORDAAN
WALK

This walk takes you from Dam Square—the "Times Square" of Amsterdam—to Anne Frank's House and then deep into the characteristic Jordaan neighborhood. It's a cultural scavenger hunt, offering you a chance to appreciate the laid-back Dutch lifestyle and catch a few intimate details that most busy tourists never appreciate.

In the Jordaan (pron. zhor-DON) you'll see things that are commonplace in Amsterdam...but you won't find in any other city in the world.

This is a short and easygoing walk—nice in the sleepy morning or en route to a Jordaan dinner in the evening. Bring your camera as you'll enjoy some of Amsterdam's most charming canal scenes.

Orientation

Route Overview: The walk begins at Dam Square and ends at the center of the Jordaan by Egelantiers canal. To return to Dam Square, it seems quicker to hike (10–15 min) than to take a tram (walk 4 blocks south to Rozengracht and catch tram #13, #14, or #17).

Length of Our Tour: Allow an hour for the walk.

St. Andrew's Hof: Free, daily 9:00–18:00, Egelantiersgracht 107.

Electric Ladyland: €5, Tue–Sat 13:00–18:00, closed Sun–Mon, Tweede Lelie Dwarsstraat 5-HS, www.electric-lady-land.com.

The Tour Begins

• *From Dam Square, leave the McDonald's, the mimes, and the tourists behind, and head to the place where real Amsterdamers live. Looking westward, between the Royal Palace and the Nieuwe Kerk, you'll see the facade of the red-brick ...*

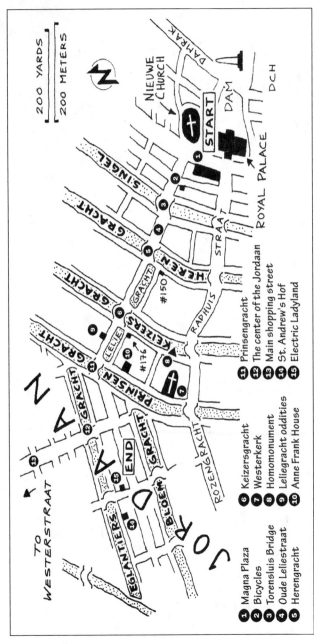

Jordaan Walk

200 YARDS
200 METERS

1 Magna Plaza
2 Bicycles
3 Torensluis Bridge
4 Oude Leliestraat
5 Herengracht
6 Keizersgracht
7 Westerkerk
8 Homomonument
9 Leliegracht oddities
10 Anne Frank House
11 Prinsengracht
12 The center of the Jordaan
13 Main shopping street
14 St. Andrew's Hof
15 Electric Ladyland

Magna Plaza Shopping Center

Built in 1899 on top of 4,560 pilings, this "modern"-looking building symbolized the city's economic revival after two centuries of decline. The revival was brought on by the opening of the North Sea Canal and increased industrialization, capped by a World's Fair in 1883. The shopping center, originally the main post office, now houses 40 stores. At the top of the mini-escalator (ground floor, on the right) a cheery cheese lady would love you to try her Gouda (free and generous samples of 3 or 4 kinds, with an explanation).

• *Exiting Magna Plaza, take two lefts—walking a few meters on busy Nieuwezijds Voorburgwal, then immediately left on tiny Molsteeg. (The pink pavement alerts you that this stretch of street is actually a bike path—keep to the sides.) From here, it's a straight shot west (though the street changes names along the way) to the Anne Frank House and into the Jordaan.*

Bicycles

At the intersection with Spuistraat, see the rows of bicycles parked along the street. Amsterdam's 700,000 residents own that many bikes. Holland's 16 million people own 16 million bikes, with many people owning two—a long-distance racing bike and an in-city bike, often deliberately kept in poor maintenance so it's less enticing to the many bike thieves. Locals are diligent about locking their bikes twice: They lock the spokes and then use a heavy chain to attach the bike to something immovable.

The Dutch appreciate the efficiency of a self-propelled machine that travels five times faster than walking, without pollution, noise, parking problems, or high fuel costs. On a *fiets* (bicycle), a speedy local can traverse the historic center in 10 minutes. Use caution when crossing Spuistraat, which has a pink-paved bike lane where inefficient walkers must yield the right of way or be "brrrringed" furiously and perhaps abused verbally. As you explore, enjoy the quiet of a people-friendly town where bikes outnumber cars.

• *After another block, the street opens onto a small square straddling the Singel canal.*

Torensluis Bridge

With cafés and art galleries, this quiet neighborhood seems farther than just three blocks from busy Dam Square. The canal today

looks much as it might have during the Golden Age of the 1600s, when the city quickly became a major urban center. Pan 360 degrees and take in the variety of buildings.

The so-called **skinniest house in Amsterdam** is the red house at #166. In fact, it's just the entryway to a normal house that opens up farther back. Most Amsterdam buildings extend far back, with interiors looking quite different from what you might expect from the facade. Real estate has always been expensive on this canal, and owners were taxed by the amount of street frontage. A local saying at the time was "Only the wealthy can live on the inside of a canal's curve" (where they would have maximum taxable frontage with a minimum of usable space).

The houses crowd together, shoulder to shoulder. Built on top of thousands of logs hammered vertically into the marshy soil, over the years they've shifted with the tides, some leaning to the sides. Houses that lean out over the street are often built that way to maximize interior space. Many brick houses have iron rods strapped onto the sides, binding the bricks to an inner skeleton of wood. Most have big, tall windows to admit as much light as possible. Mingled among the old houses are a few modern buildings—sleek, gray-metal apartments—that try to match the humble, functional spirit of the older ones.

Two **characteristic bars** spill out onto the bridge. Van Zyglen is famous for its variety of beers. Café Zeezicht is popular for its sandwiches and apple pie. Both are great for their canal setting.

The statue of **Multatuli** (1820–1887) honors the "Dutch Rudyard Kipling," whose autobiographical novel *Max Havelaar* (1860) follows a progressive bureaucrat's fight to improve the lives of Javanese natives slaving away on Dutch-owned plantations. He was the first to criticize Dutch colonial practices—very bold back then.

Amsterdam's **canals** (roughly 80 km of them) are about three meters (10 feet) deep, and are flushed daily by opening the locks as the North Sea tides come in and out. You can glimpse the locks in the distance at the north end of the Singel canal—the white flagpole thingies sprouting at 45-degree angles (beyond the green dome) are part of the apparatus to open and shut the gates. The Dutch are credited with inventing locks in the 1300s, the single greatest invention in canal-building, allowing ships to pass from higher to lower water levels.

Gables

Along the rooftops, Amsterdam's famous gables are false fronts to enhance roofs that are, generally, sharply pitched. Gables come in all shapes and sizes, sometimes decorated with animal and human heads, garlands, urns, scrolls, and curlicues. Despite the infinite variety, you can recognize several generic types.

A simple point gable just follows the triangular shape of a normal pitched roof. A bell gable—there's one two doors to the right of the skinny house—is shaped like (duh) a bell. Step gables, triangular in shape and lined with steps, are especially popular in Belgium. Spout gables have a rectangular protrusion at the peak. Neck gables rise up vertically from a pair of sloping "shoulders." Cornice gables make pointed roofs look classically horizontal. (I believe there's also a clark gable, but frankly, I don't give a damn.)

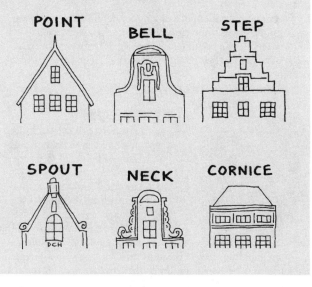

The historic Singel canal was originally the moat running around the medieval walled city. The green copper dome in the distance marks the Lutheran church. Left of that is the new city—reclaimed in the 1600s and destined to be the high-rent district. To the right is the old town.

- *Continue west on . . .*

Oude Leliestraat

Consumers will find plenty to consume on this block of shops and cafés that runs Amsterdam's gamut—Puccini's bonbons, Grey Area's marijuana, Foodism's vegetarian fare, De Lelie's Surinamese chicken *rotis*, Leg Af eetcafé's traditional meat and potatoes, and Heren Hoek's lamb *shoarmas*.

Grey Area bucks the trend of coffeeshops. While most cultivate a dark, exotic, opium-den atmosphere, this is small, clean, and well-lit. The green-and-white decal in the window identifies it as #092 in the city's licensing program, and also as a winner in the 2001 Cannabis Cup, a high honor.

• *The next canal is the . . .*

Herengracht

The house that's kitty-corner across the bridge (Herengracht 150) fronts on the canal, giving us a cut-away of its entire depth—the long white side. Most Amsterdam buildings are much bigger than they appear from the front. On the roof, rods support the false-front gable.

Parking is a problem in a city designed for boats, not cars. Parking signs (there's one along Herengracht—on the left) warn you to put money in the meter at the end of the block, or have your wheels shackled with "the boot," which stays on until you pay your fine.

• *Continue west, walking along . . .*

Leliegracht

This is one of the city's prettiest small canals, lined with trees and crossed by a series of arched bridges (some of the city's 400). Notice that some of the buildings—furniture and bookstores—have staircases leading down below the street level to residences.

Many buildings have a beam jutting out from the top with a hook on the end. Attach a pulley to that, and you can lift up a sofa and send it through a big upper-story window—much easier than lugging it up a narrow staircase.

• *The next canal you cross is . . .*

Keizersgracht

The **Westerkerk** tower rises above the rooftops, capped with a golden crown and the Amsterdam coat of arms. The crown shape

was a gift of the Hapsburg Maximilian I, as thanks for a big loan. Rembrandt is buried under the floor of this "Western Church," which dates from 1631. Its carillons toll the hour, a sound that reminded Anne Frank—who hid out just down the street—that there was, indeed, an outside world.

Kitty-corner across the bridge is the world headquarters for **Greenpeace** (Keizersgracht 176), an organization fighting for global environmental issues through lobbying and direct, nonviolent confrontation. The building recalls the modern style known as the Amsterdam School (c. 1910). The overall look is squarish and modern, but small towers and curvy bay windows relieve the minimalism.

A hundred meters left (south) along the Keizers canal, a triangular pink dock juts into the canal—the **Homomonument.** There are often flowers on it, remembering another AIDS victim. The pink triangle design co-opts the Nazi concentration-camp symbol for gays. Amsterdam often hosts international conventions on AIDS and gay awareness.

The green metal structure near the Homomonument is a public urinal (called a *pissoir*) that offers only minimal privacy. But for Dutch men ignored by worldly Dutch women, it's no problem.

The busy street just south of the Homomonument is Raadhuis Straat, where there's a taxi stand, the handy east–west trams #13, #14, and #17, and a french-fry stand featuring art with the lowly fried potato worked into some famous paintings.

• *Continue west along . . .*

More on Leliegracht

Some things are commonplace in Amsterdam but odd elsewhere in the world. The mail-slots on several doors have stickers saying *Nee* or *Ja* (no or yes), telling the postman what types of junk mail they'll accept or refuse. At #52, a handy bike

ramp slants down the steps to a home below street level. And at #62, glance up to the first story to see a rear-view mirror. Why go way down steep stairs to see who's at the door when you can just check the well-aimed mirror?

• *At the Prinsengracht, the Anne Frank House (★ see Anne Frank*

House Tour, page 125) is 100 meters to the left, and the Westerkerk is another 100 meters beyond that.

Prinsengracht

One of the most livable canals in town is lined with several of the city's estimated 2,000 houseboats. When small sail-powered cargo ships became uneconomical with the advent of modern cargo boats in the 1930s, they found a new use—as houseboats lining the canals of Amsterdam, where land was so limited and pricey. Today their cargo holds are fashioned into elegant, cozy living rooms. Moorage spots are prized and grandfathered in, making some of the junky old boats worth more than you'd think. Along this canal, boaters can plug hoses and cables into outlets along the canalside to get water and electricity. (To learn more about houseboats, visit the charming houseboat museum, described in the Sights chapter.)

Notice the canal traffic. The speed limit on canals is 7.5 kilometers (4 miles) per hour. At night, boats must have running lights on the top, side, and stern. Most boats are small and low to glide under the city's bridges. The Prinsengracht bridge is average size, with about 2 meters of headroom (it varies with the water level); some are as low as 1.7 meters. Good maps indicate the critical height of the bridges.

Just across the bridge are several typical cafés. The relaxed Café de Prins serves food and drink both day and night. The old-timey De 2 Zwaantjes occasionally features the mournful songs of the late local legend Johnny Jordaan. And the Café t' Small (not visible from here, a half-block to the right) has a deck where you can drink outside along a quiet canal (for details, see "Hungry?" on the next page).

• *Once you cross the Prinsengracht, you enter the Jordaan. Facing west (toward Café de Prins), cross the bridge and veer left (using a hypothetical clock as a compass) at 11:00 o'clock down . . .*

Nieuwe Leliestraat

The buildings are smaller, the ground-level apartments are remarkably open to the street, signs warn speeding drivers to *Let op!* for the speed bumps *(drempels)*, and the mail slots sport more *Nee*s than *Ja*s (no junk mail, please). Welcome to quiet Jordaan. Built in the 1600s as a working-class housing area, it's now home to artists and yuppies. The name Jordaan probably wasn't derived from the French *jardin*—but given the neighborhood's garden-like ambience, it seems like it should have been.

• *At the first intersection, Eerste Leliedwarsstraat, chess players may wish to detour left one block to the smoky but intensely cerebral Schaak Café (Bloemengracht 20). If chess isn't your game, turn right on Eerste*

*Leliedwarsstraat and go one block to Egelantiers canal. The bridge over
the canal is what I think of as ...*

The Center of the Jordaan

This place—with its bookstores, small cafés full of rickety tables,
art galleries, and working artists' studios—sums up the Jordaan.

Look down the quiet Egelantiers canal, lined with trees and
old, narrow, gabled buildings, and scattered with funky scows by
day that become cruising *Love Boat*s by night.

Look south at the Wester-
kerk, and see a completely
different view than the tourists
at the Anne Frank House get.
Framed by narrow streets,
crossed with streetlamp wires,
and looming over shoppers
on bicycles, this is the church
in its best light.

With your back to the church, look north down the street
called Tweede Egelantiers Dwarsstraat, the laid-back neighborhood's main shopping and people street, lined with boutiques,
antiques, hair salons, restaurants, and cafés. A few blocks down
(but don't go there now), the street intersects Westerstraat, a
wide, east–west boulevard with more everyday businesses and a
weekend street market.

• *Just past the next bridge west on Egelantiers canal is the entrance to ...*

St. Andrew's Hof

Enter—quietly—through the black door marked "Sint-Andrieshof
107 t/m 145" and encounter a slice of Vermeer—a tiny courtyard
surrounded by a dozen or so residences. Take a seat on a bench
and immerse yourself in this still world. This small-scale version
of the Begijnhof is one of scores of *hofjes* (subsidized residences
built around a courtyard), funded by churches, charities, and the
city for low-income widows and pensioners (daily 9:00–18:00,
Egelantiersgracht 107).

Hungry?

There are several recommended restaurants in the area. Especially
good are **Café Restaurant de Reiger** (daily 11:00–15:30 & 18:00–
22:30, Nieuwe Leliestraat 34, tel. 020/624-7426) and **Café 't Smalle**
(lunch 12:00–17:00; choose from 3 different places to eat or drink:
canalside, inside at the bar, or an upstairs room; at Egelantiersgracht
12 where it hits Prinsengracht, tel. 020/623-9617). For full descriptions, see the Amsterdam's Eating chapter, page 151.

• *Your tour's over. To get back to Dam Square, you can walk (10– 15 min) or catch a tram (walk 4 blocks south to Rozengracht, then take tram #13, #14, or #17).*

But old hippies have two more stops: Heading back toward the center of town along Egelantiers canal, make a right turn on Tweede Leliedwarsstraat, where you'll find . . .

Hippie Highlights

Electric Ladyland: The First Museum of Fluorescent Art,
a small shop with a flowery window display, hides a fluorescent wonderland, the creation of Nick Padalino . . . one cool cat who

 really found his black-light niche in life. Downstairs, under Nick's shop, is a unique and tiny museum featuring fluorescent black-light art. Nick lovingly guides you, demonstrating fluorescent minerals from all over the world and fluorescence in everyday objects (stamps, candy, and so on). He seems to get a bigger

kick out of it than even his customers. You can see the historic first fluorescent crayon from San Francisco in the 1950s. Wow. The label says "use with black light for church groups." Wow. (€5, Tue–Sat 13:00–18:00, closed Sun–Mon, Tweede Leliedwarsstraat 5-HS, www.electric-lady-land.com.)

This may all make more sense if you're smoking what Nick's smoking. The nearby **Paradox Coffeeshop** is the perfect coffee-shop for the nervous American who wants a mellow place to go local (light meals, fresh juice, easy music, daily 10:00–20:00, 1e Bloemdwarsstraat 2).

RIJKSMUSEUM
TOUR

At the Rijksmuseum ("Rijks" sounds like "hikes"), Holland's Golden Age shines with the best collection anywhere of the Dutch masters—from Vermeer's quiet domestic scenes to Steen's raucous family meals to Hals' snapshot portraits to Rembrandt's moody brilliance.

Watch painting evolve from narrative religious art to the Golden Age, when secular art dominated. With no local church or royalty to commission big canvases in the Protestant Dutch republic, artists had to find different patrons—the upper-middle-class businessmen who fueled Holland's capitalist economy. Artists painted their portraits, and decorated their homes with pretty still-lifes and nonpreachy slice-of-life art.

Note: The main core of the Rijksmuseum will close in the fall of 2003 until 2007 for a massive renovation. Thankfully, the most famous masterpieces—nearly everything on the typical tourist's hit list—will be kept on display in the Philips Wing (the part of the building nearest the Van Gogh Museum; enter on south side of Rijks—see photo on left). If using this self-guided tour in the Philips Wing, ignore the maps and directions and navigate simply by the photos. The early pieces may not be displayed but nearly all the great masters will be out. Hours during this period may expand to 9:00–21:00.

Orientation
Cost: €8; free under age 18; tickets good all day.
Hours: Daily 10:00–17:00, closed only on Jan 1.
Getting There: It's at Stadhousderskade 42, near the Van Gogh

Museum. From the train station, catch tram #2 or #5. The trams stop at the rear of the Rijksmuseum (at the Philips Wing—which will be the main entrance after the fall of 2003) on Hobbemastraat.
Information: The helpful information booth has free maps and a good "Tour of the Golden Age" brochure (€0.50). Free 20-minute movies are sometimes shown in English; they are restful and informative but not necessary. Tel. 020/674-7000, www.rijksmuseum.nl.
Audioguide Tour: €3.50, covers more than 500 of the exhibits with dial-a-number convenience and provides a blitz tour for those interested in a quick visit of the highlights.
Length of Our Tour: 90 minutes.
Checkrooms: Leave your bag at the free checkrooms.
Cuisine Art: The museum cafeteria is fine. The Vondelpark (picnic-perfect park and the delightful, recommended Café Vertigo) and Leidseplein (a lively square with cafés) are each a short walk away.
Photography: Permitted without a flash.
Starring: Rembrandt van Rijn, Johannes Vermeer, Frans Hals, and Jan Steen.

Overview

• *The Rijksmuseum, which straddles a road, was built to show off Rembrandt's* Night Watch. *Check your bag at the checkrooms at either of the front entrances, then climb the stairs (or take the elevator) to the second floor. To get oriented, look down the long central gallery to* Night Watch.

Built to house the nation's greatest art, the Rijksmuseum packs several thousand paintings into 200 rooms. Our tour is in about a dozen rooms on this floor to the left of *Night Watch*. (The right half of the museum is an impressive, but normally ignored, collection of Golden Age hutches and their contents; see "The Rest of the Rijks," below.

We'll concentrate on only four painters—Rembrandt, Hals, Vermeer, and Steen. All of them lived during Holland's Golden Age in the 1600s, when foreign trade made it one of Europe's richest lands. But first, a couple of quick stops to get a feel for Dutch art before its ship came in.

DUTCH ART

Dutch art is meant to be enjoyed, not studied. It's straightforward, meat-and-potatoes art for the common man. The Dutch love the beauty of everyday things painted realistically and with exquisite detail. So set your cerebral cortex on Low and let this art pass straight from the eyes to the heart with minimal detours.
• *Start in Room 201, located through the glass door marked "Dutch Painting" at the left end of the lobby.*

Rijksmuseum Overview

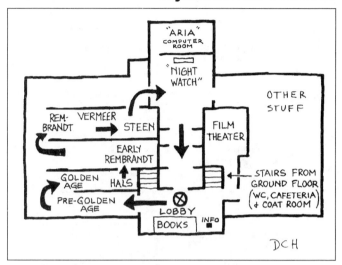

DUTCH ART BEFORE THE GOLDEN AGE (PRE-1600)

Circle of Geertgen tot Sint Jans— *The Tree of Jesse* (c. 1520)

In the days when 90 percent of Europe was illiterate, art was Sunday school. These first few rooms are filled with Bible scenes that can be read almost "page by page." Here we see Jesus' family tree— literally. At the top is Mary with the baby Jesus. His ancestors are below— David (with the harp), Solomon (with the scepter), Jesse (sleeping on the ground), and others stacked like an early version of *Hollywood Squares*.

Notice the care the artist has taken with the little details, especially the solemn faces, intricately patterned clothes, jewel-encrusted scepters, and the man (lower right) with a double chin and 5-o'clock shadow.

• *Walk through the next couple of rooms of mostly religious scenes, stopping in Room 204 at a colorful three-panel work.*

Rijksmuseum Tour

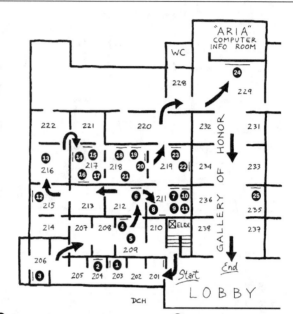

1 The Tree of Jesse
2 Dance around the Golden Calf
3 Christ in the House of Mary & Martha

4 HALS - The Merry Drinker
5 Various still lifes

6 AVERCAMP - Winter Landscape
with Ice Skaters

7 REMBRANDT - Self-Portrait at an Early Age
8 REMBRANDT - Musical Allegory
9 REMBRANDT - Portrait of Saskia
10 REMBRANDT - Jeremiah Lamenting the
Destruction of Jerusalem

11 REMBRANDT - Portrait of Maria Trip

12 The Threatened Swan
13 Various landscapes & seascapes

14 REMBRANDT - Denial of St. Peter
15 REMBRANDT - The Jewish Bride
16 REMBRANDT - De Staalmeesters
17 REMBRANDT - Self-Portrait as
the Apostle Paul

18 VERMEER - The Kitchen Maid
19 VERMEER - Woman Reading
a Letter
20 VERMEER - The Love Letter
21 VERMEER - The Little Street

22 STEEN - The Feast of St. Nicholas
23 STEEN - The Merry Family

24 REMBRANDT - The Night Watch
25 HALS - Wedding Portrait
of Isaac & Beatrix

Lucas Van Leyden—*Triptych of the Dance around the Golden Calf* (c. 1530)

In Sinai's Red Light District, the Children of Israel play while their leader is away. They dance (in the background) around a golden idol, while Moses and Aaron receive the Ten Commandments (see the two tiny, faint figures in the dark distance at the foot of a smoking mountain). Folks in colorful robes exchange good food, wine, and conversation in an outdoor setting. It's a pleasant scene to look at.

Or is it? Everyone's partying, but nobody's smiling. It's a swirl of activity as they desperately try to enjoy themselves. Look at the couple making out in the right panel. She's kissing him, but he's thinking about what will happen when Moses gets back.

• *Now enter the large Room 206 and find a big, appetizing painting.*

Joachim Bueckelaer—The plentiful kitchen with, in the background, *Christ in the House of Mary and Martha* (1566)

While Italians painted saints, angels, and Madonnas, the Dutch painted . . . food. For the middle-class merchant, food was a religion, and he worshiped thrice daily. Notice the delicious realism—the skin of the martyred birds, the temptation of the melons, Saint Artichoke in ecstasy. The sacred detail! You can practically count the hares' hairs.

But this too is a Bible scene. In the faint background someone is preaching. The title is *Christ in the House of Mary and Martha.* Compare the sketchy, sloppy work on Christ with the painstaking detail of the food. Dutch priorities.

Coincidentally, this was painted in 1566, the year of the Iconoclasm, when Protestant Dutch hard-liners vandalized religious

paintings of saints and Madonnas, condemning them as "graven images" of false gods. From then on, elaborate religious art was politically incorrect.

• *Leave the medieval world through the glass doors, and enter the Golden Age in Rooms 207–209.*

THE GOLDEN AGE (1600s)

Who bought this art? Look around and you'll see—ordinary middle-class people, merchants, and traders. Even in their Sunday best, you can see that these are hardworking, businesslike, friendly, simple people (with a penchant for ruffled lace collars).

Dutch fishermen sold their surplus catch in distant areas of Europe, importing goods from these far lands. In time, fishermen became traders, and by 1600, Holland's merchant fleets ruled the waves with colonies as far away as India, Indonesia, and America (New York was originally "New Amsterdam"). The Dutch slave trade—selling Africans to Americans—generated a lot of profit for luxuries such as the art you're looking at. Back home, these traders were financed by shrewd Amsterdam businessmen on the new frontiers of capitalism.

Look around again. Is there even one crucifixion? One saint? One Madonna? OK, maybe one. But this is people art, not church art. In most countries, Catholic bishops and rich kings supported the arts. But the Republic of the Netherlands, recently free of Spanish rule and Vatican domination, was independent, democratic, and largely Protestant, with no taste for saints and Madonnas.

Instead, Dutch burghers bought portraits of themselves, and pretty, unpreachy, unpretentious works for their homes. Even poor people bought smaller canvases by "no-name" artists designed to fit the budgets and lifestyles of this less-than-rich-and-famous crowd. We'll see examples of their four favorite subjects—still-lifes (of food and everyday objects), landscapes, portraits (often of groups), and scenes from everyday life.
• *In Room 209...*

Frans Hals—*The Merry Drinker* (1627)

You're greeted by a jovial man in a black hat, capturing the earthy, exuberant spirit of the Golden Age. Notice the details—the happy red face of the man offering us a glass of wine, the sparkle in his eyes, the lacy collar, the decorative belt buckle, and so on.

Now move in closer. All these meticulous details are accomplished with a few quick, thick, and messy brushstrokes. The beard is a tangle of brown worms, the belt buckle a yellow blur. His hand is a study in smudges. Even the expressive face is done with a few well-chosen patches of color. Unlike the still-life scenes, this canvas is meant to

Ruffs

I cannot tell you why Dutch men and women of the Golden Age found these ruffled, fanlike collars attractive, but they were the rage here and elsewhere in Europe. Ruffled collars and sleeves were first popular in Spain in the 1540s, but the style really took off with a marvelous discovery in 1565—starch. Within decades, Europe's wealthy merchant class was wearing nine-inch collars made from 18 yards of material.

The ruffs were detachable, made from a long, pleated strip of linen set into a neck (or wrist) band. You tied it in front with strings. Big ones required that you wear a wire frame underneath for support. There were various types—the "cartwheel" was the biggest, a "double ruff" had two layers of pleats, a "cabbage" was somewhat asymmetrical.

Ruffs required elaborate maintenance. You washed and starched the linen. While still wet, hot metal pokers were inserted into the folds to form the characteristic figure-eight pattern. Ruffs were stored in special round boxes to hold their shape.

By 1630, Holland had come to its senses, and the fad faded.

be viewed from a distance where the colors and brushstrokes blend together.

Frans Hals (c. 1580–1666) was the premier Golden Age portrait painter. Merchants hired him like we'd hire a wedding photographer. With a few quick strokes, Hals captured not only the features but the personality.

Rather than posing his subject, making him stand for hours saying "cheese," Hals tried to catch him at a candid moment. He often painted common people, fishermen, and barflies such as this one. He had to work quickly to capture the serendipity of the moment. Hals uses a stop-action technique, freezing the man in mid-gesture, where the rough brushwork creates a blur that suggests the man is still moving.

Two centuries later the Impressionists learned from Hals' messy brushwork. In the Van Gogh Museum you'll see how van Gogh painted, say, a brown beard by using thick dabs of green, yellow, and red that blend at a distance to make brown.

• *Also in Room 209, ponder the . . .*

Various Still-Lifes (c. 1630)

Savor the fruits of Holland's rich overseas trade—lemons from the south, pitchers from Germany, and spices from Asia, including those most exotic of spices . . . salt and pepper. These carefully

composed, photo-realistic still-lifes reflect the same sense of pride the Dutch have for their homes, cultivating them like gardens till they're immaculate, decorative, and well ordered.

Pick one. Get so close that the guard joins you. Linger over the little things: the pewterware, the seafood, the lemon peels, the rolls, and the glowing goblets that cast a warm reflection on the tablecloth. You'd swear you can see yourself reflected in the pewter vessels. At least you can see the faint reflections of the food and even of surrounding windows. The closer you get, the better it looks.

• *Enter Room 211.*

Hendrick Avercamp (1585–1634)—
Winter Landscape with Ice Skaters

A song or a play is revealed to the audience at the writer's pace. But in a painting, we set the tempo, choosing where to look and how long to linger. Exercise your right to loiter at this winter

scene by Hendrick Avercamp. Avercamp, who was deaf and mute, presents a visual symphony of small little scenes.

The village stream has frozen over, and the people all come out to play. (Even today, tiny Holland's ice-skating teams routinely beat the superpowers.) In the center, a guy falls flat on his face. A couple makes out in the haytower silo. There's a "bad moon on the rise" in the broken-down outhouse at left, and another nearby. The whole scene is viewed from a height (the horizon line is high), making it seem as if the fun goes on forever. Just skate among these Dutch people—rich,

poor, lovers hand in hand, kids, and moms—and appreciate the silent beauty of this intimate look at old Holland.
• *Enter Room 212.*

Rembrandt—Early Works

Rembrandt van Rijn (1606–1669) is the greatest Dutch painter. Whereas most painters specialized in one field—portraits, landscapes, still-lifes—Rembrandt excelled in them all.
• *Look for the following Rembrandts in Rooms 212 and 213.*

Rembrandt van Rijn—*Self-Portrait at an Early Age*

Here we see the young, small-town boy about to launch himself into whatever life has to offer. Rembrandt was a precocious kid.

His father, a miller, insisted he be a lawyer. His mother hoped he'd be a preacher (look for a portrait of her reading the Bible, nearby). Rembrandt combined the secular and religious worlds by becoming an artist, someone who can hint at the spiritual by showing us the beauty of the created world.

He moved to Amsterdam and entered the highly competitive art world. Amsterdam was a booming town and, like today, a hip and cosmopolitan city. Rembrandt portrays himself at age 22 as being divided—half in light, half hidden by hair and shadows—open-eyed but wary of an uncertain future. As we'll see, Rembrandt's paintings are often light-and-dark, both in color and in subject, exploring the "darker" side of human experience.

Rembrandt—*Musical Allegory* (1626)

Painted when Rembrandt was 19, this rather crude early work is actually a portrait of his own family in funny costumes—his father (in turban), mother, grandmother, and himself standing in back. The painting was lost for centuries, hidden in some attic, discovered by accident, and sold at auction for a small fortune.

A century ago, there were 1,000 so-called Rembrandt paintings in existence. Since then, a five-man panel of art scholars has declared most of those to be by someone else, winnowing the number of authentic Rembrandts to 300, with some 50 more under suspicion. Most of the fakes are not out-and-out forgeries, but works by admirers of his distinctive style.

In this room and elsewhere, you'll see real Rembrandts, paintings by others that look like his, portraits of Rembrandt by his students, and one or two "Rembrandts" that may soon be "audited" by the Internal Rembrandt Service. Be careful the next time you plunk down $14 million for a "Rembrandt."

Rembrandt—*Portrait of Saskia* (1633)

It didn't take long for Amsterdam to recognize Rembrandt's great talent. Everyone wanted a portrait done by the young master. He became wealthy and famous. He fell in love with and married the rich, beautiful, and cultured Saskia. By all accounts, the two were enormously happy, entertaining friends, decorating their house with fine furniture, raising a family, and living the high life. In this wedding portrait thought to be of Saskia, the bride's face literally glows. A dash of white paint puts a sparkle in her eye. Barely 30 years old, Rembrandt was the most successful painter in Holland. He had it all.

Rembrandt—*Jeremiah Lamenting the Destruction of Jerusalem* (1630)

The Babylonians have sacked and burned Jerusalem. But Rembrandt leaves the pyrotechnics (in the murky background at left) to Spielberg and the big screen. Instead, he tells the story of Israel's destruction in the face of the prophet who predicted the disaster. Jeremiah slumps in defeat, deep in thought, confused and despondent, trying to understand why this evil had to happen. Rembrandt turns his flood-light of truth on the prophet's deeply lined forehead.

Rembrandt wasn't satisfied to crank out portraits of fat merchants in frilly bibs, no matter what they paid him. He wanted to experiment, trying new techniques and more probing subjects. Many of his paintings weren't commissioned and were never even intended for

Rembrandt van Rijn (1606–1669)

Rembrandt is the greatest Dutch painter, master of many styles, and perhaps history's finest painter of self-portraits. The son of a Leyden miller (who owned a waterwheel on the Rhine—"van Rijn"), he took Amsterdam by storm with his famous painting of *The Anatomy Lesson* (1632, currently in the Mauritshuis Museum in The Hague). The commissions poured in for official portraits, and he was soon wealthy and married (1634) to Saskia van Uylenburgh. They moved to an expensive home in the Jewish Quarter (today's Rembrandt House Museum), and decorated it with their collection of art and exotic furniture. His portraits were dutifully detailed, but other paintings explored strong contrasts of light and dark, with dramatic composition.

In 1642, Saskia died, and his fortunes changed, as the public's taste shifted and commissions dried up. In 1649, he hired an 18-year-old model named Hendrickje Stoffels, and she soon moved in with him. Holland's war with England (1652–1654) devastated the art market, and Rembrandt's freespending ways forced him to declare bankruptcy (1656)—the ultimate humiliation in success-oriented Amsterdam. He moved to more humble lodgings on Rozengracht Straat.

In his last years, his greatest works were his self-portraits, showing a tired, wrinkled man stoically enduring life's misfortunes. Rembrandt piled on layers of paint and glaze to capture increasingly subtle effects.

In 1668, his lone surviving child, Titus, died, and Rembrandt died the next year. His death effectively marks the end of the Dutch Golden Age.

sale. His subjects could be brooding and melancholy, a bit dark for the public's taste. So was his technique.

You can recognize a Rembrandt canvas by his play of light and dark. Most of his paintings are a deep brown tone, with only a few bright spots glowing from the darkness. This allows Rembrandt to highlight the details he thinks are most important, and express moody emotions.

Light has a primal appeal to humans. (Dig deep into your DNA and remember the time when fire, a sacred thing, was not tamed. Light! In the middle of the night! This miracle separated us from our fellow animals.) Rembrandt strikes us at that instinctive level.

Rembrandt—*Maria Trip* (1639)

This debutante daughter of a wealthy citizen is shy and reserved—maybe a bit awkward in her new dress and adult role, but still self-assured. When he chose to, Rembrandt could dash off a commissioned portrait like nobody's business. The details are immaculate—the lace and shiny satin, the pearls behind the veil, the subtle face and hands. But Rembrandt gives us not just a person but a personality.

Look at the red rings around her eyes, a detail a lesser painter would have air-brushed out. Rembrandt takes this feature unique to her and uses it as a setting for her luminous, jewel-like eyes. Without being prettified, she's beautiful.

• *Continue on to Room 215.*

Shhh . . . Dutch Art

You can be sitting at home late one night and it's perfectly quiet. Not a sound, very peaceful. And then . . . the refrigerator motor turns off, and it's *really* quiet.

Dutch art is really quiet art. It silences our busy world so that every sound, every motion is noticed. You can hear

cows tearing off grass 50 meters away. Dutch art is still. It slows our fast-lane world so we notice the motion of birds. We notice how the cold night air makes the stars sharp. We notice that the undersides of leaves and of cats are always a lighter shade than the tops. Dutch art stills the world so we can hear our own heartbeats and reflect upon that most noble muscle that without thinking gives us life.

To see how subtle Dutch art is, realize that one of the museum's most exciting, dramatic, emotional, and extravagant Dutch paintings is probably *The Threatened Swan*, on the wall in front of you. Quite a contrast to the rape scenes and visions of heaven of Italian Baroque from the same time period.

• *Continue to Room 216.*

Various Landscapes, Seascapes, Churchscapes, and Foodscapes (Still-Lifes)

The seascapes remind us that this great art was financed by wealth from a far-flung trading empire. The meticulous paintings of church interiors show the aftermath of the wave of iconoclasm that converted rich Catholic churches into spacious, whitewashed Protestant churches.

The landscapes—often of manmade land reclaimed from the sea—all have the mark of humans in them. The things that we think of as typically Dutch—windmills, flowers, wooden shoes—are products of this flat, wet Dutch countryside. The windmills used wind power to pump water out of the soil, reclaiming land that was once part of the sea. To walk on the marshy farmland, you needed wooden shoes. The sandy soil wasn't the best for farming, but tulips (originally from Turkey) flourished. The country's hardworking people made good with little to start with. As the saying goes, "God made the Earth, but the Dutch made Holland."

• *Enter Room 217.*

Rembrandt—Later Works

In our last episode, we left Rembrandt at the height of fame, wealth, and happiness. He may have had it all, but not for long. His wife, Saskia, died. The commissions came more slowly. The money ran out. His mother died. One by one his sons died. He had to auction off his paintings and furniture to pay debts. He moved out of his fine house to a cheaper place. His bitter losses added a new wisdom to his work.

Rembrandt—*The Denial of St. Peter* (1660)

Jesus has been arrested as a criminal. Here, his disciple Peter has followed him undercover to the prison to check on the proceedings. The young girl recognizes Peter and asks him, "Don't you know Jesus?" Peter, afraid of being arrested by the Romans, denies it.

She asks him again, and Peter must decide where his loyalties lie. With the Roman soldier who glares at him suspiciously from the left, not buying Peter's story at all? Or with his doomed master in the dark background on the right looking knowingly over his shoulder, understanding Peter's complicated situation? Peter's a

bad liar. The confusion and self-doubt are written all over his face. That's his story and he's sticking to it.

The strong contrasts of light and dark heighten the drama of this psychologically tense scene. The soldier is a blotch of brown. Jesus is a distant shadowy figure, a lingering presence in Peter's conscience. The center of the picture is the light shining through the girl's translucent fingers, glowing like a lamp as she casts the light of truth on Peter. Peter's brokenhearted betrayal and sense of guilt could only have been portrayed by an older, wiser Rembrandt.

Rembrandt—*The Jewish Bride* (1667)

The man gently draws the woman toward him. She's comfortable enough with him to sink into thought, and she reaches up unconsciously to return the gentle touch. They're young but

wizened. This uncommissioned portrait (known as *The Jewish Bride*, though the subject is unknown) is a truly human look at the relationship between two people in love. They form a protective pyramid of love amid a gloomy background. The touching hands form the center of this somewhat sad but peaceful work. Van Gogh said, "Rembrandt alone has that tenderness—the heartbroken tenderness."

Rembrandt was a master of oil painting. In his later years, he rendered details with a messier, more Impressionistic style. The red-brown-gold of their clothes is a patchwork of oil laid on thick with a palette knife.

Rembrandt—*De Staalmeesters* also called *The Syndics* (1662)

While commissions were more rare, Rembrandt could still paint an official group portrait better than anyone. In the painting made famous by Dutch Masters cigars, he catches the Drapers Guild in a natural but dignified pose (dignified at least until the guy on the left sits down in his friend's lap).

It's a business meeting, and they're all dressed in black with black hats—the standard power suit of the Golden Age. They

gather around a table examining the company's books. Suddenly, someone walks in (us), and they look up. It's as natural as a snapshot, though X-rays show Rembrandt made many changes in posing them perfectly.

The figures are "framed" by the table beneath them and by the top of the wood paneling above their heads, making a three-part composition that brings this band of colleagues together. Even in this simple portrait we feel we can read the guild members' personalities in their faces. (If the table in the painting looks like it's sloping a bit unnaturally, lie on the floor to view it at Rembrandt's intended angle.)

Rembrandt—*Self-Portrait as the Apostle Paul* (1661)

Rembrandt's many self-portraits show us the evolution of a great painter's style as well as the progress of a genius' life. For Rembrandt, the two were intertwined.

Compare this later self-portrait (he's 55 but looks 70) with the youthful, curious Rembrandt of age 22 we saw earlier. With lined forehead, bulbous nose, and messy hair, he peers out from under several coats of glazing, holding old, wrinkled pages. His look is . . . skeptical? Weary? Resigned to life's misfortunes? Or amused? (He's looking at us, but remember that a self-portrait is done staring into a mirror.)

This man has seen it all—success, love, money, fatherhood, loss, poverty, death. He took these experiences and wove them into his art. Rembrandt died poor and misunderstood, but he remained very much his own man to the end.

• *Continue to Room 218. The only thing quiet and still about this often-crowded Vermeer room is its paintings.*

Johannes Vermeer (1632–1675)

Vermeer is the master of tranquility and stillness. He creates a clear and silent pool that is a world in itself. Most canvases show interiors of Dutch homes where Dutch women engage in everyday activities, lit by a side window. The Rijksmuseum has the best collection of

Vermeers in the world—all four of them. (There are only some 34 in captivity.) But each is a small jewel worth lingering over.

Vermeer—*The Kitchen Maid* (c. 1658)

Shhh...you can practically hear the milk pouring into the bowl.

Vermeer brings out the beauty in everyday things. The subject is ordinary, a kitchen maid, but you could look for hours at the tiny details and rich color tones. These are everyday objects,

but they glow in a diffused light: the crunchy crust, the hanging basket, even the rusty nail in the wall with its tiny shadow. Vermeer had a unique ability with surface texture, to show how things feel when you touch them.

The maid is alive with Vermeer's distinctive yellow and blue—the colors of many traditional Dutch homes— against a white backdrop. She is content, solid, and sturdy, performing this simple task like it's the most important thing in the world. Her full arms are built with patches of reflected light. Vermeer squares off a little world in itself (framed by the table in the foreground, the wall in back, the window to the left, and the footstool at right), then fills this space with objects for our perusal.

Vermeer—*Woman Reading a Letter* (c. 1662–1663)

Vermeer's placid scenes often have an air of mystery. The woman is reading a letter. From whom? A lover? A father on

a two-year business trip to Indonesia? Not even taking time to sit down, she reads it intently, with parted lips and a bowed head. It must be important. (She looks pregnant, adding to the mystery, but that may just be the cut of her clothes.)

Again, Vermeer has framed off a moment of everyday life. But within this small world are hints of a wider, wilder world. The light coming from the left is obviously from a large window, giving us a whiff of a much broader world outside. The map hangs prominently, reminding us of travel, perhaps where the letter is from.

Vermeer—*The Love Letter* (c. 1669–1670)

There's a similar theme here. The curtain parts, and we see through the doorway into a dollhouse world, then through the seascape on the back wall to the wide ocean. A woman is playing a lute when she's interrupted by a servant bringing a letter. The mysterious letter stops the music, intruding like a pebble dropped into the pool of Vermeer's quiet world. The floor tiles create a strong 3-D that sucks us in straight to the center of the painting—the woman's heart.

Vermeer—*The Little Street* (c. 1658)

Vermeer lived his whole life in the picturesque town of Delft. This may be the view from his front door.

Here, in this painting known as *The Little Street*, the details actually aren't very detailed—the cobblestone street doesn't have a single individual stone in it. But Vermeer shows the beautiful interplay of colored rectangles on the buildings. Our eye moves back and forth from shutter to gable to window ... and then from front to back as we notice the woman deep in the alleyway.

Fans of Vermeer may want more than these four small gems. You could take the train to The Hague (Den Haag), where his *Girl with the Pearl Earring* and *View of Delft* hang in the Mauritshuis Museum. Or content yourself with Vermeer's fellow Delftian and colleague (and lover of floor tiles), Pieter de Hooch (1629–1684), whose work is nearby.

• *Continue to Room 219.*

Jan Steen (1626–1679)

Not everyone could afford a masterpiece, but even the poorer people wanted works of art for their own homes (the way some people today hang a landscape from Sears over the sofa). Jan Steen, the Norman Rockwell of his day, painted humorous scenes from the lives of the lower classes. As a tavern owner, he observed society firsthand.

Jan Steen—*The Feast of St. Nicholas*

It's Christmas time, and the kids have been given their gifts. A little girl got a doll. The mother says, "Let me see it," but the girl turns away playfully.

Everyone is happy except... the boy who's crying. His Christmas present is only a branch in his shoe—like coal in your stocking, the gift for bad boys. His sister gloats and passes it around. The kids laugh at him. But wait, it turns out the family is just playing a trick. In the background, the grandmother beckons to him saying, "Look, I have your real present in here." Out of the limelight but smack in the middle sits the father providing ballast to this family scene, and clearly enjoying his children's pleasure.

Steen has frozen the moment, sliced off a piece, and laid it on a canvas. He's told a story with a past, present, and future. These are real people in a real scene.

Steen's fun art reminds us that museums aren't mausoleums.

Jan Steen—*The Merry Family* (1668)

This family—three generations living happily under one roof— is eating, drinking, and singing like there's no tomorrow. The

broken eggshells and scattered cookware symbolize waste and extravagance. The neglected proverb tacked to the fireplace reminds us that children will follow the footsteps of their parents. The father in this jolly scene is very drunk—ready to topple over—while in the foreground his mischievous daughter is feeding her brother wine straight from the flask. Mom and Grandma join the artist himself (playing the bagpipes) in a raucous singalong, but the child learning to smoke would rather follow dad's lead.

Golden Age Dutch families were notoriously lenient with their kids. Even today, the Dutch describe a raucous family as a "Jan Steen household."

• *Pass through Rooms 220, 227 (displaying work by van Gogh), and 228 to reach the Gallery of Honor and the museum's centerpiece.*

Rembrandt—*Night Watch*
• *The best viewing spot is to the right of center—the angle Rembrandt had in mind when he designed it for its original location.*

This is Rembrandt's most famous—though not necessarily greatest—painting. Done in 1642 when he was 36, it was one of his most important commissions—a group portrait of a company of Amsterdam's civic guards to hang in their meeting hall.

It's an action shot. With flags waving and drums beating, the guardsmen (who, by the 1640s, were really only an honorary militia of rich bigwigs) spill into the street from under an arch in the back. It's all for one and one for all as they rush to the rescue of Amsterdam. The soldiers grab lances and load their muskets. In the center, the commander (in black, with a red sash) strides forward energetically with a hand gesture that seems to say, "What are we waiting for? Let's move out!" His lieutenant focuses on his every order.

Why is *Night Watch* so famous? Compare it with the less famous group portraits on either side of the room. In those, every face is visible. Everyone is well lit, flat, and flashbulb-perfect. These people paid good money to have their mugs pre-
served for posterity, and they wanted it right up front. These colorful, dignified, and relaxed works are certainly the work of a master ...but not quite masterpieces.

By contrast, Rembrandt rousted the Civic Guards off their fat duffs. By adding movement and depth to an otherwise static scene, he took posers and turned them into warriors. He turned a simple portrait into great art.

Rembrandt caught the optimistic spirit of Holland in the 1600s. Their war of independence from Spain was heading to victory and their economy was booming. These guardsmen on the move epitomize the proud, independent, upwardly mobile Dutch.

OK, some *Night Watch* scuttlebutt: First off, "Night Watch" is a misnomer. It's a daytime scene, but over the years, as the preserving varnish darkened and layers of dirt built up, the sun set on this painting and it got its popular title. When the painting was moved to a smaller room, the sides were lopped off (and the pieces lost), putting the two main characters in the center and causing the work to become more static than intended. During World War II, the painting was rolled up and hidden for five years. More recently, a madman attacked the painting, slicing the captain's legs (now repaired skillfully).

Night Watch, contrary to popular myth, was a smashing success in its day. However, there are elements in it that show why Rembrandt soon fell out of favor as a portrait painter. He seemed to spend as much time painting the dwarf and the mysterious glowing girl with a chicken (the very appropriate mascot of this "militia" of shopkeepers) as he did the faces of his employers.

Rembrandt's life darkened long before his *Night Watch* did. This work marks the peak of Rembrandt's popularity...and the beginning of his fall from grace. He continued to paint masterpieces. Free from the dictates of employers whose taste was in their mouths, he painted what he wanted, how he wanted it. Rembrandt goes beyond mere craftsmanship to probe into and draw life from the deepest wells of the human soul.

• *As you walk down the Gallery of Honor to return to the entrance, stop at Room 233.*

Frans Hals (c. 1581–1666)—*Wedding Portrait of Isaac Abrahamsz Massa and Beatrix van der Laen* (1622)

In this wedding portrait of a chubby, pleasant merchant and his bride, Hals sums up the story of the Golden Age. This overseas trader was away from home for years at a time on business. So

Hals makes a special effort to point out his patron's commitment to marriage. Isaac pledges allegiance to his wife, putting his hand on his heart. Beatrix's wedding ring is prominently displayed, dead center between them (on her right-hand forefinger, Protestant style). The vine clinging to a tree is a symbol of man's support and woman's dependence. And in the distance at right, in the classical love garden, are other happy couples strolling arm in arm amid peacocks, a symbol of fertility.

In earlier times, marriage portraits put the man and wife in separate canvases, staring out grimly. Hals' jolly couple reflects a societal shift from marriage as business partnership to an arrangement that's more friendly and intimate.

Hals didn't need symbolism to tell us that these two are

prepared for their long-distance relationship—they seem relaxed together, but they each look at us directly, with a strong, individual identity. Good as gold, these are the type of people who propelled this soggy little country into its glorious Golden Age.

The Rest of the Rijks

The west wing (second floor) displays elaborate home furnishings—furniture, silver pitchers, dishes, and tapestries. Rooms 255–257 have a collection of ceramic objects. Delftware was the famed Dutch version of blue-and-white Chinese Ming vases, and some pieces show both influences.

Below, on the first floor, find the dollhouses. One in Room 175 gives a glimpse into an Amsterdam canal house. The two dollhouses in Room 164 were the pastime not of little girls but of bored middle-class housewives.

The first floor of the east wing (Rooms 102–112) houses Dutch history, with emphasis on the Golden Age. Ship models, paintings, a Dutch yearbook of 80 generals, and good English explanations tell the story of Holland's break with Catholicism, the rebellion against Spain, and the founding of the Dutch East India Company (V.O.C.), making the tiny country a global superpower.

VAN GOGH
MUSEUM
TOUR

The Van Gogh Museum (we say "van GO," the Dutch say "van HOCK") is a cultural high even to those not into art. It's a short, well-organized, and user-friendly look at the art of one fascinating man. If you like bright-colored landscapes in the Impressionist style, you'll like this museum. If you enjoy finding deeper meaning in works of art, you'll really love it. The mix of van Gogh's creative genius, his tumultuous life, and the traveler's determination to connect to it makes this museum as much a walk with Vincent as with his art.

Located near the Rijksmuseum, this outstanding museum houses the 200 paintings owned by Vincent's younger brother, Theo. It's a stroll through a beautifully displayed garden of Vincent's work and life. While the main floor dominates, don't miss the top two floors. The museum also focuses on the late-19th-century art that influenced Vincent (much of which happened to be in Theo's collection). The €3 audioguide includes insightful commentaries about van Gogh's paintings, along with related quotations from Vincent himself.

Each year, the Van Gogh Museum hosts special exhibits in its new wing. Had he taken better care of himself, Vincent would have been 150 years old in 2003. To celebrate, the museum will host a *Vincent's Choice* exhibit (a collection of art Vincent was influenced by) until June 15, followed by the *Van Gogh Modern* exhibit (20th-century art influenced by van Gogh) from June 27 through October 12. These promise to be wonderful bonuses included in your normal museum ticket.

Orientation
Cost: €7.25; €2 if under 18; free for those under 13 and for those with one ear.

Van Gogh Museum—Second Floor

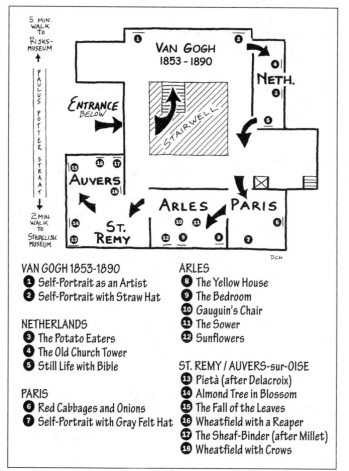

VAN GOGH 1853-1890
❶ Self-Portrait as an Artist
❷ Self-Portrait with Straw Hat

NETHERLANDS
❸ The Potato Eaters
❹ The Old Church Tower
❺ Still Life with Bible

PARIS
❻ Red Cabbages and Onions
❼ Self-Portrait with Gray Felt Hat

ARLES
❽ The Yellow House
❾ The Bedroom
❿ Gauguin's Chair
⓫ The Sower
⓬ Sunflowers

ST. REMY / AUVERS-sur-OISE
⓭ Pietà (after Delacroix)
⓮ Almond Tree in Blossom
⓯ The Fall of the Leaves
⓰ Wheatfield with a Reaper
⓱ The Sheaf-Binder (after Millet)
⓲ Wheatfield with Crows

Hours: Daily 10:00–18:00, closed only on Jan 1.

Crowd Control: There can be long lines to get into the crowded museum. But with three cashiers, the line moves quickly and the wait is rarely more than 15 minutes.

Getting There: It's behind the Rijksmuseum at Paulus Potterstraat 7. From Centraal Station, catch tram #2 or #5 to Hobbemastraat.

Information: At the information desk, pick up a free floor plan (containing a brief history of the artist's brief life). The bookstore is understandably popular, with several good basic "Vincent" guidebooks and lots of posters (with tubes). Tel. 020/570-5200, www.vangoghmuseum.nl.

Audioguide Tour: Audioguides cost €3.

Length of Our Tour: One hour.

Checkroom: Free and mandatory.

Cuisine Art: The terrace cafeteria (soup, salads, sandwiches) is pricey. Consider the Cobra café on Museumplein; the many cafés at Leidseplein (several blocks northwest); or the picnic-friendly Vondelpark and the recommended Café Vertigo.

Photography: No photos allowed.

Overview

The core of the museum and this entire tour is on the first floor (one flight up from the ground floor). The bookstore and cafeteria are on the ground floor. The second floor has a study area and more paintings (generally, van Gogh's smaller-scale works, including drawings). The third floor shows works by his friends and colleagues, from smooth-surfaced Academy art to Impressionists Claude Monet and Camille Pissarro to fellow post-Impressionists Paul Gauguin, Paul Cézanne, and Henri de Toulouse-Lautrec. The new wing (accessed from the ground floor by going down the escalator) was built to showcase temporary exhibitions (2003 exhibits explained above).

The paintings on the first floor are arranged chronologically, taking us through the changes in Vincent van Gogh's life and styles. Some background on Vincent's star-crossed life makes the museum even better, so I've included liberal doses of biographical material.

The paintings are divided into five periods of Vincent's life—Netherlands, Paris, Arles, St. Rémy, and Auvers-sur-Oise—proceeding clockwise around the floor. (Although the busy curators frequently move the paintings around, they *usually* keep them within the same room, so look around.)

Vincent van Gogh (1853–1890)

"I am a man of passions . . ."

You can see Vincent van Gogh's canvases as a series of suicide notes—or as the record of a life full of beauty, too full of beauty. He attacked life with a passion, experiencing life's highs and lows more intensely than the average person. The beauty of the world overwhelmed him and its ugliness struck him as only another dimension of beauty. He tried to absorb all of life, good and bad, and channel it onto a canvas. The frustration of this overwhelming task drove him to madness.

If all this is a bit overstated—and I guess it is—it's an attempt to show the emotional impact van Gogh's works have had on many people, myself included.

Van Gogh's life and art were one. His style changed with his circumstances and mood. For each painting I'll give a little background material and let the work itself say the rest. Since the museum divides his life and art into distinct periods, I'll do the same.

• *Climb the stairs to the first floor. The first room is an introduction to van Gogh, illustrated with a line of self-portraits.*

Self-Portraits of the Artist
Early Years (1853–1883)—Wandering

As you study the series of self-portraits consider his formative years.

Vincent, a pastor's son from a small Dutch town, started working at age 16 as a clerk for an art dealership. But his two interests, art and religion, distracted him from his dreary work and, after several years, he was finally fired.

The next 10 years were a collage of dead ends as he traveled Northern Europe pursuing one path after another. He launched into each project with incredible energy, then became disillusioned and moved on to something else: teacher at a boarding school, assistant preacher, bookstore apprentice, preacher again, theology student, English student, literature student, art student. He bounced around England, France, Belgium, and the Netherlands. He fell in love but was rejected for someone more respectable. He quarreled with his family and was estranged. He lived with a prostitute and her daughter, offending the few friends he had. Finally, in his late 20s, worn out, flat broke, and in poor health, he returned to his family in Nuenen and made peace. He started to paint.

Self-Portrait as an Artist (1888)

"I am now living with my brother Vincent, who is studying the art of painting with indefatigable zeal."

—Theo van Gogh to a friend

Here, the budding young artist proudly displays his new palette full of bright new colors, trying his hand at the Impressionist technique of building a scene using dabs of different-colored paint. A whole new world of art—and life—opened up to him in Paris.

Self-Portrait with Straw Hat (1887)

"You wouldn't recognize Vincent, he has changed so much .... The doctor says that he is now perfectly fit again. He is making tremendous strides with his work .... He is also far livelier than he used to be and is popular with people."

— Theo van Gogh to their mother

In Paris, Vincent learned the Impressionist painting technique. The shimmering effect comes from placing dabs of different colors side by side on the canvas. At a distance, the two colors blend in the eye of the viewer to become a third color. Here, Vincent uses separate strokes of blue, yellow, green, and red to create a brown beard—but a brown that throbs with excitement.

• *Let's go back in time to begin a chronological look at his art. For his stark, early work, enter the next room.*

The Netherlands (1880–1885)— Poverty and Religion

These dark gray canvases show us the hard, plain existence of the people and town of Nuenen in the rural southern Netherlands. We see simple buildings, bare or autumnal trees, and overcast skies, a world where it seems spring will never arrive. What warmth there is comes from the sturdy, gentle people themselves.

The style is crude—van Gogh couldn't draw very well, nor would he ever be a great technician. The paint is laid on thick, as though painted with Nuenen mud. The main subject is almost always dead center, with little or no background, so there's a claustrophobic feeling. We are unable to see anything but the immediate surroundings.

The Potato Eaters (1885)

"Those that prefer to see the peasants in their Sunday-best may do as they like. I personally am convinced I get better results by painting them in their roughness .... If a peasant picture smells of bacon, smoke, potato steam—all right, that's healthy."

— Vincent van Gogh

In a dark, cramped room lit only by a dim lamp, poor workers help themselves to a steaming plate of potatoes. They've earned it. Vincent deliberately wanted the canvas to be potato-colored.

Vincent had dabbled as an artist during his wandering years, sketching things around him and taking a few art classes, but it wasn't until age 29 that he painted his first oil canvas. He soon threw himself into it with abandon.

He painted the poor working peasants. He worked as a lay minister among the poorest of the poor, peasants and miners. He joined them at work in the mines, taught their children, and even gave away his own few possessions to help them. The church authorities finally dismissed him for "excessive zeal," but he came away understanding the poor's harsh existence and the dignity with which they bore it.

The Old Church Tower at Nuenen (1885)

The crows circle above the local cemetery of Nuenen. Soon after his father's death, Vincent—in poor health and depressed— moved briefly to Antwerp. He then decided to visit his brother Theo, an art dealer living in Paris, the art capital of the world. Theo's support—financial and emotional— allowed Vincent to spend the rest of his short life painting.

Still Life with Bible (1885)

"I have a terrible need of—shall I say the word?—religion. Then I go out and paint the stars."

—Vincent van Gogh

A Bible and *Lust for Life*—these two books dominated van Gogh's life. In his art he tried to fuse his religious upbringing with his love of the world's beauty. He lusted after life with a religious fervor. The burned-out candle tells us of the recent death of his father. The Bible is open to Isaiah 53: "He was despised and rejected of men, a man of sorrows . . ."

Vincent moved from rural, religious, poor Holland to Paris, the City of Lights. Vincent van Gone.

• *Continue to the next room.*

Paris (March 1886–Feb 1888)—Impressionism

The sun begins to break through, lighting up everything he paints. His canvases are more colorful, and the landscapes more spacious, with plenty of open sky, giving a feeling of exhilaration after the closed, dark world of Nuenen.

In the cafés and bars of Paris' bohemian Montmartre district, Vincent met the revolutionary Impressionists. He roomed with Theo and became friends with other struggling young painters, such as Paul Gauguin and Henri de Toulouse-Lautrec. His health improved, he became more sociable, had an affair with an older woman, and was generally happy.

He signed up to study under a well-known classical teacher but quit after only a few classes. He couldn't afford to hire models, so he roamed the streets with sketch pad in hand and learned from his Impressionist friends.

The Impressionists emphasized getting out of the stuffy studio and setting up canvases outside on the street or in the countryside to paint the play of sunlight off the trees, buildings, and water.

As you see in this room, at first, Vincent copied from the Impressionist masters. He painted garden scenes like Claude Monet, café snapshots like Edgar Degas, "block prints" like the Japanese masters, and self-portraits...like nobody else.

Still Lifes, such as *Red Cabbages and Onions* (1887)

Vincent quickly developed his own style—thicker paint, broad, swirling brush strokes, and brighter clashing colors that make even inanimate objects seem to vibrate with life. The many different colors are supposed to blend together, but you'd have to back up to Belgium before these colors resolve into focus.

Self-Portrait with Gray Felt Hat (1887–1888)

"He has painted one or two portraits which have turned out well, but he insists on working for nothing. It is a pity that he shows no desire to earn some money because he could easily do so here. But you can't change people."

   —Theo van Gogh to their mother

Despite his new sociability, Vincent never quite fit in with his Impressionist friends. As he developed into a good painter, he became anxious to strike out on his own. Also, he thought the social life of the big city was distracting him from serious work. In this painting, his face screams out from a swirling background of molecular activity. He wanted peace and quiet, a place where he could throw himself into his work completely. He headed for the sunny South of France.

• *Travel to the next room to reach . . .*

Arles (Feb 1888–May 1889)— Sunlight, Beauty, and Madness

Winter was just turning to spring when Vincent arrived in Arles near the French Riviera. After the dreary Paris winter, the colors of springtime overwhelmed him. The blossoming trees inspired him to paint canvas after canvas, pulsing with new life and drenched in sunlight.

The Yellow House, also called *The Street* (1888)

"It is my intention . . . to go temporarily to the South, where there is even more color, even more sun."
—Vincent van Gogh

Vincent rented this house with the green shutters. (He ate at the pink café next door.) Look at that blue sky! He painted in a frenzy, working feverishly to try and take it all in. For the next nine months, he produced an explosion of canvases,

working very quickly when the mood possessed him. His unique style evolved beyond the Impressionists'—thicker paint, stronger outlines, brighter colors (often applied right from the paint tube), and swirling brushwork that makes even inanimate objects pulse and vibrate with life.

Sunflowers (1889)

"The worse I get along with people the more I learn to have faith in Nature and concentrate on her."
—Vincent van Gogh

Vincent saw sunflowers as his signature subject, and he painted a half-dozen versions of them, each a study in intense yellow. If he signed the work (see the "V. G." on the vase), it means he was proud of it.

Even a simple work like these *Sunflowers* bursts with life. Different people see different things in *Sunflowers*. Is it a happy painting, or is it a melancholy one? Take your own emotional temperature and see.

The Bedroom (1888)

"I am a man of passions, capable of and subject to doing more or less foolish things—which I happen to regret, more or less, afterwards."
    —Vincent van Gogh

Vincent was alone, a stranger in Provence. And that had its downside. Vincent swung from flurries of ecstatic activity to bouts of great loneliness. Like

anyone traveling alone he experienced those high highs and low lows. This narrow, trapezoid-shaped, single-room apartment (less than 200 square feet) must have seemed like a prison cell at times. (Psychologists point out that most everything in this painting comes in pairs—two chairs, two paintings, a double bed squeezed down to a single—indicating his desire for a mate. Hmm.)

He invited his friend Paul Gauguin to join him, envisioning a sort of artists' colony in Arles. He spent months preparing a room upstairs for Gauguin's arrival.

Gauguin's Chair (1888)

"Empty chairs—there are many of them, there will be even more, and sooner or later, there will be nothing but empty chairs."
    —Vincent van Gogh

Gauguin arrived. At first they got along great, painting and carousing. But then things went bad. They clashed over art, life, and personalities. On Christmas Eve 1888, Vincent went ballistic.

Enraged during an alcohol-fueled argument, he pulled out a knife and waved it in Gauguin's face. Gauguin took the hint and quickly left town. Vincent was horrified at himself. In a fit of remorse and madness, he mutilated his own ear and presented it to a prostitute.

The Sower (1888)

A dark, silhouetted figure sows seeds in the burning sun. It's late in the day. The heat from the sun, the source of all life, radiates out in thick swirls of paint. The sower must be a hopeful man, because the field looks slanted and barren. Someday, he thinks, the seeds he's planting will grow into something great, like the tree that slashes diagonally across the scene—tough and craggy, but with small optimistic blossoms.

Vincent had worked sowing the Christian gospel in a harsh environment (see Mark 4:1–9). Now in Arles, ignited by the sun, he cast his artistic seeds to the wind, hoping.

• *Continue into the next room.*

St. Rémy (May 1889–1890)— The Mental Hospital

The people of Arles realized they had a madman on their hands. A doctor diagnosed "acute mania with hallucinations," and the local vicar talked Vincent into admitting himself to a mental hospital. Vincent wrote to Theo, "Temporarily I wish to remain shut up, as much for my own peace of mind as for other people's."

In the mental hospital, Vincent continued to paint whenever he was well enough. He often couldn't go out, so he copied from books, making his own distinctive versions of works by Rembrandt, Delacroix, Millet, and others.

We see a change from bright, happy landscapes to more introspective subjects. The colors are less bright and more surreal, the brushwork even more furious. The strong outlines of figures are twisted and tortured.

Pietà, after Delacroix (1889)

It's evening after a thunderstorm. Jesus has been crucified, and the corpse lies at the mouth of a tomb. Mary, whipped by the cold wind, holds her empty arms out in despair and confusion. She is the tender mother who receives us all in death as though saying,

"My child, you've been away so long—rest in my arms." Christ has a Vincent-esque red beard.

At first the peace and quiet of the asylum did Vincent good, and his health improved. Occasionally he was allowed outside to paint the gardens and landscapes. Meanwhile, the paintings he had sent to Theo began to attract attention in Paris for the first time. A woman in Brussels bought one of his canvases—the only painting he ever sold during his lifetime. Nowadays, a *Sunflowers* sells for $40 million.

The Garden of Saint Paul's Hospital, also called *The Fall of the Leaves* (1889)

"*...a traveler going to a destination that does not exist...*"
—Vincent van Gogh

The stark brown trees are blown by the wind. A solitary figure (Vincent?) winds along a narrow, snaky path as the wind blows leaves on him.

The colors are surreal—blue, green, and red tree trunks with heavy black outlines. A road runs away from us, heading nowhere.

Wheatfield with a Reaper (1889)

"*I have been working hard and fast in the last few days. This is how I try to express how desperately fast things pass in modern life.*"
—Vincent van Gogh

The harvest is here. The time is short. There's much work to be done. A lone reaper works uphill, scything through a swirling wheatfield, cutting slender paths of calm.

The Sheaf-Binder, after Millet (1889)

"*I want to paint men and women with that something of the eternal which the halo used to symbolize...*"
—Vincent van Gogh

Vincent's compassion for honest laborers remained

constant since his work with Belgian miners. These sturdy folk with their curving bodies wrestle as one with their curving wheat. The world Vincent sees is charged from within by spiritual fires, twisting and turning, matter turning into energy and vice versa.

The fits of madness returned. During these spells, he lost all sense of his own actions. He couldn't paint, the one thing he felt driven to do. He wrote to Theo, "My surroundings here begin to weigh on me more than I can say—I need air. I feel overwhelmed by boredom and grief."

Auvers (May–July 1890)—Flying Away

"The bird looks through the bars at the overcast sky where a thunderstorm is gathering, and inwardly he rebels against his fate. 'I am caged, I am caged, and you tell me I have everything I need! Oh! I beg you, give me liberty, that I may be a bird like other birds.' A certain idle man resembles this idle bird . . . . "

—Vincent van Gogh

Branches of an Almond Tree in Blossom (1890)

Vincent moved north to Auvers, a small town near Paris where he could stay at a hotel under a doctor friend's supervision. On the way there, he visited Theo. Theo's wife had just had a baby, whom they named Vincent. Brother Vincent showed up

with this painting under his arm as a birthday gift. Theo's wife later recalled, "I had expected a sick man, but here was a sturdy, broad-shouldered man with a healthy color, a smile on his face, and a very resolute appearance."

In his new surroundings he continued painting, averaging a canvas a day, but was interrupted by spells that swung from boredom to madness. His letters to Theo were generally optimistic, but he worried that he'd soon succumb completely to insanity and never paint again. The final landscapes are walls of bright, thick paint.

Wheatfield with Crows (1890)
"This new attack . . . came on me in the fields, on a windy day, when I was busy painting."
—Vincent van Gogh

On July 27, 1890, Vincent left his hotel, walked out to a nearby field and put a bullet through his chest.

This is the last painting Vincent finished. We can try to search the wreckage of his life for the black box explaining what happened, but there's not much there. His life was sad and tragic, but the record he left is one not of sadness but of beauty. Intense beauty.

The wind-blown wheatfield is a nest of restless energy. Scenes like this must have overwhelmed Vincent with their incredible beauty—too much too fast with no release. The sky is stormy and dark blue, almost nighttime, barely lit by two suns boiling through the deep ocean of blue. The road starts nowhere, leads nowhere, disappearing into the burning wheatfield. Above all of this swirling beauty fly the crows, the dark ghosts that had hovered over his life since the cemetery in Nuenen.

ANNE FRANK HOUSE
TOUR

ANNE FRANK
TAGEBUCH

On May 10, 1940, Germany's Luftwaffe began bombing
Schiphol Airport, preparing to invade the Netherlands. The
Dutch army fought back, and the Nazis responded by leveling
Rotterdam. Within a week, the Netherlands surrendered,
Queen Wilhelmina fled to Britain, and Nazi soldiers goose-
stepped past the Westerkerk church and into Dam Square,
where they draped huge swastikas on the Royal Palace. A five-
year occupation began. The Netherlands had been neutral in
World War I, and Amsterdam—progressive and modern but
a bit naive—was in for a rude shock.

The Anne Frank House immerses you, in a very immediate
way, in the struggles and pains of the war years. Walk through
rooms where eight Amsterdam Jews hid for two years from Nazi
persecution. Though they were eventually discovered, and seven
of the eight died in concentration camps, their story has an uplift-
ing twist—the diary of Anne Frank, preserving the human spirit
that cannot be crushed.

Orientation
Cost: €6.50.
Hours: April–Aug daily 9:00–21:00, Sept–March daily 9:00–19:00.
Crowd Control: Why do thousands
endure hour-long daytime lines when
they can walk right in by arriving
after 18:00? Avoid summer crowds
by visiting after dinner.
Getting There: It's at Prinsengracht 263, near Westerkerk
and about a 20-minute walk from
Centraal Station. Or take tram #13

or #17 or bus #21, #170, #171, or #172 to the Westermarkt stop, about a block from the museum's entrance.

Information: The museum has excellent information in English—a pamphlet at the door and fine descriptions with quotes from the diary throughout. Use this chapter as background, then let the displays and videos tell more. Tel. 020/556-7100, www.annefrank.nl.

Length of Our Tour: One hour.

Overview

We'll walk through the rooms where Anne Frank's family hid for 25 months. The front half of the building, facing the canal, remained the offices and warehouses of an operating business. The back half, where the Franks lived, was the Secret Annex, its entrance concealed by a bookcase.

• *Buy your ticket and enter the ground-floor exhibit.*

Models of the Secret Annex

Two models with dollhouse furniture help you envision life in the now-bare living quarters. Find the bookcase entrance, which leads to Anne's parents' room (with wood stove). Anne's room is next to it, with a blue bed, a brown sofa, a table-chair-bookcase ensemble, and photos on the wall. On the fourth floor was the living room and the van Pels' rooms. All told, eight people shared this tiny apartment.

• *After viewing the important five-minute video, go upstairs to the offices/warehouses of the front half of the building.*

First Floor: Offices

From these offices, Otto Frank ran a successful business called Opekta, selling spices and pectin for making jelly. When the Nazis gained power in Germany in 1933, Otto had moved his family from Frankfurt to tolerant Amsterdam, hoping for a better life.

Photos and displays show Otto with some of his colleagues. During the Nazi occupation, while the Frank family hid in the back of the building, these brave people kept Otto's business running, while secretly bringing supplies to the Franks. Miep Gies, Otto's secretary, brought food every few days, while bookkeeper Victor Kugler cheered up Anne with the latest movie magazine.

• *Go upstairs to the . . .*

Second Floor: Warehouse

At first, the Nazi overlords were tolerant, even friendly, with the vanquished Dutch. But soon they imposed restrictions that affected one in ten Amsterdamers—that is, Jews. Jews had to wear yellow-star patches and register with the police. They were forbidden in movie theaters and on trams and even forbidden to ride bikes.

In February 1941, the Nazis started rounding up Jews, shipping them by train to "work camps," which, in reality, were transit stations on the way to death camps in the East. Outraged, the people of Amsterdam called a general strike that shut down the city for two days...but the Nazis responded with even harsher laws.

In July 1942, Anne's sister Margot got her **call-up notice** for a "work-force project." Otto handed over the keys to the business to his Aryan colleagues, sent a final postcard to relatives, gave the family cat to a neighbor, spread rumors they were fleeing to Switzerland, and prepared his family to "dive under" (*onderduik*, as it was called) into hiding.

Photos of *The People in Hiding* put faces on the eight people— all Jewish—who eventually inhabited the Secret Annex. First was the Frank family—Otto and Edith and their daughters, 13-year-old Anne and 16-year-old Margot. A week later, they were joined by the van Pels (called the "van Daans" in the *Diary*), with their teenage son, Peter. A few months later, Fritz Pfeffer (called "Mr. Dussel" in the *Diary*) was invited in.

• *At the back of the third floor warehouse is...*

The Bookcase Entrance

On a Monday rainy morning, July 6, 1942, the Frank family— wearing extra clothes to avoid carrying suspicious suitcases— breathed their last fresh air, took a long look at the Prinsengracht canal, and disappeared into the back part of the building, where they spent the next two years. Victor Kugler concealed the entrance to the annex with this swinging bookcase, stacked with business files.

Though not exactly a secret (since it's hard to hide an entire building), the annex was just one of thousands of back-houses (*achterhuis*), a common feature in Amsterdam, and the Nazis had no reason to suspect anything on the premises of the legitimate Opekta business.

• *Pass through the bookcase entrance into the Secret Annex into...*

Otto, Edith, and Margot's Room

The family carried on life as usual. Otto read Dickens' **Sketches by Boz**, Edith read from a **prayer book** in their native German, and the children continued their studies, with Margot taking **Latin lessons** by correspondence course. They avidly followed the course of the war by radio broadcasts and news from their helpers. As the tides of war slowly turned and it appeared they might one day be saved from the Nazis, Otto tracked the Allied advance on a **map** of Normandy.

The room is very small, even without the furniture. Imagine yourself and two fellow tourists confined here for two years....

Pencil lines on the wall track Margot's and Anne's heights, marking the point at which these growing lives were cut short.

Anne Frank's Room

Pan the room clockwise to see some of the young girl's idols in photos and clippings she pasted there herself: American actor Robert Stack, Queen Elizabeth II, matinee-idol Rudy Vallee, figure-skating actress Sonja Henie, and on the other wall, actress Greta Garbo, actor Ray Milland, Renaissance man Leonardo da Vinci, and actress Ginger Rogers.

Out the window (which had to be blacked out) is the back courtyard—a chestnut tree and a few buildings. These things, along with the Westerkerk bell chiming every 15 minutes, represented the borders of Anne's "outside world."

Picture Anne at her small desk, writing in her diary.

In November 1942, they invited a Jewish neighbor to join them, and Anne was forced to share the tiny room. Fritz Pfeffer (known in the *Diary* as "Mr. Dussel") was a middle-aged dentist with whom Anne didn't get along. Pfeffer wrote a farewell letter to his non-Jewish fiancée, who continued to live nearby and receive news of him from Miep Gies without knowing his whereabouts.

The Bathroom

The eight inhabitants shared this bathroom. During the day, they didn't dare flush the toilet.

• *Ascend the steep staircase—silently—to the ...*

Common Living Room

This was also the kitchen and dining room. Otto Frank was well-off, and early on the annex was well stocked with food. The **menu** for a special dinner lists soup, roast beef, salad, potatoes, rice, dessert, and coffee. Later, as war and German restrictions plunged Holland into poverty and famine, they survived on canned foods and dried kidney beans.

Miep Gies would dutifully take their shopping list, buy food for her "family" of eight, and lug it up secretly. Buying

Life in the Annex

By day, it's enforced silence, so no one can hear them in the offices. They whisper, tiptoe, and step around squeaky places in the floor. The windows are blacked out, so they can't even look outside. They read or study, and Anne writes in her diary.

At night and on weekends, when the offices close, one or two might sneak downstairs to listen to Winston Churchill's BBC broadcasts on the office radio. Everyone's spirits rose and sank with news of Allied victories and setbacks.

Anne's diaries make clear the tensions, petty quarrels, and domestic politics of eight people living under pressure. Mr. van Pels annoys Anne, but he gets along well with Margot. Anne never gets used to Mr. Pfeffer, who is literally invading her space. And, most of all, pubescent Anne is often striking sparks with her German mom (Anne's angriest comments about her mom were deleted from early editions).

Despite their hardships, the group feels guilty—they have shelter, while so many other Jews are rounded up and sent off.

As the war progresses, they endure long nights when the house shakes from Allied air raids, and Anne cuddles up in her dad's bed.

Boredom tinged with fear—Existentialist hell.

such large quantities in a coupon-rationed economy was highly suspicious, but she knew a sympathetic grocer (a block away in Leliegracht) who was part of a ring of Amsterdamers risking their lives to help "divers."

At night, the living room became sleeping quarters for Hermann and Auguste van Pels.

Peter van Pels' Room

On Peter's 16th birthday, he got a **Monopoly-like board game** as a present.

Initially, Anne was cool toward Peter, but after two years

together, a courtship developed, and their flirtation culmin-
ated in a kiss.

The staircase (no visitor access) leads up to where they stored
their food. Anne loved to steal away here for a bit of privacy.
At night, they'd open a hatch to let in fresh air.

One hot August day, Otto was in this room helping Peter
learn English, when they looked up to see a man with a gun.
The hiding was over.

• *From here, we leave the Secret Annex, returning to the Opekta
storeroom and offices in the front house. As you work your way
downstairs, you'll see a number of exhibits on the aftermath of
this story.*

Front House: The Arrest, Deportation, and Auschwitz Exhibits

They went quietly. On August 4, 1944, a German policeman
accompanied by three Dutch Nazis pulled up in a car, politely
entered the Opekta office, and went straight to the bookcase
entrance. No one knows who tipped them off. The police gave
the surprised hiders time to pack. They demanded their valu-
ables, and stuffed them into Anne's briefcase ... after dumping
her diaries onto the floor.

Taken in a van to Gestapo headquarters, the eight were
processed in an efficient, bureaucratic manner, then placed on
a train to Westerbork, a concentration camp northeast of the
city (see their 3" x 5" registration cards).

From there, they were locked in a car on a normal passen-
ger train and sent to Auschwitz (see the transport list), a Nazi
extermination camp in Poland. On the platform at Auschwitz,
they were "forcibly separated from each other" (as Otto later
reported) and sent to different camps. Anne and Margot were
sent to Bergen-Belsen.

Don't miss the video of one of Anne's former neighbors
who, by chance, ended up at Bergen-Belsen with Anne. In
English, she describes their reunion as they talked through a
barbed wire fence shortly before Anne died. She says of Anne,
"She didn't have any more tears."

Anne and Margot both died of typhus in March 1945, only
weeks before the camp was liberated. Five of the other original
eight were either gassed or died of disease. Only Otto survived.

The Franks' story was that of Holland's Jews. The seven
who died were among 100,000 Dutch Jews (out of a total of
130,000) who did not survive the war. Of Anne's school class
of 87 Jews, only 20 survived.

• *In the next room is an ...*

Exhibit on the Diaries

See Anne's three diaries (and another notebook), and learn about how they were discovered and published after the war. Anne got the first diary as a birthday present when she turned 13, shortly before they went into hiding. She wrote it in the form of a letter to an imaginary friend named Kitty.

• *Go downstairs to view the . . .*

Videos

The video of Miep Gies describes how she found Anne's diaries in the Secret Annex after the arrest and gave them to Otto when he returned. Another video shows Otto's reaction. Though the annex's furniture had been ransacked during the arrest, afterward the rooms remained virtually untouched, and we see them today much as they were.

Otto decided to have the diaries published, and in 1947, *De Achterhuis (The Back-House)* appeared in Dutch, soon followed by many translations, a play, and a movie. While she was alive, Anne herself had recognized the uniqueness of her situation and had been in the process of revising her diaries, preparing them to one day be published.

• *Continue downstairs to the ground floor and enter the movie room.*

Neo-Nazi Video

The thinking that made the Holocaust possible survives. Even today, some groups promote the notion that the Holocaust never occurred and contend that stories like Anne Frank's are only a hoax. The people who run this museum offer a closing video about Neo-Nazism and racism today in hopes that the souvenir you'll take away from this visit is a heightened awareness of this evil yet persistent human trait.

AMSTELKRING MUSEUM TOUR

Our Lord in the Attic (Ons' Lieve Heer op Solder)—A Hidden Catholic Church

For two centuries (1578–1795), Catholicism in Amsterdam was illegal but tolerated (like pot in the 1970s). When hard-line Protestants took power in 1578, Catholic churches were vandalized and shut down, priests and monks were rounded up and kicked out of town, and Catholic kids were razzed on their way to school. The city's Catholics were forbidden to worship openly, so worshippers gathered secretly to say Mass in homes and offices. In 1663, a wealthy merchant built Our Lord in the Attic, one of a handful of such places in Amsterdam serving as a secret parish church until Catholics were once again allowed to worship in public. This unique church—embedded within a townhouse in the middle of the Red Light District—comes with a little bonus: a rare glimpse inside a historic Amsterdam home straight out of a Vermeer painting.

Orientation

Cost: €4.50.

Hours: Mon–Sat 10:00–17:00, Sun 13:00–17:00.

Getting There: It's at Oudezijds Voorburgwal 40, a seven-minute walk from either Centraal Station or Dam Square.

Information: Tel. 020/624-6604, www.museumamstelkring.nl.

Length of Our Tour: One hour.

The Exterior

Behind the attic windows of this narrow townhouse sits a 150-seat, three-story church the size of a four-lane bowling alley. Below it is the home of the wealthy businessman who built the church. This 17th century townhouse, like many in the city, also has a back-house *(achterhuis)* that was rented out to another family. On this tour, we'll visit the front house, then the church, then the back-house. Before entering, notice the emergency-exit door in the alley. This was once the hidden church's main entrance.

• *Step inside. Buy your ticket, and climb the stairs to the first floor, where we begin touring the front house. The first stop is a room with a big fireplace, the...*

Parlor *(Sael)*

By humble Dutch standards, this is an enormous, highly ornate room. Here, in the largest room of the house, the family received guests and hosted parties. The decor is the Dutch version of classical, where everything comes in symmetrical pairs—corkscrew columns flank the fireplace, the coffered ceiling mirrors the patterned black-and-white marble floor, and a fake exit door balances the real entrance door.

Over the fireplace is the coat of arms of Jan Hartman (1619–1668), a rich Catholic businessman who built this house for his family and the church for his fellow Catholics in the neighborhood. The family symbol, the crouching hart (deer), became the nickname of the church—*Het Hert.*

The painting over the fireplace *(The Presentation in the Temple)* has hung here since Hartman's time, and shows his taste for Italian Catholic Baroque–style beauty. On the wall opposite the windows, the family portrait is right out of the Dutch Golden Age, showing a rich Catholic businessman and his family of four... but it's not Hartman.

The tall ceramic doodad nearby is a multiarmed tulip vase. Its pagoda shape reminds us that Delftware originally came from China.

• *Now ascend the small spiral staircase that leads to a room facing the canal, called the...*

Canal Room

Unlike the rather formal parlor, this was where the family just hung out, staring out the windows or warming themselves at the stove. The furnishings are typical of a wealthy merchant's home of the time. The wood stove and the textiles on the walls are re-creations, but look like the originals. The Delftware vase would have been filled with tulips, back then still an exotic and expensive transplant from the East. In the Dutch custom (still occasionally seen today), the family covered tables with exotic Turkish rugs imported by traders of the Dutch East India Company.

Despite the family's wealth, space was tight. In the 1600s,

often entire families would sleep together in small bed cabinets. They sat up to sleep because they believed if they lay down, the blood would pool in their heads and kill them.

The black ebony knickknack cabinet is painted with a scene right out of the 1600s' Red Light District. On the right door, the Prodigal Son spends his inheritance making merry with bare-breasted, scarlet-clothed courtesans—high-rent prostitutes who could also entertain educated clients with the cello. On the left door, the Prodigal Son has spent it all. He can't pay his bill, and is kicked out of a cheap tavern—still half-dressed—by a pair of short-changed prostitutes.

• *As you climb the staircase up to the church, you can look through a window into the small . . .*

Chaplain's Room

Originally the maid's room, this humble bedroom is now furnished to look as it did in the 1800s, when the church chaplain lived here. See the tiny bed cabinet decorated with a tiny skull—a reminder of mortality—and a pipe on the table.

• *Continue up to the church.*

Our Lord in the Attic Church—Nave and Altar

The church is long and narrow, with an altar at one end, an organ at the other, and two balconies overhead to maximize the seating in this relatively small space. Compared with Amsterdam's white-washed Protestant churches, this Catholic church has an elaborate Baroque decor, with statues of saints, garlands, and baby angels. The balconies are suspended from the ceiling and held in place by metal rods.

This attic church is certainly hidden, but everyone knew it was here. In tolerant (and largely Catholic) Amsterdam, Catholics were not actually arrested or punished (after the Protestants' initial anger of 1578), they were just socially unacceptable. Hartman was a respected businessman who used his wealth and influence to convince the city fathers to look the other way as the church was built. Imagine the jubilation when the church opened its doors in 1663, and repressed Catholics could finally gather together and worship in this fine space without feeling like two-bit criminals.

The altar is flanked by classical columns and topped with an

Anti-Catholic = Anti-Spanish

The anti-Catholic laws imposed by Protestants were partly retribution for the Catholics' own oppressive rule, partly a desire to reform what was seen as a corrupted religion...and largely political. By a quirk of royal marriage, Holland was ruled from afar by Spain—Europe's most militantly Catholic country, home of the Inquisition, the Jesuits, and the Pope's own Counter-Reformation army.

In 1578 Amsterdam's hard-line Protestants staged the "Alteration"—a coup kicking out their Spanish oppressors and allying the city with the Prince of Orange's rebels. Catholics in the city—probably a majority of the population—were considered guilty by association. They were potential enemies, suspected as puppets of the pope or spies for Spanish kings or subverters of the social order. In addition, Catholics were considered immoral worshippers of false idols, bowing down to graven images of saints and the Virgin Mary.

Catholic churches were seized and looted, and prominent Catholics were dragged to Dam Square by a lynch mob, before being freed unharmed outside the city gates. Laws were passed prohibiting open Catholic worship. For two centuries, Protestant extremists gave Catholics a taste of their own repressive medicine. However, Amsterdam's long tradition of tolerance meant that Catholics were not actually arrested or prosecuted under these laws. Still, many families over many generations were torn apart by the religious and political strife of the Reformation.

arch featuring a stucco God the Father, a dove of the Holy Spirit, and trumpeting angels.

The **base of the left column**—made of wood painted to look like marble—is hollow. Inside is a fold-out wooden pulpit that could be pulled out for the priest to preach from—as explained with photos on the wall opposite.

The altarpiece painting (Jacob de Wit's *Baptism of Jesus*) is one of three that could be rotated with the feast days. Step into the room behind the altar to see the two spares. In a glass case on the back side of the altar, squint at the ship-in-a-bottle miniature home devotionals.

• *This room's alcove is called the . . .*

Lady Chapel

An altar dedicated to Our Lady—the Virgin Mary, the mother of Christ—contains more of the images that so offended and outraged hard-line Protestants. See her statue with baby Jesus and find her symbols, the rose and crown, in the blue damask altar cloth.

Catholics have traditionally honored Mary, addressing prayers to her or to other saints, asking them to intercede with God on their behalf. To Calvinist extremists, this was like bowing down to a false goddess. They considered statues of the Virgin to be among the "graven images" forbidden by the Ten Commandments (Exodus 20:4).

The **collection box** *(voor St. Pieter)* on the wall over the staircase was for donations sent to fund that most Catholic of monuments, the pope's own church, the Basilica of St. Peter in Rome—to Calvinists the center of corruption, the "whore of Babylon."

• *Later we'll head down the stairs here, but first climb the stairs to the first balcony above the church.*

Lower Balcony

The window by the altar looks south, across ramshackle rooftops (note the complex townhouse-with-backhouse design of so many Amsterdam buildings) to the steeple of the Oude Kerk. The Oude Kerk was the main Catholic church until 1578, when it was rededicated as Dutch Reformed (Protestant), the new official religion of the Netherlands.

For the next hundred years, Catholics had no large venue to gather in, until Our Lord in the Attic opened in 1663.

The 1749 organ is small but more than adequate. These days, music-lovers flock here on special evenings for a *Vondelkonzert* (wandering concert). They listen to a few tunes here, have

Calvinism

Holland's Protestant movement followed the stern reformer John Calvin more than the beer-drinking German Martin Luther. Calvin's French followers, called Huguenots, fled religious persecution in the 1500s, finding refuge in tolerant Amsterdam. When Catholic Spain began persecuting them in Holland, they entered politics and fought back.

Calvin wanted to reform the Catholic faith by condemning corruption, simplifying rituals, and returning the faith to its Bible roots. Like other Protestants, Calvinists emphasized that only God's grace—and not our good works—can get us to Heaven.

He even went so far as to say that God predestined some for Heaven, some for Hell. Later, some overly pious Calvinists even claimed to be able to pick out the lucky winners from the unlucky, sinful losers. Today the Dutch Reformed Church (and some other Reformed and Presbyterian churches) carries on Calvin's brand of Christianity.

a drink, then move on to hear more music at, say, the Oude Kerk or the Royal Palace.

Next to the organ, the painting *Evangelist Matthew with an Angel* (*De evangelist Mattheus*, c. 1625, by Jan Lievens) features the wrinkled forehead and high-contrast shadings used by Lievens' more famous colleague, Rembrandt.

• *Stairs next to the organ lead to the...*

Upper Balcony

Looking down from this angle, the small church really looks small. It could accommodate 150 seated worshippers.

• *At the back of the upper balcony is the...*

Canalside Room—Religious Art

This kind of religious hardware is standard in Catholic church services—elaborate silver and gold monstrances (ornamental holders in which the Communion wafer is displayed), chalices (for the Communion wine), ciboria (chalices with lids for holding consecrated wafers), pyxes (for storing unconsecratedwafers), candelabras, and incense burners. "Holy earth boxes" were used for Catholics denied burial in consecrated ground. Instead, they put a little consecrated dirt in the box, and placed it in the coffin.

Admiring these beautiful pieces, remember that it was this

kind of luxury, ostentation, and Catholic mumbo-jumbo that drove thrifty Calvinists nuts.

Looking out the window, you can see you're literally in the attic. Straight across the canal is a house with an ornate gable featuring dolphins. This street was once the city's best address.

• *Back down on the lower balcony, circle around to the window just to the right of the altar for a . . .*

Northern View

Look north across modern junk on rooftops to the impressive dome of St. Nicholas' church, near Centraal Station. This is the third Amsterdam church to be dedicated to the patron saint of seafarers and of the city. The first was the Oude Kerk (until 1578), then Our Lord in the Attic (1663). Finally, after the last anti-Catholic laws were repealed (1821), St. Nicholas was built as a symbol of the faith's revival.

When St. Nicholas was dedicated in 1887, Our Lord in the Attic closed up shop. The next year wealthy Catholics saved it from the wrecking ball, turning it into one of Amsterdam's first museums.

• *Head back downstairs, passing through the room behind the altar with the Lady Chapel and taking the stairs (past the offering box) down to the . . .*

Confessional

The confessional dates from 1740. The priest sat in the left half, while parishioners knelt in the right to confess their sins through a grilled window. Catholic priests have church authority to forgive sins, while Protestants take their troubles directly to God.

(The sociologist Max Weber theorized that frequently forgiven Catholics more easily accept the status quo, while guilt-ridden Protestants are driven to prove their worth by making money. Hence, northern Protestant countries—like the Netherlands—became capitalist powerhouses, while southern Catholic countries remained feudal and backward. Hmm.)

• *Go down another flight to the . . .*

Jaap Leeuwenberg Room (Room 16)

We've now left the church premises and moved to the back-house rooms that were rented out to other families. This room's colors are seen in countless old homes—white walls, ochre-yellow beamed ceiling, ox-blood-red landing, and black floor tiles. The simple colors, lit here by a light shaft, make small rooms seem bright and spacious.

• *The very steep stairs near the window lead down to the . . .*

17th-Century Kitchen

This reconstructed room was inhabited as-is up until 1952.
Blue-tiled walls show playful scenes of kids and animals. Step
into the small pantry, then open a door to see the toilet.
• *Climb the rope back up the stairs, turn left and descend a different
set of stairs into the . . .*

19th-Century Kitchen

This looks just so Dutch, with blue tiles, yellow walls, and Vermeer
lighting from a skylight. The portrait over the fireplace depicts
the last resident of this house on her First Communion day. When
she died in 1953, her house became part of this museum.

Think of how her age overlaps our age . . . of all the change
since she was born. Consider the contrast of this serene space
with the wild world that awaits just outside the door of this hidden
church. And plunge back into today's Amsterdam.

AMSTERDAM HISTORY MUSEUM TOUR

Amsterdam Historisch Museum

Dozens of rooms (with great English explanations) take you creatively through Amsterdam's story, from fishing village to sea-trading superpower to hippie haven to a city of immigrants. Simply follow the Grand Tour Route signs and you'll see every room on your hike through 1,000 years of Amsterdam history.

Orientation

Cost: €6.50.
Hours: Mon–Fri 10:00–17:00, Sat–Sun 11:00–17:00.
Getting There: It's on Kalverstraat 92, next to the Begijnhof, in downtown Amsterdam.
Information: Tel. 020/523-1822.
Length of Our Tour: One hour.
Cuisine Art: The museum has a good-value café.

MUSEUM HIGHLIGHTS

Growth of the City

Take time to watch the entire sequence as the computer-generated growth screen takes you through time. Watch the population go from zero to 700,000 in a thousand years. Witness the birth of the city—the damming of the Amstel, which created Dam Square, the commercial zone where the Damrak's sea harbor met the Rokin's river port. Then follow the subsequent canalization as the city fills in its fortified center and continues to grow.

From City of Monasteries to a Trading Power

Exhibits show how Amsterdam was once a Catholic city rich with monasteries. Then (in the room of globes) it's 1650, and it's clear that Holland has become a great trading power. Later, a room explains the Dam Square, showing it in the old days.

• *Climb the stairs to the rooms on the next level.*

Look for the interesting model showing how a primitive collar filled with air was used to float ships high over sandbars, enabling them to get out of the city's shallow harbor. The paintings show great faces, from bigshots to the orphans who used to inhabit this building.

• *Located over a sky bridge in Room 11 is . . .*

Rembrandt's *The Anatomy Lesson of Dr. Jan Deijman*

His famous *Anatomy Lesson of Dr. Tulp* (1632, now in The Hague's Mauritshuis) had put young Rembrandt on Amsterdam's artistic map two decades earlier. Now, in 1656, Rembrandt returned to the dissection room for another anatomy lesson—this time from Dr. Jan Deijman.

A fire in 1732 incinerated the surrounding spectators of this group portrait, leaving us with just the stars of the scene—Dr. Deijman and the corpse. The body of this recently hanged thief ("Black Jack" Fonteijn) was donated to the surgery theater in the Waag (today's Red Light District), where Dr. D. held a dissecting demonstration for med students and the paying public. Rembrandt attended, sketch pad in hand.

The corpse's feet are right in our face (similar to Mantegna's famous *Dead Christ*), a masterpiece of foreshortening. We stare into the gaping hole of his disemboweled stomach. An assistant (head burned off in the fire) does the work, opening the head and exposing the brain, while the doctor looks on calmly, hand on hip.

• *In the next room, climb a modern spiral staircase to the carillon display for . . .*

Carillon Lessons

Invented by Dutch bellmakers in the 1400s and perfected in the 1600s, this musical instrument is a Flemish specialty. The carillon player (called a "carillonneur"), seated at his keyboard up in the tower, presses keys with his fists and feet, jerking wires that swing clappers against tuned bells. The bells range in size from 20-pound high notes to 8-ton low notes struck by hundred-pound clappers. These days, some carillons have electric actions to make it easier, plus player-piano mechanisms to automate the playing.

Mozart, Vivaldi, Handel, and Bach—all of whom lived during the carillon's heyday—wrote Baroque music that sounds beautiful on bells.

Sit down and pound your fists on the keys (that's why they're there). Hitting the red marked keys, play a chromatic scale (successive keys) as fast as you can. Hit 'em hard. Then, push the buttons on the walls to hear recordings of actual Amsterdam carillons in action—and imagine the fists flying.

• *The next section is on . . .*

20th-Century Sociology

This gives you a close-up look at housing in contemporary Amsterdam, a city of 727,000 people crammed into small apartments, either in historic buildings or in developments of city-built housing. Recently, many Indonesian and Surinamese have immigrated here. Tracing the evolution of housing in Amsterdam in the 20th century, you study typical apartments from aerial views. The big blue board of doorbells represents the residents who live in a suburban apartment complex (in a district called "Fleerde" which has probably never seen a tourist). Hit the red buzzers to meet the residents and tour their homes.

World War II

This section includes color footage of Liberation Day in 1945. A touch-screen computer lets you witness a terrible event on Dam Square, the Grote Club Massacre. Just a few days after the war ended (May 7), German troops who were holed up in a club overlooking Dam Square opened fire on celebrating locals, killing 19 and injuring 117.

Hippie Age

In the 1960s, hippies from around the world were drawn to freewheeling Amsterdam. The socialist group called the "Provos" provoked the Establishment by publishing an outrageous magazine (the first issue contained a page of smokeable paper made from marijuana), staging pro-pot events, and promoting innovative (but ultimately unsuccessful) campaigns to provide free white bicycles and white electric-powered cars to city commuters. You can trace the evolution of Amsterdam's "no war on drugs" and even listen to a Ted Koppel interview of Mayor Ed Koch and his Dutch counterparts on the pros and cons of legalizing marijuana.

Former Orphanage and Regents' Room

As you leave, don't miss the room opposite the ticket desk (between the WC and the exit door). The first small room tells of the orphanage here. Originally a cloister, in 1570 it became an orphanage, which took in kids until the 1960s.

Finally, you enter a stately Regents' Room (for the orphanage's board of directors) where you'll see grand ego-elevating paintings honoring bigshots. Many of the Dutch Masters' paintings you'll see in the Netherlands' museums were commissioned to decorate rooms like this.

SLEEPING

€1 = about $1, country code: 31, area code: 020

Greeting a new day by descending your steep stairs and stepping into a leafy canalside scene—graceful bridges, historic gables, and bikes clattering on cobbles—is a fun part of experiencing Amsterdam. But Amsterdam is a tough city for budget accommodations, and any room under €140 will have its rough edges. Still, you can sleep well and safely in a great location for €80 per double.

Amsterdam is jammed during convention periods, the Queen's Birthday (April 30), and on summer weekends. Many hotels will not take weekend bookings for people staying less than three nights.

Parking in Amsterdam is even worse than driving. You'll pay €32 a day to park safely in a garage—and then hike to your hotel.

If you'd rather trade big-city action for small-town coziness, consider sleeping in Haarlem, half an hour away by train (see Haarlem chapter).

Sleeping near the Train Station

HIGHER PRICED

Ibis Amsterdam Hotel is a modern and efficient 187-room place towering over the station and a multistory bicycle garage. It offers a central location, comfort, and good value without a hint of charm (Db-€149, family-€176, skip breakfast and save €12 per person, CC, book long in advance, air-con, smoke-free rooms on request, Stationsplein 49, tel. 020/638-9999, fax 020/620-0156, www.ibishotel.com).

MODERATELY PRICED

Amstel Botel, the city's only remaining "boat hotel," is a shipshape, bright, and clean floating hotel with 175 rooms (Sb/Db-€81, Tb-€90, worth the extra €5 per room for canal

Sleep Code

S = Single, **D** = Double/Twin, **T** = Triple, **Q** = Quad,
b = bathroom, **s** = shower only, **CC** = Credit Cards accepted,
no CC = Credit Cards not accepted.

Nearly everyone speaks English in the Netherlands, and prices include breakfast unless noted.

To help you easily sort through these listings, I've divided the rooms into three categories, based on the price for a standard double room with bath:

Higher Priced—Most rooms €140 or more.
Moderately Priced—Most rooms €80–140.
Lower Priced—Most rooms less than €80.

view, breakfast-€8, CC, elevator, €25/day parking pass, 400 meters from train station, on your left as you leave station, you'll see the sign and the big white boat on Oosterdokskade, tel. 020/626-4247, fax 020/639-1952, www.amstelbotel.com).

Sleeping between Dam Square and the Anne Frank House

HIGHER PRICED

Hotel Toren is a chandeliered historic mansion in a pleasant, quiet canalside setting in downtown Amsterdam. This splurge, run by Eric and Petra Toren, is classy yet friendly and two blocks northeast of the Anne Frank House. The least expensive four-star in town, it's a great value (Sb-€100–120, Db-€125–160, deluxe canalside Db-€215, Tb-€160–185, "bridal suites" for €205–230, prices vary with season, 10 percent discount for cash with this book, breakfast buffet-€12, CC, air-con, Keizersgracht 164, tel. 020/622-6352, fax 020/626-9705, www.toren.nl). Bernarda, who runs the bar, is a great source of local advice.

Canal House Hotel, a few doors down, offers a rich 17th-century atmosphere. Above generous and elegant public spaces, tangled antique-filled halls lead to 26 spacious, tastefully appointed rooms. Evenings come with candlelight and soft music (Db-€150, big Db-€190, CC, elevator, Keizersgracht 148, tel. 020/622-5182, fax 020/624-1317, www.canalhouse.nl, e-mail: info@canalhouse.nl).

Hotel Ambassade—lacing together 60 rooms in eight houses—is an amazingly elegant and fresh place, sitting aristocratically but daintily on the Herengracht. Its public rooms are palatial, with a library and plush antique furnishings.

Amsterdam Hotels

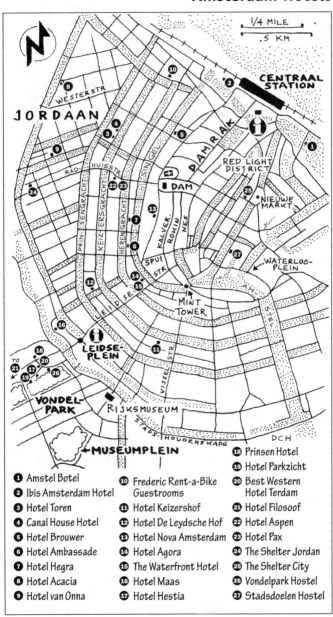

1 Amstel Botel
2 Ibis Amsterdam Hotel
3 Hotel Toren
4 Canal House Hotel
5 Hotel Brouwer
6 Hotel Ambassade
7 Hotel Hegra
8 Hotel Acacia
9 Hotel van Onna

10 Frederic Rent-a-Bike Guestrooms
11 Hotel Keizershof
12 Hotel De Leydsche Hof
13 Hotel Nova Amsterdam
14 Hotel Agora
15 The Waterfront Hotel
16 Hotel Maas
17 Hotel Hestia

18 Prinsen Hotel
19 Hotel Parkzicht
20 Best Western Hotel Terdam
21 Hotel Filosoof
22 Hotel Aspen
23 Hotel Pax
24 The Shelter Jordan
25 The Shelter City
26 Vondelpark Hostel
27 Stadsdoelen Hostel

A family-run hotel this size is rare (Sb-€158, Db-€188, Db suite-€260, Tb-€310, extra bed-€30, breakfast-€14—and actually worth it, CC, elevator, free Internet access, Herengracht 341, tel. 020/555-0222, www.ambassade-hotel.nl, e-mail: info@ambassade-hotel.nl).

MODERATELY PRICED

Hotel Brouwer, a woody and homey old-time place situated peacefully but centrally on the Singel canal, rents eight plain rooms up lots of very steep stairs (Sb-€45, Db-€85, located between train station and Dam Square, near Lijnbaanssteeg at Singel 83, tel. 020/624-6358, fax 020/520-6264, www .hotelbrouwer.nl, e-mail: akita@hotelbrouwer.nl).

Hotel Hegra is a rare simple and inexpensive, yet comfy, sedate, and cat-friendly place with 11 rooms run by Robert de Vries. The place is well worn but feels safe (D-€60, Ds-€75, Db-€85, includes breakfast, CC, Herengracht 269, tel. 020/ 623-7877, fax 020/623-8159). The lack of a Web site is in keeping with the character of Robert's management.

Sleeping in the Jordaan

MODERATELY PRICED

Hotel Acacia's 20 good rooms fill a funky cheese-wedge-shaped building on a canal and a great workaday square, buried deep in the Jordaan (Sb-€65, Db-€80, Tb-€100, Qb-€120, Quint/ b-€130, 5 percent extra to pay with CC, 3-night minimum for advance reservations, some larger studios, parking, bus #18 from station, Lindengracht 251, tel. 020/622-1460, fax 020/638-0748, www.hotelacacia.nl, e-mail: acacia@wxs.nl, Gerard). The Acacia also rents four fine rooms or apartments in two **Acacia Houseboats** moored adjacent to the hotel. This is your best opportunity for that old-time Amsterdam-houseboat experience in a quintessential Amsterdam neighborhood (Db-€95–110, Tb-€115, Qb-€130, see Web site for details).

Hotel van Onna is a smoke-free, professional-feeling place renting 41 simple, industrial-strength rooms. The beds are a bit springy—but the price is unbeatable and the location makes you want to crack out your easel (Sb-€40, Db-€80, Tb-€120, no CC, reserve only by phone, Bloemgracht 102, tel. 020/626-5801, www.netcentrum.com/onna, Luiz).

Near the Jordaan

Frederic Rent-a-Bike Guestrooms, with a bike rental shop as the reception, is a collection of private rooms on a gorgeous canal just outside the Jordaan, a five-minute walk from the train station. Frederic has amassed about 100 beds ranging from dumpy €60 doubles to spacious and elegant €160 apartments. Some places are great for families and groups of up to six. He also rents houseboat apartments. All are displayed in living color on his Web site (bike shop open daily 9:00–18:00, cash only, Brouwersgracht 78, tel. 020/624-5509, www.fredereic.nl).

Sleeping in the Spui and Leidseplein Neighborhoods

The area around Amsterdam's rip-roaring nightlife center (Leidseplein) is colorful, comfortable, and convenient. These canalside places are within a five-minute walk of Leidseplein but in generally quiet and characteristic settings.

HIGHER PRICED

Hotel Nova Amsterdam, a bright, spacious place offering professional service and reliability, rents 60 stark yellow and beech-wood rooms in a great locale (Sb-€100, Db-€140, Tb-€170, Qb-€200, CC, elevator, midway between Dam Square and Spui at Nieuwezijds Voorburgwal 276, tel. 020/623-0066, fax 020/627-2026, e-mail: novahotel@wxs.nl).

Hotel Maas is a big, quiet, and stiffly hotelesque place. Though it's on a busy street rather than a canal, it's a handy option (S-€80, Sb-€105, one D-€95, Db-€145, suite-€205, prices vary with view and room size, extra person-€20, hearty breakfast, CC, elevator, tram #1, #2, or #5 from station; Leidsekade 91, tel. 020/623-3868, fax 020/622-2613, www.hotelmaas.nl).

MODERATELY PRICED

Hotel Keizershof is wonderfully Dutch, with six bright, airy rooms in a 17th-century canal house. A steep spiral staircase leads to rooms named after old-time Hollywood stars. The enthusiastic hospitality of the de Vries family gives this place a friendly, almost small-town charm (S-€45, D-€65, Ds-€75, Db-€90, 3-night minimum, fine family-style breakfast around a big table, use CC to secure room but pay in cash for these prices, strictly non-smoking, tram #16, #24, or #25 from train station; Keizersgracht 618, where Keizers canal crosses Spiegelstraat, tel. 020/622-2855, fax 020/624-8412, www.vdwp.nl/keizershof).

Two well-located places offering mediocre value are side by side overlooking the Singel canal where it hits Koningsplein: **Hotel Agora** (16 rooms, Db-€110, view Db-€125, CC, Singel 462, tel. 020/627-2200, fax 020/627-2202, www.hotelagora.nl), and **The Waterfront Hotel,** which feels cozier with lots of steep stairs and

rustic yet nice rooms (10 rooms, Db-€105, view Db
458, tel. & fax 020/421-6621, www.waterfront.demon.nl).

LOWER PRICED

Hotel de Leydsche Hof, canalside with simple, quiet rooms,
is open only from Easter through mid-September. Its peaceful
demeanor almost allows you to overlook the flimsy cots and
old carpets (Ds-€60, Ts-€90, Qs-€110, no breakfast, no CC,
10-min walk from Leidseplein, Leidsegracht 14, near where it hits
Keizersgracht, tel. 020/623-2148, run by friendly Mr. Piller).

Sleeping near Vondelpark

These options cluster around Vondelpark in a safe neighborhood
that lacks the canal flavor but is only a short walk from the action.
The first four places are in a pleasant nook between the rollicking
Leidseplein and the breezy Vondelpark. They are easily connected
with the train station on trams #1, #2, and #5. The last place has
more personality but is farther away.

HIGHER PRICED

Best Western Hotel Terdam is an 89-room American-style
hotel well situated on a quiet street just across the bridge from
bustling Leidseplein (Db-€130–170 depending on season and
air-con, breakfast likely not included but often used as a bargain-
ing chip, CC, elevator, Tesselschadestraat 23, tel. 020/612-6876,
fax 020/683-8313, www.ams.nl).

MODERATELY PRICED

Hotel Hestia, on a safe and sane street, feels very professional
with 18 clean, bright, and generally spacious rooms (Sb-€80, very
small Db-€95, Db-€105–130, Tb-€160, Qb-€190, CC, elevator,
Roemer Visscherstraat 7, tel. 020/618-0801, fax 020/685-1382,
www.hestia.demon.nl).

   Prinsen Hotel, with 45 nicely appointed but generally
cramped rooms, is family-run and has a peaceful garden and a safe,
professional feel (small Db on weekdays-€116, small Db on week-
ends-€128, bigger Db-€138, CC, elevator, Vondelstraat 36, tel.
020/616-2323, fax 020/616-6112, www.prinsenhotel.nl).

   Hotel Parkzicht, an old-fashioned place with extremely
steep stairs, rents 13 big, plain rooms on a quiet street bordering
Vondelpark (S-€39, Sb-€49, Db-€77–90, Tb-€110–120, Qb-
€120–130, CC, closed Nov–March, Roemer Visscherstraat 33,
tel. 020/618-1954, fax 020/618-0897, e-mail: hotel@parkzicht.nl).

   Hotel Filosoof greets you with Aristotle and Plato in the
foyer and classical music in its generous lobby. Its 38 rooms are

decorated with themes; the Egyptian room has a frieze of hieroglyphics. Philosophers' sayings hang on the walls, and thoughtful travelers wander down the halls or sit in the garden, rooted in deep discussion. The rooms are small, but the hotel is endearing (Db-€111–122, Tb-€150–170, CC, elevator, 3-min walk from tram line #1, get off at Jan Peter Heierstraat, Anna Vondelstraat 6, tel. 020/683-3013, fax 020/685-3750, www.hotelfilosoof.nl).

Lower-Priced Backpacker Hotels and Hostels

Cheap hotels line the convenient but noisy main drag between the town hall and the Anne Frank House. Expect a long, steep, and depressing stairway, noisy front rooms, and quieter rooms in the back.

Hotel Aspen, a good value for a budget hotel, is tidy, stark, and well maintained (8 rooms, S-€32, D-€41, Db-€64, Tb-€75, Qb-€87, no breakfast, CC, Raadhuisstraat 31, tel. 020/626-6714, fax 020/620-0866, e-mail: info@hotelaspen.nl, run by Esam and Hanne). A few doors away, **Hotel Pax** has large, plain, but airy backpacker-type rooms (S-€25–34, D-€37–57, Db-€55-85, T-€50–68, Q-€55–77, no breakfast, prices vary with size and season, CC, 2 showers and 2 toilets for 8 rooms, Raadhuisstraat 37, tel. 020/624-9735, run by two young brothers: Philip and Peter).

The Shelter Jordan is a scruffy, friendly, Christian-run, 100-bed place in a great neighborhood. While most of Amsterdam's hostels are pretty wild, this place is drug-free and alcohol-free with boys on one floor and girls on another. These are Amsterdam's best budget beds, in 14- to 20-bed dorms (€16, includes sheets and breakfast, maximum age 35, CC, Internet access, non-smoking, 02:00 curfew, near Anne Frank House, Bloemstraat 179, tel. 020/624-4717, www.shelter.nl, e-mail: jordan@shelter.nl). The Shelter serves hot meals, runs a snack bar, offers lockers, leads nightly Bible studies, and closes the dorms from 10:30 to 13:00. Its sister hostel, **The Shelter City** in the Red Light District, is similar but definitely not preaching to the choir (€16, includes breakfast and sheets, CC, maximum age 35, curfew, Barndesteeg 21, tel. 020/625-3230, fax 020/623-2282, www.shelter.nl, e-mail: city@shelter.nl).

The city's two official hostels are **Vondelpark,** Amsterdam's top hostel (€18–24 with breakfast, D-€66, nonmembers pay €2.25 extra, no CC, lots of school groups, 4–20 beds per room, right on the park at Zandpad 5, tel. 020/589-8996, fax 020/589-8955, www.njhc.org/vondelpark) and **Stadsdoelen** (€17 with breakfast, nonmembers pay €2.25 extra, no CC, just past Dam Square, Kloveniersburgwal 97, tel. 020/624-6832, fax 020/639-1035, www.njhc.org, e-mail: stadsdoelen@njhc.org). While generally booked long in advance, a few beds open up each day at 11:00.

EATING

Traditional Dutch food is basic and hearty, with lots of bread, cheese, soups, and fish. Lunch and dinner are served at American times (roughly 12:00–14:00 and 18:00–21:00).

Dutch treats include cheese, pancakes *(pannenkoeken)*, gin *(jenever)*, light pilsner-type beer, and "syrup waffles" *(stroopwafel)*.

Experiences you owe your tongue in Holland: trying a raw herring (outdoor herring stands are all over), lingering over coffee in a "brown café," sipping an old *jenever* with a new friend, and consuming an Indonesian feast—a *rijsttafel*.

Budget Tips: Get a sandwich to go, and grab a park bench on a canal. Sandwiches *(broodjes)* of delicious cheese on fresh bread are cheap at snack bars, delis, and *broodje* restaurants. Ethnic fast-food stands abound, offering a variety of meats wrapped in pita bread. Easy to buy at grocery stores, yogurt in the Netherlands (and throughout Northern Europe) is delicious and drinkable right out of its plastic container.

Types of Eateries

Any place labeled "restaurant" will serve full, sit-down meals for lunch or dinner. But there are other places to fill the tank.

An *eetcafé* is a simple restaurant serving basic soups, salads, sandwiches, and traditional meat-and-potatoes meals in a generally comfortable but no-nonsense setting.

A *salon de thé* serves tea and coffee, yes, but also croissants, pastries, and sandwiches for a light brunch, lunch, or afternoon snack.

Cafés are all-purpose establishments, serving light meals at meal times and coffee, drinks, and light snacks the rest of the day and night. *Bruin* cafés ("brown cafés," named for their nicotine-stained walls) are usually a little more bar-like, with dimmer lighting, wood paneling, and more tobacco smoke.

A *proeflokal* is a bar (with light snacks) for tasting wine, spirits, or beer. *Coffeeshop* is the code word for an establishment where cannabis is sold and consumed, though most also offer drinks and munchies, too (see Smoking chapter on page 161 for more details).

There's no shortage of stand-up, take-out places serving fast-food, sandwiches, and all kinds of quick ethnic fare.

No matter what the type of establishment, expect it to be *gezellig*—a much-prized Dutch virtue, meaning an atmosphere of relaxed coziness.

Etiquette and Tipping

The Dutch are easygoing. Pay as you go or pay after? Usually it's your choice. Tip or don't tip? Your call. Wait for table service or order at the bar? Whatever you do, you won't be scolded for your *faux pas*, as you might in France or Italy. Dutch establishments are *gezellig*. Still, here are some guidelines:

• Tipping is not necessary in restaurants (15 percent service is usually already included in the menu price), but a tip of about 5 percent is a nice reward for good service. In bars, rounding up to the next euro ("keep the change") is appropriate if you get table service rather than order at the bar.

• When ordering drinks in a café or bar, you can just pay as you go (especially if the bar is crowded), or wait until the end to settle up, as many locals do. If you get table service, take the cue from your waiter.

• Cafés with outdoor tables generally do not charge more if you sit outside (unlike in France or Italy).

• Expect tobacco smoke—in bars, cafés, restaurants, every-where. You don't have to like it, but expect it.

• Waiters constantly say *"Alstublieft"* (pron. AHL-stoo-bleeft). It's a catch-all polite word meaning "please," "here's your order," "enjoy," and "you're welcome." You can respond with a thank you by saying *"Dank u wel"* (pron. dahnk yoo vehl).

Typical Meals

Breakfast: Breakfasts are big by Continental standards—bread, meat, cheese, and maybe an egg or omelet. Hotels generally put out a buffet spread including juice and cereal.

Lunch: Simple sandwiches are called *broodjes* (most commonly made with with cheese and/or ham). An open-face sandwich of ham and cheese topped with two fried eggs is an *uitsmijter* (pron. OUTS-mi-ter). Soup is popular for lunch.

Snacks and Take-Out Food: Small stands sell french fries

Birgit Jons' Diary

9:00   Not hungry. Had coffee with small breakfast of bread, cheese, ham, and a boiled egg.

11:00 Got hungry and stopped at a *salon de thé* for an *uitsmijter* sandwich.

12:30 Cold out, so warmed up with *erwtensoep* at an *eet-café*. Also had more bread, cheese, and ham, and a small salad.

15:00 Dirk bought me a *shoarma* with fries and mayonnaise. Topped it off at a stand selling—mmm!—*poffertjes*.

16:30 Work's done! Sat in the sun along a canal outside a *proeflokal* and sipped...was it fruit brandy? Got courage to swallow whole raw herring from kiosk—mistake!

17:30 Cappuccino and *appelgebak*.

19:00 Finally, dinner! I've been starving myself all day. First, fresh Zeeland oysters. Next, the main course—meat, potatoes, and pale asparagus, all heaped on one plate. For dessert, *pannenkoeken* topped with strawberries and whipped cream, with coffee and a weird liqueur.

21:00 Party! We met at De Prins for a *pils* and an *oude jenever*. Smoked six cigarettes (no artificial preservatives).

23:00 Need grease—inhaled two *frikandels* at late-night deli. Fortified for tomorrow—another busy day!

(frites) with mayonnaise; raw or marinated herring; *shoarmas* (lamb tucked in pita bread); falafels (fried chickpea balls in pita bread); and *doner kebabs* (Turkish gyros). Delis have deep-fried croquettes *(kroketten)*.

Dinner: It's the biggest meal of the day, consisting of meat or seafood with boiled potatoes, cooked vegetables, and a salad. Hearty stews are served in winter. These days, many people eat more vegetarian fare.

Sweets: Try *poffertjes* (small sugared doughnuts without holes), *pannenkoeken* (pancakes with fruit and cream), *stroopwaffelen* (syrup waffles), and *appelgebak* (apple pie).

Local Specialties

Cheeses: Edam (covered with red wax) or Gouda (pron. HOW-dah). Gouda can be young or old: *jong* is mellow and *oude* is salty, crumbly, and strong, sometimes seasoned with cumin or cloves.

French Fries: Commonly served with mayonnaise (ketchup and

curry sauce are often available) on a paper tray or in a newspaper cone. *Vlaamse frites* are made from whole potatoes, not pulp.

Herring: Fresh raw herring, marinated or salted, often served with onions or pickles, sometimes with sour cream on a thick, soft, white bun.

Hutspot: Hearty meat stew with vegetables, especially popular on winter days.

Kroketten (croquettes): Log-shaped rolls of meats and vegetables (kind of like corn dogs) breaded and deep-fried, such as *bitterballen* (meatballs), *frikandelen* (sausage), or *vlammetjes* (spring rolls).

Pannenkoeken: Either sweet dessert pancakes or crêpe-like dinner pancakes.

Ethnic Foods

If you're not in the mood for meat and potatoes, sample some of Amsterdam's abundant ethnic offerings.

Indonesian (Indisch): The tastiest "Dutch" food is Indonesian, from the former colony. Find any Indisch restaurant and experience a *rijsttafel* (rice table). With as many as 30 spicy dishes and a big bowl of rice (or noodles), a *rijsttafel* can be split and still fill two hungry tourists. *Nasi rames* is a cheaper, smaller version of a *rijsttafel*. Another popular dish is *bami goring*—stir-fried noodles served with meat, vegetables, and *rijsttafel* items. *Nasi goreng* is like *bami* but comes with fried rice. *Satay* is skewered meat and *gado-gado* consists of steamed vegetables and hard-boiled eggs with peanut sauce. Among the most common sauces are peanut, red chili (*sambal*), and dark soy.

Middle Eastern: Try a *shoarma* (roasted lamb with garlic in pita bread, served with bowls of different sauces), falafel, gyros, or *doner kebab*.

Surinamese (Surinaamse): Surinamese cuisine is a mix of Caribbean and Indonesian influences, featuring *roti* (spiced chicken wrapped in a tortilla) and rice (white or fried) served with meats in sauces (curry and spices). Why Surinamese food in Amsterdam? In 1667, Holland traded New York City ("New Amsterdam") to Britain in exchange for the small country of Surinam (which borders Guyana on the northeast coast of South America). For the next three centuries, Surinam (renamed Dutch Guyana) was a Dutch colony, which is why it has indigenous Indians, Creoles, and Indonesian immigrants who all speak Dutch. When Surinam gained independence in 1975, 100,000 Surinamese emigrated to Amsterdam, sparking a rash of Surinamese fast-food outlets.

Drinks

Beer: Order "a beer" and you'll get a *pils*, a light lager/pilsner-type beer in a 10-ounce glass with a thick head leveled off with a stick. (Typical brands are Heineken, Grolsch, Oranjeboom, and Amstel.) A common tap beer is Palm Speciale, an amber ale served in a stemmed, wide-mouth glass. Belgian beers are popular, always available in bottles and sometimes on tap. *Witte* (white) beer is light-colored and summery, sometimes served with a lemon slice (it's like American Hefeweizen but yeastier).

Jenever: This is Dutch gin made from juniper berries. *Jong* (young) is sharper; *oude* (old) is mellow. Served chilled, *jenever* (pron. yah-NAY-ver) is meant to be chugged with a *pils* chaser (this combination is called a *kopstoot*—head-butt). While cheese gets harder and sharper with age, *jenever* grows smooth and soft. Old *jenever* is best.

Liqueur: You'll find a variety of local fruit brandies and cognacs.

Wine: Dutch people drink a lot of fine wine, but it's almost all imported.

Coffee: The Dutch love their coffee, enjoying many of the same drinks (espresso, cappuccino) served in American or Italian coffee shops. Coffee usually comes with a small spice cookie. A *koffie verkeerd* (pron. fer-KEERT, "coffee wrong") is an espresso with a little steamed milk.

Soft Drinks: You'll find the full array.

Orange Juice: Many café/bars have a juicer for making fresh-squeezed orange juice.

Water: The Dutch (unlike many Europeans) drink tap water with meals, but many prefer mineral water, still or sparkling (Spa brand is popular).

RESTAURANTS IN AMSTERDAM

Of Amsterdam's thousand-plus restaurants, no one knows which are best. I'd pick an area and wander. The rowdy food ghetto thrives around Leidseplein. Wander along Leidsedwarsstraat, Restaurant Row. The area around Spui canal and that end of Spuistraat is also trendy and a bit less rowdy. For fewer crowds and more charm, find something in the Jordaan district. The best advice: your hotelier's. Most keep a reliable eating list for their neighborhood and know which places keep their travelers happy.

Here are some handy places to consider.

Amsterdam Restaurants

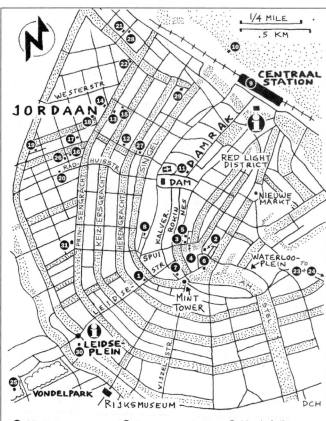

1 Albert Heijn
  Supermarket
2 Atrium Cafeteria
3 Café ´t Gasthuys
4 Pannenkoekenhuis
  Upstairs
5 Restaurant Kapitein
  Zeppos
6 De Jaren Café
7 La Place
8 Restaurant
  Haesje Claes
9 Stationsrestauratie
10 Pier 10

11 Restaurant
  de Roode Leeuw
12 Restaurant de Luwte
13 Pancake Bakery
14 De Bolhoed
15 Dimitri's
16 De Groene Lantaarn
17 Café Restaurant
  de Reiger
18 Café ´t Smalle
19 Restaurant
  Vliegende Schotel
20 Long Pura
  Restaurant

21 Moeder's Pot
22 Café ´t Papeneiland
23 To Rest. Plancius
24 To Taman Sari
  Restaurant
25 Café Vertigo

Coffeeshops:
26 Paradox
27 The Grey Area
28 Coffee Shop Relax
29 Siberia Coffeeshop
30 The Bulldog
31 La Tertulia

Eating near Spui in the Center

The first four places all cluster along the colorful, student-filled Grimburgwal lane near the intersection of Spui and Rokin (midway between Dam Square and the Mint Tower).

The city university's **Atrium** is a great budget cafeteria (€4.50 meals, Mon–Fri 11:00–15:00 & 17:00–19:30, closed Sat–Sun, from Spui, walk west down Landebrug Steeg past the canalside Café 't Gasthuys 3 blocks to Oudezijds Achterburgwal 237, go through arched doorway on the right, tel. 020/525-3999).

Café 't Gasthuys, one of Amsterdam's many brown cafés (so called for its smoke-stained walls), serves light meals and good sandwiches and offers indoor or peaceful canalside seating (daily 12:00–24:00, Grimburgwal 7, tel. 020/624-8230).

Pannenkoekenhuis Upstairs is a tiny and characteristic perch up some extremely steep stairs where Arno Jakobs cooks and serves delicious €7 pancakes to four tables (daily from noon, Grimburgwal 2, tel. 020/626-5603).

Restaurant Kapitein Zeppos—named for a Belgian TV star from the 1960s—serves French-Dutch food in a relatively big and festive setting. The light lunch specials—soups and sandwiches—cost €5–10. Dinners go for around €20 (daily 11:00–15:30 & 17:30–23:00, just off Grimburgwal at Gebed Zonder End 3, tel. 020/624-2057).

De Jaren Café (The Years Café) is a stark and trendy place for soup, salads, sandwiches, or just coffee over a newspaper. On a sunny day, its canalside patio is popular with yuppies (daily 10:00–24:00, Nieuwe Doelenstraat 20–22, just up from Muntplein, tel. 020/625-5771).

La Place, a cafeteria on the ground floor of a department store, is a festival of fresh, appealing food served cafeteria-style. It has a no-smoking section and a small outdoor terrace upstairs. This thriving place has a lively market feel and lots of great vegetables (Mon–Sat 10:00–20:00, Thu until 21:00, Sun 12:00–20:00, it's in La Marché at the end of Kalverstraat, near Mint Tower, corner of Rokin and Muntplein, tel. 020/620-2364).

Restaurant Haesje Claes, famous as *the* place for traditional Dutch cooking in the center, is big and fast enough to be a standard for tour groups (daily noon to midnight, Spuistraat 275, tel. 020/624-9998). The area around it is a huge and festive bar scene.

Eating in and near the Train Station

Stationsrestauratie is a surprisingly classy, budget, self-service option inside the station on platform 2 (Mon–Sat

7:00–22:00, Sun from 8:00). The entire platform 2 is lined with eateries, including the tall, venerable, 1920s-style First Class Grand Café.

Pier 10, once an old fishing shack, is now a charmingly simple little restaurant offering cozy harborfront dining. It's at the end of a dock in the shadow of (but ignoring) the huge train station. Reserve a place in the tiny five-table front room (two seatings: 18:30 and 21:30) where it's just you and the harbor traffic by candlelight (€30 meals, fun but small menu, seafood and modern European, daily from 18:30, De Ruyterkade Steiger 10, tel. 020/624-8276).

Eating near Dam Square

Restaurant de Roode Leeuw is a grand place offering a respite from the crush of Damrak. You'll get a menu filled with Dutch traditions, dressy service, and plenty of tourists (€18 main dish, 3-course menu with lots of intriguing choices for €30, daily 12:00–22:00, Damrak 93–94, tel. 020/555-0666).

Eating near the Anne Frank House and in the Jordaan District

All these places except for the last two are within a few scenic blocks of Anne Frank's house, providing handy lunches and atmospheric dinners in Amsterdam's most characteristic neighborhood.

Restaurant de Luwte is painfully romantic on a pictur-esque street overlooking a canal, with lots of candles, a muted but fresh modern interior, and French Mediterranean cuisine (€18 main courses, €35 for a full meal, big dinner salads for €15, daily 18:00–22:00, Leliegracht 26, tel. 020/625-8548).

The **Pancake Bakery** serves good pancakes in a nothing-special family atmosphere. The menu features a fun selec-tion of ethnic-themed pancakes—including Indonesian, for those who want two experiences in one (€8.25 pancakes, splitting OK, daily 12:00–21:30, Prinsengracht 191, tel. 020/625-1333).

De Bolhoed, across the canal, serves serious vegetarian and vegan food in an ambience Buddha would dig (€13 meals, daily 12:00–22:00, Prinsengracht 60, tel. 020/626-1803).

Dimitri's is a nondescript little place serving creative salads, with a few outdoor tables on a street filled with bikes and cobbles (€9 main-course salads, breakfasts too, daily 8:00–22:00, Prinsenstraat 3, tel. 020/627-9393).

De Groene Lantaarn (The Green Lantern) is fun for fondue. The menu offers fish, meat, and cheese (Dutch, not

Swiss) with salad and fruit for €17–22 (Thu–Sun from 18:00, closed Mon–Wed, a few blocks into the Jordaan at Bloemgracht 47, tel. 020/620-2088).

Café Restaurant de Reiger must offer the best cooking of any *eetcafé* in the Jordaan. It's famous for its fresh ingredients and delightful bistro ambience. In addition to an English menu, ask for a translation of the €15 daily specials on the chalkboard. The café, which is crowded late and on weekends, takes no reservations but you're welcome to have a drink at the bar while you wait (daily 11:00–15:30 & 18:00–22:30, glass of house wine for €2.50, veggie options, non-smoking section, Nieuwe Leliestraat 34, tel. 020/624-7426).

Café 't Smalle is extremely charming with three zones where you can enjoy a light lunch or a drink: canalside, inside around the bar, and up some steep stairs in a quaint little loft. While open daily until midnight, food is served only at lunch from 12:00 to 17:00 (plenty of interesting wines by the glass posted, at Egelantiersgracht 12 where it hits Prinsengracht, tel. 020/623-9617).

Restaurant Vliegende Schotel is a folksy, unvarnished little Jordaan eatery decorated with children's crayon art that has a cheap and fun meatless menu featuring fish and vegetarian fare. Nothing trendy about this place—just locals who like food and don't want to cook (daily 17:00–23:00, non-smoking section, wine by the glass, Nieuwe Leliestraat 162, tel. 020/625-2041).

Long Pura is a good place for authentic Indonesian. Though pricey, filled with tourists, and on a noisy street, it's conveniently located, friendly, and proudly serves reliably delicious rice-table extravaganzas in a tastefully Indonesian setting (€31 for *rijsttafel*, €37 with appetizer and dessert, daily 18:00–23:00, Rozengracht 46, tel. 020/623-8950).

Moeder's Pot, a six-table neighborhood eatery with great character and charm, is gruff with the smell of fried food and cigarettes. Hearty main courses come with fried potatoes and vegetables, applesauce, and salad. The place is not central but puts you in a charming little neighborhood at the seaside edge of the Jordaan (€7–15, Mon–Sat 11:00–22:00, closed Sun, Vinkenstraat 119, no phone).

Café 't Papeneiland is a classic brown café. With Delft tiles, an evocative old stove, and a stay-awhile perch overlooking a canal with welcoming benches, it's been the neighborhood hangout since the 17th century (overlooking northwest end of Prinsengracht at #2, tel. 020/624-1989). Though the café serves light meals, most come here to nurse a drink and chat.

Eating near the Botanical Garden and Dutch Resistance Museum

Restaurant Plancius, adjacent to the Dutch Resistance Museum, is a mod, handy spot for lunch. With good indoor and outdoor seating, it's popular with the broadcasters from the nearby local TV studios (creative breakfasts and light lunches €5–8, daily 9:00–24:00, Plantage Kerklaan 61a, tel. 020/330-9469).

Taman Sari Restaurant is the local choice for Indonesian, serving hearty, quality €9 dinners and *rijsttafel* dinners for €14 to €18 (daily 17:00–23:00, 32 Plantage Kerklaan, tel. 020/623-7130).

Eating near Vondelpark

Café Vertigo offers a fun selection of excellent soups and sandwiches. Grab an outdoor table and watch the world spin by (daily 11:00–24:00, beneath Film Museum, Vondelpark 3, tel. 020/612-3021).

SMOKING

Tobacco

A third of the Dutch people smoke tobacco. You don't have to
like it, but expect it—in restaurants, bars, bus stops, almost everywhere. Holland has a long tradition as a smoking culture, being
among the first to import the tobacco plant from the New World.
Tobacco shops such as the House of Hajenius glorify the habit
(see page 62). Smoking seems to be part of an overall diet and regi-
men that—no denying it—makes the Dutch people among
the healthiest in the world. Tanned, trim, firm, 60-something
Dutch people sip their beer, take a drag, and ask me why Americans murder themselves with Big Macs.

Still, their version of the Surgeon General is finally waking
up to the drug's many potential health problems. Since 2002,
warning stickers bigger than America's are required on cigarette
packs, and some of them are almost comically blunt, such as:
Smoking will make you impotent . . . and then you die. (The
warnings prompted gag stickers like, "If you can read this, you're
healthy enough," and "Life can kill you.")

Beginning in 2003, smoking is prohibited on trains. It's
unclear how much this will be obeyed or enforced.

Marijuana

Amsterdam, Europe's counterculture mecca, thinks the concept
of a "victimless crime" is a contradiction in terms. Heroin and
cocaine are strictly illegal in the Netherlands, and the police
stringently enforce laws prohibiting their sale and use. But,
while hard drugs are definitely out, marijuana causes about as
much excitement as a bottle of beer. If tourists call an ambulance
after smoking too much pot, medics just say, "Drink something
sweet and walk it off."

Throughout the Netherlands you'll see "coffeeshops"—pubs selling marijuana. The minimum age for purchase is 18. Coffeeshops can sell up to five grams of marijuana per person per day. Locals buy marijuana by asking, "Can I see the cannabis menu?" The menu looks like the inventory of a drug bust. Display cases show various

joints or baggies for sale. The Dutch include a little tobacco in their prerolled joints. To avoid the tobacco, you either need to get cigarette papers with your baggie (dispensed free, like toothpicks) or borrow a bong. Baggies usually cost €5—smaller contents mean better quality.

Pot should never be bought on the street in Amsterdam. Well-established coffeeshops are considered much safer. Coffeeshop owners have an interest in keeping their trade safe and healthy. They warn Americans, unused to the strength of the local stuff, to try a lighter leaf. In fact, they are generally very patient in explaining the varieties available.

Several forms of the cannabis plant are sold. Locals smoke more hashish (the sap of the cannabis plant) than the leaf of the plant (which they call "marijuana" or "grass"). White varieties (called "White Widow" or "Amsterdam White") are popular, featuring marijuana with white, fiber-like strands.

So what am I? Pro-marijuana? Let's put it this way: I agree with the Dutch people who remind me that a society either has to allow alternative lifestyles... or build more prisons. Last year alone, more than 700,000 Americans were arrested for marijuana use; only Russia incarcerates more of its citizens. The Dutch

are not necessarily pro-marijuana. They believe that a prohibition on marijuana would cause more problems than it solves. Statistics support the Dutch belief that their system works. They have fewer hard drug problems than other countries. And they believe America's policy—like so many other touchy issues in the news lately—is based on electoral politics rather than rationality.

To learn more about marijuana, drop by Amsterdam's Cannabis

College or the Hash, Marijuana, and Hemp Museum. To see where cannabis growers buy their seeds, stop by the Sensi Seed Bank Store. These three places are located on Oudezijds Achterburgwal street (see end of Red Light District Walk, page 79).

Coffeeshops

Most of downtown Amsterdam's coffeeshops feel grungy and fore-boding to anyone over 30. The neighborhood places (and those in small towns around the countryside) are much more inviting to people without piercings, tattoos, and favorite techno artists. I've listed a few places with a more pub-like ambience for Americans wanting to go local, but within reason. For locations, see map on page 156.

Paradox is the most *gezellig* (cozy) coffeeshop I found—a mellow, graceful place. The manager, Ludo, is patient with descriptions and is happy to walk you through all your options. This is a rare coffeeshop that serves light meals. The juice is fresh, the music is easy, and the neighborhood is charming. Colorful murals with bright blue skies are all over the walls, creating a fresh and open feeling (loaner bongs, games, no CC, daily 10:00–20:00, 2 blocks from Anne Frank House at 1e Bloemdwarsstraat 2, tel. 020/623-5639).

The Grey Area coffeeshop is a cool, welcoming, and smoky hole-in-the-wall appreciated among local aficionados as a seven-time winner of Amsterdam's Cannabis Cup award. Judging by the proud autographed photos on the wall, many famous Americans have dropped in. You're welcome to just nurse a bottomless cup of coffee (open Tue–Sun high noon to 20:00, closed Mon, between Dam Square and Anne Frank House at Oude Leliestraat 2, tel. 020/420-4301, www.greyarea.nl, run by two friendly Americans, Steven and John).

Coffee Shop Relax is simply the neighborhood pub serving a different drug. It's relaxed and has a helpful staff and homey atmosphere with plants, couches, and bar seating. The great straight-forward menu chalked onto the board behind the bar details what it has to offer (daily 10:00–24:00, a bit out of the way, but a pleasant Jordaan walk to Binnen Orangestraat 9).

Siberia Coffeeshop is central but feels cozy, with a friendly canal-side ambience (daily 11:00–23:00, Internet access, helpful staff, fun English menu that explains the personalities of each item, a variety of €4 bags, Brouwersgracht 11).

Coffeeshop Interlude

A tourist walks into the Bulldog coffeeshop and asks the bartender, "Can I see the cannabis menu?"

"Yes, of course," says the bartender, and directs her to a desk near the door where the list of marijuana products is displayed. The woman is no cannabis connoisseur, and she's a bit dazzled by the exotic names on the menu and the sheer variety of substances produced from the same plant. But soon, her eye zeroes in on some familiar words:

Hash
Thai baby	1 gram	€12
Jungle stick	1 gram	€13
Etc.		

Marihuana
Black Widow	2.1 g	€12
Amsterdam White	1.9 g	€10
Etc.		

Joints
With tobacco	4 joints	€12
Pure marihuana	4 joints	€12
Etc.		

Not wanting to appear unsophisticated, she thinks quickly: "I don't want hash (the waxy resin) because I'd have to mix it with tobacco to smoke it. I just want the leafy stuff, but I don't have a pipe, and I couldn't roll a joint (cigarette of marijuana leaves) to save my life."

"Four joints of marijuana, please," she tells the man at the desk. She pays the man, takes the joints to an empty table, borrows a lighter from a fellow patron, and smokes. Chiding herself for being so timid, she marvels at how legal it all is. She buys an orange juice at the bar, then goes back outside and shoots off a roll of film in half an hour.

La Tertulia is a sweet little mother-daughter-run place with pastel décor, fishpond, and a cheery terrarium ambience (Tue–Sat 11:00–19:00, closed Sun–Mon, games, sandwiches, Prinsengracht 312, www.coffeeshopamsterdam.com).

The Bulldog is the high-profile, leading touristy chain of coffeeshops. They are young but welcoming, with reliable selections. They're pretty comfortable for green tourists wanting to just hang out for a while. The flagship branch, in a former police station right on Leidseplein, is very handy, offering fun outdoor seating where you can watch the world skateboard by (daily 9:00–01:00, Leidseplein 17, tel. 020/625-6278, www.bulldog.nl).

Smartshops

These business establishments (one is listed on page 64) sell "natural" drugs that are legal. Many are harmless nutritional supplements, but they also sell hallucinogenic mushrooms, stimulants similar to Ecstasy, and strange drug cocktails rolled into joints. It's all perfectly legal, but if you've never taken drugs recreationally, don't start here.

SHOPPING

Amsterdam brings out the browser even in those who were not born to shop. Ten general markets, open six days a week, keep folks who brake for garage sales pulling U-turns. Markets include Waterlooplein (the flea market); the huge Albert Cuyp street market; and various flower markets (such as the Singelgraacht canalmarket near Mint Tower, daily except Sun).

When you need to buy something but don't know where to go, two chain stores—Hema and Vroom & Dreesman—are handy for everything from inexpensive clothes and notebooks to food and cosmetics. De Bijenkorf and Metz & Co. department stores are old-time fancy. (For more information, pick up the TI's "Shopping in Amsterdam" brochure.) To find out how to get a VAT (Value Added Tax) refund on your purchases, see page 5.

Smaller shops are open from 9:00 to 18:00 and until 21:00 on Thursdays (closed Sun). Larger stores and supermarkets are open weekdays from 8:00 to 20:00 and until 17:00 on Saturdays (closed Sun). The businesslike Dutch know no siesta, but many shopkeepers take Monday mornings off.

Amsterdam's Top Shopping Zones

Jordaan—The colorful old working-class district of the Jordaan and its main drag, Westerstraat, are a wonderland of funky, artsy shops. On Mondays you'll find busy markets at the end of Westerstraat (Noordermerkt) and the neighboring street, Lindengracht.
Leidsestraat—This is a bustling shopping street with elegant and trendy shops including the top-end department store Metz & Co.
The Nine Little Streets—De Negen Straatjes is home to 190 diverse shops mixing festive, creative, nostalgic, practical, and artistic items. The cross streets make a tic-tac-toe with a couple of canals just west of Kalverstraat. (Look for the zone where

Hartenstraat, Wolvenstraat, and Huidenstraat cross the Keizersgracht and Herrengracht.)

Kalverstraat-Heiligeweg-Spui—This is the busiest shopping corridor in town. Kalverstraat, a pedestrian street, is a human traffic-jam of low-end shoppers. It feels soulless, but if you explore the fringes, there are some interesting places.

Spiegelkwartier—Located between the Rijksmuseum and the city center, this is *the* place for art and antiques. You'll find 70 art and antique dealers offering 17th-century furniture, old Delftware, oriental art, clocks, jewelry, and Art Nouveau doodads. Wander down Spiegelgracht and Nieuwe Spiegelstraat.

Prinsheerlijk—Along Herenstraat and Prinsenstraat, you'll find top-end fashion, interior design, and gift shops. If you're looking for jewelry, accessories, trendy clothing, and fancy delicatessens, this may be an expensive but rewarding stroll.

Magna Plaza Shopping Center—Formerly the main post office, this grand 19th-century building has been transformed into a stylish mall with 40 boutiques. You'll find fashion, luxury goods, and gift shops galore. It's just behind the Royal Palace a block off Dam Square.

Popular Souvenirs

Wooden shoes—Originally key for navigating soggy Amsterdam, now something to clomp around in.

Delftware—Ceramic plates, vases, and tiles decorated with a fake Chinese blue-and-white design popularized in the 1600s. Only a few licensed places sell the real stuff (expensive) and antiques (very expensive). You can find fireplace tiles (cheap) at most gift shops.

Diamonds—Cut or uncut, expensive or really expensive. Diamond dealers offer free cutting and polishing demos at their shops (on Potterstraat behind Rijksmuseum; on Dam Square; and at Gassan Diamonds near Rembrandt's House. See page 57).

Beers—A yeasty, frothy souvenir.

Jenever—Dutch gin (made from juniper berries) sold in traditional stone bottles.

Chocolate—Belgian or Dutch Verkade or Droste cocoa in tins.

Flower seeds and bulbs—Packed with a seal that promises they are U.S. Customs–friendly.

Posters and art postcards—The Van Gogh Museum bookshop has a good selection (and sells mailing tubes to protect posters).

Marijuana pipes—Make sure they're unused. Even a little residue can get you busted at U.S. Customs.

Old maps—Capturing the Golden Age.

Old books—Browse musty bookshelves and unearth a treasure. Amsterdam has lots of one-of-a-kind specialty stores. Poke around and see what you can find.

NIGHTLIFE

Amsterdam hotels serve breakfast until 11:00 because so many people—visitors and locals—live for nighttime in Amsterdam.

On summer evenings, people flock to the main squares for drinks at outdoor tables. Leidseplein is the glitziest, surrounded by theaters, restaurants, and nightclubs. The slightly quieter Rembrandtplein (with adjoining Thorbeckeplein) is the center of gay discos. Spui features a full city block of bars. And Nieuwemarkt, on the east edge of the Red Light District, is a bit rough, but is probably the most local.

The Red Light District (particularly Oudezijds Achterburgwal) is less sleazy at night, almost carnival-like as the neon comes on and the streets fill with Japanese tour groups (see Red Light District Walk, page 68).

Information

Boom Chicago and *Uitkrant* are two free publications (available at TIs and many bars) that list festivals and performances of theater, film, dance, cabaret, and live rock, pop, jazz, and classical music.

For the best lowdown on the youth and nightlife scene, get *Boom Chicago*. This irreverent magazine is packed with practical tips and countercultural insights, and gives a €3 discount on the *Boom Chicago* R-rated comedy theater act (see below). *Uitkrant* is in Dutch, but it's just a calendar of events, and anyone can figure out the name of the event and its date, time, and location.

There's also *What's On in Amsterdam, Time Out Amsterdam*, the Thursday edition of many Dutch papers, and the *International Herald Tribune*'s special Netherlands inserts (all sold at newsstands).

The **AUB ticket office** at Stadsschouwburg Theater (Leidseplein 26, tel. 0900/0191) is the best one-stop-shopping box office for theater, classical music, and major rock shows.

Music

You'll find classical music at the Concertgebouw (at the far
south end of Museumplein, tel. 020/675-4411) and at the former
Beurs (on Damrak, tel. 020/627-0466), and opera and dance at
the new opera house on Waterlooplein (tel. 020/551-8100).
In the summer, Vondelpark hosts open-air concerts.

Two rock music (and hip-hop) clubs near Leidseplein—
Melkweg (Lijnbaansgracht 234a, tel. 020/531-8181, www
.melkweg.nl) and Paradiso (Weteringschans 6, tel. 020/626-
4521, www.paradiso.nl)—present big-name acts that you might
recognize if you're younger than I am.

Jazz has a long tradition at the Bimhuis nightclub, east of
the Red Light District (concerts Thu–Sat, Oude Schans 73–77,
box office tel. 020/623-1361, www.bimhuis.nl).

Comedy

Boom Chicago, an R-rated comedy theater act, was started 10
years ago by a group of Americans on a graduation tour. They
have been entertaining tourists and locals alike ever since. The
show is a series of rude, clever, and high-powered skits offering a
raucous look at Dutch culture and local tourism (€16, nightly at
20:15, dinner seating early in the 270-seat Leidseplein Theater,
Leidseplein 12, tel. 020/423-0101, www.boomchicago.nl). They
do two shows: *Best of Boom* (a collection of their greatest hits over
the years) and a new show for locals and return customers. Meals
are optional and a good value.

Theater

Amsterdam is one of the world centers for experimental live
theater (much of it in English). Many theaters cluster around the
street called the Nes, which stretches south from Dam Square.

Movies

Catch modern movies in the 1920s setting of the classic Tuschinski Theater (between Muntplein and Rembrandtplein, described
on page 46). The Amsterdam Film Museum, which has some
evening showings, is also worth checking out (Vondelstraat 69,
near Vondelpark, tel. 020/589-1400, www.filmmuseum.nl, see
page 37). It's not unusual for movies at many cinemas to be
sold out—consider buying tickets during the day.

HAARLEM

ORIENTATION AND SIGHTS

Cute and cozy yet authentic and handy to the airport, Haarlem is a fine home base, giving you small-town warmth overnight with easy access (15 min by train) to wild and crazy Amsterdam.

Bustling Haarlem gave America's Harlem its name back when New York was New Amsterdam, a Dutch colony. For centuries, Haarlem has been a market town, buzzing with shoppers heading home with fresh bouquets, nowadays by bike.

Enjoy the market on Monday (clothing) or Saturday (general), when the square bustles like a Brueghel painting with cheese, fish, flowers, and families. Make yourself at home; buy some flowers to brighten your hotel room.

Orientation (area code: 023)

Tourist Information: Haarlem's TI (VVV), at the train station, is friendlier, more helpful, and less crowded than Amsterdam's. Ask your Amsterdam questions here (Mon–Fri 9:30–17:30, Sat 10:00–14:00, closed Sun, tel. 0900/616-1600, €0.50/min, helpful parking brochure). The €1 *Holiday Magazine* is not necessary, but it's free if you buy the fine €2 town map. The TI also sells a €2 self-guided walking-tour map for over-achievers. The little computer terminal prints out free maps anytime on the curb outside the TI.

Arrival in Haarlem: As you walk out of the train station (which has lockers), the TI is on your right and the bus station is across the street. Two parallel streets flank the train station (Kruisweg and Jansweg). Head up either street, and you'll reach the town square and church within 10 minutes. If you need help, ask a local person to point you toward the *Grote Markt* (Main Square).

Parking is expensive on the streets and €1 an hour in several

Haarlem of the Golden Age

Parts of Haarlem still look like they did four centuries ago, when the city was a bustling commercial center rivaling Amsterdam. It's easy to imagine local merchants and their wives dressed in black with ruff collars, promenading the Market Square.

Back then, the town was a port on the large Haarlemmer Lake, with the North Sea only about eight kilometers away. As well as being the tulip capital, Haarlem was a manufacturing center producing wool, silk, lace, damask cloth, furniture, smoking pipes (along with cheap, locally grown tobacco), and mass quantities of beer. Haarlemers were notorious consumers of beer. It was a popular breakfast drink, and the average person drank six pints a day.

In 1585, the city got an influx of wealthy merchants when Spanish troops invaded the culturally rich city of Antwerp, driving Protestants and Jews north. Even when hard-line, moralistic Calvinists dominated Haarlem's politics, the city remained culturally and religiously diverse.

In the 1700s, Haarlem's economy declined along with that of the Netherlands. In the succeeding centuries, industry—printing, textiles, ship building—once again made the city an economic force.

central garages. Two main garages let you park overnight for €1 (at the train station and near Die Raeckse Hotel).

Helpful Hints

You can rent **bikes** at the train station (€6/day, €45 deposit and passport number, Mon–Sat 6:00–24:00, Sun 7:30–24:00).

The handy GWK **change office** at the train station offers fair exchange rates (Mon–Fri 8:00–20:00, Sat 9:00–18:00, Sun 10:00–18:00).

For **Internet access**, try Internet Café Amadeus (in the Hotel Amadeus overlooking Market Square, €1/15 min) or nearly any coffeeshop (if you don't mind marijuana smoke).

For **laundry,** My Beautiful Launderette is handy and cheap

Haarlem

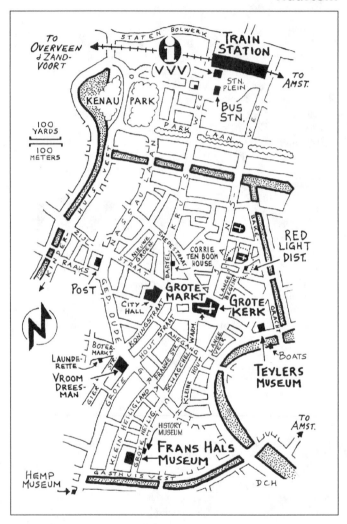

(€5 wash and dry, daily 8:30–20:30, self-service, bring change, near Vroom Dreesman department store at Boter Markt 20).

On April 26, 2003, an all-day **Flower Parade** of floats wafts through eight towns, including Haarlem.

For a local **guide,** consider Walter Schelfhout (€75/2-hr walk, tel. 023/535-5715).

Sights—Haarlem

▲▲**Market Square (Grote Markt)**—Haarlem's market square, where 10 streets converge, is the town's delightful centerpiece... as it has been for 700 years. To enjoy a coffee or beer here, sim-

mering in Dutch good living, is a quintessential European experience. In a recent study, the Dutch were found to be the most content people in Europe. In another study, the people of Haarlem were found to be the most content in the Netherlands. Observe. Sit and gaze at the church, appreciating the same scene Dutch artists captured in oil paintings that now hang in museums.

Just a few years ago, trolleys ran through the square and cars were parked everywhere. But today it's a people zone, with market stalls filling the square on Mondays and Saturdays and café tables on other days.

This is a great place to build a picnic with Haarlem finger foods—raw herring, local cheese (Gouda and Edam), a *frikandel* (little corn-dog sausage), french fries with mayonnaise, *stroopwafels* (waffles with syrup), *poffertjes* (little sugar doughnuts), or one of many different ethnic foods (falafel, *shoarma*, Indonesian dishes). Overseeing the square is the...

L. J. Coster statue: Forty years before Gutenberg invented movable type, this man carved the letter *A* out of wood, dropped it into some wet sand, and saw the imprint it left. He got the idea of making movable type out of wood (and later he may have tried using lead). For Haarlemers, that was good enough, and they credit their man, Coster, with inventing modern printing. In the statue, Coster (c. 1370–1440) holds up a block of movable type and points to himself, saying, "I made this." How much Coster did is uncertain, but Gutenberg trumped him by building a printing press, casting type in metal, and pounding out the Bible. Coster is facting the...

Town Hall: This has been the site of Haarlem's town hall since about 1100. Remember that while most of medieval Europe was ruled by kings, dukes, and barons, Haarlem has been largely self-governing since 1425. The town hall was rebuilt after a 1351 fire, and the facade is from 1630.

The town drunk used to hang out on the bench in front of the town hall, where he'd expose himself to newlyweds coming down the stairs. The Dutch, rather than arresting the man, moved the bench. Next to the church is the...

Meat Market (Vleeshall), 1603: The fine Flemish Renaissance building nearest the cathedral is the old meat hall. Built by the rich butchers and leather workers guilds, the meat market was on the ground floor, the leather upstairs, and the cellar was filled with ice to keep the meat preserved. It's decorated with carved bits of early advertising—sheep and cows for sale.

▲**Church (Grote Kerk)**—This 15th-century Gothic church (now Protestant) is worth a look, if only for its Oz-like organ (from 1738, 30 meters/100 feet high, its 5,000 pipes impressed both Handel and Mozart). Note how the organ, which fills the west end, seems to steal the show from the altar.

To enter, find the small *Entrée* sign behind the church at Oude Groenmarkt 23 (€1.50, Mon–Sat 10:00–16:00, closed Sun to tourists, tel. 023/532-4399). Consider attending (even part of) a concert to hear Holland's greatest pipe organ (regular free concerts Tue at 20:15 mid-May–mid-Oct, additional concerts Thu at 15:00 July–Aug, confirm schedule at TI or at www.bavo.nl). ✪ See Grote Kerk Tour, page 180.

▲▲**Frans Hals Museum**—Haarlem is the hometown of Frans Hals, and this refreshing museum—an almshouse for old men back in 1610—displays many of his greatest paintings (€5.40, Tue–Sat 11:00–17:00, Sun 12:00–17:00, closed Mon, Groot Heiligland 62, tel. 023/511-5775, www.franshalsmuseum.nl). Enjoy lots of Frans Hals group portraits and the take-me-back paintings of old-time Haarlem. Pieter Brueghel the Younger's painting *Proverbs* illustrates 72 old Dutch proverbs. To peek into old Dutch ways, identify some with the help of the English-language key. ✪ See Frans Hals Museum Tour, page 189.

History Museum—This small museum, across the street from the Frans Hals Museum, offers a glimpse of old Haarlem. Request the English version of the 10-minute video. Study the large-scale model of Haarlem in 1822 while its fortifications were still intact, and enjoy the new "time machine" computer and video display that shows you various aspects of life in Haarlem at different points in history (€1, Tue–Sat 12:00–17:00, Sun 13:00–17:00, closed Mon, Groot Heiligland 47, tel. 020/542-2427). The adjacent architecture museum (free) may be of interest to architects.

Corrie Ten Boom House—Haarlem is home to Corrie Ten Boom, popularized by *The Hiding Place*, an inspirational book and movie about the Ten Boom family's experience protecting Jews from the Nazis. Corrie Ten Boom gives the other half of the Anne Frank story—the point of view of those who risked their lives to hide Dutch Jews during the Nazi occupation (1940–1945).

The clock shop was the Ten Boom family business. The elderly father and his two daughters—Corrie and Betsy, both in their 50s—lived above the store and in the brick building attached in back (along Schoutensteeg alley). Corrie's bedroom was on the top floor at the back. This room was tiny to start with, but the family built a second, secret room at the very back—the hiding place, where they could hide six or seven Jews at a time.

Devoutly religious, the family had a long tradition of toler-ance, having for generations hosted prayer meetings here in their home for both Jews and Christians.

The Gestapo, tipped off that the family was harboring Jews, burst into the Ten Boom house. Finding a suspicious number of ration coupons, the Nazis arrested the family but failed to find the six Jews in the hiding place (who later escaped). Corrie's father and sister died while in prison, but Corrie survived the Ravensbruck concentration camp to tell her story in her memoir.

The Ten Boom House is open for 60-minute English tours; the tours are sometimes mixed with preaching (donation accepted, April–Oct Tue–Sat 10:00–16:00, Nov–March Tue–Sat 11:00–15:00, closed Mon, 50 meters north of Market Square at Barteljorisstraat 19, the clock-shop people get all wound up if you go inside—wait at the door, where tour times are posted, tel. 023/531-0823).

▲Teylers Museum—Famous as the oldest museum in Holland, Teylers is interesting mainly as a look at a 200-year-old museum—fossils, minerals, and primitive electronic gadgetry. New exhibition halls (with rotating exhibits) have freshened up the place. Stop by if you enjoy mixing, say, Renaissance sketches with pickled extinct fish (€4.50, Tue–Sat 10:00–17:00, Sun 12:00–17:00, Spaarne 16, tel. 023/531-9010).

Canal Cruise—Making a scenic loop through and around Haarlem, these little trips by Woltheus Cruises are more relaxing than informative (€6.50, Tue–Sun 10:00–17:00, closed Mon, 70 min, 5/day, across canal from Teylers Museum at Spaarne 11a, tel. 023/535-7723).

Red Lights—Wander through a little red light district as precious as a Barbie doll—and legal since the 1980s (2 blocks northeast of Market Square, off Lange Begijnestraat, no senior or student discounts). Don't miss the mall marked by the red neon sign reading *t'Steegje*. The nearby *t'Poortje* (office park) costs €6.

Amsterdam to Haarlem Train Tour

Since you'll be commuting from Amsterdam to Haarlem, here's a tour to keep you entertained. Departing from Amsterdam, grab a seat on the right (with your back to Amsterdam, top deck if possible). Everything is on the right unless I say on the left.

You're riding the oldest train line in Holland. Across the harbor behind the Amsterdam station, the tall brown skyscraper is the corporate office of **Shell Oil.** The Dutch had the first multi-national corporation (the United East India Company, back in the 17th century). And today this international big-business spirit survives with companies like Shell and Philips.

Leaving Amsterdam, you'll see the cranes and ships of its harbor—sizable but nothing like the world's biggest in nearby Rotterdam.

On your left, find the old **windmill.** In front of it, the little garden plots and cottages are escapes for big-city people who probably don't even have a balcony.

Coming into the Sloterdijk Station (where trains connect for Amsterdam airport), you'll see huge office buildings, such as Dutch Telecom KPN. These grew up after the station made commuting easy.

Look for the **drive-in brothel** a kilometer past Sloterdijk Station, 50 meters to the right of the tracks (just before a long line of modern windmills—see the pink urinals and the purple door). A yellow sign says, "Tippel Zone—open 21:00." (*Tippel* is the sound a mouse makes when it runs through the house at night.) There's an oval driveway with pink "bus stops" for browsing, a lounge building, and blue privacy stalls behind (including 2 for bikers). The lounge has a clinic with a nurse and counselors to keep the women healthy. If a prostitute is diagnosed with AIDS, she gets a subsidized apartment to encourage her to quit the business. Shocking as this may seem to some, it's a good example of a pragmatic solution to a problem—getting the most dangerous prostitutes off the streets to combat the spread of AIDS.

Passing through a forest and by some houseboats, you enter a *polder*—reclaimed land. This is an ecologically sound farm zone, run without chemicals. Cows, pigs, and chickens run free—they're not raised in cages. The train tracks are on a dike, which provides a solid foundation not susceptible to floods. This way the transportation system functions right through any calamity. Looking

The Haarlemmermeer

The land between Haarlem and Amsterdam—where trains speed through, cattle graze, and 747s touch down—was once a lake the size of Washington, D.C.

In the 1500s, a series of high tides and storms caused the IJ River to breach its banks, flooding this sub-sea-level area and turning a bunch of shallow lakes into a single one nearly five meters (15 feet) deep, covering 180 square kilometers (70 square miles). By the 1800s, floods were licking the borders of Haarlem and Amsterdam, and the residents needed to act. First, they dug a Ring Canal to channel away water (and preserve the lake's shipping business). Then, using steam engines, they pumped the lake dry, turning marshy soil into fertile ground. The Amsterdam–Haarlem train line that soon crossed the former lakebed was the country's first.

out at the distant dike, remember you're in the most densely populated country in Europe. On the horizon, sleek, modern windmills whirl.

On the right, just after the tall green-and-white telecom tower, find a big, beige-and-white building. This is the **mint,** where currency is printed (top security, no advertising). This has long been a family business—see the name: Johan Enschede.

As the train slows down, you're passing through the Netherlands' biggest train-car maintenance facility and entering Haarlem. Look left. The domed building is a prison, built in 1901 and still in use. The windmill burned down in 1932 and was just rebuilt in 2002.

When you cross the Spaarne River, you'll see the great church spire towering over Haarlem as it has since medieval times—back when a fortified wall circled the town. Notice the white copy of the same spire capping the smaller church between the prison and the big church. This was the original sandstone steeple that stood atop the big church until structural problems forced them to move it to another church and build a new spire for the big church. Hop out into one of Holland's oldest stations. Art Nouveau decor from 1908 survives all around.

GROTE KERK
TOUR

Haarlem's impressive Grote Kerk (Great Church), one of the best-known landmarks in the Netherlands, is visible from miles around, rising above the flat plain that surrounds it. From the Market Square, you see the church at a three-quarters angle, emphasizing both its length (72 meters, or 240 feet) and height (80 meters, or 260 feet).

Orientation

Cost: €1.50.

Hours: Mon–Sat 10:00–16:00, closed Sun to tourists, Sun service at 10:00.

Getting There: The church is on the main square, a 10-minute walk south of the train station.

Information: Tel. 023/532-4399, www.bavo.nl.

Length of Our Tour: One hour.

Music: Consider attending even part of a concert to hear Holland's greatest pipe organ. Free concerts are generally offered throughout the summer (Tue at 20:15 mid-May–mid-Oct, additional concerts Thu at 15:00 July–Aug; confirm schedule at TI or at Web site listed above).

Overview

After a fire destroyed the old church (1328), the Grote Kerk was built over a 150-year period (c. 1390–1540) in the late Gothic style of red and gray brick, topped with a lead-covered wood roof and a stacked tower bearing a golden crown and a rooster weathervane.

Builders raised money by cleverly hitting up both popes—back when there were two competing pontiffs, one in Avignon and one in Rome. The builders came home with two different "absolution bills," authorizing them to grant forgiveness to

Grote Kerk

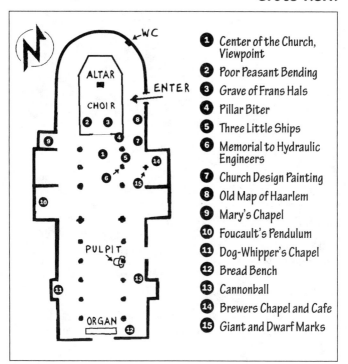

1. Center of the Church, Viewpoint
2. Poor Peasant Bending
3. Grave of Frans Hals
4. Pillar Biter
5. Three Little Ships
6. Memorial to Hydraulic Engineers
7. Church Design Painting
8. Old Map of Haarlem
9. Mary's Chapel
10. Foucault's Pendulum
11. Dog-Whipper's Chapel
12. Bread Bench
13. Cannonball
14. Brewers Chapel and Cafe
15. Giant and Dwarf Marks

parishioners for donations. Apparently Haarlem's sinners—not knowing for sure which pope was *the* pope—covered all their bases by giving twice for their forgiveness.

• *You'll enter the church from the side opposite the square. As you walk around the building, check out a few details...*

Exterior

Notice the rough buttress anchors, which were never needed. Money ran out, and the planned stone ceiling (which would have required these buttresses) was replaced by a lighter wooden one. Some windows are bricked up because the organ fills the wall.

The original stone tower crowned the church from 1522 until 1530, when they noticed that the church was sinking under its weight. It was removed and replaced by the lighter wood-covered-with-lead version you see today. (The frugal Dutch recycled the old tower, using it to cap the Bakenesser church, a short walk away.)

Because the tower was
used as a lookout by Napoleon, it was classified as
part of the town's defense.
As a result, the tower (but
not the rest of the church)
became city property and,
since Haarlem's citizens
own it, they must help
pay to maintain it.

The base of the church is crusted, barnacle-like, with shops—
selling jewelry, souvenirs, haircuts, and artwork in the colonnaded
former fish market—harkening back to medieval times, when
religion and commerce were more intertwined. The little shops
around the cathedral have long been church-owned and rented
to bring in a little cash.

Originally Catholic, the St. Bavo Church became Protestant
(Dutch Reformed) along with much of the country in the late
1500s. From then on, the anti-saint Protestants simply called it
the Great Church.

If you're in Haarlem at night, you'll hear the Great Church's
carillon chiming a simple "de dong dong, de dong dong" ("Don't
wor-ry, be hap-py") at 21:00. In days gone by, this used to warn
citizens that the city gates would soon close for the night. Today,
during the day, a machine (and occasionally live carillonneurs)
play music on its bells.

• *Enter the church at Oude Groenmarkt 23 (look for the small* Entrée
sign). Stand in the center of the church and take it all in.

Interior

Simple white walls and the black floor, brown ceiling, and
mahogany-colored organ make this spacious church feel vast,
light, and airy. Considering it was built over the span of 150 years,
its architecture is impressively homogenous. Originally much of

the church was painted in bright
patterns, similar to the carpet-
like frescoes on some columns
near the center of the church.
But in 1566, Protestant extremists stripped the church of
its graven images and ornate
Catholic trappings, leaving
the church relatively stark,
with minimal decoration.
They whitewashed everything.

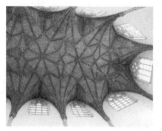

The frescoes you see today were restored when the whitewash was removed in the 1980s.

Look up to see the fan-vaulted cedar ceiling from 1530. Look down to see tomb-stones paving the floor. And look midway up the walls to catch squatting gargoyles.

The three-story organ fills the west wall.

• *We'll circle the church, but first stand at the candle-lined, fence-like brass barrier and look into an enclosed area of wooden benches ("stalls") and the altar, known as the . . .*

Choir

After the church's foundation was laid, the choir was built first and used for worship for more than a century while the rest of the building was completed.

Today, the brass-and-wood barrier keeps tourists from enter-ing the most sacred area, just as peasants were kept out in medi-eval times. While the commoners had to stand during services, local big shots got to perch their heinies on the little ledges (called miseri-cords, carved in 1512) of the **wooden stalls** that line the choir; the eighth stall along the left-hand side shows a poor peasant

bending over to bear a rich guy's bum on his back. The stalls are also deco-rated with the coats of arms of noble families, whose second sons tradition-ally became priests.

The choir's floor holds a simple slab marked with a lantern—the **Grave of Frans Hals** (Graf van Frans Hals), Haarlem's own master artist of the Golden Age. When he was a child, Hals' family moved to Haarlem, and he lived and worked here all his life, worshipping in the Grote Kerk. A friend of mayors and preachers, he chron-icled middle-class citizens and tavern life, producing hundreds of masterpieces along with 10 kids. (See the Frans Hals Museum Tour, page 189.)

At both ends of the brass barrier, look for the knee-level,

endearing carvings of the "pillar biter." The message, aimed at those who were "more Catholic than even the Pope," was this: *Don't go overboard on devotion.*

More than a thousand wealthy people are buried under the church's pavement stones. Only those with piles of money to give to the church could be buried in a way that gave them an advantage in the salvation derby. But even though the dead bodies were embalmed, they stunk. Imagine being a peasant sitting here, trying to think about God...and thinking only of the stench of well-fed bodies rotting. And the phrase "stinking rich" was born.

• *Looking down the nave (without actually walking there yet), on the left side is the...*

Pulpit

The pulpit, elaborately carved from oak in 1679, is topped with a tower-shaped roof. Brass handrails snake down the staircase, serpents fleeing the word of God. In this simply decorated Protestant church, the pulpit is perhaps the most ornate element, directing worshippers' eyes to the speaker. During the Reformation, Protestants changed the worship service. As teaching became more important than ritual, the pulpit was given a higher profile.

• *Suspended between columns between the center of the church and the place you entered are...*

Three Little Ships

Sailing under the red-white-and-blue Dutch flag and the flag of a rearing lion, ships like these helped make Holland the world's number one sea-trading nation in the 1600s.

The biggest model ship of the three is a frigate. These fast, heavily armed, three-masted, fully rigged ships rode shotgun for merchant vessels, protecting them from pirates in their two-year journey to the Far East and back. This one has a flat-bottomed hull, necessary to ply Amsterdam's shallow harbor. It could fire a 21-gun salute from each side. Extra cannons on the poop and forecastle made it more powerful than the average frigate.

The keel has an iron saw, a Dutch military specialty for slicing through the chains that commonly blocked harbors (see the chain between two towers near the bow).

• *Nearby, just to the right, find the . . .*

Memorial to Hydraulic Engineers

The marble relief shows Neptune in his water chariot. In low-lying Holland of the 1800s, when flooding could mean life or death, hydraulic engineers were heroes.

Twenty meters beyond the memorial (near where you entered, just left of the café) is a painting done when the church was commissioned. This provided a model for the architects to follow.

• *From here, circle the church counter-clockwise, starting back near the tourists' entrance. On the wall near the tourists' entrance hangs an . . .*

Old Map of Harlemum

The map shows the walled city in 1688, with ramparts and a moat. Surrounding panels showcase Haarlem's 750-year history.

The lower-left panel shows the 1572–1573 Siege of Haarlem (described below), as brave Haarlem women join their menfolk in battle—bombs exploding around them—to fight off invading Spanish troops.

The bottom-right panel shows knights kneeling before a king in the 12th century, while in the distance, ships sail right along the city walls. Up until the 1840s, when it was drained and reclaimed, there was a large lake (the Haarlemmermeer) standing between Haarlem and Amsterdam. The Grote Kerk, when viewed by distant travelers, seemed to float like a stately ship on the lake, as seen in the landscape along the bottom of the map.

• *Circle around the altar to the other side of the church, to . . .*

Mary's Chapel (Maria Kapel)

Inside the iron cage on the back wall is an old wood-and-iron chest that served as a safe for the church's cash and precious documents—such as those papers granting the power to sell forgiveness. See the board of keys for the many doors in this huge complex. Notice also the sarcophagi. Once filled with the "stinking rich," boxes like this were buried five deep below the church floor. Such high-density burying maximized the revenue generated by selling burial spots.

Foucault's Pendulum

In the north transept, a ball on a wire swings from the ceiling across a dial on the floor, recreating Foucault's pendulum experiment of 1851. Stand here patiently and watch Earth rotate on its axis.

As the pendulum swings steadily back and forth, Earth rotates counter-clockwise underneath it, making the pendulum appear to rotate clockwise around the dial. Earth rotates once every 24 hours, of course, but at Haarlem's latitude of 52 degrees, it makes the pendulum (appear to) sweep 360 degrees every 30 hours, 27 minutes (to knock over the bowling pin). Stand here for five minutes, and you'll see Earth move one degree.

As the world turns, find several small relief statues (in a niche on the right-hand wall) with beheaded heads and defaced faces— victims of the 1566 Iconoclast rampage, when angry Protestant extremists vandalized Dutch Catholic churches (as this once was).

Model of Church and Photo of Organist

A hundred times smaller than the church itself, this model still took a thousand work-hours to build. On the wall are displayed some of the building materials: matchsticks, washers, screens, glue, wire, and paper clips.

Also on the wall is a photo of the organ pit, showing the organist seated at the Grote Kerk's keyboard. Three keyboards, pedals, and 65 stops (the knobs to either side of the keyboards) make the pipes sound like anything from flutes to horns, producing an awesome majesty of sound.

Picture 10-year-old Mozart at the controls of this 5,000-pipe sound machine. In 1766, he played Haarlem at the tail end of his triumphant, three-year, whirlwind tour of Europe. He'd just returned from London, where he met J. C. Bach, the youngest son of Johann Sebastian Bach (1685–1750), the grandfather of organ music. Mozart had just written several pieces inspired by Bach and may have tried them out here.

"Hal-le-lu-jah!" That famous four-note riff may have echoed around the church when Handel played here in 1740, the year before his famous oratorio, *Messiah*, debuted. The 20th-century organist/humanitarian Albert Schweitzer also performed here.

Pass the church's little fire pumps on wheels (from 1850). One was kept in the rafters and had access to cisterns of rainwater collected for fighting fires.

Dog-Whipper's Chapel

In a sculpted relief (top of column at left end of chapel, above eye level), an angry man whips an angry dog while striding over another angry dog's head. Back when churches served as rainy-day marketplaces, this man's responsibility was to keep Haarlem's dogs out of the church.

The Organ

Even silent, this organ impresses. Finished in 1738 by Amsterdam's Christian Muller, it features a mahogany-colored casing with tin pipes and gold trim, studded with statues of musicians and an

eight-piece combo of angels. Lions on the top hold Haarlem's coat of arms—a sword, surrounded by stars, over a banner reading *Vicit Vim Virtus* (Truth overcomes force). There are larger pipe organs in the world, but this is one of the best.

The organist sits unseen amid the pipes, behind the section that juts out at the bottom. While the bellows generate pressurized air, the organist presses a key, which opens a valve, admitting forced air through a pipe and out its narrow opening, producing a tone. An eight-foot-long pipe plays middle C. A four-foot-long pipe plays C exactly one octave up. A 20-foot pipe rumbles the rafters. With 5,068 pipes ranging from over 20 feet tall to just a few inches, this organ can cover eight octaves (a piano plays seven) and each key can play a variety of sounds. By pulling one of the stops (such as "flute" or "trumpet"), the organist can channel the air into certain sets of pipes tuned to play together to mimic other instruments. For maximum power, you "pull out all the stops."

Free Bread, a Cannonball in the Wall, and the Siege of Haarlem

Left of the organ, the bread bench is a rare piece of 15th-century furniture that survives here. This was where the church gave the city's poor their daily bread and lard.

Duck! On the wall (left of the chapel with the green metal gate, above eye level) sits a cannonball, placed here in 1573 to commemorate the city's finest hour—the Siege of Haarlem.

In the winter of 1572–1573, Holland was rebelling against its Spanish oppressors. Haarlem proclaimed its alliance with William of Orange (and thus, independence from Spain). In response, the angry Spanish governor—camped in Amsterdam—laid siege to Haarlem. The winter was cold, food ran low, and the city was bombarded by Spanish cannons. Inside huddled 4,000 cold, hungry Calvinists. At one point, the city's women even joined the men on the barricades, brandishing kitchen knives and melon-ballers.

But Spain had blockaded the Haarlem Lake, and on June 12, 1573, Haarlem had to surrender. The Spanish rounded up 1,500 ringleaders and executed them to send a message to the rest of the country. Still, Haarlem's brave seven-month stand against overwhelming odds became a Dutch "Alamo," inspiring their countrymen to fight on.

Following Haarlem's brave lead, other Dutch towns rebelled. Though Holland and Spain would skirmish for another five decades, the battles soon moved southward, and Spanish troops would never again seriously penetrate the country's borders.

Brouwerskapel—Giant and Dwarf Marks

The long and short of the city's 750-year history are found on the chapel's central pillar. Black lines mark the height of Haarlem's shortest citizen, thigh-high (33 inches) Simon Paap, who supposedly died in a dwarf-tossing incident, and—wow!—8-foot-8-inch-tall Daniel Cajanus. Who said, "When you've seen one Gothic church, you've seen 'em all"?

FRANS HALS MUSEUM TOUR

For two hundred years, Frans Hals (c. 1582–1666) was considered nothing more than just another so-so Dutch portrait painter...and many visitors to the Frans Hals Museum may agree with that lukewarm assessment.

But others may see what I did—a bold humanist who painted everyday people in their warts-and-all glory, a forerunner of Impressionist brushwork, a master of composition, and an articulate visual spokesman for his generation—the generation of the Golden Age.

Stand eye-to-eye with life-size, lifelike portraits of Haarlem's citizens—brewers, preachers, workers, bureaucrats, and housewives—and see the people who built the Golden Age then watched it start to fade.

Orientation

Cost: €5.40.

Hours: Tue–Sat 11:00–17:00, Sun 12:00–17:00, closed Mon.

Getting There: The museum is at Groot Heiligland 62. Walk 15 minutes from the train station toward the city center or take bus #4 or #72 to the Frans Hals Museum stop.

Information: Tel. 023/511-5775, www.franshalsmuseum.nl.

Length of Our Tour: One hour.

Overview

This museum fancies itself as the museum of the Golden Age—your best chance anywhere to enjoy 17th-century art in a 17th-century building. Well-described exhibits unfold as the rectangular museum wraps around a peaceful central courtyard. The building's layout makes sense when you realize it was built (1610) as subsidized housing for poor old men.

Frans Hals (c. 1582–1666)

At age 10, Frans Hals, the son of a weaver, moved with his family to Haarlem. He would spend the rest of his life there, rarely traveling even to nearby Amsterdam.

His early years are known to us only through his paintings of taverns and drunks, musicians and actors, done in a free and colorful style (like the Rijksmuseum's *Merry Drinker*, see page 96). In 1610, he married and joined Haarlem's St. Luke's Guild of painters. In 1612, he was admitted to the prestigious St. George Civic Guard. In 1617, Hals married again, producing (altogether) 10 children, five of whom painted.

Hals' group portrait of the St. George Civic Guard (1616) put him on the map as Haarlem's premier portrait painter. For the next five decades, he abandoned the light-hearted slice-of-life scenes of his youth and dedicated himself to chronicling Haarlem's prosperous, middle-class world of businessmen and professionals—people he knew personally as well as professionally.

Despite his success, Hals had trouble with money. In 1654, he had to sell his belongings to pay debts, and he fought poverty the rest of his life. Commissions became scarce, as the public now preferred more elegant, flattering portraits. His final works (1650–1666) are dark and somber, with increasingly rough and simple brushwork.

In 1664, the city granted him a pension for his years of service. When he died two years later, his work quickly passed out of fashion, dismissed as mere portraits. In the 1800s, the Impressionists rediscovered him, and today he's recognized for his innovations, craftsmanship, and unique style.

Circle counter-clockwise, through the art of Hals' predecessors and colleagues, to the back. The lush still-lifes give a sense of how good life is and how important it is to embrace it before it all rots and falls away. In fact, a new wing, opening in 2003, ties this Dutch slice-of-life art to . . . slices of Dutch life. The wing displays various Golden Age paintings alongside exhibits explaining more about daily life during the 17th century.

Frans Hals Museum—Room 21

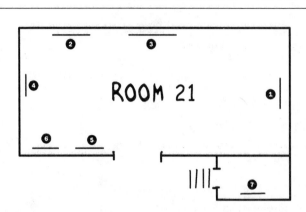

```
┌──────────────────────────────────┐
│      ②          ③                 │
│                                   │
│ │④    ROOM 21              ①│ │
│                                   │
│    ⑥      ⑤                       │
│                    ┌─┐            │
│                 ││││  └──⑦        │
└──────────────────────────────────┘
```

① Banquet of the Officers of the St. George Civic Guard, 1616

② Banquet of the Officers of the St. Adrian Civic Guard, 1627

③ Meeting of the Officers and Subalterns of the Civic Guard of St. Adrian, 1633

④ Officers and Subalterns of the St. George Civic Guard, 1639

⑤ Regents of the Old Men's Almshouse, 1664

⑥ Regentesses of the Old Men's Almshouse, 1664

⑦ Painting with Flemish Proverbs, by Pieter Breughel

Most of your visit will be a free-flow wander (including the first three Frans Hals paintings described below on your hit list). Then settle into Room 21 for your main course—six large Civic Guard portraits, each a Frans Hals masterpiece. For dessert— one more room adjacent to Room 21 has a few fanciful extras.

Portrait of Jacobus Zaffius (1611)

Arr-r-r-rh! This fierce, intense, rough-hewn man is not a pirate but a priest, the rogue leader of an outlawed religion in Haarlem—Catholicism. In the 1600s, Haarlem was a Protestant town in the midst of a war against Catholic Spain, and Catholics were guilty by association. But Zaffius refused to be silenced. He turns to glare and snarl at the Protestant town fathers. He was so personally imposing that the city tolerated his outspokenness.

The face jumps out from a background of neutral gray-brown-black. His features are alive—head turning, mouth twisting, face wrinkling up, beard bristling. Hals captures him in action, using a slow shutter speed. The rough brushstrokes of the fur coat and beard suggest the blur of motion of this agitated individual. This is Frans Hals' first known portrait, painted when he—a late starter in the art world—was nearly 30.

Portraits of Nicolaes Woutersz van der Meer and his wife, Cornelia Claesdr Vooght (1631)

Hals knew Nicolaes van der Meer, a fellow Civic Guard lodge member, personally. Van der Meer was a brewer, an important post in a city where per capita beer consumption was—get this—six

pints a day per person (man, woman, and child). He was also the mayor, so his pose is official and dignified, larger than life-size. But the face is pure Golden Age—red-cheeked and healthy, confident and intelligent, his even gaze tinged with wisdom. This mayor kept a steady hand on the tiller of Haarlem's ship of state.

The face is literally the focus of this otherwise messy painting. The ruffled collar is a tangle of simple, figure-eight swirls of white paint; the brocaded coat is a patchwork of white lines; and the lace cuffs are a few broad outlines. But out of the rough brushwork and somber background, van der Meer's crystal-clear eyes meet ours. The finely etched crow's feet around his eyes suggest that Hals had seen this imposing man break into a warm smile. Hey, I'd vote for him as my mayor.

The companion painting shows van der Meer's companion, his wife, **Cornelia.** Husband-and-wife portraits were hung together—

notice that they share the same background, and the two figures turn in toward each other. Still, both people are looking out at us, not clinging to each other, suggesting a mature partnership more than lovey-dovey newlyweds. Married couples in Golden Age Holland divvied up the work—men ran the business, women ran the home—and prided themselves on their mutual independence. (Even

Frans Hals' Style

- Hals' forte is **portraits.** Of his 240 paintings, 195 are individual or group portraits, mostly of Haarlem's citizens.

- His paintings are **life-size** and **realistic,** capturing everyday people—even downright ugly people—without airbrushing out their blemishes or character flaws.

- Hals uses **rough, Impressionistic brushwork,** where a few thick simple strokes blend at a distance to create details. He worked quickly, often making the rough sketch the final oil version.

- His **stop-action** technique captures the sitter in midmotion. Aided by his rough brushwork, this creates a blur that suggests the person is still moving.

- Hals adds **3-D depth** to otherwise horizontal, widescreen canvases. (Men with their elbows sticking out serve to define the foreground.)

- His canvases are **unified** by people wearing matching colors, using similar poses and gestures, and gathered in symmetrical groups.

- His paintings have a **relaxed, light-hearted, even comical atmosphere.** In group portraits, the subjects interact with one another. Individual portraits meet your eyes as if meeting an old friend.

- His works show **nothing religious**—no Madonnas, Crucifixions, angels, or Bible scenes. If anything, he imbues everyday objects with heavenly beauty and grants ordinary people the status of saints.

today in progressive Holland, fewer women join the work force than in many other industrial nations.) Cornelia's body is as imposing as her husband's, with big manly hands and a practical, slightly suspicious look. The detail work in her ruff collar tells us that Hals certainly could sweat the details when it suited his purpose.

Regents of the St. Elisabeth Hospital of Haarlem (1641)
These aren't the Dutch Masters cigar boys, though it looks like Rembrandt's famous (and later) *De Staalmeesters* (see the Rijksmuseum Tour, page 91). It's a board meeting, where five men in black hats and black suits with lace collars and cuffs—the Golden Age power suit—sit around a table in a brown room.

Pretty boring stuff, but Hals was hired to paint their portraits, and he does his best. Behind the suits, he captures five distinct men. The man on the far left is pondering the universe or raising a belch. The man in the middle (facing us) looks like the classic Golden Age poster boy, with moustache, goatee, ruddy cheeks, and long hair. Another is clean-shaven, while the guy on the far right adds a fashion twist with moustache wax. Hals links these five unique faces with one of his trademark techniques—similar poses and gestures. The burping man and the goateed man are a mirror image of the same pose—leaning on the table, hand on chest. Several have cupped hands, several have hands laid flat, or on their chests, or on the table. And the one guy keeps working on that burp.

• *Continue to the large Room 21, where you're well guarded by canvases full of companies of men in uniform. We'll start with the men in the bright red sashes.*

Banquet of the Officers of the St. George Civic Guard (1616)

In 1616, tiny Holland was the richest country on earth, and these Haarlem men are enjoying the fruits of their labors. The bright red sashes, the jaunty poses, the smiles, the rich food, the sweep-

ing tilt of the flags . . . the exuberant spirit of the Golden Age. These weekend warriors have finished their ceremonial parade through town, hung their ceremonial weapons on the wall, and now they sit down for a relaxed, after-the-show party.

The man in the middle (next to the flag-bearer, facing us) is about to carve the chicken when the meal is interrupted. It's us, arriving late through the back door, and heads turn to greet us. There's our old friend Nicolaes van der Meer, hand on hip, turning around with a friendly look, while the man to the right, the colonel in charge, waves us in. Frans Hals knew these men well as friends and colleagues, since he himself was a life-long member of this Civic Guard company.

This band of brothers is united by common gestures—two

Civic Guard Portraits

The fathers of the men pictured in this room fought, suffered imprisonment, and died in the great Siege of Haarlem (1572–1573) that helped turn the tide against Spanish oppression. But their sons were bankers, merchants, traders, and sailors, boldly conquering Europe on the new frontier of capitalism. Civic Guards became less of a militia and more a social club for upwardly mobile men. Their feasts—huge eating and drinking binges, punctuated with endless toasts, poems, skits, readings, dirty limericks, and ceremonial courses—could last days on end.

Standard Civic Guard portraits (see Amsterdam City Walk, page 60) always showed the soldiers in the same way—two neat rows of men, with everyone looking straight out, holding medieval weapons that tell us their ranks. It took master artists like Hals and Rembrandt to turn these boring visual documents into art.

men have hands on hips, three turn their palms up, two plant their hands downward, three clutch wine glasses, and so on. But mostly, they're joined by the uniform sashes. Most red sashes slant to the left, forming one set of diagonals, while the red flags slant the opposite way.

With this painting, Frans Hals broke the mold of stuffy group portraits. He relegates the traditional symbolic weapons to the shelf (upper right) and breaks up the traditional chorus-line of soldiers by placing the men naturally around a table. Van der Meer sticks his elbow in our face (another Hals trademark) to define a distinct foreground, while the flag-bearer stakes out the middle ground and a window at the back opens up to a distant, airy background.

Then Hals sets the scene in motion. A guy on the left side leans over to tell a joke to his friend. The dashing young flag-bearer in the middle turns back to listen to the bald-headed man. An ensign (standing, right side) enters and doffs his cap to Captain van der Meer. And then we barge in, interrupting the banquet, but welcomed as one of the boys.

Banquet of the Officers of the St. Adrian Civic Guard (1627)

The men are bunched into two symmetrical groups, left and right. The figures form a Y, with a tilted flag marking the right diagonal (echoed by several tilted ruffs), and a slanting row of heads forming

the left diagonal (echoed by several slanting sashes). The diagonals meet at the back of the table, marking the center of the composition, where the two groups of men exchange food, drink, and meaningful eye contact.

Meeting of the Officers and Subalterns of the Civic Guard of St. Adrian (1633)

Six years later, Hals painted many of these same men gathered around an outdoor table. The horizontal row of faces is punctuated by three men standing sideways, elbows out. Again, the men are united by sashes that slant (generally) in the same direction and by repeated gestures—hands on hips, hands on hearts, and so on.

Officers and Subalterns of the St. George Civic Guard (1639)

When 57-year-old Frans Hals painted this, his last Civic Guard portrait, he included himself among his St. George buddies. (Find Frans in the upper left, second from left, under the number 19.)

As he got older, Hals refined and simplified his group-portrait style, using quieter colors, the classic two horizontal rows of soldiers, and the traditional symbolic weapons. You can recognize the captain (fifth from the right, with white goatee, number 5) by his short pike (pole topped with a spearhead), the lieutenants by their longer partisans, and the rest by their ordinary hatchet-headed halberds.

A decade after this was painted, Holland officially ended its war with Spain (Treaty of Munster, 1648), Civic Guards lost their military purpose, businessmen preferred portraits showing themselves as elegant gentlemen rather than crusty soldiers, and the tradition of Civic Guard group portraits quickly died out.

Regents of the Old Men's Almshouse (1664)

These men look tired. So was Holland. So was Hals. At 82, Hals, despite years of success, was poor and dependent on the charity of the city, which granted him a small pension.

He was hired to paint the board of directors of the Old Men's Almshouse. The almshouse was located here in the building that now houses the Frans Hals Museum. Though Hals himself never lived in the almshouse, he fully understood what it was to be penniless and have to rely on money doled out by men like these.

The portrait is unflattering, drained of color. Somber men dressed in black peer out of a shadowy room. These men were trying to administer a dwindling budget to house and feed an aging population. Holland's Golden Age was losing its luster.

The style is Impressionistic—collars, cuffs, and gloves rendered with a few messy brushstrokes of paint. Hands and faces are a patchwork of light and dark splotches. Despite the sketchiness, each face captures the man's essence.

Historians speculate that this unflattering portrait was Hals' revenge on tightwad benefactors, but the fact is that the regents were satisfied with their portrait. By the way, the man just to the right of center isn't drunk, but suffering from facial paralysis. To the end, Hals respected unvarnished reality.

Regentesses of the Old Men's Almshouse (1664)

These women ran the women's wing of the almshouse, located across the street. Except for a little rouge on the women's pale-as-death faces, this canvas is almost a study in gray and black, as Hals pared his palette down to the bare essentials. The faces are subtle variations on old age. Only the woman on the right resolutely returns our gaze.

The man who painted this was old, poor, out of fashion, in failing health, perhaps bitter, and dying. In contrast with the lively group scenes of Hals' youth, these individuals stand forever isolated. They don't look at each other, each lost in their own thoughts, perhaps contemplating their own mortality (or stifling belches). Their only link to one another is the tenuous, slanting line formed by their hands, leading to the servant who enters the room with a mysterious message.

Could that message be... death? Or just that this tour is nearly over?

• *In the adjacent Room 19, go up five step to the...*

Former Chapel

Take a look inside. You'll find a **fancy dollhouse,** the hobby of the lady of the house (her portrait is on the left). Handmade by finest local craftsmen, this delicately crafted dollhouse offers a glimpse of wealthy 18th-century living.

The exquisite **bed curtain,** brought back from New England, decorated the bed of a wealthy Dutch family who lived in colonial America. It's embroidered with bulb flowers known during the 17th century—and well described in English.

Find the **painting with the proverbs.** In this fun painting, the Flemish artist Pieter Brueghel the younger—son of the more famous Brueghel—shows 72 charming Flemish scenes representing different folk sayings. Pick up the chart to identify these clever bits of folk wisdom. As is so often the case, rather than preachy religious art or political propaganda, Flemish art shares the simple and decent morals of the hardworking Dutch.

SLEEPING, EATING, AND NIGHTLIFE

€1 = about $1, country code: 31, area code: 023

The helpful Haarlem TI, just outside the train station, can nearly always find you a €20 bed in a private home (for a €4.50-per-person fee plus a cut of your host's money). Avoid this if you can; it's cheaper to reserve calling direct. Nearly every Dutch person you'll encounter speaks English.

Haarlem is most crowded in April and May (especially Easter weekend) and in July and August.

The listed prices include breakfast unless otherwise noted) and usually include the €1.70-per-person-per-day tourist tax. To avoid this town's louder-than-normal street noises, forgo views for a room in the back. Hotels and the TI have a useful parking brochure.

Sleeping in the Center

HIGHER PRICED

Hotel Lion D'Or is a classy, 34-room business hotel with all the professional comforts and a handy location. Don't expect a warm welcome (Sb-€115–125, Db-€145–165, extra bed-€10, CC, elevator, some non-smoking rooms, across the street from train station at Kruisweg 34, tel. 023/532-1750, fax 023/532-9543, www.goldentulip.nl/hotels/gtliondor).

MODERATELY PRICED

Hotel Amadeus, on Market Square, has 15 small, bright, and basic rooms. Some have views of the square. This characteristic hotel, ideally located above an early 20th-century dinner café, is relatively quiet. Its lush old lounge/breakfast room on the second floor overlooks the square, and Mike and Inez take good care of their guests (Sb-€52.50, Db-€73.50, Tb-€90, Qb-€100,

Sleep Code

S = Single, **D** = Double/Twin, **T** = Triple, **Q** = Quad,
b = bathroom, **s** = shower only, **CC** = Credit Cards accepted,
no CC = Credit Cards not accepted.

To help you easily sort through these listings, I've divided the rooms into three categories, based on the price for a standard double room with bath:

Higher Priced—Most rooms €100 or more.
Moderately Priced—Most rooms €65–100.
Lower Priced—Most rooms less than €65.

includes tax, 2-night stay and cash get you a 5 percent discount, 12-min walk from train station, CC, steep climb to lounge, then an elevator, Grote Markt 10, tel. 023/532-4530, fax 023/532-2328, www.amadeus-hotel.com). The hotel also runs a five-terminal Internet café.

Hotel Carillon also overlooks the town square but comes with a little more traffic and bell-tower noise. Many of the 22 well-worn rooms are small, and the stairs are ste-e-e-p. The front rooms come with great town-square views and street noise (tiny loft singles-€30, Db-€72, Tb-€94, Qb-€102, includes tax, 12-min walk from train station, CC, no elevator, Grote Markt 27, tel. 023/531-0591, fax 023/531-4909, www .hotelcarillon.com, e-mail: info@hotelcarillon.com).

Hotel Joops (pron. yopes; rhymes with ropes) rents 30 hotel rooms within a block of the hotel—which is just behind the cathedral (hotel Db-€65–85, Tb-€95)—and also administers a corral of 80 other rooms, scattered in buildings within a block of the church. The 80 rooms are a mixed bunch, ranging from cheap, well-worn, depressing rooms (avoid these if you can afford it; S-€30, D-€55, T-€75) to modern new suites with kitchenettes (Db-€70–90) for about the same price as the hotel rooms (breakfast-€9.50 extra, CC, 5 percent discount for cash, Oude Groenmarkt 20, Internet access, minimal service, tel. 023/532-2008, fax 023/532-9549, www.dutchhotels.nl/joops.hotel, e-mail: joops@easynet.nl).

Die Raeckse Hotel—family-run and friendly—is not as central as the others and has less character and more traffic noise, but its 21 rooms are decent and comfortable (Sb-€55, Db-€70–80 depending upon the size, Tb-€93, Qb-€105, extra bed-€20, CC, Raaks Straat 1, tel. 023/532-6629, fax 023/531-7937, www.die-raeckse.nl, e-mail: dieraeckse@zonnet.nl). A big cheap garage is across the street.

Haarlem Hotels and Restaurants

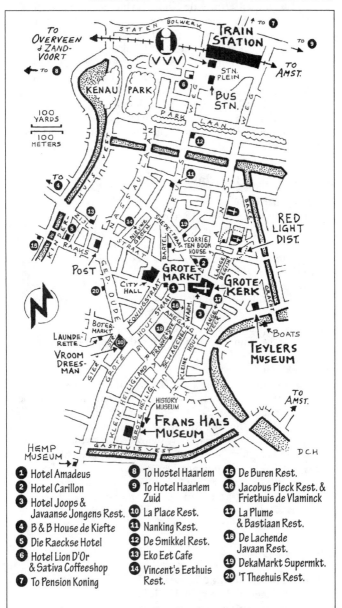

1. Hotel Amadeus
2. Hotel Carillon
3. Hotel Joops & Javaanse Jongens Rest.
4. B & B House de Kiefte
5. Die Raeckse Hotel
6. Hotel Lion D'Or & Sativa Coffeeshop
7. To Pension Koning
8. To Hostel Haarlem
9. To Hotel Haarlem Zuid
10. La Place Rest.
11. Nanking Rest.
12. De Smikkel Rest.
13. Eko Eet Cafe
14. Vincent's Eethuis Rest.
15. De Buren Rest.
16. Jacobus Pieck Rest. & Friethuis de Vlaminck
17. La Plume & Bastiaan Rest.
18. De Lachende Javaan Rest.
19. DekaMarkt Supermkt.
20. 'T Theehuis Rest.

LOWER PRICED

Bed and Breakfast House de Kiefte is your get-into-a-local-home budget option. Marjet (pron. mar-yet) and Hans, a frank, interesting Dutch couple who speak English well, rent four bright, cheery, non-smoking rooms (includes breakfast and travel advice) in their quiet, 1892 home (Ds-€50, T-€70, Qs-€90, Quint/s-€105, no CC, 2-night min, very steep stairs, family loft sleeps up to 5, kids over 4 welcome, Coornhertstraat 3, tel. 023/532-2980, cellular 06-5474-5272). It's a 15-minute walk or €7 taxi ride from the train station and a five-minute walk from the center. From Grote Markt, walk to the right of city hall straight out Zijlstraat and over the bridge and take a left on the fourth street.

Sleeping near Haarlem

MODERATELY PRICED

Hotel Haarlem Zuid—with 300 rooms and very American—is sterile but a good value for those interested only in sleeping and eating. It sits in an industrial zone, a 20-minute walk from the center on the road to the airport (Db-€80, breakfast-€12, CC, elevator, free parking, laundry service, fitness center, inexpensive hotel restaurant, Toekanweg 2, tel. 023/536-7500, fax 023/536-7980, www.hotelhaarlemzuid.nl, e-mail: haarlemzuid@valk.com). Buses #70, #71, and #72 connect the hotel with the train station and Market Square every 10 minutes. Bus #80 makes runs to the beach or Amsterdam. Fast airport bus #300 stops at the hotel.

LOWER PRICED

Pension Koning, a 15-minute walk north of the train station or a quick jaunt on bus #71, has five simple rooms in a row house in a residential area (S-€23, D-€46, T-€69, 2-night minimum, includes breakfast, no CC, Kleverlaan 179, tel. 023/526-1456).

Hostel Haarlem, completely renovated and with all the youth-hostel comforts, charges €18–21 for beds in eight-bed dorms (€2.50 extra for nonmembers, includes sheets and breakfast, CC, daily 7:30–24:00, Jan Gijzenpad 3, 3 km from Haarlem station—take bus #2 from platform A1, or a 5-min walk from Santpoort Zuid train station, tel. 023/537-3793, fax 023/537-1176, www.njhc.org/haarlem, e-mail: haarlem@njhc.org).

Eating in Haarlem

Eating between Market Square and the Train Station

Pancakes for dinner? **Pannekoekhuis De Smikkel** serves a selection of over 50 dinner (meat, cheese, etc.) and dessert pancakes. The pancakes (€8 each) are filling. With the €1.25-per-person cover charge, splitting is OK (daily 12:00–21:00, Sun from 16:00, closed Mon in winter, 2 blocks in front of station, Kruisweg 57, tel. 023/532-0631).

Nanking Chinese-Indonesian Restaurant serves Chinese and an inexpensive Indonesian *rijsttafel* (daily 16:00–22:00, Kruisstraat 16, a few blocks off Grote Markt, tel. 023/532-0706).

Enjoy a sandwich or coffee surrounded by trains and 1908 architecture in the classy **Brasserie Haarlem Station Restaurant** (daily 7:30–20:00, snacks only, between tracks #3 and #6 at the station).

Eating on or near Zijlstraat

Eko Eet Café is great for a cheery, tasty vegetarian meal (€9.50 menu, daily 17:30–21:30, Zijlstraat 39, tel. 023/532-6568).

Vincent's Eethuis serves the best cheap, basic Dutch food in town. This former St. Vincent's soup kitchen now feeds more gainfully employed locals than poor (€6, free seconds on veggies, friendly staff, Mon–Fri 12:00–14:00 & 17:00–19:30, closed Sat–Sun, Nieuwe Groenmarkt 22).

The cheery **De Buren** offers handlebar-mustache fun, serving happy locals traditional Dutch food such as *draadjesvlees* (beef stew with applesauce) and *oma's kippetje* (grandmother's chicken). Gerard and Marjo love their work. Enjoy their entertaining and creative menu, made especially for you (€11–16 dinners, "you choose the sauce," Wed–Sun 17:00–22:00, closed Mon–Tue, back garden terrace, outside the tourist area at Brouwersvaart 146, follow Raaks Straat west across the canal from Die Raeckse Hotel, tel. 023/534-3364).

Eating between the Market Square and Frans Hals Museum

Jacobus Pieck Eetlokaal is popular with locals for its fine-value "global cuisine" (€9.50 plate of the day, Mon 10:00–17:00, Tue–Sat 10:00–22:00, closed Sun, Warmoesstraat 18, behind church, tel. 023/532-6144).

Friethuis de Vlaminck is the place for a (€1.35) cone of old-fashioned French fries (Warmoesstraat 3, Tue–Sat until 18:00, closed Sun–Mon, behind church).

La Plume steak house is noisy with a happy, local, and carnivorous crowd (€12–18 meals, daily from 17:30, CC, Lange Veerstraat 1, tel. 023/531-3202).

Bastiaan serves good Mediterranean cuisine in a classy atmosphere (€16 dinners, Tue–Sat from 18:00, closed Sun–Mon, CC, Lange Veerstraat 8, tel. 023/532-6006).

Marijuana in Haarlem

Haarlem is a laid-back place in which to observe the Dutch approach to recreational marijuana. The town is dotted with 16 easygoing coffeeshops where pot is casually sold and smoked by relaxed, non-criminal types.

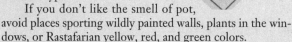

If you don't like the smell of pot, avoid places sporting wildly painted walls, plants in the windows, or Rastafarian yellow, red, and green colors.

If you want an introduction to the whole scene, stop in at the friendly **Global Hemp Museum,** the hub of Haarlem's coffeeshop action. Actually more of a hemp-products store, Global Hemp does run a humble museum upstairs (shop free, museum €2.50, Internet access-€1.50/30 min, Mon–Sat 11:00–20:00, summer Sun 12:00–20:00, Houtplein 16a, tel. 023/534-9939).

Willie Wortel Sativa Coffeeshop, next door to the Global Hemp Museum, is one of the best established coffeeshops (daily 9:00–24:00, in front of train station at Kruisweg 46). The display case–type menu explains what's on sale (€2.50 joints, €5 baggies, space cakes, but no alcohol, only soft drinks, mellow music).

'T Theehuis, which feels more like a miniature hippie teahouse, was Haarlem's first coffeeshop, with 50 different varieties on its menu and a friendly staff (daily 13:00–22:00, a block off Market Square at Smedestraat 25).

High Times offers smokers 16 varieties of joints in racks behind the bar (neatly prepacked in trademarked "Joint Packs," €2–3.50, daily 12:00–23:00, Internet access, Lange Veerstraat 47). Across the street, Crack is the wild and leathery place to go for loud music, pool, and darts (Lange Veerstraat 32).

De Lachende Javaan (The Laughing Javanese) serves the best Indonesian food in town. The €17 *rijsttafel* is great (light eaters can split this extravaganza—€3.85 for extra plate, Tue–Sun from 17:00, closed Mon, CC, Frankestraat 25, tel. 023/532-8792).

Javaanse Jongens, a new place serving Indonesian food in a fresh, woody, almost-bistro ambience, offers anyone with this book a free *tembuka* appetizer plate with their meal (€19 split-table *rijsttafel,* daily 17:00–22:00, CC, Oude Groenmarkt 8, tel. 023/531-1200).

La Place serves a healthy budget lunch with Haarlem's best view. Sit on the top floor or roof garden of the Vroom Dreesman department store (Mon 11:00–17:30, Tue–Sat 9:30–17:30, Thu until 20:30, closed Sun, on the corner of Grote Houtstraat and Gedempte Oude Gracht, tel. 023/515-8700).

Picnic shoppers head to the **DekaMarkt supermarket** (Mon 11:00–20:00, Tue–Sat 8:30–20:00, Thu until 21:00, closed Sun, Gedemple Oude Gracht 54, between Vroom Dreesman department store and post office).

Nightlife in Haarlem

Haarlem's evening scene is great. The bars around the Grote Kerk and Lange Veerstraat are colorful and lively. You'll find plenty of music. The best show in town: the café scene on Market Square. In good weather, café tables tumble happily out of the bars.

For trendy local crowds, sip a drink at **Studio Café** (daily 12:00–24:00, on Market Square, next to Hotel Carillon, tel. 023/531-0033). Tourists gawk at the old-fashioned belt-driven ceiling fans in **Café 1900** across from the Corrie Ten Boom House (daily 9:00–00:30, live music Sun night except in July, Barteljoris Straat 10, tel. 023/531-8283).

NETHERLANDS
DAY TRIPS
Zaanse Schans • Edam • Delft • Arnhem

The Netherlands are tiny. The sights listed below are easy day trips by bus or train from Amsterdam or Haarlem. Match your interest with the village's specialty: flower auctions, folk museums, cheese, Delft porcelain, beaches, or modern art.

DAY TRIPS NORTH OF AMSTERDAM
Zaanse Schans Open-Air Museum

This 17th-century Dutch village turned open-air folk museum puts Dutch culture—from cheese-making to wooden-shoe-carving—on a lazy Susan.

Located in the town of Zaandijk, this is your easiest one-stop look at traditional Dutch culture and the Netherlands' best collection of windmills. Take an inspiring climb to the top of a whirring windmill; gather a group and ask for a tour (entrance to grounds free, but you must pay a euro or two to go in windmills and other sights in the park, daily 8:30–17:30, until 17:00 in winter, parking €3.40/hr, tel. 075/616-8218, www.zaanseschans.nl). Zaanse Schans is your typical big-bus tour stop. To avoid the masses, visit early or late.

At the visitors' center at the park's main entrance, pick up the free brochure/map and ask about the day's scheduled events (bike rentals, lockers, WC, tel. 075/616-8228).

These are the park's highlights.

Rederij de Schans: This boat tour of the park and adjacent town departs near the Mustardmill (€5, daily except Mon, 90 min, tel. 075/614-6762).

Bakery Museum: The fragrant Bakkerijmuseum sells what it bakes.

Shoe Maker: The Klompenmakerij is a major stop in

Netherlands Day Trips

the park, with a three-minute video and a fascinating live demonstration that sends wood chips flying as a machine carves a shoe.

Cheese Shop: At the Kasamakerij, a local farmer is evangelical about Dutch cheeses, telling you how it's made and filling you with tasty samples.

Zaanse Museum: This fresh, modern multimedia presentation explains Holland's industrial past and present with the help of a fine, included audioguide (€4.50, Tue–Sat 10:00–17:00, Sun 12:00–17:00, closed Mon, tel. 075/616-2862).

Pancake Restaurant: The Pannenkoeken Restaurant offers delicious traditional sweet and savory pancakes—coming with all the fillings you might select for an omelet: cheese, ham, mushrooms, and so on (€4–7, cash only, closes at 18:00).

Transportation Connections—Zaanse Schans

The park is 15 minutes by train north of Amsterdam. Take the Alkmaar-bound train to Station Koog-Zaandijk and then walk,

following the teal signs—past a fragrant chocolate factory—
for 10 minutes.

If driving from Amsterdam, take the A8 (direction: Zaanstad/
Purmerend), turn off at Purmerend A7, then follow signs to
Zaanse Schans.

EDAM

For the ultimate in cuteness and peace, make tiny Edam your
home. It's sweet but palatable and 30 minutes by bus from
Amsterdam (2/hr).

While Edam is known today for cheese, it was once an industrious shipyard and port. But having a canal to the sea caused such
severe flooding in town—cracking walls and spilling into homes—
that a frustrated resident even built a floating cellar (now in Edam
Museum). To stop the flooding, the harbor was closed off with
locked gates (you'll see the gates in Dam Square next to TI). The
harbor silted up, forcing the decline of the shipbuilding trade.

Edam's Wednesday market is held year-round, but it's best
in July and early August, when the focus is on cheese, and you—
along with piles of other tourists—can meet the cheese traders,
local farmers, and even the cheese queen.

Tourist Information: The TI, often staffed by volunteers,
is on Dam Square. Pick up the free "Edam Holland" brochure
and consider the €2 "A Stroll Through Edam" self-guided walking tour (April–Sept Mon–Sat 10:00–17:00, closed Sun, Oct–
March Mon–Sat 10:00–15:00, closed Sun, WC, ATM just outside,
tel. 0299/315-125, www.vvv-edam.nl, e-mail: info@vvv-edam.nl).

Arrival in Edam: To get from the bus station to Dam Square
and the TI, it's a five-minute walk: Leaving the station, head for
the Station-Zuid Hotel/Restaurant (good place to eat). From
there, turn left on Zuidervesting, turn right at the first canal
onto Schepenmakersdijk, then left over the first walking bridge
onto Lingerzijde; follow this street until you pass the leaning
bell tower and take a right onto Kleine Kerkstraat, which leads
to Dam Square.

Sights—Edam

Introductory Walk—Start in Dam Square and walk over the
bridge to the Edam Museum. After visiting the museum, turn
right down Spui (canal on your left) and walk for one block.
Take a right down Matthijs Tinxgracht, follow this street through
the cheese market square, peek into the old cheese weigh house,
and continue down the street to see the Church of Saint Nicholas.

Edam Museum—This small, quirky museum offers a fun peek
into a 400-year-old home and a floating cellar. Learn about

Edam's trade history upstairs and about Fris Pottery on the top floor (€2, Tue–Sat 10:00–16:30, Sun 13:30–16:30, closed in winter, on Dam Square, tel. 0299/372-644).

Sleeping in Edam
(€1 = about $1, country code: 31, area code: 0299)
Sleep Code: **S** = Single, **D** = Double/Twin, **T** = Triple, **Q** = Quad, **b** = bathroom, **s** = shower only, **CC** = Credit Cards accepted, **no CC** = Credit Cards not accepted.

The **TI** (tel. 0299/315-125) has a list of inexpensive rooms in private homes.

Hotel de Fortuna—an eccentric canalside mix of flowers, a cat of leisure, a pet turtle, and duck noises—offers steep stairs and low-ceilinged rooms in several ancient buildings in the old center of Edam (Db-€85–98, includes breakfast, CC, garden patio, attached restaurant, Spuistraat 3, tel. 0299/371-671, fax 0299/371-469, www.fortuna-edam.nl, e-mail: fortuna@fortuna-edam.nl).

Damhotel, centrally located on a canal around the corner from the TI, has attractive, comfortable rooms with a plush feel (Sb-€55, Db-€90, Tb-€125, Qb-€170, includes breakfast, CC, attached restaurant, Keizersgracht 1, tel. 0299/371-766, fax 0299/374-031, www.damhotel.nl).

Eating in Edam
Tai Wah has take-out Chinese/Indonesian (eat in De Fortuna garden) and indoor seating (Mon and Wed–Sat 16:00–21:00, Sun 13:00–21:00, closed Tue, Lingerzijde 62, tel. 0299/371-088).

Picnickers stock up at the Toppers grocery (to the left of the Edam Museum).

Transportation Connections—Edam
From Amsterdam, take direct bus #114 (30 min) or bus #110 for a scenic route through the town of Volendam (45 min).

MORE DAY TRIPS NORTH OF AMSTERDAM
▲**Alkmaar**—Holland's cheese capital is especially fun (and touristy) during its weekly cheese market (April–Aug only, Fri 10:00–12:30, TI tel. 072/511-4284).

▲▲**Enkhuizen's Zuiderzee Museum**—This lively, open-air folk museum in the salty old town of Enkhuizen has a "Living on Urk" village (patterned after an old Dutch fishing town), populated by people who do a convincing job of role-playing no-nonsense 1905 Dutch villagers. No one said "Have a nice day" back then. You can eat herring hot out of the old smoker and see barrels and rope made. Children enjoy playing at the dress-up chest, trying out old-time games, and making sailing ships out of old wooden shoes (€9, early April–late Oct daily 10:00–17:00, July–Aug free tours at 13:30, private guide for €40, tel. 0228/351-111, www.zuiderzeemuseum.nl). Take the train from Amsterdam direct to Enkhuizen. To get to the museum from the station, catch a shuttle boat (4/hr) or take a pleasant 15-minute walk.

▲**Hoorn**—This elegant, quiet, and typical 17th-century Dutch town north of Amsterdam entertains tourists with a steam-engine museum, bakery, and castle. The Hoorn TI rents bikes and has a good walking tour brochure (tel. 072/511-4284).

Historic Triangle—Any TI offers a flier describing the "Historic Triangle," an all-day excursion from Amsterdam that connects the towns of Hoorn, Medemblik, and Enkhuizen by steam train and boat.

First, to get from Amsterdam to Hoorn by train, allow an hour and €15 round-trip. Then hop on the steam train from Hoorn to Medemblik (60 min), followed by a boat ride to Enkhuizen (60 min). This "Triangle" route runs twice a day in July and August. Off-season it's usually offered twice daily on weekends and once daily on weekdays except Monday—but confirm at a TI (€18, tel. 0229/214-862).

Zandvoort—For a quick and easy look at the windy coastline in a shell-lover's Shangri-La, visit the beach resort of Zandvoort, a breezy 45-minute bike ride or an eight-minute car or train ride west of Haarlem (from Haarlem, follow road signs to Bloemendaal). South of the main beach, bathers work on all-over tans.

De Rijp—This sleepy town is worth visiting if you're driving north of Amsterdam.

Volendam, Marken, and Monnikendam—These famous towns are quaint as can be (although very touristy).

DAY TRIPS SOUTH OF AMSTERDAM
Delft

Peaceful as a Vermeer painting (he was born here) and lovely as its porcelain, Delft is a typically Dutch town with a special soul. Enjoy it best by simply wandering around, watching people, munching local syrup waffles, or daydreaming from the canal bridges.

Tourist Information: The TI is a tourist's dream, offering a good €2 brochure on Delft (includes excellent map and a self-guided "Historical Walk through Delft"), guided walks (May–Aug Wed and Fri 14:00 and 15:30), and a number of brochures describing self-guided walking tours (€1.80). The 90-minute audioguide tour called "Talking Walls" is geared for kids—€6.50 for headset

Johannes Vermeer (1632–1675)

The great Golden Age painter Johannes Vermeer was born in Delft, grew up near Market Square, and set a number of his paintings here. His father, an art dealer, had given Johannes a passion for painting. Late in the artist's career, with Holland fighting draining wars against England, the demand for art and luxuries went sour in the Netherlands, forcing Vermeer to downsize—he sold his big home, packed up his wife and 14 children, and moved in with his mother-in-law. He died two years later.

After centuries of relative obscurity, Vermeer and his 20-some paintings are now much appreciated. None of his paintings are in Delft, but you'll find four of his masterpieces in Amsterdam's Rijksmuseum (see page 91) and others in The Hague's Mauritshuis Museum.

and brochure (Mon–Sat 9:00–17:30, April–Sept also Sun 11:00–15:00, tel. 015/213-0100 fax 015/215-8695, www.vvvdelft.nl).

Arrival in Delft: From the train station (free toilets, ATM on left as you leave), walk across the canal and follow blue-and-white signs to the town center. Drivers take the Delft exit 9 off A13 expressway.

Market Days: Multiple all-day markets are held on Thursdays (general on Market Square, flower on Hippolytusbuurt Square) and on Saturdays (general on Brabantse Turfmarkt and Burgwal, flea market at Hippolytusbuurt Square, and sometimes an art market at Heilige Geestkerkhof).

Sights—Delft

Royal Dutch Delftware Manufactory—The blue earthenware made at Delft's Koninklijke Porceleyne Fles is famous worldwide and the biggest tourist attraction in town. The Dutch East India Company, headquartered here, had imported many exotic goods, including Chinese porcelain. The Chinese designs became trendy and were copied by many of the local potters. Three centuries later, their descendants are still going strong, and you can see them at work in this factory. Catch an English-language tour (prices vary depending on tour, April–Oct 10:00, 11:00, 14:00, and 15:00) or take a self-guided tour at any time: Watch the short video, follow the small tile arrows, and feel free to stop and chat with any of the artisans (€2.50, April–Oct daily 9:00–17:00, Nov–March daily 9:30–17:00, Rotterdamseweg 196, from train station catch tram #1

Delft Manufacturing Process

Delft earthenware is made from a soupy mix of clay and water. To make plates, the glop is rotated on a spinning disk until it looks like a traditional Dutch pancake. This "pancake" is then placed in a plate mold, where a design is pressed into it.

To make vases, pitchers, cups, and figurines, the liquid clay is poured into hollow plaster molds. These porous molds work like a sponge, sucking the water out of the clay to leave a layer of dry clay along the mold walls. Once the interior walls have reached the correct thickness, all excess clay within is poured off and recycled.

After the clay object is removed from the mold, it's fired in the kiln for 24 hours. The pottery removed from the kiln is called "biscuit." Next, painters trace traditional decorations with sable-hair pencils onto the biscuit pottery; these are then painted with a black paint containing cobalt oxide. When fired, a chemical reaction changes the black paint into the famous Delft Blue. Before the second firing, the objects are dipped into an opaque white glaze, which melts into a translucent glass-like layer.

or bus #63, #121, or #129 and get off at TU Aula bus stop, 5-min walk from tram or bus stop, tel. 015/251-2030).

Sleeping in Delft
(€1 = about $1, country code: 31, area code: 015)
Herberg de Emauspoort, a picture-perfect family-run hotel, is relaxed, friendly, and ideally located around the family's 80-year-old bakery. Rooms overlook the canalside or peek into the courtyard. Romantics can stay in one of their gypsy caravans ("Pipo de Clown" or "Mammaloe"). Borrow bikes for free or rent a canoe for the day (16 rooms, Db-€96, Tb-€115, Qb-€140, CC, near main square at Vrouwenregt 9-11, tel. 015/219-0219, fax 015/214-8251, www.emauspoort.nl, e-mail: emauspoort@emauspoort.nl).

Hotel Leeuwenbrug, a former warehouse, has 36 cozy rooms, an Old World atmosphere, and a helpful and friendly staff (Sb-€72–105, Db-€87–120, prices varies seasonally, ask for off-season pricing, includes breakfast, CC, Koornmarkt 16, tel. 015/214-7741, fax 015/215-9759, www.leeuwenbrug.nl, e-mail: sales@leeuwenbrug.nl).

'T Raedthuys, located in the heart of Delft on the main

square, has 11 tired, basic rooms (S-€38, D-€48, Db-€65, Q-€90, Qb-€100, ask for off-season discount, CC, enter through restaurant, Markt 38–40, tel. 015/212-5115, fax 015/213-6069, www.raedthuys-delft.com).

Transportation Connections—Delft

To: Amsterdam (2 trains/hr, 40 min), **The Hague** (you can take the train, but the tram is easier, catch tram #1—Scheveningen to The Hague's city center, purchase tickets at TI).

MORE DAY TRIPS SOUTH OF AMSTERDAM

▲▲**The Hague (Den Haag)**—Locals say the money is made in Rotterdam, divided in The Hague, and spent in Amsterdam. The Hague is the Netherlands' seat of government and the home of several engaging museums. The Hague's **TI** is at the train station (Mon–Sat 9:00–17:30, later in summer, Sun 10:00–17:00, tel. 06/3403-505, €0.45/min).

The **Mauritshuis'** delightful, easy-to-tour art collection stars Vermeer and Rembrandt (€7, Tue–Sat 10:00–17:00, Sun 11:00–17:00, Korte Vijverberg 8, tel. 070/302-3456). Across the pond, the **Torture Museum** (Gevangenpoort) shows the medieval mind at its worst (€3.75, Tue–Fri 11:00–17:00, Sat–Sun 12:00–17:00, closed Mon, required tours on the hour, last one at 16:00, ask ticket taker if film and talk will be in English before you commit, tel. 070/346-0861).

For a look at the 19th century's attempt at virtual reality, tour **Panorama Mesdag,** a 360-degree painting of nearby Scheveningen in the 1880s with a 3-D sandy-beach foreground (€4, Mon–Sat 10:00–17:00, Sun 12:00–17:00, Zeestraat 65, tel. 070/310-6665). The nearby **Peace Palace,** a gift from Andrew Carnegie, houses the International Court of Justice (€3.40, Mon–Fri, required guided tours at 10:00, 11:00, 14:00, or 15:00, closes without warning—call ahead or check at TI, tram #7 or #8 from station, tel. 070/302-4137).

Scheveningen, the Dutch Coney Island, has a newly renovated pier and is liveliest on sunny summer afternoons (from the Hague train station, take tram #1, #8, or #9 to Gevers Deynootplein/Kurhaus and walk via Palace Promenade to the Boulevard).

Madurodam, a mini-Holland amusement park, is a kid-pleaser (€10, kids 4–11-€7, Sept–mid-March daily 9:00–18:00, mid-March–June until 20:00, July–Aug until 22:00, George Maduroplein 1, tram #1 or #9 from Hague train station, tel. 070/355-3900, www.madurodam.nl).

▲▲▲**Keukenhof**—This is the greatest bulb-flower garden on earth.

Each spring six million flowers, enjoying the sandy soil of the Dutch dunes and *polderland*, conspire to make even a total garden-hater enjoy them. This 100-acre park is packed with tour groups daily (€11.50, open March 21–May 28 in 2003, daily 8:00–19:30, last tickets sold at 18:00, tel. 0252/465-555, www.keukenhof.nl).

To get to Keukenhof from Amsterdam, take the train to Leiden, then catch bus #54 to the garden (allow 75 min total). From Haarlem, catch bus #50 or #51 to Lisse, then bus #54 to Keukenhof (allow 45 min total). Go late in the day for the best light and the fewest groups.

Note that Holland's 2003 Flower Parade will be held on April 26. This all-day parade, featuring floats decorated with blossoms instead of crepe paper, runs through eight towns, including Lisse and Haarlem.

▲▲**Aalsmeer Flower Auction**—Get a bird's-eye view of the huge Dutch flower industry. Wander on elevated walkways (through what's claimed to be the biggest commercial building on earth) over literally trainloads of freshly

cut flowers. About half of all the flowers exported from Holland are auctioned off here in four huge auditoriums. Stop at one of the "listening posts" for on-the-spot information (€4, Mon–Fri 7:30–11:00, closed Sat–Sun, the auction wilts after 9:30 and on Thu, gift shop, cafeteria; bus #172 from Amsterdam's station, 2/hr, 60 min; from Haarlem take bus #140 and transfer to bus #172 or #77 in Aalsmeer, 2/hr, 60 min; tel. 0297/392-185). Aalsmeer is close to the airport and a handy last fling before catching a late morning weekday flight out.

▲**Rotterdam**—This city, the world's largest port, bounced back after being bombed flat in World War II. See its towering Euromast, take a harbor tour, and stroll its great pedestrian zone (TI tel. 0900/403-4065, toll call-€0.50/min).

Utrecht—The Museum von Speelklok tot Pierement, which offers free and mandatory guided 55-minute tours on the hour, demonstrates musical clocks, calliopes, and street organs (€6, Tue–Sat 10:00–17:00, Sun 12:00–17:00, closed Mon, last tour at 16:00, 10-min walk from station, Buurkerkhof 10, tel. 030/231-2789).

ARNHEM

Arnhem, an hour southeast of Amsterdam, has two fine sights: the Arnhem Open-Air Dutch Folk Museum and the Kröller-Müller Museum, featuring modern art in a huge park.

Arnhem's **TI** is at the train station (Mon 11:00–17:30, Tue–Thu 9:00–17:30, Fri 10:00–16:00, closed Sat–Sun, tel. 026/442-6767).

Sights—Arnhem

▲▲Kröller-Müller Museum and Hoge Veluwe National Park—Near Arnhem, Hoge Veluwe National Park is the Netherlands' largest (13,000 acres) and is famous for its Kröller-Müller Museum. This huge, striking modern-art collection, including 55 paintings by van Gogh, is set deep in the forest. The park has hundreds of white bikes you're free to use to make your explorations more fun. At the Bekoezerscentrum (visitors' center) you'll find maps, WCs, a cafeteria-style restaurant, and a playground for children. While riding through the vast green woods, make a point to get off your bike and climb an inland sand dune (€5 to enter park, €5 more for museum, museum open Tue–Sun 10:00–17:00, closed Mon, easy parking, tel. 031/859-1041).

To reach the museum from Amsterdam, take the train to Ede-Wageningen, where bus #110 goes directly into the Hoge Veluwe National Park. Ask the driver where to get off for the visitors' center or the art museum.

To get to the park from the Arnhem train station, catch the bus to Otterlo, then switch to bus #110 which will take you into the park (1/hr). At this time there is no direct connection between Arnhem and the Kröller-Müller Museum. Consider a taxi (have the visitors' center call for you).

▲▲Arnhem Open-Air Dutch Folk Museum—Arnhem has the Netherlands' first and biggest folk museum. You'll enjoy a huge park of windmills, old farmhouses (gathered from throughout the Netherlands and reassembled here), traditional crafts in action, and a pleasant education-by-immersion in Dutch culture.

Visit the Entrance Pavilion to get a free map or the English guidebook (€4). See the multimedia exhibit, HollandRama. Ask about special events and activities (especially for kids) as you enter (€11, Easter–Oct daily 10:00–17:00, tel. 026/357-6111, www.openluchtmuseum.nl).

Self-Guided Tour: With limited time, just hit the highlights. Swing by the informational desk at the entrance and ask for the free park map. Start your walk by heading straight down the entrance path on the left. Walk to the **farmhouse** (4.1 on map, labeled as "cheese-covered" farmhouse); step inside and enjoy the hospitality of 1745. In the cowhouse, see the patterns the farmwife would make with fresh sand and seashells each summer to show off family status.

Then cross the **drawbridge** (4.2), dating from 1358. Stop

here to look out over the pond toward the sawmill. You might see children playing with a small rope-pulled ferryboat.

Continue across the drawbridge into the little village, stopping on the way at the **bakery and grocery** on your left (4.8). Continue to the main square, where you can play with toys from the 1800s. See if you can make the "flying Dutchman" fly, or try to ride an original "high-wheeled velocipede" without falling off. Sample a *poffertje* (mini-pancake) from the little stall in the main square. Leave the square and head toward the fisherman's cottage (4.11).

The **fisherman's cottage**—with a bright and colorful interior behind a black-tarred exterior—has a rope-controlled smoke hatch rather than a chimney. Wooden cottages like these were nicknamed "smoke houses." Leaving the cottage, walk back through the square to visit the **laundry** (5.1) and imagine washing your clothes here.

Hike up to the 17th-century **paper mill** (5.4), where you might see a demonstration of linen rags being turned into pulp and then into paper. Peek upstairs at the finished paper hanging to dry. Leave the mill and turn left; walk two minutes toward the dairy factory (7.1), noticing the beautiful herb garden to your right.

The **Freia Steam-Dairy Factory** (named after Freia, the Norse goddess of agriculture) was the Netherlands' first privately owned cheese and butter factory. Sample free cheese, and try to follow the huge belt of the steam engine as it whirls through the factory. From Freia, head toward the village school (8.2). Finally, cut across the main field and climb the platform mill (15.6) for a great view.

The park has several good budget **restaurants** and covered picnic areas. Its rustic Pancake House serves hearty (splittable) Dutch flapjacks. The De Kasteelboerderji Café-Restaurant at the Oud-Beijerland Manor (traditional €8 *dagmenu*, or plate of the day) is a friendly place that can feed 300 visitors at once.

To reach the open-air museum *(openluchtmuseum)* from the Arnhem train station, take bus #3 (direction: Alteveer) or the faster #13 (4/hr, 15 min, runs July–Aug only).

Transportation Connections—Arnhem

Trains connect Arnhem with **Amsterdam** (2/hr, 70 min, likely transfer in Utrecht).

By car from Amsterdam, take A2 south to Utrecht, then A12 east to Arnhem. Just before Arnhem, take the Arnhem Nord exit Openluchtmuseum (exit #26) and follow signs to the nearby museum. (If driving from Haarlem, skirt Amsterdam to the south on E9, then follow signs to Utrecht.)

TRANSPORTATION CONNECTIONS: NETHERLANDS

AMSTERDAM

Amsterdam's train-information center requires a long wait. Save lots of time by getting train tickets and information in a small-town station, at the airport upon arrival, or from a travel agency. For phone information, dial 0900/9292 for local trains or 0900/9296 for international trains (€0.50/min, daily 7:00–24:00, wait through recording and hold...hold...hold...). The numbers listed in this chapter are all frustrating phone trees in Dutch and—if you wait—maybe in English.

By train to: **Schiphol Airport** (6/hr, 20 min, €3), **Haarlem** (6/hr, 15 min, €5.50 same-day return), **The Hague** (2/hr, 50 min), **Rotterdam** (4/hr, 1 hr), **Bruges** (hrly, 3.5–4.25 hrs, 1–3 transfers; transfers are timed closely—be alert and check with conductor), **Brussels** (2/hr, 3 hrs, €30), **Ostende** (hrly, 4 hrs, change in Antwerp), **London** (2/day, 8 hrs, train to Hoek van Holland, then ferry across Channel, then train from Harwich to London; or 8/day, 6.5 hrs, with transfer to Eurostar Chunnel train in Brussels, Eurostar discounted with railpass, www.eurostar.com), **Copenhagen** (5/day, 10 hrs, transfer in Osnabrück and Hamburg; or 3-hr train to Duisberg and transfer to 11-hr night train), **Frankfurt** (8/day, 5–6 hrs, transfer in Köln or Duisburg), **Munich** (7/day, 9 hrs, transfer in Mannheim, Hanover, or Köln, one 11-hr direct night train), **Bonn** (10/day, 3 hrs, some direct but most transfer in Köln), **Bern** (5/day, 9 hrs, one direct but most transfer in Basel, Köln, or Brussels), **Paris** (5/day, 5 hrs, required fast train from Brussels with €11 supplement). If you don't have a railpass, the cheapest way to get to Paris is by bus (Euroline buses make the 8-hour trip five times daily, about €39 or €60 round-trip compared to €100 second-class by train; bus station in Amsterdam at Julianaplein 5, Amstel Station, 5 stops by Métro from Centraal Station, tel. 020/560-8788, www.eurolines.com).

Netherlands Transportation

Amsterdam's Schiphol Airport

The airport, like most of Holland, is English-speaking, user-friendly, and below sea level. Its banks offer fair rates (24 hrs daily, in arrival area).

Schiphol (pron. SKIP-pol) Airport has easy connections with **Amsterdam** by train (6/hr, 20 min, €3) and by KLM Hotel Bus (3/hr, 20 min, €10, leaves from lane A7 in front of the airport, 2 routes—ask attendant which comes closest to your hotel, one bus stops at Westerkerk near Anne Frank House and many recommended hotels). Allow about €35 for a taxi to Amsterdam.

Schiphol also has good connections with **Haarlem** by train (2/hr, 40 min, transfer at Amsterdam-Sloterdijk, €4.55) and by bus #300 (4/hr, 40 min, departs from lane B2 in front of the airport, €3.50). Figure about €32 to Haarlem by taxi.

The airport has a train station of its own. You can validate your Eurailpass and hit the rails immediately or, to stretch your train pass, buy an inexpensive ticket into Amsterdam today and start the pass later.

Schiphol flight information (tel. 0900/7244-7465, €0.10/min) can give you flight times and your airline's Amsterdam number for reconfirmation before going home (€0.45/min to climb through its phone tree). To reach the airlines, dial: KLM at 020/649-9123 or 020/474-7747, NW is same as KLM, Martinair at 020/601-1222, SAS at 0900/746-63727, American Airlines at 06/022-7844, British Air at 023/554-7555, and easyJet at 023/568-4880.

If you have time to kill at Schiphol, check out the Dutch Masters. The Rijksmuseum loans a dozen or so of its masterpieces from the Golden Age to the Rijksmuseum Schiphol, a free little art gallery behind the passport check between piers E and F.

HAARLEM

By train to: Amsterdam (6/hr, 15 min, €3.20 one-way, €5.50 same-day return, ticket not valid on "Lovers Train," a misnamed private train that runs hrly), **Delft** (2/hr, 40 min), **Hoorn** (4/hr, 1 hr), **The Hague** (4/hr, 35 min), and **Alkmaar** (2/hr, 30 min).

To **Schiphol Airport**: by **taxi** (about €32), by **train** (2/hr, 40 min, transfer at Amsterdam-Sloterdijk, €4.55); by **bus** (6/hr, 45 min, bus #300 leaves from Haarlem's Vroom Dreesman department store and from Haarlem's train station in the "Zuidtangent" lane, €3.50).

BELGIUM

- 31,000 square kilometers (12,000 square miles), a little larger than Maryland
- 10 million people (830 per square mile)
- €1 = about $1

Belgium falls through the cracks. It's nestled between Germany, France, and Britain, and it's famous for waffles, sprouts, endives, and a statue of a little boy peeing—no wonder many travelers don't even consider a stop here. But many who do visit remark that Belgium is one of Europe's best-kept secrets. There are tourists—but not as many as the country's charms merit.

The country is split between the French-speaking Walloons in the south and the Dutch-speaking Flemish people (60 percent of the population) in the north. Talk to locals to learn how deep the cultural rift is. Belgium's capital, Brussels, while mostly French-speaking, is officially bilingual. The country also has a small minority of German-speaking people. Because of Belgium's international importance as the capital of the European Union, more than 25 percent of its residents are foreigners.

It's here in Belgium that Europe comes together: where Romance languages meet Germanic languages, Catholics meet Protestants, and the Benelux union was established 40 years ago, planting the seed that today is sprouting into the unification of Europe. Belgium flies the flag of Europe more vigorously than any other place on the Continent.

Bruges and Brussels are the best two first bites of Belgium. Brussels is simply one of Europe's great cities. Bruges is a

Belgium

wonderfully preserved medieval gem that expertly nurtures the tourist industry, bringing the town a prosperity it hasn't enjoyed since 500 years ago, when—as one of the largest cities in the world—it helped lead northern Europe out of the Middle Ages.

Belgians brag that they eat as much as the Germans and as well as the French. They are among the world's leading beer consumers and carnivores. In Belgium, never bring chrysanthemums to a wedding—they symbolize death. And tweaking little kids on the ear is considered rude.

Ten million Belgians are packed into a country only a little bigger than Maryland. At 830 people per square mile, it's the second most densely populated country in Europe (after the Netherlands). This population concentration, coupled with a dense and well-lit rail and road system, causes Belgium to shine at night when viewed from space, a phenomenon NASA astronauts call the "Belgian Window."

BRUGES

Brugge

ORIENTATION

With Renoir canals, pointy gilded architecture, vivid time-tunnel art, and stay-awhile cafés, Bruges is a heavyweight sightseeing destination as well as a joy. Where else can you ride a bike along a canal, munch mussels, wash them down with the world's best beer, savor heavenly chocolate, and see Flemish Primitives and a Michelangelo, all within 300 meters of a bell tower that jingles every 15 minutes? And there's no language barrier.

The town is Brugge (pron. BROO-ghah) in Flemish, or Bruges (pron. broozh) in French and English. Its name comes from the Viking word for wharf. Right from the start, Bruges was a trading center. In the 11th century, the city grew wealthy on the cloth trade.

By the 14th century, Bruges' population was 35,000, as large as London's. As the middleman in sea trade between Northern and Southern Europe, it was one of the biggest cities in the world and an economic powerhouse. In addition, Bruges had become the most important cloth market in Northern Europe.

In the 15th century, while England and France were slogging it out in a 100-year-long war, Bruges was the favored residence of the powerful Dukes of Burgundy—and at peace. Commerce and the arts boomed. The artists Jan van Eyck and Hans Memling had studios here.

But by the 16th century, the harbor had silted up and the economy had collapsed. The Burgundian court left, Belgium became a minor Hapsburg possession, and Bruges' Golden Age abruptly ended. For generations, Bruges was known as a mysterious and dead city. In the 19th century, a new port, Zeebrugge, brought renewed vitality to the area. And in the 20th century, tourists discovered the town.

Today Bruges prospers because of tourism: It's a uniquely

well-preserved Gothic city and a handy gateway to Europe. It's no secret, but even with the crowds, it's the kind of city where you don't mind being a tourist.

Bruges' ultimate sight is the town itself, and the best way to enjoy that is to get lost on the back streets, away from the lace shops and ice-cream stands.

Planning Your Time

Bruges needs at least two nights and a full, well-organized day. Even non-shoppers enjoy browsing here, and the Belgian love of life makes a hectic itinerary seem a little senseless. With one day (other than a Monday, when all the museums are closed), the speedy visitor could do the Bruges town walk described below:

9:30	Climb the bell tower on the Market Square.
10:00	Tour the sights on the Burg Square.
11:00	Tour the Groeninge Museum.
12:00	Tour the Gruuthuse Museum.
13:00	Eat lunch and buy chocolates.
14:00	Take a short canal cruise (discount dock).
14:30	Visit the Church of Our Lady and see the Michelangelo Madonna.
15:00	Tour the Memling Museum.
16:00	Catch the Straffe Hendrik Brewery tour.
17:00	Calm down in the Begijnhof.
18:00	Ride a bike around the quiet back streets of town or take a horse-and-buggy tour.
20:00	Lose the tourists and find a dinner.

(If this schedule seems insane, skip the bell tower and the brewery—or stay another day.)

Orientation

The tourist's Bruges (you'll be sharing it) is one square kilometer contained within a canal, or moat. Nearly everything of interest and importance is within a convenient cobbled swath between the train station and Market Square (a 15-min walk). Many of my quiet and charming recommended accommodations lie just beyond Market Square.

Tourist Information

The main office is on Burg Square (April–Sept Mon–Fri 9:30–18:30, Sat–Sun 10:00–12:00 & 14:00–18:30, Oct–March Mon–Fri 9:30–17:00, Sat–Sun 9:30–13:00 & 14:00–17:30, lockers, money-exchange desk, WC in courtyard, tel. 050-448-686, www.brugge.com). The other TI is at the train station (generally Mon–Sat 10:00–18:00, closed Sun).

Bruges

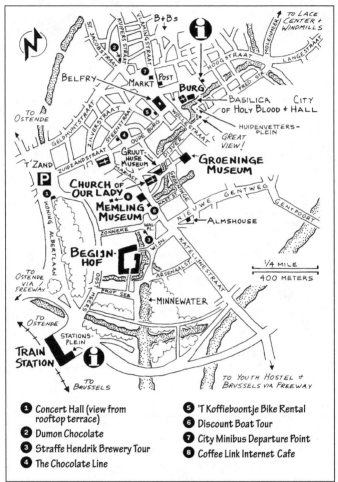

1 Concert Hall (view from rooftop terrace)

2 Dumon Chocolate

3 Straffe Hendrik Brewery Tour

4 The Chocolate Line

5 'T Koffieboontje Bike Rental

6 Discount Boat Tour

7 City Minibus Departure Point

8 Coffee Link Internet Cafe

The TIs sell a great €1 Bruges visitor's guide with a map and listings of all of the sights and services. You can also pick up a bimonthly English-language program called *events@brugge*. The TIs have information on train schedules and on the many tours available (see "Tours" below). Bikers will want the "5X on the Bike around Bruges" map/guide (€1.25) that shows five routes through the countryside. Many hotels give free maps with more detail than the map the TIs sell.

Museum Tips

Admission prices are steep but include great audioguides—
so plan on spending some time and getting into it. The
information number for all museums is 050-448-711.

Combo-Ticket: The TIs and participating museums
sell a museum combo-ticket (any 5 museums for €15). Since
the Groeninge and Memling museums cost €8 each, anyone
interested in art will save money with this pass.

Black Monday: In Bruges, nearly all sights are open
Tuesday through Sunday year-round from 9:30 to 17:00 and
closed on Monday. If you're in Bruges on a Monday, consider a boat, bus, or walking tour (see page 229).

Arrival in Bruges

By Train: Coming in by train you'll see the square bell tower
marking the main square. Upon arrival, stop by the station TI
(has lockers) to pick up the Bruges visitor's guide (map in center-
fold). There are no ATMs at the station, but you can change
money at ticket windows.

Your best way to get to the town center is by bus. All buses go
directly to the Market Square. Simply hop on any bus, pay €1, and
in four minutes you're there. The €1 tickets are good for an hour. A
day pass costs €3. Buses #4 and #8 go farther, to the northeast part of
town (to the windmills and recommended places on Carmersstraat).

Note that nearly all city buses go directly from the station to the
Market Square and fan out from there. They then return to Market
Square (bus #2 stops at post office on square; other buses stop at
library on nearby Kuiperstraat) and go directly back to the station.

The **taxi** fare from the train station to most hotels is around
€6 (tel. 050-334-444).

It's a 20-minute **walk** from the station to the center—no fun
with your luggage. If you want to walk, cross the busy street and
canal in front of the station, head up Oostmeers, and turn right
on Steenstraat to reach Market Square.

You can rent a **bike** at the station for the duration of your
stay, but other bike-rental shops are closer to the center (see
"Helpful Hints," below).

By Car: Park at the train station for just €2.50 per day;
show your parking receipt for a free bus ride into town. There
are pricier (€9/day) underground parking garages at 't Zand
and around town, and these garages are well-marked. Driving in
Bruges is very complicated because of the one-way system.

Helpful Hints

Bike Rental: **'T Koffieboontje,** just under the bell tower, is extremely well organized and the handiest. They take a credit-card imprint for a deposit, and you're on your way with a nearly new bike (€3/1 hr, €6/4 hrs, or €9/24-hr day, €6/day with an ISIC student card, free city maps and child seats, daily 9:00–22:00, the €15 "bike plus any 3 museums" deal could save enough to pay for lunch, Hallestraat 4, tel. 050-338-027).

Other rental places include the following: **Fietsen Popelier** (50 meters from Church of Our Lady at Mariastraat 26, tel. 050-343-262), the less central **De Ketting** (cheap at €5/day, daily 9:00–20:00, Gentpoortstraat 23, tel. 050-344-196), and the **train station** (ticket window #3, daily 7:00–20:00, €9/day, €6.50/half day after 14:00, €15 deposit).

Internet Access: The relaxing **Coffee Link,** with mellow music and pleasant art, is centrally located across from the Church of Our Lady (€2/30 min, daily 10:00–21:30, 14 terminals, Maria-straat 38, tel. 050-349-973).

Laundry: Bruges' most convenient place to do laundry is **Mr. Wash** (€4 self-service wash and dry, daily 8:30–22:00, just off Market Square in an arcade at Sint Jakobsstraat 33, tel. 050-335-902). A less central launderette is at Gentportstraat 28 (daily 7:00–22:00).

Shopping: Shops are open from 9:00 to 18:00, a little later on Friday. Grocery stores are usually closed on Sunday. The main shopping street, Steenstraat, stretches from Market Square to the square called 't Zand.

Market Days: Wednesday morning (Market Square) and Saturday morning ('t Zand) are market days. On Saturday and Sunday afternoons, a flea market hops along Dijver in front of the Groeninge Museum.

Festival of Canals: Bruges' famous festival won't be held again until 2004.

Post Office: It's on Market Square near the bell tower (Mon–Fri 9:00–19:00, Sat 9:30–12:30, closed Sun, tel. 050-331-411).

Best Town View: The bell tower overlooking the Market Square rewards those who climb it with the ultimate town view.

The best view without a climb is from the rooftop terrace of Bruges' concert hall (Concert-gebouw). This seven-story building, built in 2002, is the city's only modern highrise (daily 11:00–23:00, free elevator, on edge of old town on 't Zand).

Tours of Bruges

Bruges by Boat—The most relaxing and scenic (though not informative) way to see this city of canals is by boat, with the captain narrating. Boats leave from all over town (€5.50, 4/hr, 10:00–17:00, copycat 30-min rides). Boten Stael offers an €0.80 discount with this book (just over the canal from Memling Museum at Katelijnestraat 4, tel. 050-332-771).

City Minibus Tour—City Tour Bruges gives a rolling overview of the town in an 18-seat, two-skylight minibus with dial-a-language headsets and video support (€9.50, 50 min). The tour leaves hourly from Market Square (10:00–19:00 in summer, until 18:00 in spring and fall, less in winter, tel. 050-355-024). The narration, while clear, is slow-moving and boring. But the tour is a lazy way to cruise past virtually every sight in Bruges.

Walking Tour—Local guides walk small groups through the core of town (€5, daily July–Aug, Sat–Sun only in June and Sept, depart from TI at 15:00, 2 hrs, no tours off-season). Though earnest, the tours are heavy on history and in two languages, so they may be less than peppy. Still, to propel you beyond the pretty gables and canal swans of Bruges, they're good medicine. A private two-hour guided tour costs €40 (reserve at least 3 days in advance through TI, tel. 050-448-685).

Horse-and-Buggy Tour—You'll see buggies around town ready to take you for a clip-clop tour (€28/30 min, price is per carriage, not per person).

Tours from Bruges

Quasimodo Countryside Tours—This company offers those with extra time two excellent and entertaining all-day big-bus tours through the rarely visited Flemish countryside.

The "Flanders Fields" tour concentrates on World War I battlefields, trenches, memorials, and poppy-splattered fields (Sun, Tue, and Thu 9:00–16:30).

The other tour is "Triple Treat": You'll see the former port of Damme, a castle, monastery, brewery, and chocolate factory, as well as taste a waffle, chocolate, and beer (Mon, Wed, and Fri 9:00–16:30).

Hardworking Lode leads all the tours himself, in English only (€45, €38 if under 26, CC, 30-seat non-smoking bus, includes a picnic lunch, lots of walking, reserve by calling 050-370-470 or toll-free 0800-97525, www.quasimodo.be). The bus leaves from the Park Hotel on 't Zand.

Daytours in Flanders Fields Minibus Tours—This tour is like Quasimodo's (listed above) but €9 more expensive. The differences: seven travelers on a minibus rather than a big busload; hotel pick-ups (because the small bus is allowed in the town center); an included restaurant lunch rather than a picnic; and a little more serious lecturing and a stricter focus on World War I (you actually visit the Flanders Fields Museum in Ieper, called Ypres in French).

Frank, the guide, loves leading his small groups on this fascinating day trip (€59, €5 discount when booked direct with this book, Wed–Sun 9:00–17:00, no tours Mon and Tue, call 050-346-060 or toll-free 0800-99133 to book, www.visitbruges.com).

Bruges by Bike—Quasimundo Tours, an offshoot of Quasimodo Tours listed above, leads daily bike tours in and around Bruges (€16, €12 with this book, departs at 10:00, 8 km, 2 hrs) and through the nearby countryside to Damme (€16, €12 with this book, departs at 13:00, 25 km, 3–4 hrs, tel. 050-330-775). Both tours include bike rental and depart from in front of the TI on Burg Square. For a do-it-yourself bike tour, see page 235.

Bus and Boat Tour—The Sightseeing Line offers a bus trip to Damme and a boat ride back (€16.50, April–Sept daily at 16:00, 2 hrs, leaves from Market Square, tel. 050-355-024).

SIGHTS

These sights are listed in walking order from Market Square to Burg Square to the cluster of museums around the Church of our Lady to the Begijnhof (10-min walk from beginning to end).
⭐ For a self-guided walk and much more information on each sight, see the Bruges City Walk, page 237.

▲**Market Square (Markt)**—Ringed by banks, the post office, lots of restaurant terraces, great old gabled buildings, and the bell tower, this is the modern heart of the city (most city buses run from here to the train station). Under the bell tower are two great Belgian french-fry stands, a quadrilingual Braille description of the old town, and a metal model of the tower. In Bruges' heyday as a trading center, a canal came right up to this square.

Geldmuntstraat, just off the square, is a delightful street with many fun and practical shops and eateries.

▲▲**Bell Tower (Belfort)**—Most of this bell tower has presided over Market Square since 1300. The octagonal lantern was added in 1486, making it 90 meters high—that's 290 feet and 366 steps (daily 9:30–17:00, ticket window closes 45 min early, WC in courtyard). The view is worth the climb and the €5.

▲▲**Burg Square**—The opulent square called Burg is Bruges' civic center, historically the birthplace of Bruges and the site of the ninth-century castle of the first Count of Flanders. Today it's the scene of outdoor concerts and home of the TI (with a €0.25 WC). It's surrounded by six centuries of architecture.

▲**Basilica of the Holy Blood**—Originally the Chapel of Saint Basil, the church is famous for its relic of the blood of Christ which, according to tradition, was brought to Bruges in 1150 after the Second Crusade. The lower chapel is dark and solid— a fine example of Romanesque style. The upper chapel (separate entrance, climb the stairs) is decorated Gothic (museum is next to upper chapel, €1.25, April–Sept daily 9:30–12:00 & 14:00–18:00, Oct–March Thu–Tue 10:00–12:00 & 14:00–16:00, Wed 10:00–12:00 only, tel. 050-336-792).

▲**City Hall's Gothic Room**—Your ticket gives you a room full of old town maps and paintings and a grand, beautifully restored "Gothic Hall" from 1400. Its painted and carved wooden ceiling features hanging arches (€2.50, includes audioguide and admission to Renaissance Hall, daily 9:30–17:00, Burg 12).

Renaissance Hall (Brugse Vrije)—This is just one ornate room with an impressive Renaissance chimney (€2.50, includes audio-guide and admission to City Hall's Gothic Room, Tue–Sun 9:30–12:00 & 13:30–17:00, closed Mon, entrance in corner of square at Burg 11a).

▲▲▲**Groeninge Museum**—This museum houses a world-class collection of mostly Flemish art, from Memling to Magritte (€8, Tue–Sun 9:30–17:00, closed Mon, Dijver 12, tel. 050-448-751). ⬛ See Groeninge Museum Tour, page 253.

▲**Gruuthuse Museum**—Once a wealthy brewer's home, this is a sprawling smattering of everything from medieval bedpans to a guillotine (€6, Tue–Sun 9:30–17:00, closed Mon, Dijver 17).

▲▲**Church of Our Lady**—The church stands as a memorial to the power and wealth of Bruges in its heyday. A delicate *Madonna and Child* by Michelangelo is near the apse (to the right if you're facing the altar). It's said to be the only Michelangelo statue to leave Italy in his lifetime (thanks to the wealth generated by Bruges' cloth trade). If you like tombs and church art, pay to wander through the apse (Michelangelo free, art-filled apse €2.50, Tue–Sun 9:00–12:00 & 13:30–17:00, closed Mon, Mariastraat).

▲▲**St. Jans Hospital/Memling Museum**—The former mon-astery/hospital complex has two entrances—one is to a welcom-ing Visitors Center (free), the other to the Memling Museum. The Memling Museum, in the monastery's former church, was once a medieval hospital and now contains six much-loved paint-ings by the greatest of the Flemish Primitives, Hans Memling (€8 includes fine audioguide, Tue–Sun 9:30–17:00, closed Mon, across the street from the Church of Our Lady, Mariastraat 38). ⬛ See Memling Museum Tour, page 262.

▲▲**Begijnhof**—Inhabited by Benedictine nuns, Begijnhof almost makes you want to don a habit and fold your hands as you walk under its wispy trees and whisper past its frugal little homes. For a good slice of Begijnhof life, walk through the simple museum (Begijn's House, left of entry gate, €2, has English explanations, daily 10:00–12:00 & 13:45–17:30, off-season closes at 17:00).

Minnewater—Just south of the Begijnhof is Minnewater, an idyllic world of flower boxes, canals, swans, and tour boats packed like happy egg cartons.

Almshouses—Walking from the Begijnhof back to the town center, you might detour along Nieuwe Gentweg to visit one of about 20 almshouses in the city. At #8, go through the door marked "Godshuis de Meulenaere 1613" (free) into the peaceful courtyard. This was a medieval form of housing for the poor. The rich would pay for someone's tiny room here in return for lots of prayers.

Avoid the Diamond Museum (at the start of Nieuwe Gentweg); it's less interesting than an encyclopedia (€5, daily 10:30–17:30, Katelijnestraat 43, tel. 050-342-056, www.diamondhouse.net).

Bruges Experiences: Beer, Chocolate, Lace, and Biking

▲▲**Straffe Hendrik Brewery Tour**—Belgians are Europe's beer connoisseurs. This fun and handy tour is a great way to pay your respects. The happy gang at this working family brewery gives entertaining and informative 45-minute, three-language tours (often by friendly Inge, €4 including a beer, lots of very steep steps, great rooftop panorama, daily on the hour 11:00–16:00, 11:00 and 15:00 are your best times to avoid groups, Oct–March 11:00 and 15:00 only, 1 block past church and canal, take a right down skinny Stoofstraat to #26 on Walplein, tel. 050-332-697).

At Straffe Hendrik (Strong Henry), they remind their drinkers: "The components of the beer are vitally necessary and contribute to a well-balanced life pattern. Nerves, muscles, visual sentience, and a healthy skin are stimulated by these in a positive manner. For longevity and lifelong equilibrium, drink Straffe Hendrik in moderation!"

Their bistro, where you'll be given your beer (included with the tour), serves quick and hearty lunch plates. You can eat indoors with the smell of hops or outdoors with the smell of hops. This is a great place to wait for your tour or to linger afterward. For more on beer, see page 276.

▲**Chocolate**—Bruggians are connoisseurs of fine chocolate. You'll be tempted by chocolate-filled display windows all over town. While Godiva is the best big-factory/high-price/high-quality local brand, there are plenty of smaller, family-run places in Bruges that offer exquisite handmade chocolates.

Perhaps Bruges' smoothest and creamiest chocolates are at **Dumon** (€1.60/100 grams). Madam Dumon and her children (Stefaan, Christophe, and Nathalie) make their top-notch chocolate daily and sell it fresh just off Market Square (Thu–Tue 10:00–18:00, closed Wed, Eiermarkt 6, old chocolate molds on display

in basement, tel. 050-346-282, www.chocolatierdumon.com).
Their *ganache*, a dark creamy combo, wows chocoholics.
They don't have English labels because they believe it's
best to describe their chocolates in person.

Locals and tourists alike flock to **The Chocolate Line** (€3/
100 grams) for their *"gastronomique"* varieties—unique concoc-
tions such as Havana cigar (marinated in rum, cognac, and Cuban
tobacco leaves—so therefore technically illegal in the United States),
lemon grass, ginger (shaped like a Buddha), saffron curry (a white
elephant), and a spicy chili. My fave: the sheets of chocolate with
crunchy roasted cocoa beans. The kitchen—busy whipping up their
80 varieties—is on display in the back (Mon–Sat 9:30–18:30, Sun
from 10:30, Simon Stevinplein 19, between Church of Our Lady
and Market Square, tel. 050-341-090).

The smaller **Sweertvaegher,** near Burg Square, features
top-quality chocolate (€2.50/100 grams) that's darker rather
than sweeter, made with fresh ingredients and no preservatives
(Tue–Sun 9:30–18:15, closed Mon, Philipstockstraat 29, tel.
050-338-367).

Lace and Windmills by the Moat—A 10-minute walk from
the center to the northeast end of town brings you to four windmills strung along a pleasant grassy setting on the "big moat"
canal (between Kruispoort and Dampoort, on Bruges side of

the moat). One windmill
(St. Janshuismolen) is open
to visitors (€2, daily 9:30–
12:30 & 13:30–17:00, closed
Oct–April, at the end of
Carmersstraat).

To actually see lace
being made, drop by the
nearby **Lace Centre,** where
ladies toss bobbins madly while their eyes go bad (€2 includes
afternoon demonstrations and a small lace museum called Kant-
centrum, as well as the adjacent Jeruzalem Church; Mon–Fri
10:00–12:00 & 14:00–18:00, until 17:00 on Sat, closed Sun,
Peperstraat 3, tel. 050-330-072). The **Folklore Museum,** in
the same neighborhood, is cute but forgettable (€3, daily 9:30–
17:00, closed Mon, Rolweg 40, tel. 050-330-044). To find either
place, ask for the Jeruzalem Church.

▲▲**Biking**—The Flemish word for bike is *fiets* (pron. feets).
While the sights are close enough for easy walking, the town
is a treat to bike through. And a bike quickly gets you into the
dreamy back lanes without a hint of tourism. Take a peaceful
evening ride through the back streets and around the outer canal.

Consider keeping a bike for the duration of your stay. It's the way the locals get around in Bruges.

Rental shops have maps and ideas. The TI sells a handy "5X on the Bike around Bruges" map/guide (€1.25) describing five different bike routes (18–30 km) through the idyllic countryside nearby. The best trip is 30 minutes along the canal out to Damme and back (described below). The Belgium/Netherlands border is a 40-minute pedal beyond Damme.

Damme Bike Ride: For the best short bike trip out of Bruges, rent a bike and pedal seven kilometers to the nearby town of Damme. You'll enjoy a whiff of the countryside, passing windmills and a historic church, riding along a canal to this interesting city. Allow about two hours for the leisurely round-trip bike ride and a short stop in Damme. You can also take a bus/boat tour (see page 229), or pedal to Damme and come back (with your bike) by boat.

From the **Market Square,** head east to the weird, medieval, almost creepy **Jeruzalem Church,** built by Crusaders who'd seen the Church of the Holy Sepulchre in Jerusalem. (A button to the left of the entrance lights the church.) The **Lace Museum** is next door (described above).

Continue east to the ring canal, with several **windmills** (one is open to tour, described above). Go north along the canal and exit at Damport, heading northeast on Damsevaart Zuid, which borders a canal.

From Damport, you pedal along a canal directly to Damme. There's no chance to cross the canal until you reach the town. I'd ride down on the busy right-hand side and return on the more peaceful and farmy left side. About halfway to Damme (on the right side) is a roadhouse inn.

Shortly before reaching town, pull over at the Uilenspiegel parking lot for a great **view of Damme,** with its houses and square church tower rising up from the fields. You can approach the city by taking the Vonderweg dirt path from the parking lot.

Damme is a tiny version of Bruges, with a smaller-but-similar town hall, St. Jans Hospital, and Our Lady Church. Grab a coffee at the café next to the Stadhuis.

Our Lady of Damme has two statues of the Virgin Mary. To the right of the altar is a 1630 wooden statue. Mary, tall and stately with her curly hair spilling loose, welcomes you—her eyes twinkle and crinkle as she spots you and breaks into a smile. To the right (Mary's left), watch out for the well-dressed, white-gloved Church Police (Kerk Politie). And over your left shoulder, look up at the statues in the upper nave to see Belgium's oldest wooden statue, St. Andrew with his X-shaped cross.

Mary's rival is the statue to the left of the altar, Our Lady of the Fishermen (c. 1650, in a glass case). Remember, Damme was once a port as well. The canal you rode on once led past Bruges and out to the North Sea.

Outside, near the (climbable) church tower is a four-faced modern sculpture by local artist Delporte. Like his work? You'll find more at his gallery just down the road (on the west edge of town).

Cross the canal at a bridge in Damme, and return along the scenic north bank.

Sights—Near Bruges

Dolfinarium—At Boudewijnpark, just outside of town, dolphins make a splash several times a day (€8 for 40-min show, Debaeckestraat 12, call for show times, tel. 050-383-838, www.boudewijnpark.be). The theme park's roller-skating rink is open in the afternoon (becomes an ice-skating rink off-season). From Bruges, catch the Sint Michiels bus #7 or #17 from the train station or Kuipersstraat.

Flanders Fields Museum—This World War I museum, 60 kilometers southwest of Bruges, provides a moving look at the battles fought near Ieper (Ypres in French). Use interactive computer displays to trace the wartime lives of individual soldiers and citizens. Powerful videos and ear-shattering audio complete the story (€7.50, April–Sept daily 10:00–18:00, Oct–March Tue–Sun 10:00–17:00, closed Mon, last entry 1 hour before closing, Grote Markt 34, Ieper, tel. 057-228-584, fax 057-228-589, www.inflandersfields.be). From Bruges, catch a train to Ieper via Kortrijk (2 hrs) or take a tour (See Daytours in Flanders Fields Minibus Tours, page 230). Drivers follow A17 to Kortrijk, then take A19 to Ieper.

BRUGES CITY WALK

This walk, which takes you from Market Square to the Burg to the cluster of museums around the Church of Our Lady (the Groeninge, Gruuthuse, and Memling), shows you the best of Bruges in a day.

Orientation

Note that museums are open Tue–Sun 9:30–17:00, closed Mon.

Bell Tower: €5, daily 9:30–17:00, on Market Square.

Basilica of the Holy Blood: Treasury-€1.25, April–Sept daily 9:30–12:00 & 14:00–18:00, Oct–March Thu–Tue 10:00–12:00 & 14:00–16:00, Wed 10:00–12:00 only, Burg Square.

Gothic Room: €2.50, includes audioguide and entry to Renaissance Hall, daily 9:30–17:00, City Hall, Burg 12.

Renaissance Hall: €2.50, includes Gothic Room, Tue–Sun 9:30–12:00 & 13:30–17:00, closed Mon, Burg 11a.

Groeninge Museum: €8, Dijver 12.

Gruuthuse Museum: €6, Dijver 17.

Church of Our Lady: free Michelangelo, €2.50 for art-filled apse, Tue–Sun 9:00–12:00 & 13:30–17:00, closed Mon, Mariastraat.

Memling Museum: €8, includes audioguide, Mariastraat 38.

Straffe Hendrik Brewery: €4 tour includes a beer, daily on the hour 11:00–16:00, Oct–March 11:00 and 15:00 only, Walplein 26.

Begijn's House: €2, daily 10:00–12:00 & 13:45–17:30, off-season closes at 17:00.

Market Square (Markt)

Ringed by banks, the post office, lots of restaurant terraces, great old gabled buildings, and the bell tower, this is the modern heart of the city. And, in Bruges' heyday as a trading city, this was also the center. The "typical" old buildings here were rebuilt in the

Bruges City Walk

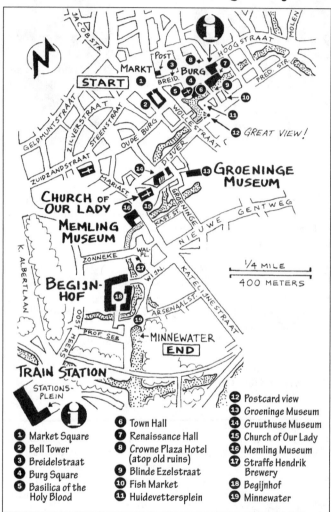

1 Market Square
2 Bell Tower
3 Breidelstraat
4 Burg Square
5 Basilica of the Holy Blood
6 Town Hall
7 Renaissance Hall
8 Crowne Plaza Hotel (atop old ruins)
9 Blinde Ezelstraat
10 Fish Market
11 Huidevettersplein
12 Postcard view
13 Groeninge Museum
14 Gruuthuse Museum
15 Church of Our Lady
16 Memling Museum
17 Straffe Hendrik Brewery
18 Begijnhof
19 Minnewater

19th century in an exaggerated neo-Gothic style (Bruges is often called more Gothic than Gothic). This pre–Martin Luther style was a political statement for this Catholic town.

Formerly, a canal came right up to this square. Imagine boats moored where the post office stands today. In the 1300s, farmers shipped their cotton, wool, flax, and hemp to the port at Bruges.

Before loading it onto outgoing boats, the industrious locals would spin, weave, and dye it into a finished product.

By 1400, the economy was shifting away from textiles and toward more refined goods such as high-fashion items, tapestry, chairs, jewelry, and paper—a new invention replacing parchment that was made in Flanders with cotton that was shredded, soaked, and pressed.

The square is adorned with **flags,** including the red-white-and-blue lion flag of Bruges, the black-yellow-red flag of Belgium, and the blue-with-circle-of-stars flag of the European Union.

The **statue** depicts two friends, Jan Breidel and Pieter de Coninc, clutching sword and shield and looking toward France during their 1302 people's uprising against the French king. The rebels identified potential French spies by demanding they repeat two words—*schild en vriend* (shield and friend)—that only Flemish locals (or foreigners with phlegm) could pronounce. They won Flanders its freedom. Cleverly using hooks to pull knights from their horses, it was the medieval world's first victory of foot soldiers over horsed knights and of common people over nobility. The French knights, thinking that fighting these Flemish peasants would be a cakewalk, had worn their dress uniforms. The peasants had a field day afterward scavenging all the golden spurs from the fallen soldiers after the Battle of the Golden Spurs (1302).

Geldmuntstraat, a block west of the square, has fun shops and eateries. Steenstraat is the main shopping street and is packed with people.

Bell Tower (Belfort)

Most of this bell tower has stood over Market Square since 1300. The octagonal lantern was added in 1486, making it 90 meters high (290 feet). The tower combines medieval crenellations, pointed Gothic arches, round Roman arches, flamboyant spires, and even a few small flying buttresses (two-thirds of the way up).

Try some french fries from either stand at the bottom of the tower. Look for the small metal model of the tower, the Braille description of the old town, and the carillon concert schedule (listed with photos of carillonneur at keyboard, just inside courtyard at base of bell tower; WC in the same courtyard).

Climb the tower (€5, 366 steps). Just before you reach the top, peek into the carillon room. The 47 bells can be played mechanically with the giant barrel and movable tabs (as they are on each quarter hour) or with a manual keyboard (as they are during concerts). The carillon-neur uses his fists and feet rather than fingers. Be there on the quarter hour, when things ring. It's *bellissimo* at the top of the hour.

Atop the tower, survey the town. On the horizon you can see the towns along the North Sea coast.

• *Descend the tower. Leaving the bell tower, turn right (east) onto pedestrian-only . . .*

Breidelstraat

Lace, waffles, chocolates, tapestry—Bruges' many treats are sold here. And beer? Turn right, down the narrow alleyway midway along the block to find the tiny de Garre bar, which serves more than a hundred Belgian beers in a smoky, local atmosphere.

• *Thread yourself through the lace and waffles to Burg Square.*

Burg Square

The opulent square called Burg is Bruges' historical birthplace, political center, and religious heart. Today it's the scene of outdoor concerts and home of the TI.

Pan the square to see six centuries of architecture. Starting with the view of the bell tower above the rooftops, sweep counterclockwise 360 degrees. You'll go from Romanesque (the interior of the fancy gray-brick **Basilica of the Holy Blood** in the corner) to the pointed Gothic arches and prickly steeples of the white sandstone **Town Hall** to the well-proportioned Renaissance windows of the **Old Recorder's House** (next door, under the gilded statues), to the elaborate 17th-century

Baroque of the **Provost's House** (past the TI and the park behind you). The **park** at the back of the square is the site of a cathedral that was demolished during the French Revolutionary period. Today the foundation is open to the public in the **Crowne Plaza Hotel** basement (described below).

• *Complete your spin and walk to the small, fancy, gray-and-gold building in the corner of the Burg Square.*

Basilica of the Holy Blood

The gleaming gold knights and ladies on the church's gray facade remind us that the double-decker church was built (c. 1150) by a brave Crusader to house the drops of Christ's blood he brought back from Jerusalem.

Lower Chapel: Enter the lower chapel through the door labeled *Basiliek*. Inside, the stark and dim decor reeks of the medieval piety that drove crusading Europeans on Christian jihads against Muslims. With heavy columns and round arches, the style is pure Romanesque.

The annex along the right aisle displays somber statues of Christ being tortured and entombed, plus a 12th-century relief panel over a doorway showing St. Basil, a fourth-century scholarly monk, being baptized by a double-jointed priest, and a man-sized Dove of the Holy Spirit.

• *Go back outside and up the staircase to reach the . . .*

Upper Chapel: After being gutted by Napoleon's secular-humanist crusaders in 1797, the upper chapel's original Romanesque decor was redone in a neo-Gothic style. The nave is color-

ful, with a curved wooden ceiling, painted walls, and stained-glass windows of the dukes who ruled Flanders and their duchesses.

The painting at the main altar tells how the Holy Blood got here. Derrick of Alsace, having helped defend Jerusalem (*Hierosolyma*) and Bethlehem (*Bethlema*) from Muslim incursions in the Second Crusade, kneels (left) before the grateful

The Legend of the Holy Blood

Several drops of Christ's blood, washed from his lifeless body by Joseph of Arimathea, were preserved in a crystal phial in Jerusalem. In 1150, the patriarch of Jerusalem gave the blood to a Flemish soldier, Derrick of Alsace, as thanks for rescuing his city from the Muslims during the Second Crusade. Derrick (also called Dedric or Thierry) returned home and donated it to the city. The old, dried blood suddenly turned to liquid, a miracle repeated every Friday for the next two centuries, and verified by thousands of pilgrims from around Europe who flocked here to adore it. The blood dried up for good in 1325.

Every year on Ascension Day (May 29 in 2003), Bruges' bankers, housewives, and waffle-vendors put on old-time costumes for the parading of the phial through the city. Crusader knights re-enact the bringing of the relic, Joseph of Arimathea washes Christ's body, and ladies in medieval costume with hair tied up in horn-like hairnets come out to wave flags, while many Bruges citizens just take the day off.

Christian patriarch of Jerusalem, who rewards him with the relic. Derrick returns home (right) and kneels before Bruges' bishop to give him the phial of blood.

The relic itself—some red stuff preserved inside a clear, six-inch tube of rock-crystal—is kept in the adjoining room (through the three arches). It's in the tall silver tabernacle on the altar. (Unless it's Friday, the tabernacle's doors will be closed, so you can't actually see the phial of blood.) On holy days, the relic is shifted across the room, and displayed on the throne under the canopy.

The Treasury (Next to Upper Chapel): For €1.25 you can see the impressive gold-and-silver, gem-studded, hexagonal reliquary (c. 1600, left wall) that the phial of blood is paraded around in on feast days. The phial is placed in the "casket" at the bottom of the four-foot structure. On the wall, flanking the shrine, are paintings of kneeling residents who, for centuries, have tended the shrine and organized the pageantry as part of the 31-member Brotherhood of

the Holy Blood. Elsewhere in the room are the Brothers' ceremonial necklaces, clothes, chalices, and so on.

In the display case by the entrance, find the lead box that protected the phial of blood from Protestant extremists (1578) and French revolutionaries (1797) bent on destroying this glaring symbol of Catholic mumbo-jumbo. The broken rock-crystal tube with gold caps on either end is a replica of the phial, giving an idea of what the actual relic looks like. Opposite the reliquary are the original cartoons (from 1541) that provided the designs for the basilica's stained glass.

Town Hall (Stadhuis)

Built around 1400, when Bruges was a thriving bastion of capitalism with a population of 35,000, this building served as a model for town halls elsewhere, including Brussels. The white sandstone facade is studded with statues of knights, nobles, and saints with prickly Gothic steeples over their heads. A colorful double band of cities' coats of arms includes those of Bruges (Brugghe) and Dunquerke. (Back then, Bruges' jurisdiction included many towns in present-day France.) The building is still the Town Hall, and it's not unusual to see couples arriving here to get married.

Entrance Hall: The free ground-level lobby (closed on weekends) is draped with colorful banners representing the different professions in town. Pick them out: candlestick-maker, painter, pig farmer, weaver, blacksmith, and cloth maker.

The adjacent hallway is a picture gallery with scenes from Belgium's history: from the Spanish king to the arrival of Napoleon, shown meeting the town mayor here at the Town Hall in 1803.

The painting at the far left end of the lobby (behind ticket desk) shows the event that symbolically ended Bruges' glory days. Mary Duchess of Burgundy lies absolutely flat on her back, having tumbled from a horse, as peasants rush to help. When she died at age 25 (in 1482), her Hapsburg husband Maximilian inherited Bruges. The town was soon swallowed up in Maximilian's huge Holy Roman Empire, ruled from afar by kings in Austria and Spain, who did nothing as the town's harbor and economy silted up.

Gothic Room: Some of modern democracy's roots lie in this ornate room where, for centuries, the city council met to discuss the town's affairs (€2.50 entry includes audioguide and Renaissance Hall). In 1464, one of Europe's first parliaments, the Estates General of the Low Countries, convened here. The fireplace at the far  end bears a proclamation from 1305, which says, "All the artisans, laborers…and citizens of Bruges are free—all of them" (providing they pay their taxes).

The elaborately carved and painted wooden ceiling (a reconstruction from 1800) features Gothic-style tracery in gold, red, and black. Five dangling arches hang down the center ("pendentives"), now adorned with modern floodlights. Notice the New Testament themes carved into the circular medallions that decorate the points where the arches meet.

The **wall murals** are late-19th-century Romantic paintings depicting episodes in the city's history. Start with the biggest painting along the left wall, and work clockwise, following the numbers found on the walls:

1. Hip, hip, hooray! Everyone cheers, flags wave, trumpets blare, and dogs bark, as Bruges' knights, dressed in gold with black Flemish lions, return triumphant after driving out French oppressors and winning Flanders' independence. The Battle of the Golden Spurs (1302) is remembered every July 11, now the Flemish national holiday.

2. Perhaps Bruges' highwater mark came at this elaborate ceremony, when Philip the Good of Burgundy (seated, in black) assembled his court here in Bruges and solemnly founded the knightly Order of the Golden Fleece (1429).

3. The Crusader knight, Derrick of Alsace, returns from the Holy Land and kneels at the entrance of St. Basil's Chapel to present the relic of Christ's Holy Blood (c. 1150).

4. A nun carries a basket of bread in this scene from St. Jans Hospital.

5. A town leader stands at the podium and hands a sealed document to a German businessman, renewing the Hanseatic League's business license. Membership in this club of trading cities was a key to Bruges' prosperity.

6. As peasants cheer, a messenger of the local duke proclaims the town's right to self-government (1190).

7. The mayor visits a Bruges painting studio to shake the hand of Jan van Eyck, the great Flemish Primitive painter (1433). Jan's wife, Margareta is there, too. In the 1400s, Bruges rivaled Florence and Venice as Europe's cultural capital. See the town in the distance, out van Eyck's window.

8. Skip it.

9. City fathers grab a ceremonial trowel from a pillow to lay the fancy cornerstone of the Town Hall (1376). Bruges' familiar towers stand in the background.

10. Skip it.

11. It's a typical market day at the Halls (the courtyard behind the bell tower). Arabs mingle with Germans in fur-lined coats and beards in a market where they sell everything from armor to lemons.

12. A bishop blesses a new canal (1404) as ships sail right by the city. This was Bruges in its heyday before the silting of the harbor. At the far right, the two bearded men with moustaches are the brothers who painted these murals.

In the adjoining room, old paintings and maps show how 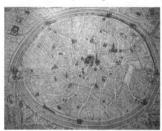 little the city has changed over the centuries. Map #8 (on the right wall) shows in exquisite detail the city as it looked in 1562. (The map is oriented with south on top.) Find the bell tower, the Church of Our Lady, and Burg Square, which back then was bounded on the north by a cathedral. Notice the canal (on the west) leading from the North Sea right to Market Square. A moat circled the city with its gates, unfinished wall, and 28 windmills (four of which survive today). The mills pumped water to the town's fountains, made paper, ground grain, and functioned as the motor of the Middle Ages. Most locals own a copy of this map that shows how their neighborhood looked 400 years ago.

• *In the southeast corner of Burg Square is the . . .*

Renaissance Hall (Brugse Vrije)

This elaborately decorated room has a grand Renaissance chimney carved from oak by Bruges' Renaissance man, Lancelot Blondeel, in 1531. If you're into heraldry, the symbolism (explained in the free English flier) makes this room worth a five-minute stop. If you're not, you'll wonder where the rest of the museum is.

The centerpiece of the incredible carving is the Holy Roman Emperor Charles V. The hometown duke, on the far left, is related to Charles V. By making the connection to the Holy Roman Emperor clear, this carved family tree of Bruges' nobility helped substantiate their power. Notice the closely guarded family jewels. And check out the expressive little cherubs.

Crowne Plaza Hotel

One of the city's newest buildings (1992) sits atop the ruins of the town's oldest structures. Around 900, when Viking ships regularly docked here to rape and pillage, Baldwin Iron Arm built a fort *(castrum)* to protect his Flemish people. In 950, the fort was converted into St. Donatian's church, which became one of the city's largest.

Ask politely at the hotel's reception desk to see the archaeological site—ruins of the fort and the church—in the basement. If there's no conference, they'll let you walk down the stairs and have a peek.

In the basement of the modern hotel are conference rooms lined with old stone walls and display cases of objects found in the ruins of earlier structures. On the immediate left hangs a document announcing the *Vente de Materiaux* (sale of material). When Napoleon destroyed the church in the early 1800s, its bricks were auctioned off. A local builder bought them at auction, and now the pieces of the old cathedral are embedded in other buildings throughout Bruges.

See oak pilings once driven into this former peat bog to support the fort and shore up its moat. Paintings show the immensity of the church that replaced it. The curved stone walls you walk among are from the foundations of the ambulatory around the church altar.

Excavators found a town water hole—a bonanza for archaeologists—turning up the refuse of a thousand years of habitation—pottery, animal skulls, rosary beads, dice, coins, keys, thimbles, pipes, spoons, and Delftware.

Don't miss the 14th-century painted sarcophagi—painted quickly for burial with the crucifixion on the west ends and the Virgin and Child on the east.

• *Back on the Burg Square, walk south under the Goldfinger family down the alleyway called . . .*

Blinde Ezelstraat

Midway down on the left side (knee level), see an original iron hinge from the city's south gate, back when the city was ringed by a moat and closed up at 22:00. On the right wall at eye level, a black patch shows just how grimy the city had become before a 1960s cleaning. Despite the cleaning and a few fanciful reconstructions, the city looks today much as it did in centuries past.

• *Cross the bridge over what was the 13th-century city moat. On your left are the arcades of the...*

Fish Market *(Vismarkt)*

The North Sea is just 20 kilometers away, and the fresh catch is sold here (Tue–Sat 6:00–13:00). Once a thriving market, today it is being replaced by souvenir stalls.

• *Take an immediate right (west), entering a courtyard called...*

Huidevettersplein

This tiny, picturesque, restaurant-filled square was originally the headquarters of the town's skinners and tanners. On the facade of the Hotel Duc de Bourgogne, four old relief panels show scenes from the leather tanners—once a leading Bruges industry. First they tan the hides in a bath of acid; then, with tongs, they pull it out to dry; then they beat it to make soft; and finally, they scrape and clean it to make ready for sale.

• *Continue a few steps to Rozenhoedkaai street, where you can look back and get a great...*

Postcard View

The bell tower reflected in a quiet canal lined with old houses— the essence of Bruges. Seeing buildings rising straight from the water makes you understand why this was the Venice of the North. Can you see the bell tower's tilt? It leans about four feet. The tilt has been carefully monitored since 1740, but no change has been detected.

Looking left (west) down the Dijver canal (past a flea market on weekends) looms the huge spire of the Church of Our Lady, the tallest brick spire in the Low Countries. Between you and the church is the Europa College (a post-graduate institution where the laws, economics, and politics of a united Europe are taught) and two fine museums.

Groeninge Museum

This sumptuous collection of paintings takes you from 1400 to 1945. While the museum has plenty of worthwhile modern art, the highlights are its vivid and pristine Flemish Primitives. ("Primitive" here means before the Renaissance.) Flemish art is shaped by its love of detail, its merchant patrons' egos, and the power of the Church. Lose yourself in the halls of the Groeninge: Gaze across 15th-century canals, into the eyes of reassuring Marys, and through town squares littered with leotards, lace, and lopped-off heads. (✪ See Groeninge Museum Tour, page 253.)

Gruuthuse Museum

The 15th-century mansion of a wealthy Bruges merchant displays period furniture, tapestries, coins, and musical instruments. Nowhere in the city do you get such an intimate look at the materialistic revolution of Bruges' glory days.

With the help of the excellent and included audioguide, just browse through rooms of secular objects that are both functional and beautiful. Here are some highlights:

In the first room (or Great Hall) the big fireplace, oak table, and tapestries attest to the wealth of Louis Gruuthuse, who got rich providing a special herb used to spice up beer.

Tapestries like the ones you see here were a famous Flemish export product, made in local factories out of raw wool imported from England and silk from the Orient (via Italy). Both beautiful and useful (as insulation), they adorned many homes and palaces throughout Europe.

These **four tapestries** (of nine originals) tell a worldly story of youthful lust that upsets our stereotypes about supposed medieval piousness. The first tapestry, the *Soup-Eating Lady* (on the left) shows a shepherd girl with a bowl of soup in her lap. The horny shepherd lad cuts a slice of bread (foreplay in medieval symbolism) and saucily asks (read the archaic French cartoon bubbles) if he can "dip into

the goodies in her lap," if you catch my drift. On the right, a woman brazenly strips off her socks to dangle her feet in water while another woman lifts her dress to pee.

The next tapestry, called *The Dance*, shows couples freely dancing together under the apple tree of temptation. *The Wedding Parade* (opposite wall) shows where all this wantonness leads—marriage. Music plays, the table is set and the meat's on the BBQ, as the bride and groom enter...reluctantly. The bride smiles, but she's closely escorted by two men, while the scared

groom (center) gulps nervously. From here, the next stop is *Old Age* (smaller tapestry), and the aged shepherd is tangled in a wolf trap. "Alas," reads the French caption, "he was once so lively, but marriage caught him, and now he's trapped in its net."

In Room 2 see the *Bust of Charles V* (on top of an oak chest) and ponder the series of marriages that made Charles (1500–1558), the grandson of a Flemish girl, the powerful ruler of most of Europe, including Bruges. Mary of Burgundy (and Flanders) married powerful Maximilian I of Austria. Their son Philip married Juana, the daughter of Ferdinand and Isabella of Spain, and when little Charles was born to them, he inherited all his grandparents' lands and more. Charles' son, Philip II (see his bust opposite), a devout Catholic, brought persecution and war to the Protestant Low Countries.

The Gruuthuse mansion abuts the Church of Our Lady. Upstairs, you'll find a chapel with a window overlooking the huge church. The family could attend services without leaving home, in their private box seats above the choir. From the balcony, you can look down on two reclining gold statues in the church, marking the tombs of Charles the Bold and his daughter, Mary of Burgundy (the grandmother of powerful Charles V).

The last room (ground floor, near the entrance) deals with old-time justice. In 1796, the enlightened city of Bruges chose the new-fangled guillotine as its humane form of execution. This 346-pound model was tested on sheep before being bloodied twice for executions on the Market Square. Also see branding irons, a small workbench for slicing off evil-doers' members, and posts to chain up criminals for public humiliation.

Leaving the museum, contemplate the mountain of bricks towering 120 meters (400 feet) above as they have for 600 years. You're heading for that church.

• *Take the interesting back way to the church. At the Arentshuis Museum entrance, duck under the arch at #16 and into a quiet courtyard. Veer right and cross a tiny 19th-century bridge.*

From the bridge, look up at the corner of the Gruuthuse mansion, where there's a teeny-tiny window, a toll-keeper's lookout. The bridge gives you a close-up look at Our Lady's big buttresses and round apse. The church entrance is around the front.

Church of Our Lady

The church stands as a memorial to the power and wealth of Bruges in its heyday.

A delicate ***Madonna and Child by Michelangelo*** (1504) is near the apse (to the right as you enter), somewhat overwhelmed by the ornate Baroque niche it sits in. It's said to be the only Michelangelo statue to leave Italy in his lifetime, bought in Tuscany by a wealthy Bruges businessman, who's buried beneath it.

As Michelangelo chipped away at the masterpiece of his youth, *David*, he took breaks by carving this (1504). Mary,

slightly smaller than life-size, sits while young Jesus stands in front of her. Their expressions are mirror images of each other— serene but a bit melancholy, with downcast eyes, as though ponder-ing the young child's dangerous future. Though they're lost in thought, their hands instinctively link, tenderly. The white Carrara marble is highly polished, some-thing Michelangelo only did when he was certain he'd got it right.

If you like tombs and church art, pay to wander through the apse. The highlight is the reclining statues marking the tombs of the last local rulers of Bruges, Mary of Burgundy, and her father, Charles the Bold. The dog and lion at their feet are symbols of fidelity and courage.

In 1482, when 25-year-old Mary of Burgundy tumbled from a horse and died, she left behind a toddler son and a husband who was heir to the Holy Roman Empire. Beside her lies her father, Charles the Bold, who also died prematurely, in war. Their twin deaths meant Bruges belonged to Austria, and would soon be swallowed up by the empire. Trade routes shifted, and goods now flowed through Antwerp, then Amsterdam, as Bruges' North Sea port silted up. After these three blows, Bruges began four centuries of economic decline.

To the left of the main altar is a balcony overlooking the altar. It's actually part of the Gruuthuse mansion next door, giving that wealthy noble family a private box seat for Mass.

• *Just across Mariastraat from the church entrance is the entry to the St. Jans Hospital's visitors' center. The entrance to the Memling Museum, which fills that hospital's church, is 20 meters south on Mariastraat.*

Memling Museum

This medieval hospital (newly opened after 2 years of renovation) contains six much-loved paintings by the greatest of the Flemish Primitives, Hans Memling. His *Mystical Wedding of St. Catherine* triptych deserves a close look. Catherine and her "mystical groom," the baby Jesus, are flanked by a headless John the Baptist and a pensive John the Evangelist. The chairs are there so you can study it. If you understand the Book of Revelation, you'll understand St. John's wild and intricate vision. The St. Ursula Shrine, an ornate little mini-church in the same room, is filled with impressive detail. (✪ See Memling Museum Tour, page 262.)

• *Continue south on Mariastraat about 150 meters. Turn right on Walstraat, which leads into the pleasant square called Walplein, where you'll find the . . .*

Straffe Hendrik Brewery Tour

Belgians are Europe's beer connoisseurs. This fun and handy tour is a great way to pay your respects. The happy gang at this working family brewery gives entertaining and informative 45-minute, four-language tours (at De Halve Moon brewpub, Walplein 26, see page 233 for details).

• *From here, the lacy cuteness of Bruges crescendos as you approach the Begijnhof.*

Begijnhof

Begijnhofs (pron. gutturally: buh-HHHINE-hof) were built to house women of the lay order called Beguines, who spent their lives in piety and service (without having to take the same vows a nun would). For military and other reasons, there were more women than men in the medieval Low Countries. The order of Beguines offered women (often single or widowed) a dignified

place to live and work. When the order died out, many Begijnhofs were taken over by towns for subsidized housing, but some, like this one, became homes for nuns.

Tour the simple museum to get a sense

of Beguine life (Begijn's House, left of entry gate, €2 with English explanations, daily 10:00–12:00 & 13:45–17:30, off-season closes at 17:00).

In the church, the rope that dangles from the ceiling is yanked by a nun around 17:15 to announce a sung Vespers service.

• *Exiting opposite the way you entered you'll hook left and see a lake with silver swans ...*

Minnewater

Just south of the Begijnhof is Minnewater, a peaceful lake-filled park with canals, swans, and tour boats. This was once far from quaint—a busy harbor where the small boats shuttled cargo from the big ocean-going ships into town. From this point the cargo was transferred again to flat-bottomed boats that went through the town's canals to their respective warehouses and Market Square.

When locals see these swans they remember the 15th-century mayor—famous for his long neck—who collaborated with the Austrians. The townsfolk beheaded him as a traitor. The Austrians warned them that similarly long-necked swans would inhabit the place to forever remind them of this murder. And they do.

• *You're a five-minute walk from the train station, where you can catch a bus to Market Square, or a 15-minute walk from Market Square—take your pick.*

GROENINGE MUSEUM TOUR

In the 1400s, Bruges was Northern Europe's richest, most cosmopolitan, and cultured city. New ideas, fads, and painting techniques were imported and exported with each shipload. Beautiful paintings were soon an affordable luxury, like fancy clothes or furniture. Internationally known artists set up studios in Bruges, producing portraits and altarpieces for wealthy merchants from all over Europe.

The Groeninge Museum, understandably, has one of the world's best collections of the art produced in the city and surrounding area. This early Flemish art is less appreciated and understood today than the Italian Renaissance art produced a century later. But by selecting about a dozen masterpieces, we'll get an introduction to this subtle, technically advanced, and beautiful style. Hey, if you can master the museum's name (pron. GROON-i-guh), you can certainly handle the art.

Orientation

Cost: €8, includes audioguide.
Hours: Tue–Sun 9:30–17:00, closed Mon.
Getting There: The museum is at Dijver 12, near the Gruuthuse Museum and Church of Our Lady.
Information: Tel. 050-448-751
Length of Our Tour: One hour.

Overview

The included audioguide allows you to wander as you like. Use this chapter as background to the huge collection's highlights, then browse, punching in the numbers of the paintings you'd like to learn more about.

Flemish Primitives

Despite the "primitive" label, the Low Countries of the 1400s (along with Venice and Florence) produced the most refined art in Europe. Here are some common features of Flemish Primitive art:

- **Primitive 3-D perspective:** Expect unnaturally cramped-looking rooms, oddly slanted tables, and flat, cardboard-cutout people with stiff posture. Yes, these works are more primitive (hence the label) than those with the later Italian Renaissance perspective.

- **Realistic:** Everyday bankers and clothmakers in their Sunday best are painted with clinical, warts-and-all precision. Even saints and heavenly visions are brought down to earth.

- **Detailed:** Like meticulous Bruges craftsmen, painters used fine-point brushes to capture almost microscopic details—flower petals, wrinkled foreheads, intricately patterned clothes, the sparkle in a ruby. The closer you get to a painting, the better it looks.

- **Oil painted on wood:** They were the pioneers of new-fangled oil-based paint (while Italy still used egg-yolk tempera), working on wood before canvas became popular.

- **Portraits and altarpieces:** Wealthy merchants and clergymen paid to have themselves painted either alone or mingling with saints.

- **Symbolic:** Since medieval times, everyone understood that a dog symbolized fidelity, a lily meant chastity, and the rose was love.

- **Materialistic:** Rich Flanders celebrated the beauty of luxury goods—the latest Italian dresses, jewels, carpets, oak tables—and the ordinary beauty that radiates from flesh-and-blood people.

Jan van Eyck (c. 1390–1441)—
Virgin and Child with Canon Joris van der Paele (1436)

Jan van Eyck was the world's first and greatest oil painter, and this is his masterpiece—three debatable but defensible assertions.

Mary, in a magnificent red gown, sits playing with her little baby Jesus. Jesus glances up as St. George, the dragon-slaying

knight, enters the room, tips his cap, and says, "I'd like to introduce my namesake, George (Joris)." Mary glances down at the kneeling Joris, a church official dressed in white. Joris takes off his glasses and looks up from his prayerbook to see a bishop in blue, St. Donatian, patron of the church he hopes to be buried in.

Canon Joris, who hired van Eyck, is not a pretty sight. He's old and wrinkled, with a double chin, weird earlobes, and bloodshot eyes. But the portrait isn't unflattering, it just shows unvarnished reality with crystal clarity.

Van Eyck brings Mary and the saints down from heaven and into a typical (rich) Bruges home. He strips off their haloes, banishes all angels, and pulls the plug on heavenly radiance. If this is a religious painting, then where's God?

He's in the details. From the bishop's damask robe and Mary's wispy hair to the folds in Jesus' baby fat and the oriental carpet to "Adonai" (Lord) written on St. George's breastplate, the painting is as complex and beautiful as God's creation. The color scheme—red Mary, white canon, and blue-and-gold saints—are Bruges' city colors, from its coat of arms.

Mary, crowned with a jeweled "halo" and surrounded by beautiful things, makes an appearance in 1400s Bruges, where she can be adored in all her human beauty by Canon Joris...and by us, reflected in the mirror-like shield on St. George's back.

Jan van Eyck—*Portrait of Margareta van Eyck* (1439)

At 35, shortly after moving to Bruges, Jan van Eyck married 20-year-old Margareta. They had two kids, and after Jan died, Margareta took charge of his studio of assistants and kept it running until her death. This portrait (age 33), when paired with a matching self-portrait of Jan, was one of Europe's first husband-and-wife companion sets.

She sits half-turned, looking out of the frame. (Jan might have seen this "Where-have-you-been?" expression in the window, late one night.) She's dressed in a red, fur-lined coat, and we catch a glimpse of her wedding ring. Her hair is invisible—very fashionable at the time—pulled back tightly, bunched into horn-like hairnets, and draped with a headdress. Stray hairs along the perimeter were plucked to achieve the high forehead look.

This simple portrait is revolutionary, being one of history's first individual portraits that wasn't a saint, king, duke, pope, or part of a religious work. It signals the advent of humanism, celebrating the glory of ordinary people. Van Eyck proudly signed the work on the original frame, with his motto saying he painted it *"als ich can"* *(ALC IXH KAN)* ... "as good as I can."

Rogier van der Weyden— *St. Luke Drawing the Virgin's Portrait* (c. 1435–40)

Rogier van der Weyden, the other giant among the Flemish Primitives, adds the human touch to van Eyck's rather detached precision.

As Mary prepares to nurse, baby Jesus can't contain his glee, wiggling his fingers and toes, anticipating lunch. Mary, dressed in everyday clothes, can't hide her love as she tilts her head down, with a proud smile. Meanwhile, St. Luke (the patron saint of painters who was said to have experienced this vision) looks on intently with a sketch pad in his hand, trying to catch the scene. These small gestures, movements, and facial expressions add an element of human emotion that later artists would amplify.

The painting is neatly divided by a spacious view out the window, showing a river stretching off to a spacious horizon. Van der Weyden experimented with 3-D effects like this, though ultimately it's just window-dressing.

Rogier van der Weyden (c. 1399–1464)— *Duke Philip the Good* (c. 1450)

Tall, lean, and elegant, this charismatic Duke transformed Bruges from a commercial powerhouse to a cultural one. In 1425, Philip moved his court to Bruges, making it the de facto capital of a Burgundian empire stretching from Amsterdam to Switzerland.

Philip wears a big hat to hide his hair, a fashion trend he himself set. He's also wearing the gold-chain necklace of the Order of the Golden Fleece, a distinguished knightly honor he gave himself.

Oil Paint

Take vegetable oil pressed from linseeds (flax), blend in dry powdered pigments, whip to a paste the consistency of room-temperature butter, then brush onto a panel of white-washed oak—you're painting in oils. First popularized in the early 1400s, oil eventually overshadowed egg-yolk-based tempera. Though tempera was great for making fine lines shaded with simple blocks of color, oil could blend colors together seamlessly.

Watch a master create a single dog's hair: He paints a dark stroke of brown, then lets it dry. Then comes a second layer painted over it, of translucent orange. The brown shows through, blending with the orange to look the color of a collie. Finally, he applies a third, transparent layer (a "glaze"), giving the collie her healthy sheen.

Many great artists were not necessarily great painters (e.g., Michelangelo). Van Eyck, Rembrandt, Hals, Velázquez, and Rubens were master painters, meticulously building objects with successive layers of paint...but they're not everyone's favorite artists.

He inaugurated the Golden Fleece in a lavish ceremony at the Bruges City Hall, complete with parades, jousting, and festive pies that contained live people hiding inside to surprise his guests.

As a lover of painting, hunting, fine clothes, and many mistresses, Philip was a role model for Italian princes such as Lorenzo the Magnificent—the *uomo universale*, or Renaissance Man.

Petrus Christus (c. 1420–c. 1475)—*Annunciation and Nativity* (1452)

Italian art was soon all the rage. Ships from Genoa and Venice would unload Renaissance paintings, wowing the Northerners with their window-on-the-world 3-D realism. Petrus Christus, one of Jan van Eyck's students, studied the Italian style and set out to conquer space.

The focus of his *Annunciation* panel is not the winged angel announcing Jesus' coming birth, and not the swooning, astonished

Mary—it's the empty space between them. Your eye focuses back across the floor tiles and through the open doorway to gabled houses on a quiet canal in the far distance.

In the *Nativity* panel, the three angels hovering overhead really should be bigger, and the porch over the group looks a little rickety. Compared to the work of Florence's Renaissance painters, this is quite . . . Primitive.

Hugo van der Goes (c. 1442–c. 1482)— *Death of the Virgin* (c. 1481)

The long death watch is over, their beloved Mary has passed on, and the disciples are bleary-eyed and dazed with grief, as though hit with a spiritual two-by-four. Each etched face is a study in sadness, as they all have their own way to cope—lighting a candle, fidgeting, praying, or just staring off into space. Blues and reds dominate, and there's little eye-catching ornamentation, letting the lined faces and expressive hand gestures do the talking.

Hugo van der Goes painted this, his last major work, the same year he attempted suicide. Hugo had built a successful career in Ghent, then abruptly dropped out to join a monastery. His paintings became increasingly emotionally charged, and his personality more troubled.

Above the bed floats a heavenly vision as Jesus and the angels prepare to receive Mary's soul. Their smooth skin and serene expressions contrast with the gritty, wrinkled death pallor on earth. Caught up in their own grief, the disciples can't see the silver lining.

Gerard David (c.1460–1523)— *Judgment of Cambyses* (1498)

That's gotta hurt.

A man is stretched across a table and skinned alive in a very businesslike manner. The crowd hardly notices, and a dog just scratches himself. According to legend, the man was a judge arrested for corruption (left panel) and flayed (right panel),

No Joke

An enthusiastic American teenager approaches the ticket seller at the Groeninge Museum:

"This is the Torture Museum, right?!"

"No," the ticket man replies, "it's art."

"Oh..." mumbles the kid, "art..."

And he walks away, not realizing that, for him, the Groeninge Museum would be torture.

then his skin was draped (right panel background) over the new judge's throne.

Gerard David, Memling's successor as the city's leading artist, painted this for the City Hall. City councilors could ponder what might happen to them if they abused their office.

By David's time, Bruges was in serious decline, with a failing economy and struggles against the powerful Austrian Hapsburg family. The Primitive style was also fading. Italian art was popular, so David tries to spice up his retro-Primitive work with pseudo-Renaissance knickknacks—*putti* (baby angels, over the judgment throne), Roman-style medallions, and garlands. But he couldn't quite master the Italian specialty of 3-D perspective. We view the flayed man at an angle from above, but the table he lies on is shown more from the side.

Attributed to Hieronymous Bosch (c. 1450–1516)— *Last Judgment* (early 16th century)

It's the end of the world, and Christ descends in a bubble to pass judgment on puny humans. Little naked people dance and cavort in a theme park of medieval symbolism, desperately trying to squeeze in their last fun. Meanwhile, some wicked souls are being punished, victims either of their own stupidity or of genetically

engineered demons. The good get sent to the left panel to frolic in the innocence of Paradise, while the rest are damned to Hell (right panel) to be tortured under a burning sky. Bosch paints the scenes with a high horizon line, making it seem that the chaos extends forever.

The bizarre work of Bosch (who, by the way, was not from Bruges) is open to many interpretations, but some see it as a warning for the turbulent times. It was the dawn of a new age. Secular ideas and materialism were encroaching, and the pious and serene medieval world was shattering into chaos.

Jan Provoost (c. 1465–1529)—*Death and the Miser*

A Bruges businessman in his office strikes a deal with Death. The grinning skeleton lays coins on the table, and in return, the

man—looking unhealthy and with fear in his eyes— reaches across the divide in the panels to give Death a promissory note, then marks the transaction in his ledger book. He's trading away a few years of his life for a little more money. The worried man on the right (the artist's self-portrait) says, "Don't do it."

Jan Provoost worked for businessmen like this. He knew their offices, full of money bags, paperwork, and books. Bruges' materialistic capitalism was at odds with Christian poverty, and society was divided over whether to praise or condemn it. Ironically, this painting's flip side is a religious work bought and paid for by...rich merchants.

• *Fast-forward a few centuries, past paintings by no-name artists from Bruges' years of decline, to a couple of Belgium's 20th-century masters.*

Paul Delvaux (1897–1994)— *Serenity* (1970)

Perhaps there's some vague connection between van Eyck's medieval symbols and the surrealist images of Paul Delvaux. Regardless, Delvaux gained fame for his nudes sleepwalking through moonlit video-game landscapes.

René Magritte (1898–1967)— *The Assault* (c. 1932)

Magritte had his own private reserve of symbolic images. The cloudy sky, female torso, windows, and horsebell (the ball with the slit) appear in other works as well. They're arranged here side by side

as if they should mean something, but they—as well as the title—only serve to short-circuit your thoughts when you try to make sense of them. Magritte paints real objects with photographic clarity, then jumbles them together in new and provocative ways.

Scenes of Bruges

Remember, Jan van Eyck, Petrus Christus, Hans Memling, Gerard David, Jan Provoost, and possibly Rogier van der Weyden (for a few years) all lived and worked in Bruges.

In addition, many other artists included scenes of the picturesque city in their art, proving that the city looks today much as it did way back when. Enjoy the many painted scenes of old Bruges as a slice-of-life peek into the city and its people back in its glory days.

MEMLING
MUSEUM
TOUR

Set in the former church of St. Jans Hospital, the Memling Museum displays surgical instruments, documents, and visual aids, offering a glimpse into medieval medicine as you work your way to the museum's climax: several of Memling's glowing masterpieces.

Orientation

Cost: €8, includes fine audioguide.
Hours: Tue–Sun 9:30–17:00, closed Mon.
Getting There: The museum is at Mariastraat 38, across the street from the Church of Our Lady.
Length of Our Tour: One hour.

Overview

Hans Memling's art was the culmination of Bruges' Flemish Primitive style. His serene, soft-focus, motionless scenes capture a medieval piety that was quickly fading. The popular style made Memling (c. 1430–1494) one of Bruges' wealthiest citizens, and his work was gobbled up by visiting Italian merchants, who took them home, cross-pollinating European art.

The displays are all on one floor of the former church, with the Memlings in a chapel at the far end.

The Church As a Hospital

Some 500 years ago, the nave of this former church was lined with beds filled with the sick and dying. Nuns served as nurses. At the far end was the high altar, which once displayed Memling's *St. John Altarpiece* (which we'll see). Bed-ridden patients could gaze on this peaceful, colorful vision and gain a moment's comfort from their agonies.

As the museum displays make clear, medicine of the day was

Some Memling Trademarks

- Serene symmetry, with little motion or emotion
- Serious faces that are realistic but timeless, with blemishes airbrushed out
- Eye-catching details like precious carpets, mirrors, and brocaded clothes
- Glowing colors, even lighting, no shadows
- Cityscape backgrounds

well intentioned but very crude. In many ways, this was less a hospital than a hospice, helping the down-and-out make the transition from this world to the next. Religious art (displayed further along in the museum) was therapeutic, addressing the patients' mental and spiritual health. The  numerous Crucifixions reminded the sufferers that Christ could feel their pain, having lived it himself.

• *Continue on the ground floor through the displays of religious art to the final two rooms, displaying Memling's paintings. A large triptych (three-paneled altarpiece) dominates the room.*

Hans Memling

St. John Altarpiece (also called The Mystical Marriage of St. Catherine)

 Sick and dying patients lay in their beds in the hospital and looked at this colorful, three-part work, which sat atop the hospital/church's high altar (1474). The piece was dedicated to the hospital's patron saints, John the Baptist and John the Evangelist (see the inscription along the bottom frame), but Memling broadened the focus to take in a vision of heaven and the end of the world.

Central Panel: Mary, with baby Jesus on her lap, sits in a canopied chair, crowned by hovering blue angels. It's an imaginary

gathering of conversing saints (*sacra conversazione*), though nobody in this meditative group is saying a word or even exchanging meaningful eye contact.

Mary is flanked by the two Johns—John the Baptist to the left and John the Evangelist (in red) to the right. Everyone else sits symmetrically around Mary. An organist angel to the left is matched by a book-holding acolyte to the right. St. Catherine (left, in white, red, and gold) balances St. Barbara in green, who's absorbed in her book. Behind them, classical columns are also perfectly balanced left and right.

At the center of it all, Jesus tips the still balance by leaning over to place a ring on Catherine's finger, sealing the "mystical marriage" between them.

St. Catherine of Alexandria, born rich, smart, and pagan to Roman parents, joined the outlawed Christian faith. She spoke out against pagan Rome, attracting the attention of the emperor Maxentius, who sent 50 philosophers to talk some sense into her—but she countered every argument, even converting the emperor's own wife. Maxentius killed his wife, then asked Catherine to marry him. She refused, determined to remain true to the man she'd already "married" in a mystical vision—Christ.

Frustrated, Maxentius ordered Catherine to be stretched across a large, spiked wheel (the rather quaint-looking object at her feet), but the wheel flew apart, sparing her and killing many of her torturers. So they just cut her head off, which is why she has a sword along with her "catherine wheel."

Looking through the columns, we see scenes of Bruges. Just to the right of the chair's canopy, the wooden contraption is a crane, used to hoist barrels from barges on Kraanplein.

Left Panel—*The Beheading of John the Baptist:* Even this gruesome scene, with blood still spurting from John's severed neck, becomes serene under Memling's gentle brush. Everyone is solemn, graceful, and emotionless—including both halves of the decapitated John. Memling depicts Salome (in green) receiving the head on

her silver platter with a humble servant's downcast eyes, as if accepting her role in God's wonderful if sometimes painful plan.

In the background left, we can look into Herod's palace, where he sits at a banquet table with his wife while Salome dances modestly in front of him. Herod's lust is only hinted at with the naked statues—a man between two women—that adorn the palace exterior.

Right Panel—*John the Evangelist's Vision of the Apocalypse:* John sits on a high, rocky bluff on the island of Patmos and sees the end of the world as we know it...and he feels fine.

Overhead in a rainbow bubble, God appears on his throne, resting his hand on a sealed book. A lamb steps up to open the seals, unleashing the awful events at the end of time. Standing at the bottom of the rainbow, an angel in green gestures to John and says, "Write this down." John starts to dip his quill into the inkwell (his other hand holds the quill-sharpener), but he pauses, absolutely transfixed, experiencing the Apocalypse now.

He sees wars, fires, and plagues on the horizon, the Virgin in the sky rebuking a red dragon, and many other wonders. Members of millennial cults should bring their Bibles along because there are many specific references brought to life in a literal way.

In the center ride the dreaded Four Horsemen, wreaking havoc on the cosmos (galloping over either islands or clouds). Horseman #4 is a skeleton, followed by a human-eating monster head. Helpless mortals on the right seek shelter in the rocks but find none.

Memling has been criticized for building a career by copying the formulas of his predecessors, but this panel is a complete original. Its theme had never been so fully expressed, and the bright, contrasting colors and vivid imagery are almost modern. In *St. John Altarpiece*, Memling shows us the full range of his palette, from medieval grace to Renaissance symmetry, from the real to the surreal.

• *In a glass case, find the...*

St. Ursula Shrine

On October 21, 1489, the mortal remains of St. Ursula were brought here to the church and placed in this gilded oak shrine, built specially for the occasion and decorated with paintings by Memling. Ursula, yet another Christian martyred by the ancient Romans, became a sensation in the Middle Ages when builders in

Germany's Köln (Cologne) unearthed a huge pile of bones believed to belong to her and her 11,000 slaughtered cohorts.

The shrine, carved of wood and covered with gold, looks like a miniature Gothic Church (similar to the hospital church). Memling was asked to fill in the "church's" stained glass windows with six arch-shaped paintings telling Ursula's well-known legend.

• *Circle counter-clockwise from the room entrance to get the story . . .*

1. Ursula—in white and blue—arrives by boat at the city of Köln and enters through the city gate. She's on a pilgrimage to Rome, accompanied by 11,000 (female) virgins. That night (look in the two windows of the house in the background, right), an angel appears and tells her this trip will mean her death, but she is undaunted.

2. Continuing up the Rhine, they arrive in Basel. (Memling knew the Rhine, having grown up near it.) Memling condenses the 11,000 virgins to a more manageable 11, making each one pure enough for a thousand. From Basel, they set out on foot (in the background, right) over the snowy Alps.

3. They arrive in Rome—formally portrayed by a round Renaissance tower decorated with *putti*—where Ursula falls to her knees before the Pope at the church steps. Kneeling behind Ursula is her fiancé, Etherus, the pagan prince of England. She has agreed to marry him only if he becomes a Christian and refrains from the marriage bed long enough for her to make this three-year pilgrimage as a virgin (making, I guess, number 11,001). Inside the church on the right side, he is baptized a Christian.

4. They head back home. Here, they're leaving Basel, boarding ships to go north on the Rhine. The Pope was so inspired by these virgins that he's joined them. These "crowd" scenes are hardly realistic—more like a collage of individual poses and faces. And Memling tells the story with extremely minimal acting. Perhaps his inspiration was the pomp and ceremony of Bruges parades, introduced by the Burgundian dukes. He would have seen *tableaux vivants*, where Brugeois would pose in costume like human statues to enact an event from the Bible or from city history. (American "living Christmas crèches" carry on this dying art form.)

5. Back in Köln, a surprise awaits them—the city has been taken over by vicious Huns. They grab Etherus and stab him. He dies in Ursula's arms.

6. The Hun king (in red with turban and beard) woos Ursula,

placing his hand over his heart, but she says "No way." So a Hun soldier draws his arrow and prepares to shoot her dead. Even here, at the climax of the story, there are no histrionics. Even the dog just sits down, crosses his paws, and watches. The whole shrine cycle is as posed, motionless, and colorful as the *tableaux vivants* that may have inaugurated the shrine here in this church in 1489.

In the background behind Ursula, a Bruges couple looks on sympathetically. This may be Memling himself (in red coat with fur lining) and his wife, Anna, who bore him three children. Behind them, Memling renders an accurate city skyline of Köln, including a side view of the Köln Cathedral (missing its still-unfinished tall spires).

• *In the small adjoining room, find several more Memlings.*

Portrait of a Young Woman (1480)

Memling's bread-and-butter was portraits done for families of wealthy merchants (especially visiting Italians and Portuguese). This portrait takes us right back to that time.

The young woman looks out the frame as if she were look-ing out a window. Her hands rest on the "sill," with the finger-tips sticking over. The frame is original but the banner and van Eyck–like letter-ing are not.

Her clothes look somewhat simple but were high-class in their day. A dark damask dress is brightened with a red sash and a detachable white collar. She's pulled her hair into a tight bun at the back, pinned there with a fez-like cap, and draped with a transparent veil. She's shaved her hairline and plucked her brows to get that clean, high-forehead look. Her ensemble is animated by a well-placed necklace of small stones.

Memling accentuates her fashionably pale complexion and gives her a pensive, sober expression, portraying her like a medieval saint. Still, she keeps her personality, with distinct features like the broad nose, neck tendons, and realistic hands. She peers out from her subtly painted veil, which sweeps down over the side of her face. What's she thinking?

Diptych of Martin van Nieuwenhove (1489)

Three-dimensional effects—borrowed from the Italian Renaissance style—enliven this traditional two-panel altarpiece. Both Mary-and-Child and the 23-year-old Martin, though in different panels, inhabit the same room.

Stand right in front of Mary, facing her directly. If you line up the paintings' horizons (seen in the distance, out the room's windows), you'll see that

both panels depict the same room—a room with two windows at the back and two along the right wall.

Want proof? In the convex mirror on the back wall (just to the left of Mary), the scene is reflected back at us, showing Mary and Martin from behind, silhouetted in the two "windows" of the picture frames. Apparently, Mary makes house calls, appearing right in the living room of the young donor Martin, the wealthy, unique-looking heir to his father's business.

SLEEPING

€1 = about $1, country code: 32

Most places are located between the train station and the old center, with the most distant (and best) being a few blocks beyond Market Square to the north and east. B&Bs offer the best value (listed after "Hotels"). All include breakfast, are on quiet streets, and (with a few exceptions) keep the same prices throughout the year. Bruges is most crowded Friday and Saturday evenings Easter through October—with July and August weekends being worst.

Bruges is a great place to sleep, with Gothic spires out your window, no traffic noise, and the cheerily out-of-tune carillon heralding each new day at 8:00 sharp. (Thankfully the bell tower is silent from 22:00 to 8:00.)

Hotels

HIGHER PRICED

Hansa Hotel offers 24 rooms in a completely modernized old building. It's tastefully decorated in elegant pastels and has all the amenities. It's a great splurge (standard Db-€130, superior Db-€170, deluxe Db-€210, singles take a double for nearly the same cost, extra bed-€40, suites available, CC, air-con, non-smoking, elevator, free Internet access, sauna, tanning bed, fitness room, bike rental for €6.50/half day, €10/day, Niklaas Desparsstraat 11, a block north of Market Square, tel. 050-444-444, fax 050-444-440, www.hansa.be, e-mail: information @hansa.be, run by cheery and hardworking Johan and Isabelle).

Hotel Egmond is quietly located in the middle of the melancholy Minnewater. Its eight 18th-century rooms have all the comforts (Sb-€102, Db-€120, Tb-€150, no CC, for longer stays ask about their apartments a few blocks away, free parking, Minnewater

Sleep Code

S = Single, D = Double/Twin, T = Triple, Q = Quad,
b = bathroom, s = shower only, CC = Credit Cards accepted,
no CC = Credit Cards not accepted. Everyone speaks English.

To help you easily sort through these listings, I've
divided the rooms into three categories, based on the price
for a standard double room with bath:

Higher Priced—Most rooms €110 or more.
Moderately Priced—Most rooms €75–110.
Lower Priced—Most rooms less than €75.

15, tel. 050-341-445, fax 050-342-940, www.egmond.be, e-mail:
info@egmond.be).

Crowne Plaza Hotel Brugge is the most modern, comfortable, and central hotel option. It's just like a fancy American hotel,
each of its 96 air-conditioned rooms equipped with a magnifying
mirror and trouser press (Db-€225–240, prices drop as low as
€180 on weekdays and off-season, CC, elevator, pool, Burg 10,
tel. 050-446-844, fax 050-446-868, www.crowneplaza.com).

MODERATELY PRICED

Hotel Adornes is small, new, and classy—a great value. It has
20 comfy rooms with full, modern bathrooms in a 17th-century
canalside house, and offers free parking, free loaner bikes, and a
cellar lounge with games and videos (Db-€90–110 depending
upon size, singles take a double for nearly the same cost, Tb-€125,
Qb-€135, CC, elevator, near Van Nevel B&B, mentioned below,
and Carmersstraat at St. Annarei 26, tel. 050-341-336, fax 050-
342-085, www.adornes.be, e-mail: hotel.adornes@proximedia.be,
Nathalie runs the family business, Britt provides a warm welcome).

Hotel Patritius, family-run and centrally located, is a grand
circa-1830 neoclassical mansion with 16 stately rooms, and a plush
lounge and breakfast room (small Db-€85, Db-€90–95, CC,
free parking, Riddersstraat 11, tel. 050-338-454, fax 050-339-634,
www.hotelpatritius.be, e-mail: hotel.patritius@proximedia.be,
Garrett and Elvi Spaey).

Hotel Botaniek has three stars, nine small rooms, and a
quiet location a block from Astrid Park (Db-€92, big Db-€96,
Tb-€105, Qb-€115, 8 percent discount for 3 nights, CC, elevator, Waalsestraat 23, tel. 050-341-424, fax 050-345-939, e-mail:
hotel.botaniek@pi.be).

In a jam you might try these large, well-located hotels of

Bruges Hotels

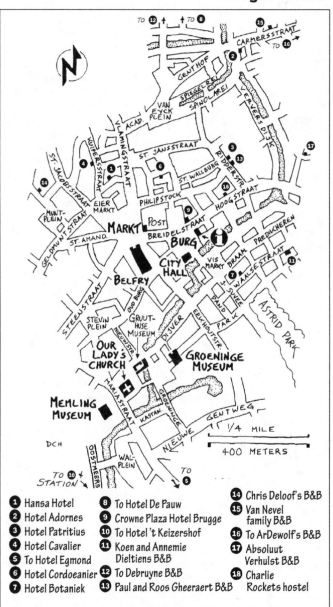

1 Hansa Hotel
2 Hotel Adornes
3 Hotel Patritius
4 Hotel Cavalier
5 To Hotel Egmond
6 Hotel Cordoeanier
7 Hotel Botaniek
8 To Hotel De Pauw
9 Crowne Plaza Hotel Brugge
10 To Hotel 't Keizershof
11 Koen and Annemie Dieltiens B&B
12 To Debruyne B&B
13 Paul and Roos Gheeraert B&B
14 Chris Deloof's B&B
15 Van Nevel family B&B
16 To ArDewolf's B&B
17 Absoluut Verhulst B&B
18 Charlie Rockets hostel

lesser value: **Hotel ter Reien** (26 rooms, Db-€90, Langestraat 1, tel. 050-349-100, e-mail: hotel.ter.reien@online.be) and **Hotel Sablon** (the "oldest hotel in town" with 36 rooms, Db-€110, Noordzandstraat 21, tel. 050-333-902, e-mail: info@sablon.be).

LOWER PRICED
Hotel Cavalier, which has more stairs than character, rents 10 decent rooms and serves a hearty buffet breakfast in a royal setting (Sb-€50–52, Db-€55–62, Tb-€70–75, Qb-€77–82, lofty "back-packers' doubles" on fourth floor-€41 or €46, CC, Kuipersstraat 25, tel. 050-330-207, fax 050-347-199, e-mail: hotel.cavalier @skynet.be, run by friendly Viviane de Clerck).

Hotel Cordoeanier, a family-run place, rents 22 bright, simple, modern rooms on a quiet street two blocks off Market Square (Sb-€52–62, Db-€62–70, Tb-€72–80, Qb-€85, Quint/b-€97, higher prices are for bigger rooms, small groups should ask about holiday house across the street, CC, cheap Internet access, Cordoeanierstraat 16, tel. 050-339-051, fax 050-346-111, www.cordoeanier.be, Kris, Veerle, Guy, and family).

Hotel de Pauw is tall, skinny, and family-run, with straight-forward rooms on a quiet street across from a church (Sb-€50, Db-€68, CC, free and easy street parking or pay garage, Sint Gilliskerkhof 8, tel. 050-337-118, fax 050-345-140, www.hoteldepauw.be, e-mail: info@hoteldepauw.be, Philippe and Hilde).

Near the Train Station: **Hotel 't Keizershof** is a dollhouse of a hotel that lives by its motto, "Spend a night, not a fortune." It's simple and tidy, with seven small, cheery, old-time rooms split between two floors, a shower and toilet on each (S-€25, D-€36, T-€54, Q-€65, no CC, free and easy parking, laundry service-€7.50, Oostmeers 126, a block in front of station, tel. 050-338-728, e-mail: hotel.keizershof@12move.be, Stefaan and Hilde).

Bed-and-Breakfasts
These places, run by people who enjoy their work, offer a better value than hotels. Each is central and offers lots of stairs and three or four doubles you'd pay €100 for in a hotel. Parking is generally easy on the street.

MODERATELY PRICED
Absoluut Verhulst is a modern-feeling B&B in a 400-year-old building (Sb-€50, Db-€75, huge and lofty suite-€93 for 2, €115 for 3, and €125 for 4, no CC, 5-min walk east of Market Square at Verbrand Nieuwland 1, tel. & fax 050-334-515, www .b-bverhulst.com, Frieda and Benno).

LOWER PRICED

Koen and Annemie Dieltiens are a friendly couple who enjoy getting to know their guests and sharing a wealth of information on Bruges. You'll eat a hearty breakfast around a big table in their bright, comfortable, newly renovated house (Sb-€50, Db-€55, Tb-€75, 1-night stays pay €10 extra per room, no CC, non-smoking, Waalse Straat 40, 3 blocks southeast of Burg Square, tel. 050-334-294, fax 050-335-230, http://users.skynet.be/dieltiens, e-mail: koen.dieltiens@skynet.be). The Dieltiens also rent a cozy studio and apartment for 2–6 people in a nearby 17th-century house (2 people pay €350 per week for studio, €400 per week for apartment, prices higher for shorter stays and more people, 20 percent cheaper off-season).

Debruyne B&B, run by Marie-Rose and her architect husband, Ronny, offers artsy, original decor (check out the elephant-sized doors—Ronny's design) and genuine warmth. If the Gothic is getting medieval, this is refreshingly modern (Sb-€45, Db-€50, Tb-€65, 1-night stay-€7.50 extra per room, no CC, non-smoking, 5-min walk north of Market Square, Lange Raamstraat 18, tel. 050-347-606, fax 050-340-285, www.bedandbreakfastbruges.com).

Paul and Roos Gheeraert live on the first floor, while their guests take the second. This neoclassical mansion with big, bright, comfy rooms is another fine value (Sb-€45, Db-€50, Tb-€70, no CC, strictly non-smoking; rooms have coffeemakers, TVs, and fridges; Riddersstraat 9, 4-min walk east of Market Square, tel. 050-335-627, fax 050-345-201, http://users.skynet.be/brugge -gheeraert, e-mail: gheeraert.brugge @skynet.be). They also rent three modern, fully equipped apartments and a large loft nearby (3-night minimum).

Chris Deloof's big, homey rooms are a good bet in the old center. Check out the fun, lofty A-frame room upstairs (Sb-€50, Ds/Db-€53, pleasant breakfast room and a royal lounge, no CC, non-smoking, Geerwiynstraat 14, tel. 050-340-544, fax 050-343-721, www.sin.be/chrisdeloof, e-mail: chris.deloof@pi.be). Chris also rents a nearby apartment (Qb-€70–80) and a holiday house for a family or group of up to five (€100–150).

The **Van Nevel family** rents three attractive top-floor rooms with built-in beds in a 16th-century house (D-€45–55, Ds-€60, third person pays €17, CC but cash preferred, non-smoking, 10-min walk from Market Square, or bus #4 or #8 from train station or Market Square to Carmersbridge, Carmersstraat 13, tel. 050-346-860, fax 050-347-616, http://home.tiscali.be/rvanneve, e-mail: Robert.VanNevel@advalvas.be). Robert, who works at the Memling Museum, enthusiastically shares the culture and history of Bruges with his guests.

ArDewolf's B&B is a family-friendly place warmly run by Nicole and Arnold in a stately, quiet neighborhood at the edge of the old town near the windmills and moat (S-€30, D-€35–37, T-€50, Q-€60, Quint-€70, no CC, Oostproosse 9, tel. 050-338-366, www.ardewolf.be). From the train station, take bus #4 to Sasplein. Walk to the path behind the first windmill and turn left on Oostproosse.

Hostels

Bruges has several good hostels offering beds for around €10–12 in two- to eight-bed rooms (singles go for about €15). Breakfast is about €3 extra. The American-style **Charlie Rockets** bar and hostel is the liveliest and most central (56 beds, €13 per bed, 2–6 per room, no CC, Hoogstraat 19, tel. 050-330-660, fax 050-343-630, www.charlierockets.com). The dull **Snuffel Travelers Inn** (Ezelstraat 47, tel. 050-333-133) and the funky **Passage** (Dweerstraat 26, tel. 050-340-232; its hotel next door rents €40 doubles) are both small, loose, and central.

EATING

Belgium is where France meets the North, and you'll find a good mix of both Flemish and French influences in Bruges and Brussels.

Belgian Specialties
These are popular throughout Belgium.

Moules: Mussels are served everywhere, either cooked plain *(nature)*, with white wine *(vin blanc)*, with shallots or onions *(marinière)*, or in a tomato sauce *(provençale)*. You get a big-enough-for-two bucket and a pile of fries. Go local by using one empty shell to tweeze out the rest of the *moules.* When the mollusks are in season, from about mid-July through April, you'll get the big Dutch mussels. Locals take a break in May and June, when only the puny Danish kind is available.

Frites: Belgian fries (*Vlaamse frites,* or Flemish fries) taste so good because they're deep-fried twice—once to cook, and once to brown. The natives eat them with mayonnaise, not ketchup.

Flemish Specialties
These specialties are traditional to Bruges, but available in Brussels.

Carbonnade: Rich beef stew flavored with onions and beer.
Chou rouge à la flamande: Red cabbage with onions and prunes.
Flamiche: Cheese pie with onions.
Flemish asparagus: White asparagus (fresh in springtime) in cream sauce.
Lapin à la flamande: Marinated rabbit braised in onions and prunes.
Soupe à la bière: Beer soup.
Stoemp: Mashed potatoes and vegetables.
Waterzooi: Creamy meat stew (chicken, eel, or fish).
...à la flamande: Anything cooked in the local Flemish style.

Brussels Specialties

These specialties are "native" to Brussels (which tends toward French cuisine), but you'll find them in Bruges, too.

Anguilles au vert: Eel in green herb sauce.

Caricoles: Sea snails. Very local and seasonal and hard to find, these usually are sold hot by street vendors.

Cheeses: Remoudou and Djotte de Nivelles are made locally.

Choux de Bruxelles: Brussels sprouts (in cream sauce).

Crevettes: Shrimp, often served as croquettes (minced and stuffed in breaded, deep-fried rolls).

Croque Monsieur: Grilled ham and cheese sandwich.

Endive: Typical Belgian vegetable (also called *chicoree* or *chicon*) served as a side dish.

Filet Américain: Beware, for some reason steak tartare (raw) is called American.

Tartine de fromage blanc: Open-face cream-cheese sandwich, often enjoyed with a cherry Kriek beer.

...à la brabançonne: Anything cooked in the local Brabant (Brussels) style, such as *faisant (*pheasant) *à la brabançonne.*

Desserts and Snacks

Gaufres: Waffles, sold hot in small shops.

Dame blanche: Hot fudge sundae.

Spekuloos: Spicy gingerbread biscuits, served with coffee.

Pralines: Belgian filled chocolates.

Pistolets: Round croissants.

Cramique: Currant roll.

Craquelin: Currant roll with sugar sprinkles.

Belgian Beers

Belgians drink 32 gallons of beer per person per year. Belgium has about 350 different varieties of beer, more than any other country. Even connoisseurs can be confused by the choices. You probably won't like every kind you try, since some Belgian beers don't even taste like beer. They're generally yeastier and higher in alcohol than beers in other countries.

Here's a breakdown of beers, with some common brand names you'll find either on tap or in bottles. This list is just a start, and you'll find many beers that don't fall into these neat categories.

Lagers: Light, sparkling Budweiser-type beers (Jupiler, Stella-Artois, Maes).

Lambics: Perhaps the most unusual and least beer-like, *lambics* are stored for years in wooden casks, fermenting from wild yeasts that occur naturally in the air. Tasting more like a dry and bitter cider or champagne, pure *lambic* is often blended with fruits or herbs to improve the taste. Local homebrewed *lambics*—such as *gueuze, faro, lambic doux,* and *lambic blanche*—are on tap in old cafés. Only *gueuze* is sold commercially in bottles.

Fruit *lambics:* Pure *lambic* is mixed with cherries *(kriek)*, raspberries *(frambozen)*, or other fruits. The result is tart, like a dry pink champagne.

White *(Witte):* Beers based on wheat (not hops), these are milky-yellow summertime beers, often served with a lemon slice. They're similar to a Hefeweizen in the United States, but yeastier (Hoegaarden is a common brand).

Trappist beers: Made by real monks, these use the *méthode champenoise,* which entails two fermentations (by either starting with a mix of young and old yeasts, or by adding more yeast after an initial fermentation). Because the second fermentation occurs in thebottle, Trappist beers are generally found only in bottles. A Trappist single denotes an amber-colored ale; *dubbel* is stronger and dark brown; and triple is pale and very strong. Try Westmalle Single/Dubbel/Triple or Chimay Red/Blue/White. For all the details on the art of Trappist beers, check out this amazing Web site: http://perso.wanadoo.fr/cyril.pagniez/trappist.htm.

Ales (Blonde/Red/Amber/Brown): This catch-all term tries to describe the enormous variety of Belgium's other beers, best recognized by their color. Try a blonde or golden ale (Leffe Blonde, Duvel, Straffe Hendrik, Kwak), a rare and bitter red (Rodenbach), an amber (Palm, De Koninck), or a brown (Leffe Bruin).

Most beers come with their own special glass. Whether wide-mouthed, tall and fluted, or with or without a stem, the glass is meant to highlight the beer's qualities. Many Belgians are offended if served, say, a Duvel in a pint glass or a *witte* beer in a stemmed glass. One of my favorite Belgian beer experiences is drinking a Kwak beer in its traditional tall glass. The glass, which widens at the base, stands in a wooden holder, and you pick the whole apparatus up—frame and glass—and drink. As you near the end, the beer in the wide bottom comes out at you quickly, with a "Kwak! Kwak! Kwak!"

Restaurants in Bruges

Bruges' specialties include mussels cooked a variety of ways (one order can feed two), fish dishes, grilled meats, and french fries. Don't eat before 19:30 unless you like eating alone. Tax and service are always included.

You'll find plenty of affordable, touristy restaurants on flood-lit squares and along dreamy canals. Bruges feeds 3.5 million tourists a year, and most are seduced by a high-profile location. These can be fine experiences for the magical setting and views,

Bruges Restaurants

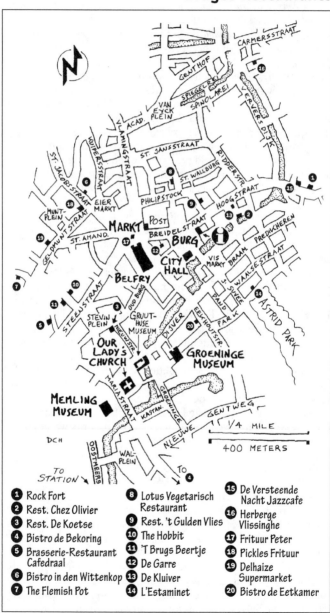

1. Rock Fort
2. Rest. Chez Olivier
3. Rest. De Koetse
4. Bistro de Bekoring
5. Brasserie-Restaurant Cafedraal
6. Bistro in den Wittenkop
7. The Flemish Pot
8. Lotus Vegetarisch Restaurant
9. Rest. 't Gulden Vlies
10. The Hobbit
11. 'T Brugs Beertje
12. De Garre
13. De Kluiver
14. L'Estaminet
15. De Versteende Nacht Jazzcafe
16. Herberge Vlissinghe
17. Frituur Peter
18. Pickles Frituur
19. Delhaize Supermarket
20. Bistro de Eetkamer

but the quality of food and service is low. I wouldn't blame you for eating at one of these places, but I won't recommend any. I prefer the candle-cool bistros that flicker on back streets.

Rock Fort is a chic new eight-table place with a modern, fresh coziness and a high-powered respect for good food. Two young chefs (Peter and Hermes) give their French cuisine a creative twist, and after just a few months in business became the talk of the town (€10 Mon–Fri lunch special with coffee, €15–20 beautifully presented dinner plates, Thu–Tue 12:00–14:30 & 18:00–23:00, closed Wed and at lunch on Sun, great pastas and salads, reservations smart for dinner, Langestraat 15, tel. 050-334-113).

Restaurant Chez Olivier—a classy, white-tablecloth, 10-table place—is considered the best fancy French cuisine splurge in town. While delicate Anne serves, her French husband, Olivier, is busy cooking up whatever he found freshest that day. While you can order à la carte, it's wise to go with the recommended daily menu (3-course lunch €35, 4-course dinner-€50, wine adds €20, 12:00–13:30 & 19:00–21:30, closed Sun and Thu, reserve for dinner, Meestraat 9, tel. 050-333-659).

Restaurant de Koetse is a good bet for central, affordable, quality local-style food. The ambience is traditional, yet fun and kid-friendly. The cuisine is Belgian and French with a stress on grilled meat, seafood, and mussels (3-course meals for €25, €20 plates include vegetables and a salad, Fri–Wed 12:00–15:00 & 18:00–22:00, closed Thu, smoke-free section, wheelchair accessible, Oude Burg 31, tel. 050-337-680).

Bistro de Eetkamer (the Living Room) is an intimate eight-table place offering stay-awhile elegance, uppity service, and fine French/Italian cuisine—but only to those with a reservation (fine 4-course €40 menu, Thu–Mon 12:00–14:00 & 18:30–22:00, closed Tue–Wed, just south of Market Square, Eekhout 6, tel. 050-337-886).

Bistro de Bekoring—a cute candlelit Gothic place—is tucked within two almshouses that were joined together. Rotund and friendly Chef Roland and his wife Gerda love serving traditional Flemish food from a small menu (€30 dinners, Wed–Sat open from 12:00 and from 18:30, closed Sun–Tue, out past Begijnhof at Arsenaalstraat 53, tel. 050-344-157).

Brasserie-Restaurant Cafedraal is boisterous and fun-loving, serving a local crowd good-quality modern European cuisine with the accent on French and fish. The high-ceilinged room is rustic but elegantly candlelit and the back bar sparkles in a brown way (€10 2-course lunches, €24 dinner plates, Tue–Sat 12:00–15:00 & 18:00–23:00, closed Sun–Mon, Zilverstraat 38, tel. 050-340-845).

Bistro in den Wittenkop, very Flemish, is a cluttered, laid-back, old-time place specializing in the beer-soaked equivalent of beef Bourguignon (€12–17 main courses, Tue–Sat 18:00–24:00, closed Sun–Mon, terrace in back, Sint Jakobsstraat 14, tel. 050-332-059).

The Flemish Pot (a.k.a. The Little Pancake House) is a cute restaurant serving delicious, inexpensive pancake meals (savory and sweet) and homemade *wafels* for lunch. Then at 18:00, enthusiastic chefs Mario and Rik stow their waffle irons and pull out a traditional menu of vintage Flemish plates (good €15 dinner menu, daily 10:00–22:00, just off Geldmuntstraat at Helmstraat 3, tel. 050-340-086).

Lotus Vegetarisch Restaurant serves good vegetarian lunch plates (€8 plat du jour offered daily) and salads in a smoke-free, pastel-elegant setting without a trace of tie-dye (Mon–Sat 11:45–14:00, closed Sun, just off Burg at Wapenmakersstraat 5, tel. 050-331-078).

Restaurant 't Gulden Vlies—romantic and candlelit, quiet and less "ye olde" than the other places—serves when the others are closed. The menu is Belgian and French with a creative twist (€16 plates, €25 monthly menu, Wed–Sun 19:00–03:00, closed Mon–Tue, Mallebergplaats 17, tel. 050-334-709).

The Hobbit is a popular grill house across the street from the recommended bar 't Brugs Berrtje (listed below). It features an entertaining menu, including all-you-can-eat spareribs with salad for €13—nothing fancy, just good basic food in a fun traditional setting (daily 18:00–24:00, Kemelstraat 8–10, tel. 050-201-827).

Bars Offering Light Meals, Beer, and Ambience

Stop into one of the city's atmospheric bars for a light meal or a drink with great Bruges ambience. Straffe Hendrik (Strong Henry), a potent and refreshing local brew, is—even to a Bud Lite kind of guy—obviously great beer. Among the more unusual to try: Dentergems (with coriander and orange peel) and Trappist (a malty, usually dark, monk-made beer). Non–beer drinkers enjoy Kriek (a cherry-flavored beer) and Frambozen Bier (raspberry-flavored beer). For more on beer, see page 276.

Any pub or restaurant carries the basic beers, but for a selection of more than 300 types, including brews to suit any season, drink at **'t Brugs Beertje.** For a light meal, consider their traditional cheese plate (Thu–Tue 16:00–24:00, closed Wed, Kemelstraat 5, tel. 050-339-616).

Another good place to gain an appreciation of the Belgian beer culture is **de Garre.** Rather than a noisy pub scene, it has a more dressy sit-down-and-focus-on-your-friend-and-the-fine-beer ambience (huge selection, off Breidelstraat, between Burg and Markt, on tiny Garre alley, daily 12:00–24:00, tel. 050-341-029).

De Kluiver is a lost-at-sea pub serving hot snacks, light €10 meals, and great sea snails in spiced bouillon *(warme wulken)* all simmered in a whispering jazz ambience (Wed–Mon 18:00–24:00, closed Tue, Hoogstraat 12, tel. 050-338-927).

L'Estaminet is a youthful, trendy, jazz-filled eatery. Away from the tourists, it's popular with local students who come for hearty €6 spaghetti (11:30–24:00, closed Mon afternoon and all day Thu, facing peaceful Astrid Park at Park 5, tel. 050-330-916).

De Versteende Nacht Jazzcafe is another popular young hangout serving vegetarian dishes, salads, and pastas on Langestraat 11 (€12.50 meals, Tue–Thu 19:00–24:00, Fri–Sat 18:00–24:00, closed Sun–Mon, live jazz on Wed from 21:00, tel. 050-343-293).

Herberge Vlissinghe, the oldest pub in town (1515), serves hot snacks in a great atmosphere (Wed–Sun open from 11:00 on, closed Mon–Tue, Blekersstraat 2, tel. 050-343-737).

Fries, Fast Food, and Picnics

Local french fries *(frites)* are a treat. Proud and traditional *frituurs* serve tubs of fries and various local-style shish kebabs. Belgians dip their *frites* in mayonnaise, but ketchup is there for the Yankees (along with spicier sauces). For a quick, cheap, and scenic meal, hit a *frituur* and sit on the steps or benches overlooking Market Square, about 50 meters past the post office. The best fries in town are from **Frituur Peter**—twin take-away carts on the Market Square at the base of the bell tower (daily 10:00–24:00).

Pickles Frituur, a block off Market Square, is handy for sit-down fries. Run by Marleen, its forte is greasy, fast, deep-fried Flemish corn dogs. The "menu 2" comes with three traditional gut bombs (Mon–Sat 11:00–24:00, at the corner of Geldmuntstraat and Sint Jakobstraat, tel. 050-337-957).

Delhaize Supermarket is great for picnics (push-button produce pricer lets you buy as little as one mushroom, Mon–Sat 9:00–18:30, Fri until 19:00, closed Sun, 3 blocks off the Market Square on Geldmuntstraat). The small **Delhaize grocery** is on Market Square opposite the bell tower (Mon–Sat 9:00–12:00 & 14:00–18:00, Sun 14:00–18:00). For midnight munchies, you'll find Indian-run corner grocery stores.

Belgian Waffles

While Americans think of "Belgian" waffles for breakfast, the Belgians (who don't eat waffles or pancakes for breakfast) think of *wafels* as Liège-style (dense, sweet, eaten plain, and heated up) and Brussels-style (lighter, often with powdered sugar or whipped cream and fruit, served in teahouses only in the afternoons from 14:00–18:00). You'll see waffles sold at restaurants and take-away stands.

For good €1.50 Liège-style *wafels*, stop by **Tea-Room Laurent** (Steenstraat 79) or **Restaurant Hennon** (between Market Square and Burg at Breidelstraat 16).

BRUSSELS

ORIENTATION

Six hundred years ago, Brussels was just a nice place to stop and buy a waffle on the way to Bruges. With no strategic importance, it was allowed to grow as a free trading town. Today it's a city of 1.25 million, the capital of Belgium, the center of the European Union, and the headquarters of NATO.

The Bruxelloise are cultured and genteel, even a bit snobby. As the unofficial capital of Europe, the city is very multicultural, featuring a variety of restaurants and hosting businessmen from around the world.

Brussels enjoyed a Golden Age of peace and prosperity (1400–1550) while England and France were duking it out in the Hundred Years' War. It was then that many of the fine structures that distinguish the city today were built. In the 1800s, Brussels had another growth spurt, fueled by industrialization, exploited wealth from the Belgian Congo, and the exhilaration of the country's recent independence (1830).

Brussels speaks French. Bone up on *bonjour* and *s'il vous plaît*. Though the city (and country) are officially bilingual and filled with foreign visitors, 80 percent of the locals speak French first and English second. Language aside, the whole feel of the town is urban French, not rural Flemish.

Because Brussels sits smack-dab between Belgium's two linguistic groups (60 percent of Belgians speak Flemish, 40 percent speak French), most of Brussels' street signs and maps are in both languages. In this chapter, generally French names are used.

Tourists zipping from Amsterdam to Paris by train usually miss Brussels, but its rich, chocolaty mix of food and culture pleasantly surprise those who stop.

Orientation

Central Brussels is defined by a ring of roads (which replaced the old city wall) called the Pentagon. All hotels and nearly all the sights I mention are within this circle. The epicenter holds the main square (the Grand Place), TI, and Central Station (all within 3 blocks of each other).

What isn't so apparent from maps is that Brussels is a city divided by gravity. A ridgeline running north–south splits the town into the Upper Town (east half, elevation 60 meters/ 200 feet) and Lower Town (west). The Upper Town, traditionally the home of nobility and the rich, has big marble palaces, broad boulevards, and the major museums. The Lower Town, with the Grand Place, narrow streets, old buildings, modern shops, colorful eateries, and little boys peeing, has more character.

Outside the pentagon- (or heart-) shaped center, sprawling suburbs contain some tourist attractions (the Atomium, EU headquarters, and Parc Cinquantenaire with the auto and military museums).

Planning Your Time

Brussels is low on great sights and high on ambience. On a quick trip, a day and a night are enough for a good first taste. It could even be done as a day trip by train from Bruges (2/hr, 60 min) or a stopover on the Amsterdam–Paris or Amsterdam–Bruges ride (hrly trains). The main reason to stop—the Grand Place (Grote Markt in Flemish)—takes only a few minutes to see. With very limited time, skip the indoor sights and enjoy a coffee or a beer on the square.

Even travelers not "into art" can spend a couple of enjoyable hours at Brussels' Ancient and Modern Art Museums, and even the tone-deaf can appreciate the Musical Instruments Museum. To see the auto and military museums (side by side), plan on a three-hour excursion from the town center.

If you're in Brussels on a Monday, when most sights are closed, consider Autoworld, Atomium, shopping, a walking tour, or a minibus tour. Most important, this is a city to browse and wander.

Tourist Information

Although the office at rue du Marché-aux-Herbes 63 is for all of Belgium, it does Brussels just fine (July–Aug daily 9:00–19:00; Sept– June Mon–Fri 9:00–18:00, Sat–Sun 9:00–13:00 & 14:00–18:00, Jan–March closed Sun afternoon, downhill 3 blocks from Central Station, tel. 02-504-0390; two fun Europe stores are across the street). Another TI is in the City Hall in the Grand Place (daily 9:00–18:00, closed Sun off-season, tel. 02-513-8940).

Brussels Overview

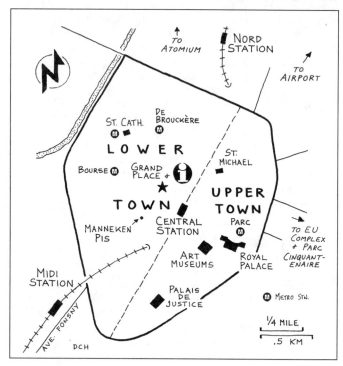

Among the TIs' countless fliers, pick up "Brussels: Yours to Discover," the weekly *What's On*, a city map, and a public transit map. The €2 "Brussels Guide & Map" booklet is worthwhile if you want a series of neighborhood walks and a more complete explanation of the city's many museums. If your next destination is Bruges, get your Bruges information here (and save a euro).

Helpful Hints

Theft Alert: As the unofficial capital of a united Europe, Brussels is on the rise. Unfortunately so is its violent crime rate. Muggings do occur. Some locals warn that it's not safe to be out late, especially after the Métro shuts down at midnight; trouble-makers prey on people who missed that last ride. As in any other big city, use common sense and consider taking a taxi back to your hotel at night (try Taxi Bleu, tel. 02-268-0000).

Travel Agency and Discount Flights: The Usit Agency has a line on the cheapest transportation connections—plane, boat, and train—which they book for a €7 fee (Mon–Fri 9:30 –18:30, Sat 10:00–16:00, closed Sun, Rue du Midi 19, tel. 02-550-0100, www.connections.be).

Internet Access: While there are many small Internet cafés and many hotels let customers get online, the dominant place is easyInternet café on Place de Brouckere (open all day, every day).

Arrival in Brussels

By Train: Brussels can't decide which of its three stations (Central, Nord, and Midi) is the main one. Most international trains leave and arrive at the Nord and Midi Stations. The Eurostar leaves from the Midi Station (also called Zuid or South), getting you to London in three hours. The area around the Midi Station is a rough-and-tumble immigrant neighborhood (with a towering Ferris wheel); the area around the Nord Station is a seedy red light district.

The Central Station has handy services (grocery store, fast food, luggage storage, waiting rooms, and so on) and is nearest to the sights and recommended hotels. Normally only Belgian and Amsterdam trains stop at Central. (Don't assume your train stops at more than one station; ask your conductor.)

If you arrive at Nord or Midi, take a connecting train to Central Station. Trains zip under the city, connecting all three stations every two minutes or so. It's an easy three-minute chore to connect from Nord or Midi to Central. You technically must buy a €1.40 ticket (or use your railpass) to go between Brussels' stations, but the conductors rarely check. As you wait on the platform for your train, look at the track notice board that tells which train is approaching. They zip in and out constantly. Anxious travelers, who think their train has arrived early, often board the wrong train on the right track.

Once you're at Central Station, you can get to the Grand Place by walking downhill from the station (through the arch in Le Meridien Hôtel, across the street) and turning right in front of the church; after a block, you'll reach a small square with a fountain. For the Grand Place, turn left at the far end of the square (at rue de la Colline); for the TI, continue straight past the square for one block. For the restaurant streets, take the first right (an alley) past the TI (see Eating in Brussels, page 330).

By Plane: Shuttle trains run between the three stations (Midi, Central, and Nord) and Brussels International Airport, 14 kilometers away (€2.35, 4/hr, 25 min). The airport–city shuttle bus is less convenient but free for those purchasing a city transit pass. Figure on spending €25 for a taxi to or from the airport. Airport info: tel. 0900/70-000.

French Phrases

Though many people in Brussels speak English, it's helpful to know some French phrases. (When using the phonetics, try to nasalize the "n" sound.)

Good day.	**Bonjour.**	bohn-ZHOOR
Mrs.	**Madame**	mah-DAHM
Mr.	**Monsieur**	muhs-YUR
Please?	**S'il vous plaît?**	see voo play
Thank you.	**Merci.**	mehr-SEE
You're welcome.	**De rien.**	duh ree-AHN
Excuse me?	**Pardon?**	par-DOHN
Yes. / No.	**Oui. / Non.**	wee / nohn
Okay.	**D'accord.**	dah-KOR
Cheers!	**Santé!**	sahn-TAY
Goodbye.	**Au revoir.**	oh vwahr
women / men	**dames / hommes**	dahm / ohm
one / two / three	**un / deux / trois**	uhn / duh / twah
Do you speak English?	**Parlez-vous anglais?**	PAR-lay voo ahn-GLAY

Getting around Brussels

Most of central Brussels' sights are walkable. But public transport is handy for connecting the train stations, climbing to the Upper Town, or visiting sights outside the central core. Those staying in hotels northwest of the Grand Place have good access to the Métro system at the De Brouckere and Ste. Catherine stops.

By Métro, Tram, Train, and Bus: A single €1.40 ticket is good for one hour on all public transportation—Métro, buses, trams, and even trains shuttling between the three train stations (notice the time when you first stamp it; buy tickets on bus or at Métro stations). Deals are available at TIs, newsstands, and Métro stations (10 tickets/€9). TIs also sell a one-day pass for €3.60 (cheaper than 3 tickets, transit info: tel. 02-515-2000. The TI's free "Métro Tram Bus Plan" is excellent.

Near the Grand Place are two transportation hubs—the Central Station and Bourse. Helpful buses #95 and #96 depart from the Bourse for the Upper Town.

Convenient taxi stands are at the Bourse (near Grand Place) and Sablon Square (in the Upper Town).

To reach sights outside the central core—such as Atomium

and Autoworld—take the Métro or a hop-on, hop-off tour bus from Central Station.

By Taxi: Cabbies charge a €2.50 drop fee, then €1 per kilometer. After 22:00, you'll be hit with a €2 surcharge.

Tours of Brussels

De Boeck's Brussels Hop-on, Hop-off Bus—This bus makes a 90-minute, 14-stop circuit (including the corny Atomium), allowing you to hop off, see a sight, and catch a later bus (€12.50/ 48 hrs, includes discounts to various sights, daily 10:00–16:00, until 17:00 July–Aug, departs Central Station every half hour at :00 and :30, headphone narration, tel. 02-513-7744, www .brussels-city-tours.com).

De Boeck's City Tours—This typical three-hour, guided (up to five languages) bus tour provides the handiest way to get the grand perspective on Brussels. You'll start with a walk around the Grand Place, then jump on a tour bus (€19, April–Oct daily at 10:00, 11:00, and 14:00, Nov–March daily at 10:00 and 14:00, depart from their office a block off Grand Place at rue de la Colline 8, can buy tickets there or at TI, tel. 02-513-7744). You'll actually get out at a lace workshop (shopping stop) and the Atomium.

Red Bus Tours—This is the only outfit giving De Boeck any competition. They offer 90-minute city tours hourly from 10:00 to 18:00, leaving from in front of the Central Station (€12, you stay on bus, recorded narration in whatever language you like).

Private Guide—Claude Janssens is good (€85/half-day, €160/ day, cellular 0485-025-423, e-mail: claude.janssens@pandora.be).

SIGHTS

Sights—Grand Place

✪ Brussels' Grand Place area sights, listed briefly below, are described in more detail in the Grand Place Walk, page 297.

▲▲▲**Grand Place**—Brussels' main square, aptly called Grand Place (pron. grahn plahs), is the heart of the old town and Brussels' greatest sight. Any time of day, it's worth swinging by to see what's going on. Concerts, flower markets, sound-and-light shows, endless people watching—it entertains (as do the streets around it). In mid-August during the Flower Festival, the square will be carpeted with 600,000 flowers.

The museums on the square are well advertised but dull. The **Hôtel de Ville,** or City Hall, with the tallest spire, is the square's centerpiece but no big deal to see (€2.50, visits only by 30-min tours, April–Sept Tue–Wed at 15:15, Sun at 12:15; Oct–March Tue–Wed at 15:15, no Sun tour). Opposite the City Museum is the **Brewery Museum,** with one room of old brewing paraphernalia and one room of new (all explained in Flemish and French). It's pretty lame . . . but a good excuse for a beer (€3 includes an unnamed local beer, daily 10:00–17:00, sometimes open later July–Sept, Grand Place 10). The **Museum of Cocoa and Chocolate,** next door, is a delightful concept. But at €5 for a meager set of displays, a second-rate video, a look at a "chocolate master" at work, and a choco-sample, it's way overpriced (Tue–Sun 10:00–17:00, last entry 16:30, closed Mon, Grand Place 13).

▲**Chocolate on Grand Place**—For many, the best thing about Grand Place is chocolate at one of the four venerable chocolate shops: Godiva, Neuhaus, Galler, and Leonidas. Each has inviting displays and sell mixes of 100 grams (your choice of 6–8 pieces) or individual pieces for less than €1. It takes a lot of sampling to judge. See the choco-crawl described in the Grand Place Walk (page 297).

Brussels Sights

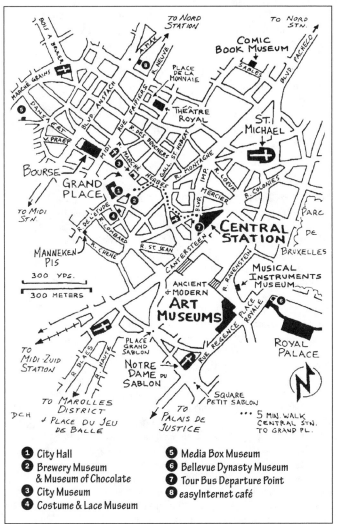

1 City Hall
2 Brewery Museum & Museum of Chocolate
3 City Museum
4 Costume & Lace Museum
5 Media Box Museum
6 Bellevue Dynasty Museum
7 Tour Bus Departure Point
8 easyInternet café

▲**City Museum**—This museum, opposite City Hall, is in a neo-Gothic building (1875) called the "King's House" (in which no king ever lived). The top floor has an enjoyable room full of costumes the *Manneken* statue has dampened, the middle floor features maps and models of old Brussels, and the bottom floor has some tapestries and paintings (€2.50, Tue–Fri 10:00–17:00, Sat–Sun 10:00–13:00, closed Mon, tel. 02-279 43 50).

Manneken-Pis—Brussels is a great city, but its mascot (apparently symbolizing the city's irreverence and love of the good life) is a statue of a little boy urinating. Read up on his story at any post-card stand. It's three short blocks off Grand Place, but, for exact directions, I'll let you ask a local, *"Où est le Manneken-Pis?"* The little squirt may be wearing some clever outfit, as costumes are sent to Brussels from around the world. Cases full of these are on display in the City Museum (described above).

Costume and Lace Museum—This is worthwhile only to those who have devoted their lives to the making of lace (€2.50, Mon–Tue and Thu–Fri 10:00–12:30 & 13:30–17:00, Sat–Sun 14:00–16:30, closed Wed, Violette 6, a block off Grand Place, tel. 02-512-7709).

Media Box Museum—This tiny new museum is dedicated to helping people better understand the power of the media that permeates society in Europe as well as the United States. The exhibit changes twice a year to be timely, covering the September 11 attacks, the World Cup, elections, and so on (€2–5 depending upon how long you stay, Tue–Sat 14:00–18:00, closed Sun–Mon, rue du Chartreux 25, near the Bourse).

Sights—Upper Town

✪ Brussels' grandiose Upper Town, with its huge palace, is described in the Upper Town Walk, page 308. Along that walk, you'll pass these next three sights.

▲▲▲**Ancient and Modern Art Museums**—These are two separate museums, connected by a tunnel and covered by the same €5 ticket (enter either through the main foyer). The Ancient Art museum, featuring Flemish and Belgian art of the 14th–18th centuries, is packed with a dazzling collection of masterpieces by van der Weyden, Breughel, Bosch, and Rubens. The Museum of Modern Art gives an easy-to-enjoy walk through the art of the 19th and 20th centuries from neoclassical to surrealism (Tue–Sun 10:00–17:00, closed Mon, half the rooms close for lunch 12:00–13:00, the other half close 13:00–14:00, audioguide-€2.50, last entry 30 min before closing time, decent cafeteria with salad bar, rue de la Régence 3, tel. 02-508-3211).

✪ See Ancient and Modern Art Museums Tour, page 317.

▲**Musical Instruments Museum**—One of Europe's best musical museums is housed in one of Brussels' most impressive Art Nouveau buildings, the newly renovated Old English department store. Inside you'll be given a pair of headphones and set free to wander several levels: folk instruments from around the world on

the ground floor, a history of Western musical instruments on the first, and an entire floor devoted to strings and pianos on the second. It has more than 1,500 instruments—from Egyptian harps to medieval lutes to groundbreaking harpsichords to the Brussels-built saxophone. As you approach an instrument, you hear it playing on your headphones (which actually work, most of the time). The museum is skimpy on English information—except for a €16 visitors' guide—but the music you'll hear is an international language. The sixth floor has a restaurant, terrace, and great view of Brussels (€5, Tue–Fri 9:30–17:00, Thu until 20:00, Sat–Sun 10:00–17:00, closed Mon, last entry 30 min before closing time, concerts every Thu at 20:00, rue Montagne de la Cour 2, just downhill and toward Grand Place from the art museum, tel. 02-545-0130).

Bellevue Dynasty Museum—The Belgian royal family has put together an interesting museum adjacent to the Royal Palace to give their subjects as well as tourists a look at that family's 150 years on the Belgian throne and the monarchy today. The English text you'll borrow from the ticket booth helps, but the exhibit suffers from a lack of English descriptions. Still, there's no better peek at the popular Belgian royal family (€3, Tue–Sun 10:00–18:00, closed Mon, Oct–March until 17:00, to the right of the palace at place des Palais 7, tel. 02-548-0448). A display of the excavation of the palace of Charles V, upon which today's palace sits, uses the same entry and ticket booth as the Bellevue Dynasty Museum, but it's not worth the hike or €2 extra.

Sights—North of Central Station

▲**St. Michael's Cathedral**—St. Michael's Cathedral has been the center of Belgium's religious life for nearly 1,000 years. Belgium is Catholic. While the Netherlands went in a Protestant direction in the 1500s, Belgium remains 80 percent Catholic (although only about 20 percent go to Mass). One of Europe's classic Gothic churches, built between roughly 1200 and 1500, Brussels' cathedral is made from white stone and topped with twin towers (open daily 8:00–18:00).

The church is where royal weddings and funerals take place. Photographs (to the right of the entrance) show the funeral of the popular King Baudouin, who died in 1991. He was succeeded by his son, Albert II (whose face is on Belgium's euro coins). Albert will be succeeded by his son, Prince Philippe. Formerly, the ruler was always a man. But in 1992, the constitution was changed, making it clear that the oldest child—boy or girl—would take the throne. In 1999, Prince Philippe and his bride Mathilde—after a civil ceremony at the Town Hall—paraded up here for a two-hour Catholic ceremony with all the fixins'. They had a baby girl in 2001, and she is in line to become Belgium's Queen Elizabeth.

Before leaving, enjoy the great view of the Town Hall spire with its gold statue of St. Michael from the outside porch.

▲**Belgian Comic Strip Centre**—Belgium has produced some of the world's most popular comic characters, like the Smurfs, Tintin, and Lucky Luke. You'll find these and many less-famous Belgian comics in the Comics Museum.

Just pop into the lobby to see the museum's groundbreaking Art Nouveau building (a former department store designed in 1903 by Belgian architect Victor Horta), browse through comic books in the bookshop, and snap a photo with a three-foot-tall Smurf...and that's enough for many people. Kids especially might find the museum, like, totally boring. But those who appreciate "art" in general will enjoy this sometimes humorous, sometimes probing, often beautiful medium. The displays are in French and Flemish, but they loan out a helpful if hard-to-follow English guidebook.

You'll see how comics are made, watch early animated films (such as *Gertie the Dinosaur*, c. 1909), and see a sprawling exhibit on Tintin (the intrepid boy reporter with the button eyes and wavy shock of hair, launched in 1929 by Hergé and much loved by older Europeans). The top floor is dedicated to "serious" comics where more adult themes and high-quality drawing aspire to turn kid's stuff into that "Ninth Art." These works can be grimly realistic, openly erotic or graphic, or darker in tone, featuring flawed anti-heroes (€6.20, Tue–Sun 10:00–18:00, closed Mon, rue des Sables 20, tel. 02-219-1980).

Sights—Away from the Center

▲**European Parliament**—Europe's governing body now welcomes visitors. This towering complex of glass skyscrapers is a cacophony of black-suited politicians speaking 11 Euro languages. The only way in is to take the 30-minute tour (free, Mon–Thu at 10:00 and 15:00, Fri only at 10:00, bus #95 or #96 from the Bourse to place du Luxembourg, find the visitors' entrance around the corner downhill from rue Wertz 43, tel. 02-284-3453).

At the proper time, you enter through the visitors' entrance to meet an escort, who equips you with an audio-guide and takes you to a balcony overlooking the huge "hemi-cycle" where the members of the European Parliament sit. From there you listen to a political-science lesson about the all-Europe system of governance.

You'll learn how early visionary utopians (like Churchill, who in 1946 called for a "United States of Europe" to avoid future wars) led the way as Europe gradually evolved into the European Union (1992). The 620 parliament members represent-ing 15 countries shape Europe's future with a $100 billion budget (from import duties, a 1.4 percent sales tax, and a percent of each member country's GNP).

It's exciting just to be here—a mouse in the corner of a place that charts the future of Europe "with respect for all political thinking... consolidating democracy in the spirit of peace and solidarity." With the current president from Italy, it is indeed an inclusive group, rather than a mock parliament dominated by Germany or France.

▲**Park of the Cinquantenaire**—This park sprawls out from under a massive triumphal arch, which was built in 1880 to cele-brate the 50th anniversary of Belgian independence. While pre-cious few of the governmental buildings of the European Union (EU) are visually exciting, you can emerge from the Métro's Schuman stop to be surrounded by the political headquarters of a more or less united Europe. The huge, star-shaped Berlay-mont Building was built in 1963 to house the Commission of the European Union. From there, you can walk 10 minutes through the park to the Autoworld and military museums (under giant arch). The next Métro stop (Merode) is closer to the museums.

▲**Autoworld**—Starting with Mr. Benz's motorized tricycle of 1886, you'll stroll through a giant hall filled with 400 historic cars. It's well described in English (€5, April–Sept daily 10:00–18:00, Oct–March 10:00–17:00, in Palais Mondial, Parc du Cinquantenaire, Métro: Merode, tel. 02-736-4165).

▲**Royal Museum of the Army and Military History**— Wander through a vast collection of 19th-century weaponry and uniforms and a giant hall dedicated to warplanes of the 20th century (free, Tue–Sun 09:00–12:00 & 13:00–16:30, closed Mon, tel. 02-737-7811). There's a good display about the Belgian struggle for independence (early 1800s).

Museum of Natural Sciences—Dinosaur enthusiasts come here for the world's largest collection of iguanodon skeletons (€3.75, Tue–Fri 9:30–16:45, Sat–Sun 10:00–18:00, closed Mon, last entry 30 min before closing time, rue Vautier 29, bus #34 from the Bourse, tel. 02-627-4238).

Antoine Wiertz Museum—Next to the Museum of Natural Sciences is a collection of works by Antoine Wiertz. This 19th-century artist painted some of the world's largest canvases, with themes ranging from Biblical to political (free, Tue–Sun 10:00–12:00 & 13:00–17:00, closed Mon and every other weekend, rue Vautier 62, bus #34 from the Bourse, tel. 02-648-1718).

Royal Museum of Central Africa—Remember the Belgian Congo? Brussels has an excellent museum of the Congo and much more of Africa (ethnography, sculptures, jewelry, colonial history, flora, and fauna) an hour from the center. Take Métro 1B to Montgomery (direction: Stockel) and then catch tram #44 to its final stop, Tervuren. From there, walk 200 meters through the park to a palace (€4, Tue–Fri 10:00–17:00, Sat–Sun until 18:00, closed Mon, tel. 02-769-5211).

Atomium—This giant molecule, with escalators connecting the various "atoms" and a restaurant with a view in the top sphere, was the symbol of the 1958 Universal Exhibition held in Belgium (€6, combo-ticket with Mini-Europe-€15, April–Aug daily 9:00–19:30, Sept–March daily 10:00–17:30, Métro: Heysel and walk 5 min, tel. 02-474-8977, www.atomium.be). Today it's the cheesy nucleus of a park on the edge of town that has the kid-pleasing **Mini-Europe,** with 1:25-scale models of 350 famous European landmarks such as Big Ben, the Eiffel Tower, and Venice (€11, combo-ticket with Atomium-€15, March–June and Sept daily 9:30–17:00, July–Aug until 19:00 weekdays and 23:00 weekends, Oct–Feb 10:00–17:00, tel. 02-474-1313).

GRAND
PLACE
WALK

This walk takes in this city's delightful old center. After exploring the Grand Place itself, we'll loop a couple blocks north, see the Bourse, then end south of the Grand Place at the *Manneken-Pis*.

Orientation

Brewery Museum: €3, daily 10:00–17:00, sometimes open later July–Sept, Grand Place 10.

Museum of Cocoa and Chocolate: €5, Tue–Sun 10:00–17:00, last entry 16:30, closed Mon, Grand Place 13.

City Museum: €2.50, Tue–Fri 10:00–17:00, Sat–Sun 10:00–13:00, closed Mon, Grand Place, tel. 02-279-4350.

Chocolate Shops: Generally open daily from 9:00-22:00, along the north side of the Grand Place.

Church of St. Nicolas: Rue de Tabora 6, tel. 02-734-9027.

Length of Our Tour: Allow two hours.

THE GRAND PLACE

This colorful, cobblestone square is the heart—historically and geographically—of heart-shaped Brussels. As the town's market square for a thousand years, this was where farmers and merchants sold their wares in open-air stalls, enticing travelers from the main east–west highway across Belgium, which ran a block north of the square. Today, shops and cafés sell chocolates, *gaufres* (waffles), beer, mussels and fries, lace, and flowers.

Brussels was born about a thousand years ago around a long-gone castle put up by Germans to fight off the French (long before either of those countries actually existed). The villagers supplied the needs of the soldiers. The city grew up on the banks of the Senne (not Seine) River, which today is completely bricked over. The river crossed the main road from Köln to Bruges.

Grand Place Walk

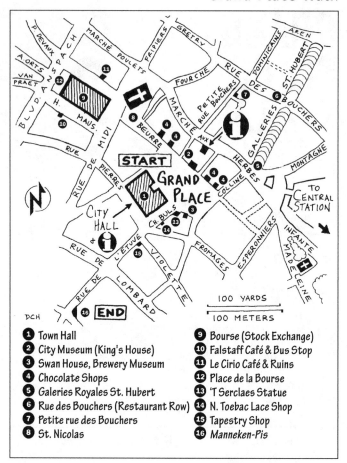

1 Town Hall
2 City Museum (King's House)
3 Swan House, Brewery Museum
4 Chocolate Shops
5 Galeries Royales St. Hubert
6 Rue des Bouchers (Restaurant Row)
7 Petite rue des Bouchers
8 St. Nicolas
9 Bourse (Stock Exchange)
10 Falstaff Café & Bus Stop
11 Le Cirio Café & Ruins
12 Place de la Bourse
13 'T Serclaes Statue
14 N. Toebac Lace Shop
15 Tapestry Shop
16 Manneken-Pis

Pan the square to get oriented. The **Town Hall** (Stadhuis) dominates the square with its 100-meter-tall tower. This was where the city council met to rule this free trading town. Brussels proudly maintained its self-governing independence while much of Europe was ruled by dukes, kings, and clergymen. These days, the Town Hall hosts weddings—Crown Prince Philippe got married on the balcony in 1999.

(The Belgian government demands that all marriages first be performed in simple civil ceremonies.) The tower is topped with the golden angel St. Michael.

Opposite the Town hall is the impressive, gray **King's House** (Maison du Roi), used by the Hapsburg kings not as a house but as an administrative center. Rebuilt in the 1890s, the stately Baroque-style building turns to prickly neo-Gothic at the top. Inside is the mildly interesting City Museum (described below).

The fancy smaller buildings giving the square its uniquely grand medieval character are former **guild halls** (now mostly shops and restaurants), their impressive gabled roofs topped with statues. Once the home offices for the town's different professions (bakers, brewers, tanners, and *Manneken-Pis*-corkscrew-makers), they all date from shortly after 1695—the year Louis XIV's troops surrounded the city, sighted their cannons on the Town Hall spire, and managed to level everything around it (4,000 wooden buildings)—except the spire. As a matter of pride, these Brussels businessmen rebuilt their offices better than ever—all within seven years. They're in stone, taller, and with ornamented gables and classical statues.

The **Swan House** (#9, just to the left of the Town Hall) once housed a bar where Karl Marx and Frederich Engels met in February 1848, to write their *Communist Manifesto*. Later that year, when the treatise sparked socialist revolution around Europe, Brussels exiled them. Today, ironically, the proletarian bar is one of the city's most expensive restaurants. Next door (#10) was and still is the brewers guild, now housing the **Brewery Museum** (see page 290). The **Museum of Cocoa and Chocolate** is next door (see page 290).

The **statues** on the rooftops each come with their own uninteresting legend, but the Bruxelloise have earthier explanations: "What's that smell?" say the statues on the roof of the Swan House, "Someone farted." "Yeah," says the golden man riding a horse atop the Brewery Museum next door, "it was that guy over there," and he points north across the square to another statue. "It wasn't me," says that statue, "it was him—way over

there." Follow his gaze to the southwest corner of the square where a statue of St. Nicholas . . . hangs his head in shame.

The **City Museum,** in the King's House, is the only museum of any importance on the square. Its top floor has an entertaining room full of costumes the *Manneken* statue has pissed through, the middle floor features maps and models of old Brussels, and the bottom floor has a few old paintings and tapestries. Most visitors head for the *Manneken-Pis* outfits.

But be sure to find the model of the city in the 12th century (second floor). View it from the window opposite the door. (To follow the directions in this description, uphill is east.) The largest structure is St. Michael's Cathedral (northeast). The Upper Town hasn't a hint of its monumental future. The Grand Place's embryonic beginning is roughly in the center of town, amid a cluster of houses.

The city was a port town—see the crane unloading barges— since it was at this point that the shallow Senne became navigable. Grain from the area was processed in the watermills, then shipped downstream to the North Sea.

By the 1200s, Brussels—though tiny by today's standards—was an important commercial center, and St. Michael's was the region's religious hub. Still, most of the area inside the 4-kilometer city wall was farmland, dotted with a few churches, convents (like the Carmelite convent hugging the south wall), towers, and markets.

The model in the far end of the room shows the city a couple centuries later—much bigger but still within its same wall.

Taste Treats on the Grand Place

Cafés: Mussels in Brussels, Belgian fries, yeasty local beers, waffles . . . if all you do is plop down at a café on the square, try some of these specialties, and watch the world go by—hey, that's a great afternoon in Brussels.

The outdoor cafés are casual and come with fair prices (a good Belgian beer costs €3.50—with no cover or service charge). Have a seat, and a waiter will serve you. The half-dozen or so cafés are all roughly equal in price and quality for simple drinks and foods—check the posted menus.

History of Chocolate

In 1519, Montezuma served Cortes a cup of hot cocoa (*xocoatl*), igniting a food fad in Europe. By 1700, elegant "chocolate houses" in Europe's capitals served hot chocolate (with milk and sugar added) to wealthy aristocrats. By the 1850s, the process of making chocolate candies for eating was developed, and Brussels, with a long tradition of quality handmade luxuries, was at the forefront.

Cocoa beans (native to the New World) are husked, fermented, and roasted, then ground into chocolate paste. (Chocolate straight from the bean is very bitter.) The vegetable fat is pressed out to make cocoa butter. Cocoa butter and chocolate paste are mixed together and sweetened with sugar to make chocolates. In 1876, a Swiss man named Henry Nestlé added concentrated milk, creating milk chocolate, a lighter, sweeter variation, with less pure chocolate.

Chocolate: For many, the best thing about the Grand Place is chocolate at one of four venerable chocolate shops. They all lie along the north side of the square starting with Godiva at the high end. Each has an inviting display case of 20 or so chocolates and sells mixes of 100 grams—your choice of 6–8 pieces— or individual pieces for less than €1. Pralines are filled chocolates—uniquely Belgian (and totally different from the French praline). Shops are generally open daily from 9:00 to 22:00.

Godiva, with the top reputation internationally, is synonymous with fine Belgian chocolate. The Godiva almond and honey goes way beyond almond roca (100 grams of your choice for €3.70).

Neuhaus, a few doors down, has been encouraging local chocoholics since 1857. Look through the glass floor at the old-time choco-kitchen in the basement. The enticing varieties are described in English and Neuhaus publishes a fine little pamphlet (free, on the counter) explaining the products. The "caprese" (toffee with vanilla crème) tastes like Easter. Neuhaus claims to be the inventor of the filled chocolate, or praline.

Galler, more homey, is less famous because it doesn't export. Still family-run (and the royal favorite), it proudly serves less-sugary chocolate—dark. The new top-end choice is called simply "85 percent"—and worth a sample if you like chocolate without the sweetness. A 100-gram mixed bag costs €3. Galler's products are also well described in English.

At **Leonidas,** most locals sacrifice 10 percent in quality to double their take by getting their fix here (machine-made, only €1.50/100 grams). White chocolate is the specialty.

• *Exit the Grand Place next to Godiva (from the northeast corner of the square) and go north one block on Rue de la Colline. At Grasmarket Square, look left down Rue du Marché-aux-Herbes, which was once the main east–west highway through Belgium, from Köln to Bruges. Look right, and notice that it's all uphill from here, past the Gothic church to the Upper Town, another four blocks beyond. Straight ahead you enter the arcaded shopping mall called . . .*

Galeries Royales St. Hubert

Europe's oldest still-operating shopping mall was built in 1847 and served as the glass-covered model for others. It celebrated the town's new modern attitude, having recently gained its independence from the Netherlands, and embarking on a century of expansion and industrialization. It was a model of efficient modern living with elegant apartments upstairs above fine shops, theaters, and cafés.

Looking down the arcade, you'll notice that it bends halfway down, designed to lure shoppers further. Its iron-and-glass look is still popular today, but the decorative columns, cameos, and pastel colors evoke a more elegant time. It's neo-Renaissance, like a pastel Florentine palace.

There's no Gap (yet), no Foot Locker, no Karmel Korn. Instead, you'll find hat and cane stores that sell . . . hats and canes, that's it, made on the premises, cut to fit. Have shoes made especially for the curves of your feet by a family that's done it for generations. Since 1857, **Neuhaus** has sold chocolates from here at its flagship store—many locals buy their pralines here. The **Taverne du Passage** restaurant serves the same local specialties (for about €12) that singer Jacques Brel used to come here for: *croquettes de*

crevettes (shrimp croquettes), *tête de veau* (calf's head), *anguilles au vert* (eels with herb sauce), and *fondue au fromage* (cheese fondue).
• *Midway down the mall, where the two sections bend, turn left and exit the mall onto Rue des Bouchers.*

Rue des Bouchers

Yikes! During meal times, the street is absolutely crawling with visitors browsing through wall-to-wall, mid-level-quality restaurants. Brussels is known worldwide for its food, serving all kinds of cuisines, but specializing in seafood (particularly mussels and shrimp). You'll have plenty to choose from here on this table-clogged restaurant row. To get an idea of prices, compare their posted "menus"—the fixed-price, several-course meal offered by most restaurants.

Many diners here are day-trippers. Colin from London, Marie from Paris, Martje from Holland, and Dietrich from Bonn could easily all "do lunch" together in Brussels—just three hours away.

The first intersection, Petite Rue des Bouchers, is the heart of the restaurant quarter, which sprawls for several blocks around. The street names tell what sorts of shops used to stand here— butchers (*bouchers*), herbs, chickens, cheese.
• *Turn left on Petite Rue des Bouchers and walk straight back to the Grand Place. At the Grand Place, turn right (west) on Rue du Beurre. Comparison-shop at the Galler and Leonidas chocolate stores. A block along is the . . .*

Church of St. Nicolas

Since the 12th century, there's been a church here. Inside, see rough stones in some of the arches from the early church. Outside, notice the barnacle-like shops, like De Little Jewelers, built right into the church. The church was rebuilt 300 years ago with money provided by the town's jewelers. As thanks, they were given these shops with apartments upstairs. Close to God, this was prime real estate. And jewelers are still here.

• *Just west of the church, the big neoclassical building you run into is the back entrance of . . .*

The Bourse (Stock Exchange) and Art Nouveau Cafés

The stock exchange was built in the 1870s in a neo-everything style.

Several **historic cafés** huddle around the Bourse. To the right are the recommended woody, atmospheric Le Cirio and A la Bécasse cafés (see page 333), to the left is the Falstaff Café.

Some Brussels cafés, like the Falstaff, are still decorated in the turn-of-the-century style called Art Nouveau. Ironwork columns twist and bend like flowers, and lots of glass and mirrors make them light and spacious. Slender, elegant, willowy Gibson Girls decorate the wallpaper, while waiters in bowties glide by.

The **ruins** under glass on the right side of the Bourse are from a 13th-century convent.

• *Circle around to the front of the Bourse, crossed by busy Boulevard Anspach.*

Place de la Bourse and Boulevard Anspach

Brussels is a political nerve center of Europe (only Washington, D.C., has more lobbyists), and there are several hundred demonstrations a year. When the local team wins a soccer match or some political group wants to make a statement, this is where people flock to wave flags and honk horns.

It's also where the old town meets the new. To the right along Boulevard Anspach are two shopping malls and several first-run movie theaters. Rue Neuve, which parallels Anspach, is a pedestrian-only shopping street.

Boulevard Anspach covers the Senne River (which was open until 1850). Remember that Brussels was once a port with North Sea boats coming as far as this point to unload their goods. But with frequent cholera epidemics killing thousands of its citizens, the city decided to cover up its stinky river.

• *Return to the Grand Place and leave the square kitty-corner, heading south on Rue Charles Buls (which soon changes its name to Stoofstraat). Just under the arch five meters off the square is a well-polished, well-loved brass statue.*

Lace

In the 1500s, rich men and women decided that lace collars, sleeves, headdresses, and veils were fashionable. For the next two hundred years, the fashion raged (peaking around 1700). It all had to be made by hand, and many women earned extra income from the demand. The French Revolution of 1789 suddenly made lace for men undemocratic and unmanly. Then, around 1800, machines replaced human hands and, except for ornamental pieces, the fashion died out.

These days, handmade lace is usually also homemade—not produced in factories but at home by dedicated, sharp-eyed hobbyists who love their work. Unlike knitting, it requires total concentration, as you are following intricate patterns. Women create their own patterns or trace tried-and-true designs. A piece of lace takes days, not hours, to make—which is why a handmade tablecloth can easily sell for €250.

There are two basic lace-making techniques: bobbin lace (which originated in Bruges) and needle lace. To make bobbin lace, women juggle many different strands tied to bobbins, "weaving" a design by overlapping the threads. Because of the difficulties, the resulting pattern is usually rather rough and simple compared with other techniques.

Needle lace is more like sewing—stitching pre-made bits onto a pattern. For example, the "Renaissance" design is made by sewing a premade ribbon onto a pattern in a fancy design. This would then be attached as a fringe to a piece of linen—to make a fancy tablecloth, for instance.

In the "Princess" design, premade pieces are stitched onto a cotton net to make anything from a doily to a full wedding veil.

"Rose point"—no longer done—uses authentic bits of handmade antique lace as an ornament in a frame or filling a pendant. This can be very expensive.

From the Grand Place to the *Manneken-Pis*

You'll see tourists and locals rubbing a **brass statue** of a reclining man. This was Mayor Evrard 't Serclaes, who in 1356 bravely refused to surrender the keys of the city to invaders, so was tortured and killed. Touch him and his misfortune becomes your good luck. Judging by the reverence with which locals go through this ritual, there must be something to it.

The **N. Toebac Lace Shop** is a welcoming place with fine lace, a knowledgeable staff, and an interesting three-minute video. Brussels is perhaps the best-known city for traditional lace-making, and this shop still sells handmade pieces in the old style: lace clothing, doilies, tablecloths, and ornamental pieces (daily 9:30–19:30, Rue Charles Buls 10). For more on lace, the Costume and Lace Museum is just around the corner (see page 292).

• *A block farther down the street, step into Textilux Center (Rue Lombard 41) for a good look at Belgian tapestries.*

Tapestries

In 1500, tapestry workshops in Brussels were famous, cranking out high-quality tapestries for the walls of Europe's palaces. They were functional (as insulation and propaganda for a church, king, or nobleman) and beautiful, an intricate design formed by colored thread. Even great painters (like Rubens and Raphael) designed tapestries, which rivaled Renaissance canvases.

First, they stretched neutral-colored threads (made from imported English wool) vertically over a loom. A tapestry design is made with the horizontal weave, from colored threads that interlace the vertical so they (mostly) cover it. Tapestry-making is much more difficult than basic weaving because each horizontal thread is only as long as the detail it's meant to create, so a single horizontal row can be made up of many individual pieces of thread. The weavers follow a pattern designed by an artist, called a "cartoon."

Flanders and Paris (the Gobelins workshop) were the two centers of tapestry-making until the art died out along with Europe's noble class.

Today's stores mostly feature tapestry purses and luggage in traditional designs.

• *Follow the crowds, noticing the excitement build, as in another block you reach the . . .*

Manneken-Pis

Even with low expectations, this bronze statue is smaller than you'd think—the little squirt's only half a meter tall, practically the size of a newborn. Still, the little peeing boy is an appropriately low-key symbol for the earthy Bruxelloise. The statue was made in 1619 to provide drinking water for the neighborhood.

To the right, look through a shop window to see a few of the 600 different costumes (including Elvis Pissley) that visiting VIPs have brought for him.

There are several different legends—take your pick. He was a naughty boy who peed inside a witch's house, so she froze him. A rich man lost his son and declared, "Find my son and we'll make a statue of him doing what he did when found." Or—the locals' favorite version—the little tyke loved his beer, and it came in handy when a fire threatened the wooden city and he bravely put it out. Want the truth? The city commissioned it to show the joie de vivre of living in Brussels—where happy people eat, drink . . . and drink . . . and then pee.

The scene is made interesting by the crowds that gather. Hang out for a while and watch the commotion this little guy makes as tour groups come and go. When I was there, a Russian man marveled at the statue, shook his head, and said, "He never stop!"

UPPER TOWN
WALK

The Upper Town has always had a more aristocratic feel than the medieval, commercial streets of the Lower Town. With broad boulevards, big marble buildings, palaces, museums, and so many things called "royal," it also seems much newer and a bit more sterile. But in fact, the Upper Town has a history stretching back to Brussels' beginnings.

Use this 10-stop walk to get acquainted with a less-touristed part of town, sample some world-class museums, see the palace, explore art galleries, and stand on a viewpoint to get the lay of the land.

The tour starts half a block from the one essential art sight in town, the Ancient and Modern Art Museums. Consider a visit while you're here (some rooms close during lunch, closed Mon, see tour on page 317). The Musical Instruments Museum is also in the neighborhood (closed Mon, see page 292).

Orientation

Getting There: The walk begins at place Royale in the Upper Town. There are several ways to get there: 1. From the Grand-Place, it's a 15-minute walk (follow your map). 2. From the Bourse, in front of the Falstaff Café, buses #95 and #96 leave every few minutes for place Royale (bus signs call it "Royale"). 3. Catch a taxi from the Bourse (€5). 4. Hop off during a hop-on, hop-off bus tour (both companies stop here; for details, see page 289).

Route Overview: From place Royale, walk south along the ridge, popping into a stained-glass-filled Gothic church, and on to the best view of the city, from the towering Palace of Justice. Then descend through the well-worn tapestries of the Sablon Quarter's antiques, art, and cafés, and on to the foot of the hill at the *Manneken-Pis*.

Upper Town Walk

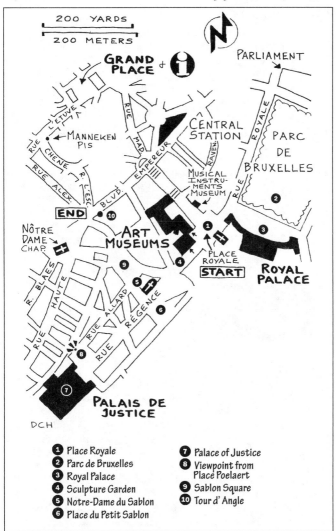

200 YARDS
200 METERS

GRAND PLACE & 🛈

PARLIAMENT

RUE L'ETUVE

← MANNEKEN PIS

RUE CHENE

RUE ALEX

RUE MAD

RUE EMPEREUR

RUE L'ESC

BLVD

CENTRAL STATION

RUE RAVEN

RUE ROYALE

PARC DE BRUXELLES

MUSICAL INSTRUMENTS MUSEUM

END ⑩

ART MUSEUMS

❶

❹

PLACE ROYALE

START

❷

❸

ROYAL PALACE

NÔTRE DAME CHAP ✝

⑨

⑤ ✝

❻

R. BLAES

RUE HAUTE

RUE ALLARD

RUE RÉGENCE

RUE

⑧

⑦

PALAIS DE JUSTICE

DCH

❶ Place Royale
❷ Parc de Bruxelles
❸ Royal Palace
❹ Sculpture Garden
❺ Notre-Dame du Sablon
❻ Place du Petit Sablon
❼ Palace of Justice
❽ Viewpoint from Place Poelaert
⑨ Sablon Square
⑩ Tour d'Angle

Length of Our Tour: Two hours.
Cuisine Art: For lunch, try the restaurant on the top floor of the Musical Instruments Museum (open to the public, with a great view) or the two recommended eateries on place du Grand Sablon, where this walk ends.

The Tour Begins

1. Place Royale

At the crest of the hill sits place Royale, enclosed by white, neo-classical buildings, forming a mirror-image around a cobblestone square with a big, green statue of a horseman in the center.

The statue—a Belgium-born Crusader, Godfrey de Bouillon (who led the First Crusade in 1096)—rides forward carrying a flag, gazing down on the Town Hall spire. If Godfrey turned and looked left down Rue de la Régence, he'd see the domed Palace of Justice at the end of the boulevard. Over his right shoulder, just outside the square, is the Royal Palace, the king's residence.

In the 1800s, as Belgium exerted itself to industrialize and modernize, this area was rebuilt as a sign that Brussels had arrived as a world capital. Broad vistas down wide boulevards ending in gleaming white, Greek-columned monuments—the look was all the rage, seen at Versailles, London, Washington, D.C.... and here.

The cupola of the Church of St. Jacques sur Coudenberg—the central portion of the square's ring of buildings—makes the church look more like a bank building. But St. Jacques goes back much further than this building (from 1787). It originated in the 13th century near a 12th-century castle. Nobles chose to build their mansions in the neighborhood, and later, so did the king.

The Musical Instruments Museum (see page 292) is 30 meters downhill from the square, housed in a turn-of-the-century iron and glass former department store. Its Art Nouveau facade was a deliberate attempt to get beyond the retro-looking Greek columns and domes of the place Royale. Even if you don't visit the museum, you can ride the elevator up to the museum café for a great Lower Town view.

Brussels' world-class Ancient and Modern Art Museums are 30 meters south of place Royale on Rue de la Régence.

• *Before heading south, exit place Royale on the north side (to Godfrey's right), which opens up to a large, tree-lined park.*

2. Parc de Bruxelles

Copying Versailles, Empress Maria-Theresa of Austria (Marie Antoinette's mom) had this symmetrical park laid out in 1776 when she ruled (but never visited) the city. This is just one of many large parks in a city that expanded with an eye to city planning.

At the far (north) end of the park is the Parliament Building. Which Parliament? The city hosts several—the EU Parliament, the Belgian, and several local city-council type parliaments. This is the Belgian Parliament, often seen

on nightly newscasts as a backdrop for the country's politicians.

In 1830, Belgian patriots rose up and converged on the park, where they attacked the troops of the Dutch king. This was the first blow in a short, almost-bloodless revolution that drove out the foreign-born king and gave the Belgians independence . . . and a different foreign-born king.

• *The long building facing the park is the . . .*

3. Royal Palace (Palais Royale)

After Belgium struck out twice trying to convince someone to be their new king, Leopold I (ruled 1831–1865), a nobleman from Germany, agreed. Leopold was a steadying influence as the country modernized. His son rebuilt this palace—near the site of earlier palaces dating back to the

10th century—by linking together a row of townhouse mansions with a unifying facade around 1870.

Leopold's great-great-great-grandnephew, King Albert II, uses the palace today as an office. (His head is on Belgium's euro coins.) Albert and his wife, Queen Paola, live in a palace north of here (near the Atomium) and on the French Riviera. If the Belgian flag (black-yellow-red) is flying from the palace, the king is somewhere in Belgium.

Albert (born 1932) is a figurehead king, as in so many European democracies, but he serves an important function as a common bond between bickering Flemish and Walloons. His son Prince Philippe is slated to succeed him, though Philippe—awkward and standoffish—is not as popular as his wife, Mathilde, a Belgian native.

The bulk of the palace is off-limits to tourists (except on special occasions), but you can visit some well-decorated rooms via the Bellevue Dynasty Museum, which tells the story of the royal family (€3, entrance on the far right end, closed Mon; described on page 293).

• *Return to place Royale, then continue south along Rue de la Régence, noticing the entrance to the Ancient and Modern Art Museums. Just past the museums, on the right, you'll see a ...*

4. Sculpture Garden (Jardin de Sculpture)

This pleasant public garden looks like a great way to descend into the Sablon Quarter, but the gates at the bottom are often locked.

• *A hundred meters farther along, you reach the Sablon neighborhood, dominated by the ...*

5. Notre-Dame du Sablon Church

The round, rose stained-glass windows in the clerestory of this 14th-century Flamboyant Gothic church are nice by day, but the real thrill is at night, when the church is lit from inside. It glows like a lantern, enjoyed by locals at the cafés in the surrounding square.

Inside, next to the altar, see a small wooden **statue of Mary** dressed in white with a lace veil. This is a copy, made after the original was destroyed by Protestant iconoclastic vandals. The original statue was thought to have had miraculous powers, saving the town from plagues. In 1348, when he original statue was in Antwerp, it spoke to a godly woman named Beatrix, prompting her to board a boat (see the small **wooden boat,** high above the entry door) and steal the statue away from Antwerp. When they tried to stop her, the Mary statue froze the Antwerp citizens in their tracks.

Beatrix and the statue arrived here, the Bruxelloise welcomed her with a joyous parade, and this large church was erected in her honor. Every year, in Brussels' famous Ommegang, locals in tights and flamboyant costumes recreate the joyous arrival. With colorful banners and large puppets, they carry Mary from here through the city streets to the climax on the Grand Place.

• *On the other side of Rue de la Régence from the church is a leafy, fenced-off garden called the ...*

6. Place du Petit Sablon

This is a pleasant refuge from the busy street, part of why this neighborhood is considered so livable. The 48 small statues atop the wrought-iron fence represent the guilds—butchers, bakers, and candlestick-makers—of medieval Brussels. Inside the garden, 10 large statues represent hometown thinkers of the 16th century—a time of great intellectual accomplishments in Brussels. Gerardus

Mercator (1512–1594), the Belgian mapmaker who devised a way

to show the spherical Earth on a flat surface, is holding a globe.

• *We'll visit the Sablon neighborhood below the church later, but before losing elevation, let's continue along Rue de la Régence, passing the Music Academy and Brussels' main synagogue (its sidewalk fortified with concrete posts to keep car bombs at a distance), before reaching the long-scaffolded . . .*

7. Palace of Justice (Palais de Justice)

This domed mountain of marble sits on the edge of the Upper Town ridge, dominating the Brussels skyline. Built in wedding-cake layers of Greek columns, it's topped with a dome bigger than St. Peter's in Rome, rising up 105 meters (340 feet). Covering more than six acres, it's the size of a baseball stadium. Everyone seems to pooh-pooh this over-the-top monument, but I find it jaw-dropping.

The palace was built in the time of King Leopold II (son of Leo I, reigned 1865–1909), and epitomizes the brassy, look-at-me grandeur of his reign. Leopold became obscenely wealthy by turning Africa's Congo region—80 times the size of Belgium—into his personal colony. Whip-wielding Belgian masters forced African slaves to tend lucrative rubber plantations, exploiting the new craze for bicycle tires. Leopold spent much of this wealth expanding and beautifying the city of Brussels.

Leo's architect, Joseph Poelaert (1817–1879), wrestled with the mathematics of the building's construction for 20 years before it finally drove him mad and he ended up in an insane asylum, leaving the project to be completed by others in 1883. The dome, often covered with maintenance scaffolding, is still somewhat shaky.

The building still serves as a Hall of Justice where major court cases are tried. If you pop into the lobby, you may see lawyers in black robes buzzing about.

• *One of the best views of Brussels is from right next to the Palace of Justice.*

8. Viewpoint from Place Poelaert

You're standing 60 meters (200 feet) above the former Senne River Valley. Gazing west over the Lower Town, pan the valley from right (north) to left:

Near you is the clock tower of the Minimen Church (which hosts lunchtime concerts in the summer). To the left of that, in the distance past a tall square skyscraper, comes the lacy white Town Hall spire.

In the far distance, 10 kilometers away, you can see one of the city's better-known sights, the **Atomium.** Its nine steel balls form the shape of an iron molecule the size of the Palace of Justice (100 meters). Built for a 1958 World's Fair, it's now a middle-aged symbol of the dawn of the Atomic Era. There's a panoramic restaurant on top with great views of the Palace of Justice.

Next (closer to you), comes the black-topped dome of the Notre-Dame de la Chapelle church, the city's oldest (from 1134, with a spire that starts Gothic and ends Baroque). On the horizon, see five boxy skyscrapers, part of the residential sprawl of this city of 1.2 million, which now covers 62 square miles. The green dome belongs to the Basilica of Koekelberg (fourth biggest in the world). And finally (panning quickly to the left), you see a black glass skyscraper marking the Midi (or South) train station.

At your feet lies the Marolles neighborhood. Once a funky, poor place where locals developed their own quirky dialog, it remains somewhat seedy—and famous for its sprawling flea market (daily 7:00–13:00, best on weekend). Two of the streets just below you—Rue Haute and Rue Blaes—are lined with second-hand shops. There is now an **elevator** (free, daily 6:00–23:00) connecting place Poelaert with the Marolles neighborhood.

(People who brake for garage sales may want to cut out of this walk early and head to Marolles from here.)

Gazing off into the distance to the far left (south), you can't see the suburb of Waterloo, 16 kilometers away. But try to imagine it, because it was there that history turned. On the morning of June 18, 1815, Napoleon waited two hours for the ground to dry before sending his troops into battle. That delay may have cost him the battle. His 72,000 soldiers could have defeated Wellington's 68,000. But the two-hour delay was just enough time for Wellington's reinforcements to arrive—45,000 Prussian troops. Napoleon had to surrender, his rule of Europe ended, and Belgium was placed under a Dutch king—until the Belgians won their independence in the 1830 revolution.

Behind you in place Poelaert are two memorials to the two World Wars, both of which passed through Belgium with deadly force.

• *Backtrack east, descending to Sablon Square by walking down Rue Ernest Allard.*

9. Sablon Square (Place du Grand Sablon)

The Sablon neighborhood features cafés and restaurants, antiques stores, and art galleries. Every weekend, there's an antiques market on the square. On warm summer evenings, the square

sparks magic, as sophisticated locals sip apéritifs at the café tables, admiring the glowing stained glass of the church.

Chocolatier Wittamer (on the far side of the square) often features elaborate window displays, like a life-sized chocolate *Manneken-Pis*.

Le Pain Quotidien serves healthy lunches, fresh-baked goods, and coffee in an unstuffy atmosphere (11 Rue des Sablons, on near side of square, close to church; see Eating in Brussels, page 330). The café at the base of the sloping square offers cheap, no-nonsense meals any time of day. For a classy lunch, try L'Estrille du Vieux Bruxelles, just downhill from place du Grand Sablon (Rue de Rollebeek 7, see page 333).

• *Sloping Sablon Square funnels downhill into the pedestrian-only street called Rue de Rollebeek, which leads past fun shops and the recommended L'Estrille restaurant to the busy boulevard de l'Empereur. To the right on the boulevard, just past the bowling alley, is the ...*

10. Tour d'Angle

This tower is a rare surviving section of Brussels' 13th-century city wall. The plan of the old town (on a plaque on the ruin) shows how this was one of seven gates along the four-kilometer-long wall.

• *Continue downhill past interesting architecture and colorful shops back to the Grand Place.*

ANCIENT AND MODERN ART MUSEUMS
TOUR

Musées Royaux des Beaux Arts—
Musée d'Art Ancien et Musée d'Art Moderne

Two large buildings house a vast collection covering the entire history of Western painting. The collection, while enjoyable, can be overwhelming. So here's a top-10 list highlighting the museum's strength—Flemish and Belgian artists.

Orientation

Cost: €5, same ticket covers both museums.

Hours: Tue–Sun 10:00–17:00, closed Mon, half the rooms close for lunch 12:00–13:00, the other half close 13:00–14:00, last entry 30 min before closing time.

Getting There: The museums are at Rue de la Régence 3. From Central Station, take bus #20, #38, #60, #71, #95, or #96; or tram #92, #93, or #94.

Information: Consider the €2.50 audioguide or the €2.50 tour booklet ("Twenty Masterpieces of the Art of Painting—A Brief Guided Tour"). Tel. 02-508-3211, www.fine-arts-museum.be.

Length of Our Tour: One hour.

Cuisine Art: Decent cafeteria with salad bar.

Overview

Though there are technically two museums—Ancient Art (pre-1800) and Modern Art (post-1800)—they're connected and covered by the same ticket. The museum sprawls over several wings and a dozen floors, and to see it all is a logistical nightmare.

Armed with the museum's free map (and supplemented with the excellent English audioguide), you'll breeze through the maze with these 10 stops as guideposts.

• *Start with the Flemish masters, one floor up in the Ancient Art Museum.*

ANCIENT ART

Rogier van der Weyden (c. 1399–1464)—*Portrait of Anthony of Burgundy (Portrait d' Antoine de Bourgogne)*

Anthony was known in his day as the Great Bastard, the bravest and most distinguished of the many bastards fathered by prolific Duke Philip the Good (a Renaissance prince whose sense of style impressed Florence's young Lorenzo the Magnificent, patron of the arts).

Anthony, a member of the Archers Guild, fingers the arrow like a bow-string. From his gold necklace dangles a Golden Fleece, one of Europe's more prestigious knightly honors. Wearing a black cloak, a bowl-cut hairdo, and a dark-red cap, with his pale face and hand emerging from a dark background, the man who'd been called a bastard all his life gazes to the distance, his clear, sad eyes lit with a speckle of white paint.

Van der Weyden, Brussels' official portrait painter, faithfully rendered life-sized, lifelike portraits of wealthy traders, bankers, and craftsmen. Here he captures the wrinkles in Anthony's neck, and the faint shadow his chin casts on his Adam's apple. Van der Weyden had also painted Philip the Good, and young Anthony's long, elegant face and full lips are a mirror image—pretty convincing DNA evidence in a paternity suit.

Capitalist Flanders in the 1400s was one of the richest, most cultured, and progressive areas in Europe, rivaling Florence and Venice.

Hans Memling (c. 1430–1494)— *Martyrdom of St. Sebastian (Volets d'un Triptyque)*

Serene Sebastian is filled with arrows by a serene firing squad in a serene landscape. Sebastian, a Roman captain who'd converted to Christianity, was ordered to be shot to death. (He miraculously survived, so they clubbed him to death.)

Ready, freeze! Like a *tableaux vivant* (popular with Philip the Good's crowd), the well-dressed archers and saint freeze this moment in the martyrdom so the crowd can applaud the colorful costumes and painted cityscape backdrop.

Hans Memling, along with his former employer, Rogier van der Weyden, are called Flemish Primitives. Why "Primitive"? For the lack of 3-D realism so admired in Italy at the time. Sebastian's arm is tied to a branch that's not arching overhead, as it should be, but instead behind him. An archer aims slightly behind, not at, Sebastian. The other archer strings his bow in a stilted pose. But Memling is clearly a master of detail, and the faces, beautiful textiles, and hazy landscape combine to create a meditative mood appropriate to the church altar in Bruges where this was once placed.

Pieter Brueghel I, the Elder (c. 1527–1569)— *The Census at Bethlehem*

Perched at treetop level, you have a bird's-eye view over a snow-covered village near Brussels. The canals are frozen over but life goes on, everyone doing something. Kids throw snowballs and sled across the ice. A crowd gathers at the inn (lower left), where a woman holds a pan to catch blood while a man slaughters a pig. Most everyone has his or her back to us or head covered, so the figures speak through poses and motions.

Into the scene rides a woman on a donkey led by a man— it's Mary and husband Joseph hoping to find a room at the inn (or at least a manger) because Mary's going into labor.

The year is 1566—the same year that Protestant extremists throughout the Low Countries vandalized Catholic churches, tearing down "idolatrous" statues and paintings of the Virgin Mary. Brueghel (more discreetly) brings Mary down to earth from her Triumphant Coronation in heaven, and places Jesus' birth in the humble here and now. The busy villagers put their heads down and keep working, oblivious to the future Mother of God and the miracle about to take place.

Brueghel the Elder was famous for his landscapes filled with crowds of peasants in motion. His religious paintings place the miraculous in everyday settings.

In this room you'll see Brueghel's works as well as those of his less-famous sons. Pieter Brueghel II, the younger Pieter, copied dad's style (and even some paintings, like the *Census at*

Bethlehem). Another son, Jan, was known as the "Velvet Brueghel" for his glossy still-lifes of flower arrangements.

Peter Paul Rubens (1577–1640)—
The Ascent to Calvary (La Montée au Calvaire)

Life-sized figures scale this 18-foot-tall canvas on the way to Christ's Crucifixion. The scene ripples with motion, from the wind-blown clothes to steroid-enhanced muscles to billowing flags and a troubled sky. Christ stumbles, and might get trampled by the surging crowd. Veronica kneels to gently wipe his bloody head.

This 200-square-foot canvas was manufactured by Rubens at his studio in Antwerp. Hiring top-notch assistants, Rubens could crank out large altarpieces for the area's Catholic churches. First, Rubens himself did a small-scale sketch in oil (like many such studies in Room 52), then he did other sketches highlighting individual details. His assistants would reproduce it on the large canvas, and Rubens himself would add the final touches.

This work is from late in Rubens' long and very successful career. He got a second wind in his 50s when he married 16-year-old Helene Fourment. She was the model in this painting for Veronica, who consoles the faltering Christ.

• *To get to the Modern Art wing, return to the ground floor and the large main entrance hall of the Ancient Museum. From there, a passageway leads to Modern Art. Once in the Modern Art wing (entering on Level -2), take the elevator to the top floor (Level +3) and work your way down the museum's eight floors.*

MODERN ART

Panorama

At the very top of Level +3 is a great view westward over Brussels' Lower Town. See the Town Hall spire and, three kilometers away, the twin green domes of the gigantic basilica built by Leopold II. Looking as far right (north) as you can, you can make out the Atomium on the horizon.

• *Watch Impressionism turn to Post-Impressionism in this wing featuring both. Paul Gauguin and Georges Seurat emerged from Paris' Impressionist community to forge their own styles.*

Paul Gauguin (1848–1903)— *Breton Calvary (Calvaire Breton)* or *The Green Christ (Le Christ vert)*, 1889

Paul Gauguin returned to the bold, black, coloring-book outlines of more "primitive" (pre-3D) art. The Christian statue and countryside look less like Brittany and more like primitive Tahiti, where Gauguin would soon settle.

Georges Seurat 1859–1891)—*The Seine at Grand-Jatte (La Seine à La Grande-Jatte)*, 1888

Seurat paints a Sunday-in-the-park view from his favorite island in the Seine. Taking Impressionism to its extreme, he builds the scene out of small points of primary colors that blend at a distance to form objects. The bright colors capture the dazzling, sunlit atmosphere of this hazy day.

James Ensor (1860–1949)—*Shocked Masks* (1883)

At 22, James Ensor, an acclaimed child prodigy, proudly presented his lively Impressionist-style works to the Brussels

Salon for exhibition. They were flatly rejected.

The artist withdrew from public view and, in seclusion, painted *Shocked Masks*, a dark, murky scene set in a small room of an ordinary couple wearing grotesque masks.

Once again, everyone disliked this disturbing canvas and heaped more criticism on him. For the next six decades, Ensor painted the world as he saw it—full of bizarre, carnival-masked, stupid-looking crowds of cruel strangers who mock the viewer.

Jacques-Louis David (1748–1825)—
The Death of Marat (1793)

In a scene ripped from the day's headlines, Marat—a well-known French crusading journalist—has been stabbed to death in his bathtub by Charlotte Corday, a conservative fanatic. Marat's life drains out of him, turning the bathwater red. With his last

strength, he pens a final, patriotic, "Vive la Révolution" message to his fellow patriots. Corday, a young noblewoman angered by Marat's campaign to behead the French king, was arrested and guillotined three days later. Jacques-Louis David, one of Marat's fellow Revolutionaries, set to

work painting a tribute to his fallen comrade. (He signed the painting: "*A Marat*"—to Marat.)

David makes it a secular pietà, with the brave writer as a martyred Christ in a classic dangling-arm pose. Still, the deathly pallor and harsh lighting pull no punches for in-your-face realism.

David, the official art director of the French Revolution, supervised propaganda and the costumes worn for patriotic parades. A year later (1794), his extreme brand of Revolution (which included guillotining thousands of supposed enemies) was squelched by moderates, and David was jailed. He emerged again as Napoleon's court painter. When Napoleon was exiled in 1815, so was David, spending his last years in Brussels.

• *Proceed to Level -5 to see . . .*

Paul Delvaux (1897–1994)

Delvaux, who studied, worked, and taught in Brussels, gained fame for his surrealistic nudes sleepwalking through moonlit, video-game landscapes. They cast long shadows, wandering bare-breasted among classical ruins. Some women grow roots.

• *Proceed to Level -6 to see . . .*

René Magritte (1898–1967)

Magritte paints real objects with photographic clarity, then jumbles them together in new and provocative ways.

Magritte had his own private reserve of symbolic images.

You'll see clouds, blue sky, windows, the female torso, men in bowler hats, rocks, and castles arranged side by side as if they should mean something. People morph into animals or inanimate objects. The juxtaposition only short-circuits your brain when you try to make sense of it.

Magritte also trained and worked in Brussels. Though world-famous now, it took decades before his peculiar brand of surrealism caught on.

SLEEPING

€1 = about $1, country code: 32

Hotel prices are high in central Brussels, but you do have budget options. The modern hostels are especially good and rent double rooms. Business hotels offer super summer or weekend specials, cutting as much as two-thirds off their prices. And I've found a few fine little family-run hotels with good prices. April, May, September, and October are very crowded, and finding a room without a reservation can be impossible.

Business Hotels with Summer Rates

The fancy hotels of Brussels (Db-€150–200) survive off the business and diplomatic trade. They are desperately empty in July and August (sometimes June, too) and on weekends (most Fri, Sat, and Sun nights). If you ask for a summer/weekend rate you'll save about a third. If you go through the TI, you'll save up to two-thirds. Four-star hotels in the center abound with summer rates around €70. If you're willing to sink as low as three stars, you'll probably get a double room with enough comforts to keep a diplomat happy, including a fancy breakfast, for as low as €60.

The TI assured me that every day in July and August there are tons of business-class hotel rooms on the push list. You'll get a big discount by just showing up at either TI (for same-day booking only). In July and August—trust me—your best value is to arrive without a reservation, walk from the Central Station down to either TI, and let them book you a room within a few blocks. These seasonal rates apply only to business-class hotels. Because of this, budget accommodations, which charge the same throughout the year, go from being a good value one day (say, a Thursday in summer) to a bad value the next (a Friday in summer).

Sleep Code

S = Single, **D** = Double/Twin, **T** = Triple, **Q** = Quad, **b** = bathroom, **s** = shower only, **CC** = Credit Cards accepted, **no CC** = Credit Cards not accepted. Everyone speaks English.

To help you easily sort through these listings, I've divided the rooms into three categories, based on the price for a standard double room with bath:

Higher Priced—Most rooms €100 or more.
Moderately Priced—Most rooms €80–100.
Lower Priced—Most rooms less than €80.

Hotels near the Grand-Place

HIGHER PRICED

Hotel Ibis has six locations in or near Brussels; the best is well situated halfway between the Central Station and the Grand-Place—a sprawling modern place offering 184 quiet, simple, industrial-strength-yet-comfy rooms (Sb or Db-€129 Mon–Thu, €109 Fri–Sun, Tb-€144 or €139, rooms €15 more in Sept, extra person-€15, breakfast-€9, CC, air-con, elevator, smoke-free rooms, Grasmarkt 100, tel. 02-514-4040, fax 02-514-5067, www.ibishotel.com, e-mail: h1046-re@accor-hotels.com).

Hotel le Dixseptième, a four-star luxury place ideally located a block below the Central Station, is an expensive oasis in the heart of town. Prim, proper, and peaceful, with chandeliers and squeaky hardwood floors, it comes with all the comforts (24 rooms, Db-€260, €172 in summer and on weekends, suites €340 and up, extra bed-€25, includes breakfast, CC, no-smoking rooms, air-con, free Internet access, elevator, rue de la Madeleine 25, tel. 02-517-1717, fax 02-502-6424, www.ledixseptieme.be).

MODERATELY PRICED

Hotel la Madeleine, on the small square between the station and the Grand Place, rents 52 plain rooms with a good location and a friendly staff (S-€50, no shower at all for this room; Ss-€70, Sb-€90, Db-€90; "executive" rooms: Sb-€110, Db-€115, Tb-€130, includes breakfast, CC, elevator, Rue de la Montagne 22, tel. 02-513-2973, fax 02-502-1350, www.hotel-la-madeleine.be). You can't check in before 15:00, but you can drop off your bags.

Hotel the Moon, which just opened in 2002, is a concrete and efficient place with 17 fresh if industrial-strength rooms,

Brussels Hotels

1. Hotel La Madeleine
2. Hotel The Moon
3. Hotel Pacific
4. Hotel Ibis
5. Hotel Opera
6. Hotel Floris
7. Hotel Le Dixseptieme
8. Mozart Hotel
9. Hotel La Legende
10. Hotel Welcome
11. Hotel Noga
12. Residence Les Ecrins
13. Citadines Sainte-Catherine Apart'hotel
14. Brueghel Hostel
15. Sleepwell

good beds, and almost no public spaces. While it has absolutely no character, you'll sleep fine and it's super-convenient, right in the old center (Sb-€65, Db-€80, Tb-€100, 10 percent cheaper on weekends and in July–Aug, includes skimpy breakfast, CC, rue de la Montagne 4, tel. 02-508-1580, fax 02-508-1585, e-mail: hotelthemoon@hotmail.com).

Hotel Opéra, on a great, people-filled street near the Grand-Place, is professional, dark, and classy, with street noise and 49 boxy rooms (Sb-€68, Db-€85, Tb-€93, Qb-€107, 10 percent less on weekends, includes breakfast, CC, courtyard rooms are quieter, elevator, Internet access, rue Gretry 53, tel. 02-219-4343, fax 02-219-1720, www.hotel-opera.be, e-mail: hotel.opera@skynet.be).

Hotel Floris, with wood floors and some beamed ceilings, has 12 spacious rooms just off the Grand Place and right across from the TI (Sb-€90, Db-€100, 2-person suite-€140, third person-€30, includes breakfast, CC, elevator, rue des Harengs 6–8, tel. 02-514-0760, fax 02-548-9039, www.grouptorus.com, e-mail: floris.grandplace@grouptorus.com).

Mozart Hotel, lacquered in marble and antiques and filled with old paintings, offers 47 comfortable rooms for a good price on a small café-filled lane just off the Grand-Place (Db-€95, includes breakfast, CC, elevator, rue Marché aux Fromages 23, tel. 02-502-6661, fax 02-502-7758, www.hotel-mozart.be, e-mail: mozart@skynet.be).

Hotel la Légende rents 26 rooms a block from the *Manneken-Pis* statue. While on a busy road, it has a pleasant courtyard. The furnishings are cheap, the "hardwood" panels on the floor are obviously fake, and the management is paranoid. But the location and price are right and the rooms are comfortable enough (small Db facing courtyard-€81, bigger fancier Db-€99, Tb-€125, Qb-€135, weekends are 6 percent cheaper but you must stay 2 nights, includes breakfast, CC, elevator, rue du Lombard 35, tel. 02-512-8290, fax 02-512-3493, www.hotellalegende.com).

LOWER PRICED

Hotel Pacific is gently run by Paul Powells, whose motto is "safe, clean, and cheap." While the charming breakfast room is from the 19th century, the ramshackle upstairs (with 15 backpacker rooms) feels like a Jackson Pollock thrift shop in a tree house. Even with the wrinkly linoleum and funky furnishings, Paul gives the place an enjoyable calmness (S-€35, D-€55, T-€75, prices include cheese-omelet breakfast, no CC, non-smoking rooms, elevator, 24:00 curfew, easy phone reservations, rue Antoine Dansaert 57, tel. 02-511-8459).

Hotels around the Fish Market

The next four listings are a 10-minute walk from the intensity of the old center, near the Ste. Catherine Métro stop. This charming neighborhood, called "the village in Brussels," faces the canalside fish market and has plenty of the town's best restaurants.

HIGHER PRICED

Citadines Sainte-Catherine Apart'hotel, part of a Europe-wide chain, is a huge "apart-hotel" with modern, shipshape rooms. Choose from efficiency studios with fold-out double beds or two-room apartments with a bedroom and a fold-out couch in the living room. All 170 units come with a kitchen, stocked cupboards, a stereo, and everything you need to settle right in (studio for one or two-€102, apartment for up to four-€146, 10 percent cheaper by the week, 50 percent cheaper by the month, breakfast-€11, parking-€8, 51 quai au Bois à Bruler, tel. 02-221-1411, fax 02-221-1599, e-mail: stecatherine@citadines.com).

MODERATELY PRICED

Hotel Welcome, owned by a bundle of hospitality and energy named Meester Smeesters, offers small but business-class rooms. Each of the 16 rooms has a different geographic theme—from India to Japan to Bali (prices are the same for 1 or 2 people: Db-€70, "business-class" Africa Db-€80, "executive-class" Db-€100, "junior suite" Egypt Db with view-€120, large suite-€130, extra bed-€13, breakfast-€8, CC, elevator, parking-€8, 23 Quai au Bois à Bruler, tel. 02-219-9546, fax 02-217-1887, www.hotelwelcome.com, e-mail: reservation@hotelwelcom.com, run by Sophie and Michael Smeesters with the assistance of Vanessa). Guests get a 5 percent discount at the pricey attached restaurant, La Truite d'Argent.

    Hotel Noga feels extremely homey with a welcoming game room and old photos of Belgian royalty lining the hallways. It's carefully run by Frederich Fouchon and his family (19 rooms, Sb-€75, Db-€95, Tb-€125, Qb-€150, all rooms 20 percent less on weekends and every day in Aug, includes breakfast, CC, very quiet, rue du Beguinage 38, tel. 02-218-6763, fax 02-218-1603, www.nogahotel.com, e-mail: info @nogahotel.com).

LOWER PRICED

Résidence les Ecrins, on a quiet street, is a friendly guesthouse run by helpful Alan and Luc. Its 11 cheery, pastel rooms have simple furnishings (Sb-€45–70, Db-€50–80, Tb-€60–90, all double beds, includes breakfast, CC, no elevator, rue du Rouleau

15, tel. 02-219-3657, fax 02-223-5740, www.lesecrins.com,
e-mail: les.ecrins@skynet.be).

Hostels

Three classy and modern hostels, in buildings that could
double as small, state-of-the-art, minimum-security prisons,
are within a 10-minute walk of the Central Station. Each
accepts people of all ages, serves cheap hot meals, takes credit
cards, and charges about the same price. All rates include breakfast and showers down the hall.

Brueghel Hostel, a fortress of cleanliness, is handiest and
most comfortable. Of its many rooms, 22 are bunk-bed doubles
(S-€23, D-€38, beds in quads-€15, beds in bigger dorms-€13,
nonmembers-€2.50 extra per night, open 7:00–10:00 & 14:00–
24:00, rue de St. Esprit 2, midway between Midi and Central
Stations, behind Chapelle church, tel. 02-511-0436, fax 02-512-
0711, www.vjh.be, e-mail: brussel@vhj.be).

Sleepwell, surrounded by high-rise parking lots, is also
comfortable (S-€25, D-€38, T-€19 per person, €12–15 for
beds in larger rooms, non-smoking, Internet access, walking
tours-€2.50/person, Rue de Damier 23, tel. 02-218-5050, fax
02-218-1313, www.sleepwell.be, e-mail: info@sleepwell.be).

Jacques Brel is a little farther out but still a reasonable
walk from everything (180 beds, S-€23, D-€38, T/Q-€15 per
person, bed in dorm-€13, includes breakfast and sheets, no
curfew, non-smoking rooms, laundry available, rue de la Sablon-
nière 30, tel. 02-218-0187, fax 02-217-2005, www.laj.be, e-mail:
brusselsbrel@laj.be).

EATING

Brussels is known for its high-quality French-style cuisine and for multicultural variety. Seafood—fish, eels, shrimp, and oysters—is especially well prepared here. For information on Belgian cuisine, see page 275.

Mussels in Brussels

Mussels are served all over town. For an atmospheric cellar or a table right on the Grand Place, eat at 't Kelderke (daily 12:00–24:00, Grand Place 15, tel. 02-513-7344). It serves local specialties, including mussels (a splittable kilo bucket for €16).

The touristy **Restaurant Chez Leon** is a mussels factory—slamming out piles of good and cheap buckets in the intense restaurant lane (see below). It's a big, welcoming place with busy green-aproned waiters offering a "Formula Leon" for €12.25, a light meal consisting of a small bucket of mussels, fries, and a beer (daily 12:00–23:00, non-smoking section, kids eat free, rue des Bouchers 18, tel. 02-511-1415).

Restaurant Lane—Rue des Bouchers

Brussels' restaurant streets—two blocks north of the Grand Place—are touristy and notorious for aggressively sucking you in and ripping you off. But the area is an exhilarating spectacle and fun for at least a walk. Order carefully and understand the prices thoroughly.

Restaurant Chez Leon is the place for buckets of cheap and good mussels (see above). **Aux Armes de Bruxelles** is a venerable eatery that has been serving reliably good food to locals in a dressy setting for generations (indoors only, €30 menus, Tue–Sun 12:00–23:00, closed Mon, Rue des Bouchers 13, tel. 02-511-5550). **Scheltema** creates a wonderful old-time brasserie elegance in the midst of this food ghetto. The presentation is four-star, the sea-food is fresh, and the kitchen is gleaming and a part of the bustling ambience (€30 menus, Mon–Sat 18:30–23:00, closed Sun, a block off rue des Bouchers at 7 Rue des Dominicains, tel. 02-512-2084).

More Eateries near the Grand Place

La Maison des Crêpes is a sweet little place serving delicious €7 crêpes (savory and sweet) and salads, just a half-block south of the Bourse (daily 11:30–23:30, good beers, rue du Midi 13, cellular 0477-301-388).

Osteria a l'Ombra, a tiny three-table place across the lane from the TI a block off the Grand Place, is perfect for anyone needing a quality bowl of pasta with a fine glass of Italian wine served by good-looking pony-tailed Italian stallions. It's pricey but the woody bistro ambience and tasty food make it a good value (daily 12:00–15:00 & 18:30–24:00, rue des Harengs 2, tel. 02-511-6710).

You'll find *frites* (french fries) and sandwich shops through-out Brussels. **Panos** (on Grasmarkt, across from entrance of Galleries Royales St. Hubert) and **La Suisse** (across from the Bourse) are both reliably good.

Two **supermarkets** are about a block from the Bourse and a few blocks from the Grand Place. **AD Delhaize** is at the intersection of Anspachlan and Marché-aux-Poulets (Mon–Sat 9:00–20:00, Fri until 21:00, Sun 9:00–18:00), and **Super GB** is a half-block away at Halles and Marché-aux-Poulets (Mon–Sat 9:00–20:00, Fri until 21:00, closed Sun).

Around the Sainte Catherine Fish Market

A five-minute walk from the old center puts you in "the village within the city" area of Sainte Catherine, where the historic fish market has spawned a tradition of fine restaurants specializing mostly in seafood. The old fish canal survives and if you walk around it you'll see plenty of enticing restaurants. Consider these:

Bij den Boer, a fun and noisy eatery popular with locals and tourists, feels like a traditional and very successful brasserie. The specialty: fish (€25 menu, Mon–Sat 12:00–14:30 & 18:00–22:30, closed Sun, quai aux Briques 60, tel. 02-512-6122). Its neighbor, **Restaurant Jacques** (at #44), also has a good reputation.

La Marie Joseph, a stylish modern place with the focus only on the fish, has earned raves among locals (€30 meals, Tue–Sun 12:00–15:00 & 18:30–23:00, closed Mon, smoke-free zone, Brandhoutkaai 47, tel. 02-218-0596).

Restaurant le Loup-Galant is a wonderfully local place a block beyond the market, with a rustic-yet-dressy charm, serving

Brussels Restaurants

1. 't Kelderke
2. Restaurant Chez Leon
3. Aux Armes de Bruxelles
4. Scheltema
5. Bij Den Boer
6. La Marie Joseph
7. Restaurant Le Loup-Galant
8. La Pain Quotidien
9. L'Estrille du Vieux Bruxelles
10. La Maison des Crepes
11. In 't Spinnekopke
12. Osteria A l'Ombra
13. Le Cirio
14. A la Becasse
15. A la Mort Subite

fine contemporary Belgian cuisine from a menu that changes monthly with what's fresh (€25 three-course menu of the week, Tue–Sat 19:00–22:00, closed Sun–Mon, air-con, no tourists, reservations wise, quai aux Barques 4, tel. 02-219-9998).

In 't Spinnekopke, a five-minute walk from the Fish Market or Bourse (through an unappealing but safe neighborhood), is the king of traditional old Brussels eateries—the Spider's Head. Its dark, tangled halls of heavy wooden tables surrounded by antique paintings are filled with serious eaters (€15–20 plates, Mon–Sat 18:00–23:00, closed Sun, place du Jardin aux Fleurs 1, tel. 02-511-8695).

Near Place Grand Sablon

La Pain Quotidien ("The Daily Bread") is an incredibly atmospheric bakery that extends out back into an elegant "Marie-Antoinette has a picnic" terrace. You'll find classy open-face sandwiches, soups, and salads—expensive but fresh and tasty (daily 8:00–19:00, rue des Sablons 11, tel. 02-513-5154).

L'Estrille du Vieux Bruxelles is a dressy, half-timbered place just downhill from place Grand Sablon serving a fine €10 daily lunch special (daily 12:00–14:00, rue de Rollebeek 7, tel. 02-512-5857).

Sampling Belgian Beer with Food and Ambience

Looking for a good place to enjoy that famous Belgian beer? Brussels is full of atmospheric cafés to savor. The places lining the Grand Place are a little touristy, but the setting's hard to beat. I've listed three places a few minutes walk off the square with magical old-time ambience. For a few euros, you can generally get a cold meat plate, an open-face sandwich, or a salad.

All varieties of Belgian beers are available, but Brussels' most unusual beers are *lambic*-based. Look for *lambic doux, lambic blanche, gueuze* (pron. kurrs), *faro,* and fruit-flavored *lambics* such as *Kriek* and *Framboise.* These beers look and taste more like a dry, somewhat bitter cider. The brewer doesn't add yeast—the beer ferments naturally from yeast found floating only in the marshy air around Brussels. For more on Belgian beer, see page 276.

At **Le Cirio,** across from the Bourse, the dark wooden tables boast the skid marks of over a century's worth of beer steins (rue de la Bourse 18–20, tel. 02-512-1395).

A la Bécasse is lower profile, with a simple wood-panel and wood-table decor that appeals to both poor students and businessmen at lunch. The home-brewed *lambic doux* is like a cider, served in a clay jar. It's just around the corner toward the Grand Place, hidden away at the end of a courtyard (daily from 10:00, rue de Tabora 11, tel. 02-511-0006).

A la Mort Subite, beyond the restaurant streets, is a classic old bar that retains its 1928 decor and many of its 1928 customers (rue Montagne-aux-Herbes Potagères 7, tel. 02-513-1318). Named 80 years ago after the "sudden death" playoff that workingmen used to end their lunchtime dice games, the place still has an unpretentious, working-class feel. The decor is simple, with wood tables, grimy yellow wallpaper, and some-other-era garland trim. A typical lunch or snack here is a *tartine* (open-face sandwich) spread with *fromage blanc* (cream cheese) or pressed meat. Eat it with one of the home-brewed *lambic*-based beers.

TRANSPORTATION CONNECTIONS: BELGIUM

Belgium's train system is tops, and its various rail deals are worth considering (these are well-described in English at www.b-rail.be).
- The second-class Multipass gives groups of 3–5 people any two trips in Belgium (3 people-€35, 4 people-€40, 5 people-€44, at least one pass user must be 26 or older).
- People under age 26 can get a Go Pass: €39 for 10 rides anywhere in Belgium.
- Seniors age 60-plus can get any six rides for €46 (available in first class only).
- Those traveling on the weekend should ask for the weekend discount for round-trips (40 percent off for 1 person, 60 percent off for any traveling companions).

Transportation Connections—Bruges
From Brussels, an hour away by train, all of Europe is at your fingertips (see below). Train info: tel. 050-302-424.

By Train: To Brussels (2/hr, usually at :33 and :59, 1 hr, €10), **Ghent** (4/hr, 40 min), **Ostende** (3/hr, 15 min), **Köln** (6/day, 4 hrs), **Paris** (hrly via Brussels, 2.5 hrs, must pay supplement of €10.50 second class, €21 first class, even with a railpass), **Amsterdam** (hrly, 3.5 hrs, transfer in Antwerp or Brussels), **Amsterdam's Schiphol Airport** (hrly, 3.5 hrs, transfer in Antwerp or Brussels, €35).

Trains from England: Bruges is an ideal "welcome to Europe" stop after London. Take the Eurostar train from London to Brussels under the English Channel (9/day, 3 hrs), then transfer, backtracking to Bruges (2/hr, 1 hr). Or, if you'd prefer to cross the Channel by boat, catch the London-to-Dover train (2 hrs, from London's Victoria station), then the catamaran to Ostende (2 hrs; train station at Ostende catamaran terminal), then the Ostende-to-

Belgium Transportation Connections

Bruges train (15 min). Five boats run daily from London to Bruges and vice versa (€37 one-way, 5-hrs, same price for cheap 5-day round-trip ticket, reserve by phone with CC and pick up your ticket at the dock, tel. 059-559-955).

Transportation Connections—Brussels

By Train: To Bruges (2/hr, 1 hr, from Central, Midi, and Nord stations), **Amsterdam** (stopping at Amsterdam's Schiphol Airport on the way, hrly, 3 hrs, from Central, Midi, or Nord, sometimes from just one but sometimes all three), **Berlin** (7/day, 7.5–8 hrs, from Central or Midi, transfer in Köln, 9-hr direct night train from Midi), **Bern** (5/day, 8–9.5 hrs, from Central, Midi, or Nord with complicated transfers; consider the direct 8.5-hr night train from Nord), **Frankfurt** (9/day, 5.5 hrs, from Midi; or transfer in Köln from Central, Midi, and Nord), **Munich** (9/day, 8.5–9.5 hrs, from Central, Midi, and Nord, most transfer in Köln and sometimes also Mannheim), **Rome** (3/day, 17 hrs, from Nord, transfer in Milan, Zurich, or Paris), **Paris** (fast trains zip to Paris—hrly, 90 min, from Midi—it's best to book by 20:00 the day before or risk limited availability on same day; even railpass holders need to pay the supplement of €11 second class, €21 first class). Every day there are two slow, no-supplement trains leaving Brussels Midi for Paris: the 17:11 departure (4.5 hrs, requires transfer in Charleroi Sud) and the night departure at 1:30 (direct, 5.5 hrs; confirm schedule at station). Train info: tel. 02-528-2828 (long wait).

To London: Brussels and London are just three hours apart by Eurostar train (9/day, under the English Channel in 20 min). To find out the latest prices or to book a ticket, call U.S. tel. 800/EUROSTAR or Belgian tel. 0900-10366, or visit www.raileurope.com or www.eurostar.be.

In 2002, full-fare one-way tickets cost $199 for second class and $279 for first class (full-fare tickets are exchangeable and fully refundable even after your departure date). The cheaper second-class "Leisure" ticket costs $139 (Leisure tickets are nonrefundable but exchangeable up to 3 days before departure). Railpass holders get discounts ($75 one-way for second-class, $155 one-way for first-class). Cheaper 7- and 14-day advance-purchase tickets are usually available if you order your ticket in Europe (can call from home or book online).

To order your ticket in Belgium by phone, call 0900-10177 (expensive toll line costs €0.50/min from pay phone and €1.50/min from hotel); you can either pay with a credit card or simply reserve a seat (and pay at the station at least an hour before the train leaves). If you buy tickets in person in Belgium, go to a major train station rather than a travel agency; you'll get your tickets immediately (travel agencies can't deliver until the next day). You can also buy your Eurostar ticket at any major train station in Europe.

A cheap way to get from Brussels to London is by Eurolines bus (€46 one-way, €70 round-trip, tel. 02-203-0707 in Brussels, www.eurolines.com).

By Plane: Virgin Express flies cheaply between Brussels and London (hrly, starting at $72), plus Milan, Rome, Nice, Barcelona, Madrid, Ireland, and Copenhagen (Belgian tel. 02-752-0505, www.virgin-express.com).

Brussels Airport

Brussels Airport is 14 kilometers northeast of the city center. Shuttle trains run between the airport and Brussels' three train stations (€2.35, 4/hr, 25 min). Expect to pay about €25 for a cab into central Brussels. Airport info: tel. 0900-70-000, www.brusselsairport.be.

HISTORY

TWENTY CENTURIES IN FOUR PAGES

A.D. 1 to 1300—Romans and Invasions

When Rome falls (c. 400), the Low Countries shatter into a patchwork of local dukedoms, ravaged by Viking raids. Out of this poor, agricultural, and feudal landscape emerge three self-governing urban centers—Amsterdam, Bruges, and Brussels—each in a prime location for trade. Amsterdam and Bruges sit where rivers flow into the North Sea, while Brussels hugs a main trading highway.

Sights:
- Amsterdam's Dam Square
- Amsterdam History Museum displays
- Haarlem's Market Square
- Bruges' original fort and church ruins
- Bruges' Basilica of the Holy Blood (1150)
- Brussels' St. Michael's Church, model in City Museum, and Tour d'Angle from city wall

1300–1500—Booming Trade Towns

Bruges, the midway port between North Sea and Mediterranean trade, becomes one of Europe's busiest and richest cities. Amsterdam augments its beer and herring trade with budding capitalism: banking, loans, and speculation in stock and futures. Brussels sells waffles and beer to passing travelers. Politically, the Low Countries are united by marriage with the cultured empire of the Dukes of Burgundy.

Sights:
- Churches: Amsterdam's Oude Kerk and Nieuwe Kerk, and Haarlem's Grote Kerk
- Amsterdam's Waag (in Red Light District), Mint Tower from original city wall, and wooden house at Begijnhof 34
- Bruges' Bell Tower, City Hall Gothic Room, and Church of Our Lady
- Flemish Primitive art (van Eyck, Memling, van der Weyden) in Bruges' Groeninge Museum and Memling Museum, and in Brussels' Ancient Art Museum
- Brussels' Grand Place, medieval-street Restaurant Row, and Sablon Church

1500s—Protestants vs. Catholics, Freedom-Fighters vs. Spanish Rulers

Protestantism spreads through the Low Countries, particularly in Holland (while Belgium remains more Catholic). Thanks to other royal marriages, the Low Countries are ruled from afar by the very Catholic Hapsburg family in Spain. In 1566, angry Protestants rise up against Spain and Catholicism, vandalizing Catholic churches and deposing Spanish governors. King Philip II of Spain sends troops to restore order and brutally punish the rebel-heretics, beginning an 80-year war of independence (1568–1648).

Sights:
- Amsterdam's whitewashed, simply decorated, post-iconoclasm churches
- Amsterdam's old houses at Zeedijk 1 and Oudezijds Voorburgwal 14 (in Red Light District)
- Civic Guard portraits in Amsterdam History Museum
- Mementos of the Siege of Haarlem in Haarlem's Grote Kerk
- Brussels' tapestry designs

1600s—Holland's Golden Age

Holland gains its independence from the Hapsburgs (officially in 1648), while Belgium languishes under Spanish rule. Amsterdam invents the global economy, as its hardy sailors ply the open seas, trading in Indonesian spices, South American sugar, and African slaves. Their combined nautical and capitalist skills make Amsterdam the world's wealthiest city.

Sights:
- Amsterdam's Rijksmuseum and Haarlem's Frans Hals Museum—paintings by Rembrandt, Hals, Vermeer, and Steen
- Old townhouses and gables in Amsterdam's Jordaan and Red Light District
- Amsterdam's Begijnhof, Royal Palace, Westerkerk, and Rembrandt's house
- Brussels' *Manneken-Pis*

1700s—Elegant Decline

Holland and Belgium are both surpassed by the rise of superpowers France and England. Wars with those powers drain their economies and scuttle Holland's fleet. Still, they survive as bankers, small manufacturers, and craftsmen in luxury goods—but on a small scale fitting their geographical size. They hit rock-bottom in 1795

when French troops occupy the Low Countries (1795–1815) and Europe's powers subsequently saddle them with a monarchy.

Sights:
- Amsterdam's Amstelkring Hidden Church
- Herengracht Mansion
- Jewish Museum synagogues
- Brussels' Grand Place guildhalls
- Lace (popularity peaks c. 1700)

1800s—Revival

Though slow to join the Industrial Revolution, Holland picks up speed by century's end. A canal to the North Sea rejuvenates Amsterdam's port, railroads lace cities together, and Amsterdam hosts a World Exhibition. Belgium, having been placed under a Dutch king, revolts and gains its own king, a German this time.

Wealth from its colony in Africa's Congo region helps rebuild Brussels in grand style.

Sights:
- Amsterdam's Centraal Station, Rijksmuseum, and Magna Plaza
- Van Gogh paintings at the Van Gogh Museum
- Indonesian foods from the colonial era
- Brussels' Upper Town buildings and boulevards
- Brussels' Galeries St. Hubert
- Chocolate

1900s—Invasions by Germans, Hippies, and Immigrants

Belgium is a major battleground in both World Wars. Holland, neutral in World War I, suffers brutal occupation under the Nazis in World War II. After the war, Brussels becomes the center of the budding movement toward European economic unity. In Amsterdam, post-war prosperity and a tolerant atmosphere in the 1960s and 1970s make it a global magnet for hippies, freaks, and your co-authors. In the 1970s and 1980s, Amsterdam and Brussels are flooded with immigrants from former colonies, producing tensions but diversifying the population.

Sights:
- Amsterdam's Beurs, Tuschinski Theater, and National Monument on Dam Square
- Amsterdam's Anne Frank House and Dutch Resistance Museum
- Amsterdam's Heineken Brewery, rock-and-roll clubs Paradiso and Melkweg, and the new "Stopera" opera house
- Haarlem's Corrie Ten Boom House
- Paintings by René Magritte in Bruges' Groeninge and Brussels' Modern Art Museums
- Brussels' Atomium and European Parliament quarter

TIMELINE OF THE NETHERLANDS AND BELGIUM

57 B.C.—Julius Caesar invades the Low Countries, conquering local Batavian, Frisian, and Belgae tribes, beginning four centuries of Roman rule.

A.D. 406—Frankish tribes from Germany drive out the last Roman legions as Rome's Europe-wide empire collapses. Christian missionaries work to prevent the area from reverting to paganism.

c. 800—Charlemagne, born in Belgium, rules the Low Countries as part of a large North European empire. After his death, his grandsons divide the kingdom and bicker among themselves.

c. 880–1000—Vikings rape and pillage the Low Countries during two centuries of raids.

c. 900—The Low Countries are a patchwork of small dukedoms ruled by bishops and local counts (of Holland, Flanders, Brabant, and so on) who owe allegiance to greater kings in France, Germany, and England.

c. 1250—In Amsterdam, fishermen build a dike (dam) where the Amstel River flows into the North Sea, creating a prime trading port. Soon the town gains independence and trading privileges from the local count and bishop. Meanwhile, Bruges becomes a major weaver of textiles, and Brussels becomes a minor trading town along the Germany–Bruges highway.

c. 1300—Italian and Portuguese sailors forge a coast-hugging trade route from the Mediterranean to the North Sea, with Bruges as the final stop.

1302—In Bruges, Flemish rebels drive out French rulers at the Battle of the Golden Spurs.

1345—Amsterdam's Miracle of the Host. A flame-resistant communion wafer causes miracles and attracts pilgrims.

1384—The discovery of a process to cure herring with salt makes Amsterdam a major fish exporter (to augment its thriving beer trade).

1384—Mary of Flanders marries Duke Philip the Bold of Burgundy, making Holland and Belgium part of a Burgundian empire that eventually stretches from Amsterdam to Switzerland.

c. 1400—Bruges is Europe's greatest trade city, the middleman between North and South.

1433—Burgundy's empire peaks when Duke Philip the Good takes over the titles of the local counts. His cultured court makes the Low Countries a center of art, literature, ideas, and pageantry.

1482—Mary of Burgundy, the last heir to the Burgundian throne, falls from a horse and dies. Her possessions (including Holland and Belgium) pass to her Austrian husband, Maximilian, and get swallowed up in his family's large Holy Roman Empire, ruled from Austria and later Spain.

1492—Columbus' voyage demonstrates the potential wealth of New World trade.

1517—The German Martin Luther's 95 theses inspire Protestantism, which becomes popular in the Low Countries (especially Holland). Later refugees of religious persecution, including Calvinists and Anabaptists, find a home in tolerant Amsterdam.

1519—King Charles V (1500–1558), the grandson of Mary of Burgundy and Maximilian, inherits all of his family's combined possessions. Charles rules Holland and Belgium as well as Austria, Spain, Germany, Spain's New World colonies, and much more. A staunch Catholic, Charles battles rebellious Protestant princes.

1535—On Amsterdam's Dam Square, Anabaptist rebels are hanged, drawn, and quartered.

1540—Emperor Charles' son, Philip of Spain invites the Inquisition to Spain.

1556—Philip II, based in Spain, succeeds his father as ruler of the Netherlands and intensifies the wars on Protestants (especially Calvinists).

1566—In a wave of anti-Catholic and anti-Spanish fury, extreme Protestants storm Catholic churches, vandalizing religious objects and converting the churches to Protestant (the Iconoclasm). Philip II sends soldiers to the Low Countries to establish order and punish rebels and heretics.

1568—Holland's Protestant counts rally around William "The Silent" of Orange, demanding freedom from Spanish Hapsburg rule (the Beggars' Revolt). This begins 80 years of on-again-off-again war with Spain, called . . . the Eighty Years' War.

1572–1573—The Spanish conquer Haarlem after a long siege, but Haarlem's brave stand inspires other towns to carry on the fight.

1578—Amsterdam switches sides (the Alteration), joining the Protestant independence movement. Extreme Calvinists control the city for several decades, officially outlawing Catholic services. Within a few years, Spanish troops are driven south out of Holland, and future battles take place mostly on Belgian soil.

1580—Holland and Belgium go separate ways in the war. Holland's towns and counts form a Protestant, military alliance against Catholic Spain (the United Provinces), while Belgium remains Catholic, with Brussels as the capital of Spanish Hapsburg rule.

1585—Antwerp, Northern Europe's greatest trading city (pop. 150,000), falls to Spanish troops. In the chaos, business plummets, and many Protestant merchants leave town. Industrious Amsterdam steps in to fill the vacuum of trade.

1588—Elizabeth I of England defeats the Spanish Armada (navy), breaking Spain's monopoly on overseas trade.

1602—The Dutch East India Company (V.O.C.), a government-subsidized trading company, is formed, soon followed by the West India Company (1622). Together, they make Amsterdam (pop. 100,000) the center of a global trading empire. Spices from Indonesia, sugar from America, and slaves from Africa funded Holland's Golden Age (c. 1600–1650).

1609—Henry Hudson's *Half Moon*, sailing for the Dutch East India Company, departs Amsterdam in search of a western passage to the Orient. Instead, Hudson finds the island of Manhattan, which soon becomes New Amsterdam (New York, 1625).

1616—Frans Hals paints the *St. George Civic Guards* (Frans Hals Museum, Haarlem).

1620—Pilgrims from England stop in Holland on their way to America.

1631—Rembrandt moves to Amsterdam, a wealthy city of 120,000 people, including René Descartes (1596–1650) and Erasmus (1585–1638), plus many different religious sects and a thriving Jewish Quarter.

1637—After a decade of insanely lucrative trade in tulip bulbs ("tulip mania"), the market crashes.

1648—The Treaty of Munster (and the Treaty of West-phalia) officially end the Eighty Years' War with Spain. The United Provinces (today's Netherlands) are now an independent nation.

1652–1654—Holland battles England over control of the seas. This is the first of three wars with England (also in 1665 and 1672) that sap Holland's wealth.

1672–1678—Louis XIV of France invades Holland, gets 25 kilometers from Amsterdam, but is finally stopped when the citizens open the Amstel locks and flood the city. After another draining war with France (1701–1713), England and France overtake Holland in overseas trade.

1689—Holland's William of Orange is invited by England's Parliament to replace the despot they'd deposed. He, ruling with wife Mary, becomes King William III of England.

1695—Louis XIV of France bombs and incinerates Brussels, punishing them for allying against him.

1776—The American Revolution inspires European democrats and worries nobles.

1787—Holland's budding democratic movement, the Patriots, is suppressed and exiled when Prussian troops invade Holland.

1789—French Revolution begins.

1795—France, battling Europe's monarchs to keep their Revolution alive, invades and occupies Holland (establishing the "Batavian Republic," 1795–1806) and Belgium.

1806—Napoleon Bonaparte, who turned France's Revolution into a dictatorship, proclaims his brother, Louis Napoleon, to be King of Holland (1806–1810).

1815—After Napoleon's defeat at Waterloo (near Brussels), Europe's nobles decide that the Low Countries should be a monarchy, ruled jointly by a Dutch prince, who becomes King William I. (Today's Queen Beatrix is descended from him.)

1830—Belgium rebels against the Dutch-born king, becoming an independent country under King Leopold I.

1860—The novel *Max Havelaar* by the Dutch writer Multatuli exposes the dark side of Holland's repressive colonial rule in Indonesia.

1876—The North Sea Canal opens after 52 years of building, revitalizing Amsterdam's port. In the next decade, the city builds the Centraal Station, Rijksmuseum, and Concertgebouw and hosts a World Exhibition (1883) that attracts three million visitors.

1881—King Leopold II of Belgium acquires Africa's Congo region, tapping its wealth to rebuild Brussels with broad boulevards and big marble buildings (neoclassical style).

1914—In World War I, Holland remains neutral, while Belgium becomes the horrific battleground where Germany dukes it out with England and France—for example, at Ieper (Ypres in French).

1932—The Dutch Zuiderzee dike is completed, making the former arm of the North Sea into a freshwater lake (the IJsselmeer) and creating many square kilometers of reclaimed land.

1940—Nazi Germany bombs Holland's Rotterdam and easily occupies the Netherlands and Belgium. Belgium's king officially surrenders, while Holland's Queen Wilhelmina (1880–1962) flees to England. In Amsterdam, Anne Frank and her Jewish family go into hiding in an attempt to avoid arrest by the Nazis (1942–1944). Late in the war, Belgium is the site of Germany's last-gasp offensive, the Battle of the Bulge.

1945—Holland and Belgium are liberated by Allied troops.

1949—Indonesia gains its independence from Holland.

1953—Major floods in Holland kill almost 2,000 people, prompting more dams and storm barriers (the Delta Project, 1958–1997).

1957—Belgium and the Netherlands join the EEC (Common Market)—the forerunner of today's European Union—with headquarters in Brussels.

1960—The Benelux economic union is formed, linking Belgium, the Netherlands, and Luxembourg. Belgium, after years of protests, grants independence to the Belgian Congo.

1967—Amsterdam is Europe's center for hippies and the youth movement.

1975—Surinam (Dutch Guyana) gains its independence from Holland, and many emigrants flock to Holland.

1980—Queen Beatrix (1938–) becomes ruler of Holland.

1992—Belgium and the Netherlands sign the Treaty of Maastricht, which creates the European Union (EU).

1995—Floods cause a billion dollars in damage.

2002—Dutch soldiers, part of an international force, aid America's invasion and occupation of Afghanistan.

2003—You arrive in Amsterdam, Bruges, and Brussels and make your own history.

APPENDIX

Let's Talk Telephones

Here's a primer on making phone calls. For information specific to the Netherlands and Belgium, see "Telephones" in the introduction.

Making Calls within a European Country: About half of all European countries use area codes (like we do); the other half uses a direct-dial system without area codes.

To make calls within a country that uses a direct-dial system (Belgium, the Czech Republic, Denmark, France, Italy, Portugal, Norway, Spain, and Switzerland), you dial the same number whether you're calling across the country or across the street.

In countries that use area codes (such as the Netherlands, Austria, Britain, Finland, Germany, Ireland, and Sweden), you dial the local number when calling within a city, and you add the area code if calling long-distance within the country.

Making International Calls: You always start with the international access code (011 if you're calling from the U.S. or Canada, or 00 from Europe), then dial the country code of the country you're calling (see chart below).

What you dial next depends on the phone system of the country you're calling. If the country uses area codes, drop the initial 0 of the area code, then dial the rest of the number.

Countries that use direct-dial systems (no area codes) vary in how they're accessed internationally by phone. For instance, if you're making an international call to the Czech Republic, Denmark, Italy, Norway, Portugal, or Spain, simply dial the international access code, country code, and the local phone number. But if you're calling Belgium, France, or Switzerland, drop the initial 0 of the local phone number.

European Calling Chart

Just smile and dial, using this key:
AC = Area Code, LN = Local Number.

European Country	Calling long distance within...	Calling from the U.S.A./ Canada to...	Calling from another European country to...
Austria	AC (Area Code) + LN (Local Number)	011 + 43 + AC (without the initial zero) + LN	00 + 43 + AC (without the initial zero) + LN
Belgium	LN	011 + 32 + LN (without initial zero)	00 + 32 + LN (without initial zero)
Britain	AC + LN	011 + 44 + AC (without initial zero) + LN	00 + 44 + AC . (without initial zero) + LN
Czech Republic	LN	011 + 420 + LN	00 + 420 + LN
Denmark	LN	011 + 45 + LN	00 + 45 + LN
Estonia	LN	011 + 372 + LN	00 + 372 + LN
Finland	AC + LN	011 + 358 + AC (without initial zero) + LN	00 + 358 + AC (without initial zero) + LN
France	LN	011 + 33 + LN (without initial zero)	00 + 33 + LN (without initial zero)
Germany	AC + LN	011 + 49 + AC (without initial zero) + LN	00 + 49 + AC (without initial zero) + LN
Gibraltar	LN	011 + 350 + LN	00 + 350 + LN From Spain: 9567 + LN
Greece	LN	011 + 30 + LN	00 + 30 + LN

European Country	Calling long distance within...	Calling from the U.S.A./ Canada to...	Calling from another European country to...
Ireland	AC + LN	011 + 353 + AC (without initial zero) + LN	00 + 353 + AC (without initial zero) + LN
Italy	LN	011 + 39 + LN	00 + 39 + LN
Morocco	LN	011 + 212 + LN (without initial zero)	00 + 212 + LN (without initial zero)
Nether- lands	AC + LN	011 + 31 + AC (without initial zero) + LN	00 + 31 + AC (without initial zero) + LN
Norway	LN	011 + 47 + LN	00 + 47 + LN
Portugal	LN	011 + 351 + LN	00 + 351 + LN
Spain	LN	011 + 34 + LN	00 + 34 + LN
Sweden	AC + LN	011 + 46 + AC (without initial zero) + LN	00 + 46 + AC (without initial zero) + LN
Switzer- land	LN	011 + 41 + LN (without initial zero)	00 + 41 + LN (without initial zero)
Turkey	AC (if no initial zero is included, add one) + LN	011 + 90 + AC (without initial zero) + LN	00 + 90 + AC (without initial zero) + LN

- The instructions above apply whether you're calling a fixed phone or cell phone.
- The international access codes (the first numbers you dial when making an international call) are 011 if you're calling from the U.S.A./Canada, or 00 if you're calling from virtually anywhere in Europe. Finland and Lithuania are the only exceptions. If calling from either of these countries, replace the 00 with 990 in Finland and 810 in Lithuania.
- To call the U.S.A. or Canada from Europe, dial 00 (unless you're calling from Finland or Lithuania), then 1 (the country code for the U.S.A. and Canada), then the area code and number. In short, 00 + 1 + AC + LN = Hi, Mom!

International Access Codes

When making international calls, first dial the international access code of the country you're calling from. For the United States and Canada, it's 011. Virtually all European countries use 00 as their international access code; the only exceptions are Finland (990) and Lithuania (810).

Country Codes

After you've dialed the international access code, dial the code of the country you're calling.

Austria—43	Greece—30
Belgium—32	Ireland—353
Britain—44	Italy—39
Canada—1	Morocco—212
Czech Rep.—420	Netherlands—31
Denmark—45	Norway—47
Estonia—372	Portugal—351
Finland—358	Spain—34
France—33	Sweden—46
Germany—49	Switzerland—41
Gibraltar—350	United States—1

U.S. Embassies

The Netherlands

U.S. Embassy: Lange Voorhout 102, The Hague (Mon-Fri 8:15-17:00, tel. 070/310-9209, www.usemb.nl).

U.S. Consulate: Museumplein 19, Amsterdam (for passport concerns, open Mon-Fri 8:30-11:30, tel. 020/575-5309, www.usemb.nl/consul.htm).

Belgium

U.S. Embassy: Regentlaan 27 Boulevard du Regent, Brussels (Mon-Fri 9:00-18:00, tel. 02/508-2111, www.usembassy.be).

Festivals and Public Holidays

Here's a partial list of festivals and public holidays in the Netherlands and Belgium. For more information, see www.amsterdampromotion.nl, www.visitbelgium.com, and www.whatsonwhen.com.

Jan 1	New Year's Day
	Netherlands & Belgium
April 20	Easter
	Netherlands & Belgium
April 30	Queen's Day (Koninginnedag): birthday of

2003

JANUARY
S	M	T	W	T	F	S
			1	2	3	4
5	6	7	8	9	10	11
12	13	14	15	16	17	18
19	20	21	22	23	24	25
26	27	28	29	30	31	

FEBRUARY
S	M	T	W	T	F	S
						1
2	3	4	5	6	7	8
9	10	11	12	13	14	15
16	17	18	19	20	21	22
23	24	25	26	27	28	

MARCH
S	M	T	W	T	F	S
						1
2	3	4	5	6	7	8
9	10	11	12	13	14	15
16	17	18	19	20	21	22
23/30	24/31	25	26	27	28	29

APRIL
S	M	T	W	T	F	S
		1	2	3	4	5
6	7	8	9	10	11	12
13	14	15	16	17	18	19
20	21	22	23	24	25	26
27	28	29	30			

MAY
S	M	T	W	T	F	S
				1	2	3
4	5	6	7	8	9	10
11	12	13	14	15	16	17
18	19	20	21	22	23	24
25	26	27	28	29	30	31

JUNE
S	M	T	W	T	F	S
1	2	3	4	5	6	7
8	9	10	11	12	13	14
15	16	17	18	19	20	21
22	23	24	25	26	27	28
29	30					

JULY
S	M	T	W	T	F	S
		1	2	3	4	5
6	7	8	9	10	11	12
13	14	15	16	17	18	19
20	21	22	23	24	25	26
27	28	29	30	31		

AUGUST
S	M	T	W	T	F	S
					1	2
3	4	5	6	7	8	9
10	11	12	13	14	15	16
17	18	19	20	21	22	23
24/31	25	26	27	28	29	30

SEPTEMBER
S	M	T	W	T	F	S
	1	2	3	4	5	6
7	8	9	10	11	12	13
14	15	16	17	18	19	20
21	22	23	24	25	26	27
28	29	30				

OCTOBER
S	M	T	W	T	F	S
			1	2	3	4
5	6	7	8	9	10	11
12	13	14	15	16	17	18
19	20	21	22	23	24	25
26	27	28	29	30	31	

NOVEMBER
S	M	T	W	T	F	S
						1
2	3	4	5	6	7	8
9	10	11	12	13	14	15
16	17	18	19	20	21	22
23/30	24	25	26	27	28	29

DECEMBER
S	M	T	W	T	F	S
	1	2	3	4	5	6
7	8	9	10	11	12	13
14	15	16	17	18	19	20
21	22	23	24	25	26	27
28	29	30	31			

	Queen Mother Juliana—party in the streets! Netherlands
May 1	Labor Day Netherlands & Belgium
May 4	WII Remembrance Day Netherlands
May 5	Liberation Day Netherlands
May 8	VE Day Netherlands & Belgium
May 9	Ascension Day Netherlands & Belgium
May (2nd Sat)	National Windmill Day—sails whirl and many mills are opened to public Netherlands

May 29	Procession of the Holy Blood Bruges
May 29–31	Ascension weekend Netherlands & Belgium
Month of June	Holland Arts Festival—concerts, theater, etc. Netherlands
June (1st week)	Kunst RAI—contemporary art exhibition Netherlands
June (1st week)	Amsterdam Kite Festival Halfweg, Netherlands
June (2nd Sat)	Grachtenloop (run around canals) Amsterdam
June 7–9	Pentacost weekend Netherlands & Belgium
Early July	Ommegang festival—pomp and pageantry Grand Place, Brussels, Belgium
Mid July	North Sea Jazz Festival The Hague, Netherlands
July 21	Independence Day Belgium
Aug 15	Assumption Day Belgium
Aug 15	Carpet of Flowers (celebrated even years) Brussels, Belgium
Mid Aug	Prinsengracht canal concert on barges Amsterdam, Netherlands
Sept (1st week)	Bloemencorso—flower parade on canals Aalsmeer to Amsterdam, Netherlands
Mid Sept	Jordaan Festival—neighborhood street party Netherlands
Nov 1	All Saints' Day Belgium
Nov 11	Armistice Day Belgium
Nov (second or third Sat)	Sinterklaas and Zwarte Piet arrive— Santa Claus procession Netherlands
Dec 5	Sinterklaasavond, traditional Christmas Netherlands
Dec 25	Christmas in Belgium (also becoming increasingly popular in the Netherlands)

Climate

First line, average daily low temperature; second line, average daily high; third line, days of no rain.

J	F	M	A	M	J	J	A	S	O	N	D

Amsterdam

J	F	M	A	M	J	J	A	S	O	N	D
30°	31°	35°	40°	45°	52°	55°	55°	51°	43°	37°	33°
41°	42°	49°	55°	64°	70°	72°	71°	66°	56°	48°	41°
8	9	16	14	16	16	14	12	11	11	10	9

Brussels

J	F	M	A	M	J	J	A	S	O	N	D
30°	32°	34°	40°	45°	53°	55°	55°	52°	45°	38°	32°
41°	44°	51°	58°	65°	71°	73°	72°	69°	60°	48°	42°
9	11	14	12	15	15	13	12	15	13	10	11

Numbers and Stumblers

- Europeans write a few of their numbers differently than we do. 1 = 1 , 4 = 4 , 7 = 7 . Learn the difference or miss your train.
- In Europe, dates appear as day/month/year, so Christmas is 25/12/03.
- Commas are decimal points and decimals commas. A dollar and a half is 1,50, and there are 5.280 feet in a mile.
- When pointing, use your whole hand, palm down.
- When counting with fingers, start with your thumb. If you hold up your first finger to request one item, you'll probably get two.
- What Americans call the second floor of a building is the first floor in Europe.
- Europeans keep the left "lane" open for passing on escalators and moving sidewalks. Keep to the right.

Metric Conversion (approximate)

1 inch = 25 millimeters	32 degrees F = 0 degrees C
1 foot = 0.3 meter	82 degrees F = about 28 degrees C
1 yard = 0.9 meter	1 ounce = 28 grams
1 mile = 1.6 kilometers	1 kilogram = 2.2 pounds
1 centimeter = 0.4 inch	1 quart = 0.95 liter
1 meter = 39.4 inches	1 square yard = 0.8 square meter
1 kilometer = .62 mile	1 acre = 0.4 hectare

Faxing Your Hotel Reservation

Use this handy form for your fax or find it online at
www.ricksteves.com/reservation. Photocopy and fax away.

One-Page Fax

To: _____ @ _____
                    hotel   *fax*

From: _____ @ _____
                    name   *fax*

Today's date: ____ /_____ /____
                 day   *month* *year*

Dear Hotel _____,

Please make this reservation for me:

Name: _____

Total # of people: _____   # of rooms: _____   # of nights: _____

Arriving: ____ /_____ /____   My time of arrival (24-hr clock): _____
              day   *month* *year*   (I will telephone if I will be late)

Departing: ____ /_____ /____
               day   *month* *year*

Room(s): Single___ Double___ Twin___ Triple___ Quad___

With: Toilet___ Shower___ Bath___ Sink only___

Special needs: View___ Quiet___ Cheapest___ Ground Floor___

Credit card: Visa___ MasterCard___ American Express___

Card #: _____

Expiration date:_____

Name on card: _____

You may charge me for the first night as a deposit. Please fax, e-mail, or
mail me confirmation of my reservation, along with the type of room
reserved, the price, and whether the price includes breakfast. Please also
inform me of your cancellation policy. Thank you.

_____
Signature

_____
Name

_____
Address

_____
City   *State*   *Zip Code*   *Country*

_____
E-mail Address

Road Scholar Feedback for
AMSTERDAM, BRUGES & BRUSSELS 2003

We're all in the same travelers' school of hard knocks. Your feedback help us improve this guidebook for future travelers. Please fill this out (or use the online version at www.ricksteves.com/feedback), attach more info or any tips/favorite discoveries if you like, and send it to us. As thanks for your help, we'll send you our quarterly travel newsletter free for one year. Thanks! **Rick**

Of the recommended accommodations/restaurants used, which was:

Best _____

Why? _____

Worst _____

Why? _____

Of the sights/experiences/destinations recommended by this book, which was:

Most overrated _____

Why? _____

Most underrated _____

Why? _____

Best ways to improve this book:

_____

_____

I'd like a free newsletter subscription:

_____ Yes _____ No _____ Already on list

_____
Name

_____
Address

_____
City, State, Zip

_____
E-mail Address

Please send to: ETBD, Box 2009, Edmonds, WA 98020

INDEX

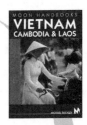

FREE-SPIRITED TOURS FROM

Rick Steves

Great Guides
Big Buses
Small Groups
No Grumps

Best of Europe ■ Village Europe ■ Eastern Europe ■ Turkey ■ Italy ■ Village Italy ■ Britain
Spain/Portugal ■ Ireland ■ Heart of France ■ South of France ■ Village France ■ Scandinavia
Germany/Austria/Switzerland ■ London ■ Paris ■ Rome ■ Venice ■ Florence ■ Prague

Looking for a one, two, or three-week tour that's run in the Rick Steves style? Check out Rick Steves' educational, experiential tours of Europe.

Rick's tours include much more in the "sticker price" than mainstream tours. Here's what you'll get with a Europe or regional Rick Steves tour ...

- **Group size:** Your tour group will be no larger than 26.

- **Guides:** You'll have two guides traveling and dining with you on your fully guided Rick Steves tour.

- **Bus:** You'll travel in a full-size bus, with plenty of empty seats for you to spread out and read, snooze, enjoy the passing scenery, get away from your spouse, or whatever.

- **Sightseeing:** Your tour price includes all group sightseeing. There are no hidden extra charges.

- **Hotels:** You'll stay in Rick's favorite small, characteristic, locally-run hotels in the center of each city, within walking distance of the sights you came to see.

- **Price and insurance:** Your tour price is guaranteed for 2003. Single travelers do not pay an extra supplement (we have them room with other singles). ETBD includes prorated tour cancellation/ interruption protection coverage at no extra cost.

- **Tips and kickbacks:** All guide and driver tips are included in your tour price. Because your driver and guides are paid salaries by ETBD, they can focus on giving you the best European travel experience possible.

Interested? Call (425) 771-8303 or visit www.ricksteves.com for a free copy of Rick Steves' 2003 Tours booklet!

Rick Steves' Europe Through the Back Door
130 Fourth Avenue North, PO Box 2009, Edmonds, WA 98020 USA
Phone: (425) 771-8303 ■ Fax: (425) 771-0833 ■ www.ricksteves.com

FREE TRAVEL GOODIES FROM

Rick Steves

EUROPEAN TRAVEL NEWSLETTER

My *Europe Through the Back Door* travel company will help you travel better *because* you're on a budget—not in spite of it. To see how, ask for my 64-page *travel newsletter* packed full of savvy travel tips, readers' discoveries, and your best bets for railpasses, guidebooks, videos, travel accessories and free-spirited tours.

2003 GUIDE TO EUROPEAN RAILPASSES

With hundreds of railpasses to choose from in 2003, finding the right pass for your trip has never been more confusing. To cut through the complexity, visit www.ricksteves.com for my online *2003 Guide to European Railpasses.* Once you've narrowed down your choices, we give you unbeatable prices, including important extras with every Eurailpass, **free:** my 90-minute *Travel Skills Special* video or DVD and your choice of one of my 24 guidebooks.

RICK STEVES' 2003 TOURS

We offer 20 different one, two, and three-week tours (200 departures in 2003) for those who want to experience Europe in Rick Steves' Back Door style, but without the transportation and hotel hassles. If a tour with a small group, modest family-run hotels, lots of exercise, great guides, and no tips or hidden charges sounds like your idea of fun, ask for my 48-page 2003 Tours booklet.

YEAR-ROUND GUIDEBOOK UPDATES

Even though the information in my guidebooks is the freshest around, things do change in Europe between book printings. I've set aside a special section at my website (www.ricksteves.com/update) listing *up-to-the-minute changes* for every Rick Steves guidebook.

Visit *www.ricksteves.com* to get your...

- ☑ **FREE EUROPEAN TRAVEL NEWSLETTER**
- ☑ **FREE 2003 GUIDE TO EUROPEAN RAILPASSES**
- ☑ **FREE RICK STEVES' 2003 TOURS BOOKLET**

Rick Steves' Europe Through the Back Door

130 Fourth Avenue North, PO Box 2009, Edmonds, WA 98020 USA
Phone: (425) 771-8303 ■ Fax: (425) 771-0833 ■ www.ricksteves.com